MENTAL MODELS
IN COGNITIVE SCIENCE

Mental Models in Cognitive Science

Essays in Honour of Phil Johnson-Laird

edited by

Jane Oakhill
and
Alan Garnham

Laboratory of Experimental Psychology,
University of Sussex

Psychology Press

An imprint of Erlbaum (UK) Taylor & Francis

Psychology Press
27 Church Road
Hove
East Sussex, BN3 2FA
U.K.

British Library Cataloguing in Publication Data

A catalogue record for this book is available from the British Library.

ISBN 0–86377–448–2

Typeset by DP Photosetting, Aylesbury, Bucks.
Printed and bound by BPC Wheatons Ltd., Exeter

Contents

List of Contributors

Tony Anderson, Centre for Research into Interactive Learning, Department of Psychology, University of Strathclyde, Graham Hills Building, 40 George Street, Glasgow G1 1QE, UK.

Bruno Bara, Centro di Scienza Cognitiva, Dipartimento di Psicologia, Università degli Studi di Torino, Via Po 14, 10123 Torino, Italy.

Ruth M.J. Byrne, Department of Psychology, Trinity College, University of Dublin, 24–28 Westland Row, Dublin 2, Republic of Ireland.

Antonella Carassa, Centro di Scienza Cognitiva, Dipartimento di Psicologia, Università degli Studi di Torino, Via Po 14, 10123 Torino, Italy.

Kate Ehrlich, Lotus Development Corporation, 55 Cambridge Parkway, Cambridge MA 02142, USA.

Jonathan St. B. T. Evans, Department of Psychology, University of Plymouth, Drake Circus, Plymouth, Devon PL4 8AA, UK.

Alan Garnham, Laboratory of Experimental Psychology, Biology Building, University of Sussex, Falmer, Brighton BN1 9QG, UK.

Giuliano Geminiani, Centro di Scienza Cognitiva, Dipartimento di Psicologia, Università degli Studi di Torino, Via Po 14, 10123 Torino, Italy.

Vittorio Girotto, CREPCO, Université de Provence, 29 Av. R. Schuman, 13100 Aix-en-Provence, France.

David W. Green, Department of Psychology, Centre for Cognitive Science, University College London, Gower Street, London WC1E 6BT, UK.

Christine Howe, Centre for Research into Interactive Learning, Department of Psychology, University of Strathclyde, Graham Hills Building, 40 George Street, Glasgow G1 1QE, UK.

Paolo Legrenzi, Istituto de Psicologia, Universita degli Studi di Milano, Via Larga 19, 20122 Milano, Italy.

George Miller, Department of Psychology, Princeton University, Green Hall, Princeton, NJ 08544-1010, USA.

Jane Oakhill, Laboratory of Experimental Psychology, Biology Building, University of Sussex, Falmer, Brighton BN1 9QG, UK.

Keith G. Oatley, Centre for Applied Cognitive Science, Ontario Institute for Studies in Education and Department of Psychology, University of Toronto, Toronto, Canada M5A 1V6.

Mick Power, Department of Psychiatry, The University of Edinburgh, Kennedy Tower, Royal Edinburgh Hospital, Morningside Park, Edinburgh EH10 5HF, UK.

Eldar Shafir, Department of Psychology, Princeton University, Green Hall, Princeton, NJ 08544-1010, USA.

Mark Steedman, Department of Computer and Information Science, University of Pennsylvania, 200 South 33rd Street, Philadelphia, PA 19104-6389, USA.

Rosemary Stevenson, Human Communication Research Centre, Department of Psychology, University of Durham, South Road, Durham DH1 3LE, UK.

Patrizia Tabossi, Dipartimento di Psicologia, Via dell'Universita 7, 34123 Trieste, Italy.

Andrew Tolmie, Centre for Research into Interactive Learning, Department of Psychology, University of Strathclyde, Graham Hills Building, 40 George Street, Glasgow G1 1QE, UK.

Peter C. Wason, Apartment 37, Burford Lodge, Pegasus Grange, Whitehouse Road, Oxford OX1 4NA, UK.

Til Wykes, Department of Psychology, Institute of Psychiatry, De Crespigny Park, Denmark Hill, London SE5 8AF, UK.

Preface

We were both fortunate to work with Phil Johnson-Laird in the late 1970s and early 1980s (initially as DPhil students) and, like many of the other people who have collaborated with him, our thinking has been greatly influenced by the concept of a "mental model". We have brought together this collection of papers from Phil's current and past collaborators on the occasion of his 60th birthday, but more importantly as a tribute to the wide-ranging impact of his theoretical ideas. It is also a personal tribute to Phil, in that everyone we asked—with two exceptions (one of whom is no longer working in the mental models area, and the other of whom found himself impossibly busy)—readily and enthusiastically agreed to contribute a chapter. Likewise, Michael Forster agreed (equally readily) to publish this collection. Thus, we feel that this book not only reflects Phil's great intellectual influence, but also the affection and esteem in which he is held by those who have worked with him.

The title of the book is, of course, taken from Phil's seminal paper, published in 1980 in *Cognitive Science*. The contents of the book reflect the range of influence of his ideas: from children's reading and learning of physics concepts to adults' reasoning, decision making and emotional responses, and even to jazz improvisation.

Jane Oakhill and Alan Garnham
Laboratory of Experimental Psychology, University of Sussex, UK.

Foreword

Peter Wason

EARLY IMPRESSIONS OF A RESEARCH WORKER
(1963–1980)

It is both a pleasure and a privilege to be asked to say a few words about Phil during the time he worked with me in the 1960s and 1970s. Most of us in the trade know something of Phil's ideas from his pioneering papers and books. And if these seem a bit demanding for a warm Sunday afternoon, there is that brilliant introduction to cognitive science, *The computer and the mind* (1993) which is accessible to a wider audience—always a great achievement.

My task is to step back from all this mature work, and to capture some memories of Phil as a student and young research worker. On 6 September 1963, Sheila Jones brought Phil to our room in 17 Gordon Square. When I had been at Harvard's Center for Cognitive Studies during the previous year, she had suggested that he might do his undergraduate project (on negation) under my supervision. He struck me at once as unusually shy (even for an undergraduate) and rather withdrawn—ideal research worker material. A few days later he reappeared with an alternative experimental design to the one I had suggested. For various reasons this was less satisfactory, but I was impressed. As expected, he took a brilliant First, and then proceeded to his PhD, his examiners being George Drew and myself. He told me afterwards that I had given him a "rough ride", a compliment, of course, to his abilities. At Phil's suggestion, we agreed to collaborate on a project concerned with the effect of linguistic and logical variables on comprehension, and with typical generosity the Medical Research Council awarded us a grant for scientific assistance.

What did we have in common apart from our love of research? Most of our friends thought we were similar. We shared the same launching-pad of formal logic as a template for human reasoning. Phil went into it more deeply than I did: he told me that he had even read that magisterial book, *The development of logic* (1962) by Walter and Martha Kneale, from cover to cover, 700-odd pages. We had breathed the same air of intellectual freedom at our universities, but achieved little at our schools, where I suppose we had been forcibly fed. Phil had left school at the age of 15 because of financial difficulties. This at least would have enabled him to escape from the tribalism that pervaded the English public school system at that time. We shared the same politics although I could not go along with his pacifism.

But in spite of these similarities, we tended to differ in our approach to intellectual problems. When Phil was developing an idea he would typically construct a tentative model to reveal its implications. I often went to the cinema with my note-book or pocket chess set so as *not* to think about it. Models, for Phil, became, not just a picture, but an instrument. "The struggle to make an intuitive idea explicit is a truly dialectical process" (Johnson-Laird & Wason, 1977, p.10). When we were designing an experiment he once told me that, he "trusted my intuition", which meant, of course, that his formal procedures were inapplicable at this stage. I recall, quite vividly, that some early chapters of his PhD thesis consisted mainly of flow diagrams. I remarked (gently, I hope) that continuous prose was generally required. It seems horribly school-masterish to say it, but his own style really did "improve". This was unlike the output of most of my students who either wrote indifferently throughout, or elegantly throughout. Phil showed progress. Of my style, he said he sometimes liked the purple passages, and sometimes disliked them: what might be called a balanced view.

But Phil remained faithful to his models. I sometimes thought that if he were to be struck by some "signal of transcendence" he would try to express the experience in a model. I had to point out that not everyone puts such reliance on models to clarify their thoughts. I use the writing of continuous prose—a technique I learned from Oxford tutorials when the meaning of every sentence may have to be explained. Drafting and re-drafting is just as much a "dialectical process". More so, perhaps, because it leaves the problem open.

Connected with this penchant for models, Phil's strongest asset was his gift for theorising. Even in his PhD thesis there is an appendix on a theory of "appropriate usage", which deals in a general way with pragmatic factors in language. And, of course, this spirit of theorising culminated in the influential theory of mental models.

On the other hand, I came to think that his aptitude for building theories exceeded that for experimentation. With one famous exception I got the feeling that Phil did not cherish his own experiments: they took second place to theoretical insights. Indeed, this attitude towards experiments is made objective (or rationalised) in a trenchant way in our book *Thinking* (1977, p.2): "[The discipline] ... has an Empiricist obsession with experiments—with designing, executing, analysing, reporting and criticizing them." In an early draft he wrote: "People do extraordinary things in psychological experiments." (To my mind extraordinary things can be more interesting than routine responses.)

My own powers were the converse. During the time we worked together I breathed and dreamed experiments, and I was satisfied if one threw light on existing theory. I must have played with several ideas for every one submitted for publication. I learned how to relax in order to provide space for new ideas, how to distrust first impressions, and how not to talk to others about possible experiments. Had we been identical twins, we would, I suppose, have felt quite comfortable in the research, a couple of theoreticians, or experimentalists, mimicking each other's moves. It was just because we differed in important ways that our project was deemed a success. I am reminded of the analogous difference between the contributions of Crick and Watson in discovering the structure of DNA.

But it seems to me true that *The psychology of reasoning* (1972), which was mainly based on our collaboration, owes more to Phil's vision than to my judgement. And apart from that, the energy required to produce such a book (and this goes for all our books) came from Phil; the paper is my ideal mode of communication. I count myself very fortunate to have been able to work with Phil.

There were some nuances in Phil's personality that are consistent with his attitude towards research. He had a great admiration for Bertrand Russell (direct and explicit), but none for Wittgenstein (indirect and allusive). If it had been the other way round, I would have been very surprised. His favourite author was Jane Austen, but, as far as I could tell, he was not moved by poetry (allusive). I find it hard to imagine him recalling even the most "cerebral" verse (e.g. Donne or Empson) just for the sake of indulging in verbal magic. But, as elsewhere in this impressionistic account, I could be wrong. Moreover, I once showed him a metaphorical passage by Francis Bacon and I was astonished when he gave it a literal interpretation. (I would not have recalled it, had it not made a deep impression on me.)

It is worth noting that I wrote our joint papers guided by Phil's trenchant observations and subsequent criticisms. I think really that for Phil words got in the way of those insights which he demanded of himself in order to grasp a problem. This dislike of verbosity was also evident in his preference for simple words in the titles of books. Typical, too, was his main emotional outlet—improvisation in jazz, about which he was very knowledgeable. In addition to this reticence with words, and perhaps connected with it, I sometimes found his judgement of others was somehow askew. I once characterised x as "highly uncreative". "Oh no", replied Phil, "—lazy".

To end on a serious note: Phil's research on mental models in reasoning has itself become a model for researchers in cognitive science—that relatively new discipline which depends, in principle, on collaboration with other specialists, e.g. anthropologists, linguists, the artificial intelligentsia, in pursuit of common aims. I only hope it will work out well. There is a danger in inter-disciplinary research that each tends to think their own a little bit superior, sometimes disguised as an insistence on rigour ("the feel-good factor"?), with a consequent lack of progress. Here is scope for the social psychologist with an interest in group processes. I hope that cognitive science will not be dominated by a few elitist scientists who talk only to each other without feeding their results back into the mainstream of psychology. How, for instance, can their projects aid those of clinical psychology, arguably the most important sub-discipline in psychology? Schizophrenia, depression, alienation, etc. have aspects that ultimately fall under the rubric of cognitive science, and they might profitably be attacked by the tools of cognitive science.

Peter Cathcart Wason
Pegasus Grange, Oxford

REFERENCES

Johnson-Laird, P.N. (1993). *The computer and the mind* (2nd Edn.). London: Fontana.
Johnson-Laird, P.N., & Wason, P.C. (Eds.) (1977). *Thinking: Readings in cognitive science.* Cambridge: Cambridge University Press.
Kneale, W., & Kneale, M. (1962). *The development of logic.* Oxford: Clarendon Press.
Wason, P.C., & Johnson-Laird, P.N. (1972). *The psychology of reasoning: Structure and content.* London: Batsford.

1

Contextuality

George A. Miller
Cognitive Science Laboratory, Princeton University, USA

In 1976, when Miller and Johnson-Laird published on "psycholexicology", polysemy was a topic that was judiciously avoided. It was assumed that words have certain core senses, and that the semantic decomposition of those senses would cast interesting light on the minds that use them. Although polysemy seemed peripheral to that analytic enterprise, in the closing pages of the book a careful reader will find this admission: "We have relied on incomplete definitions to give us the larger dimensions of lexical organization and have tried to leave open the question of how best to account for polysemy" (Miller & Johnson-Laird, 1976, p.677).

Leaving the question of polysemy open is still excellent advice for anyone who can take it. But in the years since those early explorations I have become increasingly aware that, in any practical project involving natural language as it is ordinarily spoken and written, polysemy is very hard to ignore. So I offer this chapter as a supplement to *Language and perception*, intended to treat at least one psycholexical matter that we sidestepped originally.

Just as the original book began with perception and moved slowly into language, this chapter begins with broad psychological considerations and moves slowly into some linguistic consequences. As will quickly become

Preparation of this chapter was supported in part by Grant No. N66001-94-C-6045 from the Advanced Projects Research Agency. A version was presented at the Annual Conference of the Cognitive Science Society at the University of Pittsburgh, 24 July 1995.

1

apparent, I regard the human ability to cope with polysemy as a basic cognitive skill. The skill involves the use of context in ways that must be closely related to the ways people formulate mental models of discourse. It seems doubly appropriate, therefore, to offer it for inclusion in a book devoted to matters near to the heart of P.N. Johnson-Laird.

MULTIPLE MEANINGS

One of the most interesting aspects of the lexical component of language is polysemy. "Lexical polysemy" is a polysyllabic way of saying that a word can be used to express more than one meaning. I will discuss polysemy, but first I want to make a case that polysemy is not limited to words. It is not even limited to language. Multiplicity of meaning is a very general cognitive phenomenon. Words simply provide one good place to study it.

As I have puzzled over lexical polysemy it has struck me many times that words and acts have many similarities. Both involve an association between a tangible form—a sound or action—and an intangible meaning—a sense or purpose. In the linguistic case, however, tools of representation and analysis are more developed and standardised than in the nonlinguistic case. I would never claim that behaviour is nothing but a text, but I do believe that there are enough similarities to make the comparison worth pursuing. In particular, there is polysemy in both cases: the same tangible form can be associated with different meanings in different contexts. It has occurred to me, therefore, that our capacity to handle multiple linguistic meanings may be a special case of some general capacity to deal with multiplicity of meanings.

The most interesting aspect of this multiplicity is that it seldom causes any problems. You might think that it would. Something that can have multiple meanings is potentially ambiguous—that is to say, there is always a possibility of selecting the wrong meaning and so being misled or confused. Consequently, when we want to communicate very precisely, we try to avoid terms that are subject to such ambiguities. In developing scientific terminology, for example, we try not to use the same symbol to mean two different things. But under the uncontrolled conditions we loosely call "everyday life", multiplicity of meaning abounds—and only rarely does it result in any trouble or misunderstanding.

Consequently, the ubiquity of multiple meanings is easily overlooked. We navigate daily through a sea of potential ambiguities, resolving them so easily that we seldom even notice they are there. We resolve potential ambiguities by taking into account the *contexts* in which they occur. Using context to resolve ambiguities can be a complex cognitive operation, yet we do it so effortlessly that we seldom realise we are doing anything at all.

People are remarkably clever contextualisers. I believe that human beings have a native talent for accommodating to contexts, and I want to try to make the case that the capacity to do this—a capacity that I will call *contextualisation*—is a general cognitive process.

SITUATIONS, FIELDS, AND CONTEXTS

I first puzzled over contextuality many years ago as an undergraduate at the University of Alabama when I became actively interested in theatre. The stage is a place for make-believe; it provides a situation very different from the everyday world. It fascinated me, for example, that a marriage ceremony could be repeated on a stage every night, whereas exactly the same ceremony in a church would be performed only once. And nobody had a problem distinguishing theatrical matrimony from the real thing. At the time it didn't occur to me that any special intelligence was required to maintain this distinction, but eventually Roger Barker (Barker, 1968) taught me that life goes on in many different behaviour settings, most of them characterised in much subtler ways than the theatrical one.

A few years later as a graduate student at Harvard I took a course from Harry Murray. I remember his argument that behaviourism must be misguided because exactly the same behaviour can satisfy totally different needs in different settings. I remember one of his examples: the action of lifting a spoon to the lips is different when the spoon contains food and when the spoon contains poison. The same pattern of muscle contractions has one meaning as part of the act of eating and a totally different meaning as part of the act of committing suicide. And not long after that I learned that Pavlov's dogs did not salivate at the sound of a bell unless they were in the experimental harness. Apparently, even a dog appreciates situational differences.

In short, my teachers long ago gave me many examples of the importance of the situation, and I could easily go on this way pointing out others. Anyone could. These are all cases that a behaviourist might describe in terms of discriminative stimuli—the discriminative stimuli are simply more complex than usual. My teachers had terminology for these distinctions. A *stimulus* was a simple energy change that affected a sense organ; a *stimulus object* was a more complicated entity that gave rise to a stimulus; and a *situation* was a very complicated configuration of stimulus objects. A red light is a stimulus; a sentry's command to halt is a situation.

There were problems, however. For example, when you set out to describe a situation, what do you include? Where do you stop? How far should the description extend and how detailed should it be? Kurt Lewin (1936) proposed one answer. In his topological psychology, Lewin distinguished between your physical situation and your psychological *field*. Your field—or your "life space", as Lewin called it—includes just those parts or aspects of the real situation that affect your thought or behaviour at a given moment. A bit of food might be part of the field for a hungry animal, but not for an animal that is satiated.

This distinction between a physical situation and a psychological field has long been familiar to cognitive psychologists. But now I want to introduce a further distinction. I want to use "context" in a related but different, more cognitive sense. As I shall try to use the term, *context* will refer to the part of the situation (or the field) that is used to determine meaning in general, and in particular is used to resolve potential ambiguities of meaning. And by *contextualisation* I will mean the use of context to determine meanings and resolve potential ambiguities.

This connection between context and meaning should be familiar; it is what I think people have in mind when they complain about being quoted "out of context". Change the context and you can change the meaning. This observation holds for the meaning of our acts as well as for the meaning of our words.

In simple cases, of course, what we call situation, field, and context may be practically indistinguishable. In other cases, however, they can be very different. The activity of reading illustrates the difference. When you read a novel you may be lying in a hammock in your back yard, but the context in which you understand what you are reading has little or nothing to do with your physical situation or your psychological field as you read. The context needed to understand the novel is encoded in its text and does not depend on your situation when you encounter it. Written language may be a special case, but it is an important special case and I will return to it later. For the moment I use it to illustrate how context can differ from situation.

So the claim is that context and situation are distinguishable, and that context concerns those aspects of a situation that can be used to determine meaning and resolve potential ambiguities. I recognise that by linking a definition of context so closely to the concept of meaning, it inherits all of the well-known uncertainties associated with the concept of meaning. But it also inherits the broad scope of meaningfulness; things and events, as well as spoken and written words, have meanings, and so by this definition they have contexts. That is to say, context is not limited to text. Whenever meanings are present, contexts must be considered.

I believe it is but a short step from that observation to the claim that an ability to contextualise—an ability to use context to determine meaning and resolve potential ambiguities—must be a general cognitive process, distinct from other cognitive processes that are more familiar.

CONTEXTUALISATION AND MEMORY

If contextualisation and meaning are so closely related, then surely memory must also be involved. That is to say, meanings have to be learned and remembered, or else the task of deciding which meaning is appropriate in a given context could never arise. But contextualising is something more than remembering.

Suppose we begin by comparing contextualisation and memory at a very abstract level. When antecedent experience has an effect, we say that memory is involved. The claim here is that when experience is meaningful, contextualisation is involved. Critics who already have enough problems and do not wish to clutter their cognitive theories with another cognitive process might argue that contextualisation is merely a special form of memory. They could say that recognising a context is simply a matter of remembering similar situations in the past. And I would agree that contexts become familiar and are remembered in the same way that all knowledge is acquired and remembered. But the fact that something is recognised does not explain how the recognition can determine meaning and resolve potential ambiguities. Something more than storage and retrieval is involved in contextualisation.

Contextualising, like recognising, is usually spontaneous. You don't decide to contextualise one way rather than another. Everything that you perceive or remember or think comes pre-wrapped in its own context. But the fact that contexts are recognised does not imply that contextualising is merely a variety of recognition memory. The capacity to contextualise presupposes a capacity to remember, but contextualisation involves something more than memory, just as putting the cat out involves something more than remembering to put the cat out.

Recognition involves matching a percept against some kind of internal representation. So recognising a context implies the existence of some kind of internal representation of that class of contexts. Miller and Charles (1991) call it a *contextual representation*, a cognitive representation of a class of equivalent contexts. Not only do we have to remember (or infer) the possible meanings of some word or deed, but we also have to remember the contextual representations that determine the particular meaning in specific cases.

CONTEXTUALISATION, ATTENTION, AND PERCEPTION

Just as there are relations between contextualisation and memory, so there are relations between contextualisation and perception and attention. When we attend to some object or event, it becomes a figure against the rest of the perceptual field, which then becomes the ground. This figure–ground relation is not limited to perception, of course. When we attend to a particular idea, related ideas become part of its cognitive background. Is this not what is going on between a meaning and its context? Isn't the meaningful object or event simply the figure and isn't the context its ground? Then, just as we can talk about reversing the perceptual figure–ground relation, we can ask about reversing the meaning–context relation.

Once again, these cognitive processes are related but not identical. That is to say, the capacity to appreciate the meaning of some object or event presupposes a capacity to isolate that object or event as a figure against a ground. But the thing that is attended and the meaning that is assigned to it are not the same; a given figure can be clear but its meaning obscure, or the figure can be obscure but its meaning crystal clear. If, while attending to some figure, you are reminded of something, the meaning of the figure can change completely while the figure itself remains constant.

Perceptual experiments are generally conducted in situations that are as simple as possible: in an "experimental situation" where everything but the stimuli is constant. An experimental situation is meaningful, however, and so must involve a context—the experimental context—that the experimenter creates and the subject accepts. It is usually a simple context—so simple, in fact, that the results are sometimes dismissed as irrelevant to the more complex world of practical affairs. But its simplicity does have certain advantages: sometimes it is possible to determine what aspects of the experimental situation determined a subject's response.

Experimental psychologists who work with human subjects usually try to control the meaning of an experiment by giving the subject instructions about what to expect and what to do. As German psychologists at Würzburg discovered many years ago, the instructions that a subject is given in an experimental situation can have important consequences. The instructions create an *Einstellung* or *set* that leads the subject to respond in a particular manner: hopefully, in the manner that the experimenter expected. The instructions set the subject to interpret the stimuli and to respond as the experimenter desired. There are a variety of different sets that have been discussed in the experimental journals, but I will not explore them here. Most cognitive scientists have now equated set to the notion of a goal hierarchy that guides thought and behaviour.

Giving instructions is the experimenter's way to control what the subject expects and what responses are available. That is to say, instructions provide a context that makes the experimental situation meaningful. Moreover, if you treat context as an independent variable, you can vary the meaning of an experiment.

Suppose, for example, that you instruct a subject to report which one of two stimuli, stimulus A or stimulus B, has been presented; call this the two-choice context. Then you compare this context with the case where you instruct the subject to report which one of a thousand stimuli has been presented, where the thousand include stimuli A and B and 998 others; call this the thousand-choice context. In both experiments, however, you present stimulus A—that is to say, the stimuli are the same and only the context is different. You will find that the perception of stimulus A is much more accurate in the two-choice context than in the thousand-choice context. When I first observed this difference (Miller, Heise, & Lichten, 1951), I was interested in Shannon's measure of selective information (Shannon, 1948), and I interpreted the result to mean that a choice requiring one bit of information is easier than a choice requiring ten bits of information. That still seems the easy way to summarise the results.

Even then, however, I was impressed that subjects could follow the instructions so readily. They were told to get set for a one-bit decision and they did so immediately; then they were told to get set for a ten-bit decision and they would do that immediately, too. At the time I saw no way to pursue this remarkable capacity and I went on to other things, grateful that the subjects had been able to follow instructions. Now, however, I would base some different observations on those studies. First, subjects are very skilful contextualisers—which repeats a claim I have already made. And second, context can enable a person to restrict the range of possible alternatives. This observation may be peculiar to perceptual experiments, but I think it is quite general. I believe that an important feature of our ability to form contextual representations is that it enables us to narrow the range of possibilities that we must cope with.

As a young student, I was taught that the difference between sensation and perception is that sensations are bare awarenesses, whereas perceptions are elaborated and interpreted sensations—perceptions, in the terminology I would use today, are meaningful, whereas sensations are not. In those days there were hot arguments about whether it is possible to have uninterpreted, unrecognised sensations, which I would now classify as arguments about whether any sensory process can occur without some context. Unfortunately, however, these arguments rather obscured the question of what it is that adds this meaningful interpretation to the raw sensory input. An older term, *apperception*, provides a possible name for this process. Unfortunately, the term has disappeared from psychological discussions—perhaps because philosophers and psychologists have used it in such different ways that no-one is sure what it means. But at least some who talked about apperception were referring to a final clear phase of perception where there is recognition and identification. Perhaps they meant the final stage when the range of possible alternatives has been reduced to one.

It would be desirable, if only in the name of parsimony, to subsume contextualisation under some already familiar cognitive rubric, and apperception might be a candidate. Rather than try to breathe life back into a dead term, however, I propose to continue speaking of contextualisation and to try to understand afresh how meaningful cognition depends on context.

CONTEXTUALISATION AND LANGUAGE ACQUISITION

One place where the role of context has been clearly recognised, of course, is language. Language dramatically illustrates our skill in exploiting context, and so provides a valuable test tube in which this cognitive process can be observed and analysed.

The relation between language and context has probably been discussed most extensively in connection with work on language acquisition. Because infants lack any language in which language could be explained to them, all aspects of first-language learning pose fascinating questions. Apparently, children have a native ability to infer phonology, syntax, and lexicon by observing and interacting in contexts in which language is used. But the role of meaning in that process is still debated. One view holds that meaning is irrelevant: only an innate ability to recognise the formal structure of your language is important. The alternative view is that meaning is critical: an understanding of the contexts in which language is used must precede and support the acquisition of language.

Whether or not meaning plays an important role in mastering the phonology and syntax of your mother-tongue is not a question I want to discuss. But I do have rather strong opinions concerning the acquisition of vocabulary. There would be no need for thousands of different words if they did not have different meanings, and learning which meanings are associated with which phonological forms is a central component of vocabulary acquisition.

One way to demonstrate the close connection between knowing the meaning of a word and knowing the contexts in which it can be used is to ask people to use a word in a simple sentence. This task is frequently assigned to children in American schools as a vocabulary building exercise: "Look up the following words in a dictionary and write a sentence using each one." Gildea and I (Miller & Gildea, 1987) collected examples of what fourth-grade children wrote when given this assignment for unfamiliar words. Some of the results were amusing. My own favourite was the little girl who read the definition of the verb "erode" and then wrote the sentence, "Our family erodes a lot." This response seems quite baffling until you look at the definition the child was given: "erode" was defined as "to eat out, eat away".

That research was quite instructive on the different ways to misread a dictionary, but I think the important impression we gained from those childish sentences was that the sentence-writing task provides a useful clue as to whether a child understands a word or not. Much better than, say, asking the child to define the word, a task that they fail even when they know the word quite well and can use it fluently. Knowing the meaning of a word is most simply demonstrated by an ability to use the word in an appropriate context.

It is a familiar fact that people who know a language are able to acquire a new word simply by hearing it used in one or two dozen contexts (McKeown & Curtis, 1987). You do not need a dictionary to understand it. That is to say, we are not only able to use context in order to select the context-appropriate meaning from a menu of prelearned meanings that a word can be used to express. We are also able to use context in order to construct new context-appropriate meanings for unfamiliar words. And we can even use context to understand non-literal usages—metaphor, irony, hyperbole, and the like. So contextualisation is a critical part of word learning.

When we ask how young children acquire vocabulary it is natural to assume that they also use context. But because at the outset they possess very little knowledge of their language, it cannot be the linguistic context that they are using. So it must be the nonlinguistic context. A more familiar phrasing of the same idea might be that children understand the situation in which a word is used, and from that understanding they are somehow able to infer a meaning for the word itself. I assume that understanding the situation involves, in this case, understanding which features of the situation determine the meaning of the word. And the features of the situation that determine meaning are precisely what I mean by the nonlinguistic context.

Whether you say that young children use certain features of the situation or use the nonlinguistic context is merely a terminological quibble. In either case, the problem of describing what young children do when they learn new words remains. But it is obvious that context plays an important role in acquiring vocabulary from the very beginning.

CONTEXTUAL REPRESENTATIONS

Some very insightful work has been done on word acquisition. One of those insights that I find most interesting is that very young children apparently begin with an assumption that objects have names and that each name denotes a different object. That is to say, they begin by ignoring the possibility of synonymy (Markman, 1989). They believe in one word–one meaning. As their knowledge of language grows, of course, lexical facts must eventually modify this simple learning strategy, but I am unable to say how that modification occurs.

My own interest is how children learn that the same word form can be used to express alternative meanings. It is my impression that alternative meanings of simple words occur in such different contexts that the fact that the same word form—the same phonological string—is involved in both cases is not even noticed. The formal coincidence is a later discovery, one that can carry with it a feeling of surprise. For example, many English-speaking adults have not noticed that the word "door" can be used either to refer to an aperture (as in "He stuck his head in the door") or to the solid object that closes the aperture (as in "He painted the door red"). The idea that these two meanings might be expressed by different words in another language is hard to grasp. But once the distinction is noticed, it is possible to be amused by the ambiguity of "The terminator walked through the door".

If this impression is correct, then it must be the case that, as each possible meaning of a word is learned, some representation of the specific contexts in which that meaning is appropriate is also acquired. For example, to learn in one context that "foot" can refer to a body part must initially have little to do with learning in another context that "foot" can refer to a distance. As long as the context of use is clear, the fact that "foot" can be used to express two different meanings need not even be noticed. So, learning the referential value of a word is only part of learning the word. It is also necessary to acquire a contextual representation for each meaning. A contextual representation is the cognitive content—the knowledge—that enables you to recognise a particular context as belonging to the set of contexts in which the word can be used to express a specific meaning.

Suppose we take a simple polysemous English word: "board". And suppose we collect from the available textual corpora a large collection of sentences using "board" (or "boards" or "Board" or "Boards"). Next, we read through this collection of sentences, sorting them into three piles:

1. those in which "board" refers to a piece of wood,
2. those in which "board" refers to some kind of committee, and
3. all the miscellaneous other uses of the word.

Now, take a sample of, say, 25 sentences from piles (1) and (2), delete the word "board" from all of them, and submit the resulting 50 contexts—sentences minus the word we are interested in—to English-speaking subjects who are asked to sort them into piles on the basis of similarity of meaning. We don't tell our subjects what word has been deleted nor do we tell them how many piles to use.

The results of this simple test are quite uniform (Charles, 1988). English-speaking subjects sort the contexts into two piles corresponding to the correct senses of "board", and when asked to guess the missing word will respond either with "board" or with a context-appropriate synonym—"wood" or "committee". The results demonstrate, if a demonstration were needed, that "board" is used with at least two recognisably different meanings, and that the basis for identifying each meaning is provided by the context—by the other words in the sentences in which "board" occurs. It is possible, of course, to construct contexts that do not resolve this potential ambiguity, but in a haphazard sample of sentences that someone had actually used we did not find any.

Lexicographers understand that the dictionary definition of a word has two distinct but related parts: (1) an explanation of the word's meaning, and (2) an indication (usually by example) of the contexts in which the word can be used to express that meaning. The present claim is that a mental dictionary must also contain both kinds of information. That is to say, someone who knows a word knows both (1) the meanings that the word can be used to express, and (2) a contextual representation for each meaning. Defining the alternative meanings of a word is reasonably well understood, but characterising the contexts in which each meaning occurs is not at all well understood. This is curious, as people who know a word can use it in appropriate contexts far more easily than they can give a definition for it.

Not all words have this kind of two-part dictionary entry. There is a special class of words that we use very frequently which have no meaning outside their contexts of use. These words presuppose knowledge of the situation in which they are used. Karl Bühler referred to the phenomenon as *deixis*. For example, if someone says, "I need you here right now", the referents of "I" and "you" are the speaker and a listener, who can only be identified from the actual context of use; that is deixis of person. Similarly, the referents of "here" and "now" also depend on where and when the utterance occurred; those illustrate deixis of place and time.

Deixis is familiar to psycholinguists, of course, and I mention it here only to illustrate once again how skilful people are at contextualising. The point is that a deictic word can have a different referent every time it is used, so it would be futile to try to list all of its possible referents in any dictionary. All a dictionary can provide for such words is a rule for using them appropriately in context. For deictic words, the contextual representation is all you know, and all you need to know.

CONTEXTUALISING AND WRITTEN LANGUAGE

Written language seems to offer the clearest place in which to study the phenomenon of contextualisation. As I noted earlier, in written language the only context is linguistic. Everything you need to know in order to resolve any potential ambiguities should be right there in the text. So by studying texts we can get some information about the extent of the phenomenon.

Moreover, polysemous words seem to offer the simplest place to study how potential ambiguities are resolved. There has been much interest in such potentially ambiguous sentences as "They are flying planes", but I am less interested in the source of ambiguity, whether it is lexical or syntactic, than in how the potential ambiguity is avoided in everyday language use. If we can understand how context is used to resolve lexical polysemy, we should be well along the way towards understanding how context resolves syntactic polysemy.

If polysemous words were rare, of course, they would not be a problem, but in fact they are far from rare. It is a perverse feature of natural languages that the more frequently a word is used, the more polysemous it tends to be (Jastrezembski, 1981; Jastrezembski & Stanners, 1975; Zipf, 1945). That is to say, most of the words we write or utter have multiple meanings—and so are potentially ambiguous. Even if we ignore the notoriously polysemous closed-class words of English (the prepositions, pronouns, articles, conjunctions, and so on) the open-class words that carry the burden of the content (the nouns, verbs, adjectives, and adverbs) are still predominantly polysemous. According to my estimates (Miller et al., 1994), less than 20% of the open-class words in a standard dictionary are polysemous, but more than 70% of the open-class words in a sample of running text (the Brown Corpus: Kučera and Francis, 1967; Francis and Kučera, 1982) are polysemous. That is to say, more than 70% of the substantive words we write are potentially ambiguous and have to be interpreted according to the contexts in which they are used.

It is an interesting fact, therefore, that so much polysemy results in so little ambiguity. We are so good at understanding the intended sense of a polysemous word that alternative senses seldom rise to conscious awareness. How do we do it? The contextualising machinery must work overtime.

I have said that we associate contextual representations with each sense of every polysemous word, and that these representations enable us to recognise a particular context and so to select the appropriate meaning. But "contextual representation" is not an explanation; it is merely a name for the thing that needs to be explained. What do we know about contextual representations?

We know, for one thing, that the domain of discourse is part of the context, and that it can help us select an intended meaning (Kintsch, 1972). For example, if the domain of discourse is, say, house construction, then "flight" probably means a flight of stairs, whereas if we are making travel reservations, "flight" probably means a scheduled trip by aeroplane. Each domain of discourse has its own vocabulary, and that fact must be part of the contextual representation.

We also know, however, that the topical context is seldom needed to resolve a potential ambiguity. In 1955 Kaplan reported an informal experiment in which he presented limited amounts of context before and after a polysemous word and found that readers could identify the correct sense with very few errors when they were given just two words on both sides. A similar result has been reported by Choueka and Lusignan (1985). I am not convinced that the experiment has been done properly—with controls, say, for frequency of use and part of speech and degree of polysemy in addition to different contexts before and after the target word—but when I begin to calculate how many combinations of conditions need to be tested, I lose my enthusiasm for doing it. So I am content that the available data confirms my own subjective impression that I can identify the sense of an ambiguous word without reading very far on either side of it. Local context is an important part of a contextual representation.

Furthermore, we know that some senses of a polysemous word are more probable than others. The word "horse", for example, can be used to refer to a vaulting horse or a carpenter's sawhorse, but the chances are better than 99–1 that when you encounter "horse" in a written text the appropriate meaning will be the animal. In the 1930s Lorge (1937) had Columbia University students count how often senses in the *Oxford English Dictionary* occurred in some 4,500,000 running words of prose taken from magazines of the day, and these counts were used by Thorndike in the *Thorndike-Barnhart Junior Dictionary* (1935), which enabled him to list senses in the order of their frequency, thus ensuring that the senses included would be the ones that children most needed to know.

At Princeton we have recently made a similar semantic count for open-class words on a much smaller sample of text from the Brown Corpus (Miller, Leacock, Tengi, & Bunker, 1993). Although it was not as large as we would like, we used the count to estimate what fraction of the time the most frequent meaning of the open-class words was the intended meaning (Miller et al., 1994). Our estimate was 69%. That is to say, if you simply pretended that every open-class word was monosemous, you would be wrong 31% of the time.

And, finally, we know that people make these judgements rapidly. Swinney (1979) used cross-modality priming to show that all senses of a polysemous word are retrieved during sentence comprehension, but that within a fraction of a second the contextually appropriate choice is made. If sense identification were not fast, of course, we could not talk to one another at the rate of 150 words per minute. So one suspects that the contextual representations that play a role in identifying word senses must be stored in advance, not generated on the fly.

No doubt there is more that psycholinguists could tell us about lexical disambiguation, but I want to conclude by considering the possibility of automatic word-sense identification.

CONTEXTUALISATION AND COMPUTATIONAL LINGUISTICS

Although it may be easy for us, word-sense identification is not easy for computers. It was this contrast that forced me to recognise the special human ability to exploit context. When I first considered how to program a computer to do automatic word-sense identification, I hoped to discover some clever trick that we use but that computational linguists hadn't thought of yet. After several years of working at it, I have concluded that we don't have some special trick; we have a general cognitive ability to contextualise; an ability that is a central component of our use of language and one that we have not yet learned to simulate with computers.

The problem of automatic word-sense identification remains a stumbling-block in nearly all natural language-processing tasks. A possible exception might be the processing of domain-limited texts, as only one sense of a polysemous word may be appropriate when the text is limited to a specific topic. But the problem is quite general, even though its seriousness varies from one application to the next. It is widely acknowledged that better methods of automatic word-sense identification would facilitate language processing in a wide variety of applications.

The difficulty of automatic word-sense identification was initially recognised during the surge of research on machine translation in the 1950s and 1960s. Bar-Hillel, who was an early enthusiast for fully automatic machine translation, eventually concluded that the task is impossible; he was led to that conclusion because he believed that automatic word-sense identification is impossible (Bar-Hillel, 1960). He said that although it is a trivial matter for an English speaker to assign the appropriate sense of "pen" in the sentence, "the box is in the pen", (an enclosure rather than a writing implement) no computer program could do so. We can assign the context-appropriate sense to "pen" because our world knowledge includes information about the relative sizes of boxes, writing implements, and play pens. Bar-Hillel believed that a general solution to such problems would involve a complete characterisation of world knowledge, which is unbounded.

In that same essay Bar-Hillel (1960, p.163) estimated that it might be possible to automatically select the context-appropriate sense 80% of the time, but "the remaining 20% will require not one quarter of the effort spent for the first 80%, but many, many times this effort, with a few percent remaining beyond the reach of any conceivable effort." He referred to that prediction as an instance of the "80% fallacy", which he felt was common in artificial intelligence. I refer to it as The Curse of Bar-Hillel. At Princeton we have indeed reached 80% accuracy, although not as easily as Bar-Hillel might have expected, but our efforts to do better are still under his Curse.

Although interest in machine translation lapsed during the 1970s, the problem of word-sense identification was so central to natural language processing that research on it actually increased. This is not the place for a review of the past quarter century (see Hirst, 1987, for an excellent survey), so I will try to be schematic.

Begin with the fact that some meanings of a word occur more often than others. Let me call this most frequent meaning the *default sense* of the word. That is to say, when you have no other information, your best guess is the most frequent sense. According to our results, the default sense will be right 69% of the time. Clearly, that is not good enough for any practical applications.

There seem to be three ways to attack this problem. One way is simply to avoid it by limiting the domain of discourse. Within a narrow domain, default senses (for that domain) are likely to be right far more often than 69% of the time. Moreover, in addition to knowing the vocabulary for that domain, a language-comprehension system will ordinarily be given enough specific knowledge about the topic to be able to deal with any residual polysemy. The trouble, of course, is that the system is limited to that domain. One of our remarkable human skills seems to be an ability to change the vocabulary—and the default sense—when moving from one domain of discourse to another.

If it is not possible to limit the domain of discourse, then the problem is to find heuristics that will recognise when the less-frequent meanings are being used. And there are two ways that this more difficult problem has been attacked. One is to write short programs that will examine the context looking for signs of a less-frequent sense; programs that are sometimes called "word experts" (Small, 1980). A word expert might consist of templates describing the local contexts in which different senses occur; when one of the templates is found, it usually indicates a correct sense; if none of the templates fits the context, then fall back on the default sense. Writing such programs is tedious work, however, and the results have not escaped the Curse of Bar-Hillel.

The alternative approach takes advantage of the statistical learning systems and the large machine-readable corpora that are now available. This approach has enjoyed success in speech-recognition systems and in systems for identifying parts of speech, and the possibility of extending it to word-sense identification seems promising.

Statistical classifiers identify polysemous word senses based on the analysis of co-occurrence patterns in a textual corpus. They typically train on a set of contexts where the sense is known for each instance of the polysemous target, and test on a different set of contexts. Most statistical classifiers will automatically favour the default sense; indeed, with a Bayesian system it may be difficult to over-ride the priors.

So far, however, I do not believe that any of these approaches has produced satisfactory results, although sometimes it is hard to tell. One problem with research in this area is the shortage of semantically disambiguated corpora on which to train and test. Creating such corpora is very labour-intensive, but without them it is hard to compare different systems for automatic word-sense identification.

In summary, then, this important problem of automatic word-sense identification has proved to be surprisingly difficult, but recent advances in computational linguistics and computer technology have opened new approaches to it. However, there is a serious need for semantically classified materials that can be used to develop, test, and compare alternative methods of automatic word-sense identification. Unfortunately, however, these computational models of word-sense identification have not taught us much about how human beings are able to cope with polysemy so rapidly and accurately.

It is possible, of course, that people deal with contexts in some manner different from anything we have so far imagined. But until we do understand better how people contextualise, I fear we will not understand one of the basic aspects of our mental life.

CONCLUSION

In conclusion, a word about meaning. I emphasised the importance of context in these remarks, and I defined context as those parts of a situation that we use to determine meaning, but I left the definition of meaning as an exercise for the reader. When I got around to linguistic examples, I assumed implicitly that the meaning of a word is something you should be able to look up in a good dictionary.

As I have argued with myself about these relations—on the one hand context, on the other hand meaning—I have frequently felt that I was struggling to combine theories of meaning that take *reference* as basic with theories of meaning that take *use* as basic. Definitions can be viewed as stating what a word can refer to; contexts can be viewed as determining how to use the word to make such references. Or, to put my dilemma differently, if I were forced to choose between theories of meaning based on reference and theories of meaning based on use, I would be helpless. Neither approach can stand alone.

At present, however, we understand reference much better than we understand use. So there is a problem here; an unsolved problem that is both fascinating and important: what cognitive operations are involved in our remarkable ability to contextualise?

REFERENCES

Bar-Hillel, Y. (1960). A demonstration of the nonfeasibility of fully automatic high quality translation. In F.L. Alt (Ed.), *Advances in computers*, vol. 1, pp.158–163. New York: Academic Press.

Barker, R.C. (1968). *Ecological psychology: Concepts and methods for studying the environment of human behavior*. Stanford: Stanford University Press.

Bühler, K. (1934). *Sprachtheorie: die Darstellungsfunktion der Sprache*. Jena: Gustav Fischer.

Charles, W.G. (1988). The categorization of sentential contexts. *Journal of Psycholinguistic Research, 17*, 403–411.

Choueka, Y., & Lusignan, S. (1985). Disambiguation by short contexts. *Computers and the Humanities, 19*, 147–157.

Francis, W.N., & Kučera, H. (1982). *Frequency analysis of English usage: Lexicon and grammar*. Boston, MA: Houghton Mifflin.

Hirst, G. (1987). *Semantic interpretation and the resolution of ambiguity*. Cambridge: Cambridge University Press.

Jastrezembski, J.E. (1981). Multiple meanings, number of related meanings, frequency of occurrence, and the lexicon. *Cognitive Psychology, 13*, 278–305.

Jastrezembski, J.E., & Stanners, R.F. (1975). Multiple word meanings and lexical search speed. *Journal of Verbal Learning and Verbal Behavior, 14*, 534–537.

Kaplan, A. (1955). An experimental study of ambiguity and context. *Mechanical Translation, 2*, 39–46.

Kintsch, W. (1972). *The representation of meaning in memory*. Hillsdale, NJ: Lawrence Erlbaum Associates Inc.

Kučera, H., & Francis, W.N. (1967). *Computational analysis of present-day American English*. Providence, RI: Brown University Press.

Lewin, K. (1936). *Principles of topological psychology*. New York: McGraw-Hill.

Lorge, I. (1937). The English semantic count. *Teachers College Record, 39*, 65–77.

Markman, E. (1989). *Categorization and naming in children: Problems of induction*. Cambridge, MA: MIT Press.

McKeown, M.G., & Curtis, M.E. (1987). *The nature of vocabulary acquisition*. Hillsdale, NJ: Lawrence Erlbaum Associates Inc.

Miller, G.A., & Charles, W.G. (1991). Contextual correlates of semantic similarity. *Language and Cognitive Processes, 6*, 1–28.

Miller, G.A., Chodorow, M., Landes, S., Leacock, C., & Thomas, R.G. (1994). Using a semantic concordance for sense identification. *Proceedings of ARPA Workshop on Human Language Technology* (pp.240–243). San Francisco, CA: Morgan Kaufmann.

Miller, G.A., & Gildea, P.M. (1987). How children learn words. *Scientific American, 257*, 94–99.

Miller, G.A., Heise, G.A., & Lichten, W. (1951). The intelligibility of speech as a function of the context of the test materials. *Journal of Experimental Psychology, 41*, 329–335.

Miller, G.A., & Johnson-Laird, P.N. (1976). *Language and perception*. Cambridge, MA: Harvard University Press.

Miller, G.A., Leacock, C., Tengi, R., & Bunker, R. (1993). A semantic concordance. *Proceedings of ARPA Workshop on Human Language Technology* (pp.303–308). San Francisco, CA: Morgan Kaufmann.

Shannon, C.E. (1948). A mathematical theory of communication. *Bell System Technical Journal, 27*, 379–423, 623–656.

Small, S. (1980). *Word Expert parsing: A theory of distributed word-based natural language understanding*. Doctoral dissertation, Department of Computer Science, University of Maryland, College Park, MD.

18   MILLER

Swinney, D. (1979). Lexical access during sentence comprehension: (Re)consideration of context effects. *Journal of Verbal Learning and Verbal Behavior*, *5*, 219–227.
Thorndike, E.L., & Barnhart, C.L. (1935). *Junior Dictionary*. Glenview, IL: Scott Foresman.
Zipf, G.K. (1945). The meaning–frequency relationship of words. *Journal of General Psychology*, *33*, 251–256.

2 The Interpretation of Words

Patrizia Tabossi
Trieste University, Italy

One of the main goals of psycholinguistics is to explain how people understand language. A satisfactory theory of this crucial human ability requires the clarification of the many subprocesses it involves: to name only a few, the perception of spoken and written language, the syntactic parsing of sentences, the use of lexical information.

In the early days of cognitive psychology, one of the issues extensively investigated was what does it mean to understand language or, to put it in a different way, what is the outcome of the processes of comprehension. One view, widely accepted at the time and still popular (McKoon & Ratcliff, 1992), was that to understand a sentence is to build a mental representation of its meaning in a propositional form. According to Kintsch's theory (1974), a proposition contains a predicate and a number of arguments. Relations among elements in the propositions are specified by means of verbal frames in the lexicon, described according to Fillmore's grammar (1968). The propositional representation of a sentence such as "The man broke the window with a stone", for instance, is (BREAK, A: MAN, I: STONE, O: WINDOW), where A, I, and O specify the functions of the noun phrases: agent, instrument, and object respectively.

Propositional representations need not correspond exactly to the information explicitly contained in a text. Inferential processes may operate so that the representation of a text includes propositions whether or not the information they express is explicitly given. The proposition (ANIMAL,

DOG), for instance, may be included in the representation of either one of the following texts (Kintsch, 1974, p.156):

A strong hand was needed to restrain the dog. The dog was an animal whose instincts had been aroused by the sight of the fleeing deer.

A strong hand was needed to restrain the dog. The dog's instincts had been aroused by the sight of the fleeing deer.

In this theory, the semantic information conveyed by the individual words in a text is extracted from a subset of semantic memory which contains lexical concept-types. These lexical entries are organised and contain various kinds of information: phonemic, graphemic, syntactic, semantic, imaginal, and sensory. Moreover, they include information about one's personal experiences related to the concept. All this information is assumed to be retrieved whenever one comes across the corresponding word in a sentence. Thus, lexical information, in addition to information drawn from one's general knowledge, contributes to the representation of a sentence. Sentential context, however, does not contribute to the comprehension of lexical items, which is identical in all contexts.

This claim was at odds with studies showing effects of context on the interpretation of individual words. Perhaps, the best-known of these studies is Barclay, Bransford, Franks, McCarrell, and Nitsch (1974) whose subjects found it easier to recall a sentence like "The man lifted the piano" than a sentence like "The man tuned the piano" when they were given "something heavy" as a memory cue, whereas the reverse was true when the cue was "something with a nice sound".

Being heavy and having a nice sound are both aspects of the meaning of *piano*, but their salience varies depending on the context of occurrence of the word. The selective use of different aspects of a word's meaning, which Barclay et al. (1974) referred to as semantic flexibility, was later shown not to be a memory effect (Tabossi & Johnson-Laird, 1980), calling therefore for a theory of comprehension that could account for context effects on lexical interpretation.

The need for a similar theory was also made apparent by studies on instantiation. This is a well-established phenomenon whereby people use context and general knowledge in order to give specific interpretations to general terms. *Container*, for instance, is encoded either as *basket* or as *bottle*, depending on whether it occurs in a sentence like "The container held the apples" or else in a sentence like "The container held the cola" (Anderson & Ortony, 1975).

In order to explain the various phenomena related to the contextual interpretation of words, several authors proposed that words do not have distinct meanings, but a whole set of potential meanings. As Halff, Ortony, and Anderson (1976, p.378) put it, "...words do not have discrete, qualitatively distinct meanings. Instead, they act in different contexts to establish boundaries in our underlying continuum of knowledge".

Noticing how poor and/or variable the lexical information used at times in the process of language comprehension is, some authors went as far as to claim that the meaning of a word depends entirely on context, and there may be no overlap between two uses of the same word (Jacoby, Craik, & Begg, 1979; Olson, 1970).

In the debate on how lexical information is used in language comprehension, Johnson-Laird took a position in favour of the relevance of context on the interpretation of words. He observed, for instance (1975, p.130):

> ...it is plausible to suppose that a listener does not necessarily retrieve all the information he possesses about each word occurring in a sentence... [W]hat is retrieved for a given word probably depends upon its context. Different features of a word become salient as its context is varied, e.g., "He sat on a tomato" (tomatoes are squashy, messy), "The sun was an over-ripe tomato" (tomatoes are red), "He likes tomatoes" (tomatoes are eaten).

Elsewhere (1983, p.233), for ambiguous words Johnson-Laird noted:

> ...the processes that determine the intended sense of a word are extremely efficient. They readily bring to mind the appropriate sense of a word from the context in which it occurs. Indeed, one has the impression that it is harder to think of all the different meanings of a word presented in isolation than to retrieve a relevant sense when the word occurs in context.

While assuming that words are interpreted in context, and not all the information attached to them needs to be used to understand the sentence in which they occur, he also argued against the idea that lexical items have no specific meanings (1983, p.238):

> Suppose, for the sake of argument, that one of the original sentences in the experiment by Anderson et al. ["The fish attacked the swimmer"] had been:
>
> It attacked the swimmer
>
> then doubtless *shark* would be a better retrieval cue than *it*. But no one would make the egregious error of arguing that *it* has indefinitely many meanings of which one is *shark*.

Johnson-Laird's view on the meanings of words and their use in context derived, on the one hand, from his theory of the mental lexicon (Miller & Johnson-Laird, 1976), and, on the other hand, from the theory of mental models which offers a unified view of language comprehension and reasoning (Johnson-Laird, 1983). According to the mental model theory, understanding a sentence is not to build a description of the sentence, i.e. the propositional representation of its meaning. Rather, it requires the construction of a mental model of the state of affairs described by the sentence, and its structure is analogous to the corresponding events in the world. A central assumption of the theory is that linguistic capability interacts with world knowledge. In particular, information provided by the individual words of a sentence is understood in relation to one's knowledge of situations similar to those described by the sentence. Hence, depending on the linguistic and extra-linguistic context, selected aspects of a word's meaning will become salient in different sentences and will contribute differently to the construction of their mental models. On this hypothesis, individual words have a limited number of meanings, whose various aspects are related among themselves and to other concepts in complex ways (Miller & Johnson-Laird, 1976). These meanings can be selectively used in the comprehension of sentences, allowing the instantiation of specific referents in the different mental models. Thus, in "it attacked the swimmer", *it* has a single meaning—the same as in "it smashed the window". Yet, *it* can refer to many entities, including fish and stone, and what is instantiated in the different contexts is not one of its meanings, but a specific referent.

Since those early years, research on language has made progress on the comprehension of words in context, clarifying on the one hand which aspects of a word's meaning are context-sensitive and which are not, and specifying, on the other hand, the different processes involved in the use of lexical information during sentence comprehension. In the remainder of this chapter, these developments on both unambiguous and ambiguous words will first be described. Then their impact on the debate about the functional architecture of the mind will be considered. Finally, current theories of concepts will be briefly introduced, and their close resemblance to Johnson-Laird's views of human cognition discussed.

INTERPRETING UNAMBIGUOUS WORDS

With respect to how unambiguous words are understood in context, researchers have focused their attention mainly on two issues. First, to what extent does context affect lexical interpretation? Is each aspect of a word's meaning equally sensitive to context, or are some aspects more sensitive than others? Second, by means of what processes can an unambiguous word be interpreted in context? Two hypotheses are tenable: (a) the retrieval of the meaning of a word is not immediately sensitive to context, and phenomena of interpretation take place at a later stage, after retrieval has occurred; (b) the interpretation of a word takes place immediately at the time of accessing the word meaning, and context guides this process. Although related, the two problems are clearly distinct, one concerning what information about a word is context-sensitive, and the other how context operates in selecting whatever information is sensitive to it.

Empirical evidence on the former issue indicates that not all the aspects of a word's meaning are equally dependent on context: although some become available regardless of context, others do so only when they are contextually relevant. In a property verification task, Barsalou (1982) had his subjects decide whether the meaning of a word (e.g. *skunk, roof*) that they had previously read in a sentential context did or did not have a subsequently specified feature. The feature could be central (e.g. a skunk has a smell) or peripheral to the word's meaning (e.g. a roof can be walked upon). The subjects had to decide as soon as possible whether the object denoted by the word had the property. The following example illustrates the experimental conditions:

	Central properties
Unrelated	The *skunk* was under a large willow
Related	The *skunk* stunk up the entire neighbourhood
Control	The *fire* was easily visible through the trees
	HAS A SMELL
	Peripheral properties
Unrelated	The *roof* had been renovated prior to the rainy season
Related	The *roof* creaked under the weight of the repairman
Control	The *tightrope* was high off the ground
	CAN BE WALKED UPON

Barsalou found that responses to the central properties were slower in the control condition than in either the related or the unrelated condition. By contrast, responses to the peripheral properties were slower in both the unrelated and control condition than in the related condition.

Similarly, in Greenspan (1986) subjects were asked to judge on a 7-point scale the level of association between a word and a sentence. In the scale, 1 indicated no association and 7 a strong association. The word denoted either a central or a peripheral property of an object named in the sentence (e.g. ice is cold and slippery). The sentences either emphasised one of the properties (e.g. "The fresh meat was protected by the ice", "Robert fell on the ice"), or was a control. The results indicated that both central and peripheral properties were more highly associated to the experimental than to the control sentences. However, peripheral properties were found to be reliably more associated to the sentence that emphasised them than to the other experimental sentence, whereas no corresponding difference was found for central properties.

This type of evidence suggests that not all the information about the meaning of a word is instantiated in the mental representation of a sentence, and while some aspects are invariably present, others are not. But what are the processes that lead to the contextual interpretation of lexical items? Is interpretation the result of a unique process or are there different processes underlying it? In Barsalou's study, peripheral properties are most unlikely to be among the properties one uses to name or identify objects: a roof can certainly be walked upon, but is not made for walking on, and this information cannot be considered part of the meaning of *roof*. Moreover, the sentential context follows the occurrence of the word, whose access must therefore take place before contextual information is available. Under these conditions, it is impossible for the context to guide the initial access to the word's semantic information, and interpretation can only result from initial context-insensitive access followed by post-access inferential processes.

Likewise, post-access inferential processes underlie the instantiation of general terms. In fact, regardless of whether or not the biasing context is prior to the general term, its meaning does not include the meaning of the more specific concepts: *basket* and *bottle* are not part of the meaning of *container*. It is only through an inferential process that in the mental model of a sentence a general term may be represented as more specific.

The situation is different in Greenspan (1986), where the biasing contexts precede the relevant nouns, and make salient either central or peripheral features, both of which are part of the meanings of the nouns. Here, whether interpretation results from selective access or from context-insensitive access followed by a post-access selection can only be established empirically. In fact, in the same study Greenspan conducted a cross-modal experiment, whose results closely matched the association judgements, suggesting that context may guide initial access to selected aspects of a noun's meaning.

Comparable results have been obtained, also with the cross-modal paradigm, by Tabossi (1988a). The subjects listened to sentences that either primed an aspect of the meaning of an unambiguous noun in a sentence (priming condition), or primed another aspect of its meaning (inhibiting condition), or primed no specific aspect of the noun's meaning (neutral condition). The aspect was selected so that it was considered by an independent panel of subjects to be relevant to the noun's meaning, but not the most relevant one. The following is an example of the experimental conditions:

Priming: In the light, the blond hair of the little girl had the lustre of gold (gold is yellow)

Neutral: At the lecture, the clever teacher spoke at length about gold (no specific aspect of gold)

Inhibiting: In the shop, the artisan shaped with ease the bar of gold (gold is malleable)

The results showed that deciding that YELLOW, visually presented at the offset of *gold*, is a word, was fastest after the priming context, next fastest after the neutral context, and slowest after the inhibiting context. Moreover, the same study ruled out the possibility that the findings could be attributed to the facilitation produced by a previous word in the sentence or by the sentence itself directly priming the target.

In disagreement with Greenspan (1986) and Tabossi (1988a), were the results obtained by Whitney, McKay, Kellas, and Emerson (1985), who investigated the effect of context on the access to the meaning of unambiguous nouns with a modified Stroop procedure. Their subjects listened to a sentence that either biased a high-dominant aspect of the meaning of the last noun in the sentence (e.g. "The boy skinned the trout"), or a low-dominant aspect of it (e.g. "The boy dropped his trout"), or else was a control (e.g. "The boy skinned his knee", "The boy dropped his milk"). After a delay of 0, 300, or 600 ms, the sentence was followed by a visual word denoting the high- or the low-dominant property of the object referred to by the noun (e.g. SCALES, SLIMY). The visual word was printed in coloured ink and the subjects' task was to name the colour. The interference produced by the visual word on colour naming measured the activation of the property denoted by the visual word: at 0 ms delay both SCALES and SLIMY interfered with colour naming after either of the biasing sentences significantly more than after the control sentences. At 300 ms and 600 ms delays the same pattern of results was obtained only with the dominant property. The low-dominant property, however, interfered with colour naming significantly more after the appropriate biasing context than after the inappropriate biasing context or the control context.

Whitney et al.'s results (1985) suggest an initial complete insensitivity of the processes of lexical access to contextual information. However, in order to test whether prior sentential context guides access to selected aspects of a noun's meaning, one needs to have the sentential frames prior to the relevant noun pointing to some specific property, which several of Whitney et al.'s sentences failed to do. "The man used the oak", for instance, was used by Whitney et al. in order to emphasise that oak can be used as timber. The whole sentence does prime that property, but the sentential frame prior to *oak* provides very few constraints as to the semantic information that should be contained in the incoming word. Therefore, it would be surprising if a similar context produced selective effects on immediate access.

The general picture that emerges from the studies on unambiguous words seems to indicate that words are interpreted in context, but the processes leading to such interpretation differ. In some cases, like the instantiation of general terms or the activation of features that are not part of the meaning of a noun, context does not lead to selective access. Rather, access occurs autonomously, and later inferential processes select the contextually appropriate interpretation of the word. On other occasions, however, a sufficiently constraining context may guide access. Central features, however, are always retrieved, regardless of context, whenever the word is encountered.

INTERPRETING AMBIGUOUS WORDS

How is it possible that context can guide access to selected aspects of the meaning of an unambiguous word, but has no effect on the access of ambiguous words? Intuitively, if context ought to have a different effect on ambiguous and unambiguous words, the opposite would seem more plausible. There are many contexts in which one may wonder what particular aspects of the meaning of unambiguous words are made salient (e.g. "At the lecture, the clever teacher spoke at length about gold"). It is very rare, however, that context does not disambiguate between the meanings of an ambiguity and one is left uncertain as to how the word should be interpreted. In fact, people hardly ever realise they have come across an ambiguous word.

Yet, contrary to intuition, Swinney (1979)—and others after him—found that context does not initially direct access to the appropriate meaning of an ambiguous word. Even more surprisingly, in a cross-modal study Onifer and Swinney (1981) replicated those results with unbalanced ambiguous words, i.e. ambiguities whose meanings are very different in frequency of use. Their subjects listened to sentences such as:

1. The housewife's face literally lit up as a plumber extracted her lost wedding ring from the sink.

2. The office walls were so thin that they could hear the ring of their neighbour's phone whenever a call came in.

Sentence 1 biases the dominant meaning of *ring*, whereas sentence 2 biases its subordinate meaning. The visual words, which were presented at the offset of *ring*, were related to the dominant or the subordinate meaning of *ring*, or else were control words (e.g. FINGER–TALENT; BELL–WHIP). The results showed that both sentences 1 and 2 facilitated lexical decision on both FINGER and BELL. No effect of context or dominance was found.

In order to reconcile the contradiction between the results on ambiguous words and those on unambiguous words, some authors suggested different processes for the two types of words (Potter & Faulconer, 1979). A theory, however, should be kept as simple as possible and, unless there are strong reasons to the contrary, it does not seem advisable to assume the existence of different mechanisms. Moreover, it is not clear how people could select the appropriate process before accessing a word (i.e. before knowing whether it is ambiguous or not). But how then can the discrepancy be accounted for? Tabossi reasoned that the most obvious difference between the studies on unambiguous words, yielding selective results, at least in contexts biasing central properties, and those on ambiguity, showing no context effects on access, was in the nature of prior contexts. High- and low-constraining sentences are known to have differential effects on the identification of an upcoming word (Schwanenflugel & LaCount, 1988). In the studies on unambiguous words, sentences prime specific aspects of a word's meaning and context operates by establishing constraints on the information related to the to-be-accessed word. Instead, in Swinney's work, as in most of the work on ambiguity, sentences bias one meaning of the ambiguous word, but prime no particular aspect of it. The sentence "The housewife's face literally lit up as a plumber extracted her lost wedding ring from the sink" clearly disambiguates *ring*, but emphasises no specific aspect of the biased meaning. As far as feature priming is concerned, Swinney's materials are very similar to the neutral contexts in Tabossi's study (1988a), which produced only weak effects on lexical decision as compared to the priming contexts. Hence, in a series of studies Tabossi and colleagues investigated whether sentential contexts that bias one meaning of an ambiguous word by making salient one of its aspects could yield selective access to the biased meaning. In Tabossi, Colombo, and Job (1987), the subjects performed a lexical decision task while listening to a sentence. In the test trials, the sentence contained an ambiguous word and biased an aspect either of its dominant or of its subordinate meaning. The visual target word, presented at the offset of the ambiguity, denoted the biased aspect of the dominant or of the subordinate meaning of the ambiguity, or else was a control, as in the following example:

1. The violent hurricane did not damage the ships that were in the port, one of the best equipped along the coast.

2. Deceived by the identical colour, the host took a bottle of barolo instead of port, and offered it to his guests.
    SAFE (dominant)
    RED (subordinate)
    SHORT (control)

The findings indicated that after sentence 1, responses to SAFE were faster than responses to either RED or SHORT, which did not reliably differ from each other. In contrast, after sentence 2, both SAFE and RED were responded to faster than the control.

Subsequent work showed that the difference between Onifer and Swinney (1981) and Tabossi et al. (1987) was due to the different types of sentential contexts. In fact, after a constraining context, i.e. a context biasing the dominant meaning of an ambiguity by making salient one central aspect of its meaning (e.g. "The violent hurricane did not damage the ships that were in the port, one of the best equipped along the coast"), only the target related to the dominant, contextually appropriate meaning of the ambiguity was facilitated. By contrast, after a non-constraining context, i.e. a context biasing the dominant meaning by making the subordinate one implausible (e.g. "The man had to be at the port at five o'clock for a very important meeting"), both targets related to the ambiguous word were responded to faster than the unrelated control (Tabossi, 1988b).

Consistent with findings on unambiguous words, and insofar as current methodologies are adequate to tap initial access processes, these studies indicate that both context and dominance may affect the time course of activation of the meaning(s) of an ambiguous word. In isolation, as observed by Simpson and Burgess (1985), the activation of the dominant meaning of an ambiguity is stronger, faster, and longer-lasting than the activation of its subordinate meaning. This pattern of activation is not altered by the occurrence of the ambiguity in a context that is not sufficiently constrained. A constraining context, however, produces effects, strengthening and speeding up the activation of the congruent meaning at the expense of the incongruent one. When the contextually congruent meaning is also the dominant one, the subordinate meaning, which is already slower and weaker in isolation, receives some initial activation from the perceptual input, but this may never become strong enough to be detected by current experimental methodologies. Instead, when context constrains the subordinate meaning, the activation received from the perceptual input by the dominant meaning is still sufficient to render it detectable, so that both meanings are found to be active (Tabossi & Zardon, 1993).

LEXICAL PROCESSING AND THE ARCHITECTURE OF THE MIND

Swinney's studies are among the most popular in current psycholinguistics, and a large part of their popularity, in addition to their intrinsic value, is due to the role they play in the debate on the functional architecture of the mind. There are two competing conceptions of cognitive architecture that are currently being studied in detail. In modular architectures, there is a set of encapsulated processors, each of which computes an output based on input from a restricted domain. Furthermore, intra-modular processes are characterised as mandatory, fast, automatic, attention- and interference-free, whereas extra-modular, integrative processes are characterised as slow, subject to interference, attention-demanding, and voluntarily controlled (Fodor, 1983). One consequence of a strictly modular architecture is that mutually relevant constraints will often be separated into different processing modules. In constraint-based systems, however, processing is based on different types of information, and the architecture is organised to allow the system to make use of constraints from different domains (McClelland, 1987; Rumelhart & McClelland, 1986).

Ambiguity resolution is handled differently in modular and constraint-based systems. Modular systems handle ambiguity either by having a module compute multiple outputs that are then filtered by subsequent modules (Forster, 1979), or incorporating decision principles within a module, so that it computes a single output without appealing to extra-modular information (Frazier, 1987). In contrast, a constraint-based system will make use of the available constraints that are relevant to resolve the ambiguity. Alternatives will be more or less active, depending on their likelihood and the degree of support from the constraints.

In this debate, Swinney's results are among the strongest pieces of evidence in support of the modular view, in that they suggest that the lexical processor does not make use of the available extra-lexical contextual information. But, as the foregoing discussion indicates, an extreme modular view is unlikely to be tenable, as context effects can be obtained under certain conditions. However, in contrast with the predictions of a strictly constraint-based view, not all the available information can be freely used by the different processors, (Swinney, 1979; Tabossi, 1988b).

Seemingly inconclusive results are not confined to ambiguity resolution. Even associative priming, which is one of the most typical instances of automatic intra-lexical effects, is not always mandatory, and hence violates a crucial characteristic of modular processes (Hoffman & MacMillan, 1985; Simpson, Peterson, Casteel, & Burgess, 1989). Likewise, outside language, research on perception has shown that the most basic, typically automatic processes, such as visual feature extraction may be influenced by focal attention (Prinzmetal, Presti, & Posner, 1986). On balance, the best conclusion that can be drawn from all these studies, and one on which many researchers are now converging, has been clearly expressed by Tanenhaus, Dell, and Carlson (1987), according to whom complete modularity and complete interaction can be best viewed as the two extremes along a continuum in which top-down and contextual information can act on cognitive processes in different ways. Discovering exactly how various types of information affect specific processes remains one of the main goals of current research.

LEXICAL INTERPRETATION AND CONCEPT
REPRESENTATION

The contextual interpretation of words and the different mechanisms underlying it call for a complex theory of the mental representation of lexical concepts which, while allowing for the flexible and dynamic use of semantic information, avoids the trap whereby word comprehension is completely context-dependent. The need for such a theory is also suggested by neuropsychological and developmental data.

A commonly observed phenomenon in neurological patients with lexical disorders is that some kinds of information about words' meanings (typically, superordinate information) are better preserved or more easily accessed than others (typically, specific attributes) (Martin & Fedio, 1983; Warrington, 1975). Warrington (1975) reported the case of a patient who could assign the appropriate category to objects denoted by 20 words, responding correctly to 18 out of 20 questions such as "Is cabbage a plant, an animal, or an inanimate object?". The same patient, however, made 28% of errors when required to answer questions concerning the objects' specific characteristics (e.g. "Is a cabbage green, brown or grey?").

Other patients show a clear dissociation in their ability to identify and name different categories of objects, most notably living and non-living ones (Warrington & Shallice, 1984). An explanation often proposed to account for such a dissociation—admittedly problematic (see Shallice, 1988 for a discussion)—is the selective loss in some patients of either perceptual or functional aspects of concepts, the former being crucial to the identification of living objects, the latter to the identification of artifacts. The pairing living objects/perceptual characteristics, and non-living objects/functional characteristics, however, is not a necessary one. Silveri and Gainotti (1988), for instance, described a patient, LA, who correctly named 58% of animals that were metaphorically or functionally defined (e.g. the man's best friend → dog; the farm animal which bleats and gives milk → sheep), but only 9% of animals defined descriptively (e.g. a wild black and white striped animal → zebra).

In language development, differences in the acquisition and use of various aspects of words' meanings are also well documented. In fact, a now-classic debate in the field is that between those who stressed the relevance of perceptual features in the organisation of meanings in young children and those who emphasised the pre-eminence of functional features (Clark, 1973; Nelson, 1973).

Once investigators abandoned the Fregean view of meaning, and were faced with the problem of how lexical concepts should be mentally represented, they argued that lexical concepts should contain two distinct types of information, variously characterised as analytic vs. prototypical information, core concept vs. identification procedures, defining vs. characteristic features. In essence, the distinctions were meant to capture the fact that a concept such as *grandmother*, should include both necessary information (e.g. being mother of a parent), and characteristic information (e.g. being old, with white hair, etc.) (Cohen & Murphy, 1984). Implicit in these distinctions was the notion that criteria akin to those used in science must play a role in how human beings conceptualise the world. Accordingly, the first studies on the organisation of semantic memory for natural domains, such as animals, hypothesised zoologic-like classification systems (Collins & Quillian, 1969). For years, this strong logical bias dominated many areas of cognitive psychology, in spite of Miller and Johnson-Laird's claims (1976) that logic and scientific knowledge have little room in human cognition, and it took the weight of a large body of evidence for people to fully appreciate the role of experience in human mentality. As a result of this change of attitude, the distinction between necessary and typical information in concepts has given way to more realistic views, which differ from previous approaches in at least two respects that are not disjoint. First, concepts are no longer treated as separate entities, and their interrelations are now considered crucial to the correct characterisation of the individual concepts. Second, what counts as more or less relevant in identifying an object as a category member depends on one's implicit theory of the whole domain (Barsalou & Medin, 1986; Murphy & Medin, 1985). In accordance with this view, Keil (1987) has shown that children's shift from the use of more peripheral to more central features in object identification is domain-specific. A child may correctly refuse to identify an object as an island unless it is entirely surrounded by water, while being prepared to call any elderly lady a grandmother, regardless of kinship relations. According to Keil, a child's changing ability to categorise is not the result of a shift of strategy that applies to all categories. Moreover, when a shift occurs for a specific object (e.g. the island), the change reflects a modification in the child's knowledge of the whole domain to which the object belongs.

Current theories of concepts are clearly reminiscent of the views expressed on the issue by Johnson-Laird years ago, and now proven correct. This is not dissimilar from what has happened in the area of reasoning. Here, the logical view has a long and explicit tradition that has made the natural logic theory dominant for a long time (Braine, 1990). Contrary to that view, Johnson-Laird has proposed his theory of mental models, which while acknowledging people's ability to reason with connectives and quantifiers, can also explain the powerful effect of content on their performance. There is now a growing consensus that this theory is correct. In addition, unlike competing views, it shows an explanatory power that is not restricted to deductive reasoning, but extends to induction, probabilistic reasoning and decision-making (Johnson-Laird, 1994; Legrenzi, Girotto, & Johnson-Laird, 1993). The basis of Johnson-Laird's theorising, ranging from lexical concepts to language and reasoning, is the notion that psychological facts need explanations radically different from those proposed in other domains. People may produce formal systems, and indeed logic is a product of the human mind. However, it does not follow from this that our mind works like a formal system. Likewise, the classification systems offered by natural sciences or the semantic principles of linguistics cannot simply be borrowed by psychology. Cognitive psychology has often taken, though not always consciously, this approach; and it is not surprising that in the process of recovering from this attitude it meets the ideas of those who, like Johnson-Laird, did not make that logical error.

ACKNOWLEDGEMENTS

The research reported here was supported in part by a grant 40% and in part by a grant 60% MURST. I would like to thank Nicoletta Caramelli and Riccardo Luccio for discussing with me some of the issues addressed in the chapter.

REFERENCES

Anderson, R.C., & Ortony, A. (1975). On putting apples into bottles—A problem of polysemy. *Cognitive Psychology*, 7, 167–180.

Barclay, J.R., Bransford, J.D., Franks, J.J., McCarrell, N.C., & Nitsch, K. (1974). Comprehension and semantic flexibility. *Journal of Verbal Learning and Verbal Behavior*, 13, 471–481.

Barsalou, L.W. (1982). Context-independent and context-dependent information in concepts. *Memory and Cognition*, 10, 82–93.

Barsalou, L.W., & Medin, D.L. (1986). Concepts: Static definitions or concept-dependent representations? *Cahiers de Psychologie Cognitive*, 6, 187–202.

Braine, M.D.S. (1990). The "natural logic" approach to reasoning. In W.F. Overton (Ed.), *Reasoning, necessity, and logic: Developmental perspectives*. Hillsdale, NJ: Lawrence Erlbaum Associates Inc.

Clark, E.V. (1973). What's in a word. On the child's acquisition of semantics in his first language. In T.E. Moore (Ed.), *Cognitive development and the acquisition of language*. New York: Academic Press.

Cohen, B., & Murphy, G.L. (1984). Models of concepts. *Cognitive Science*, 8, 27–58.

Collins, A.M., & Quillian, M.R. (1969). Retrieval time from semantic memory. *Journal of Verbal Learning and Verbal Behavior*, 8, 240–247.

Fillmore, C.J. (1968). The case for case. In E. Bach & R.T. Harms (Eds.), *Universal in linguistic theory*. New York: Holt, Rinehart, & Winston.

Fodor, J.A. (1983). *The modularity of mind*. Cambridge, MA: MIT Press.

Forster, K.I. (1979). Levels of processing and the structure of the language processor. In W.E. Cooper & E.C.T. Walker (Eds.), *Sentence processing: Psycholinguistic studies presented to Merrill Garrett*. Hillsdale, NJ: Lawrence Erlbaum Associates Inc.

Frazier, L. (1987). Theories of syntactic processing. In J. Garfield (Ed.), *Modularity in knowledge representation and natural language processing*. Cambridge, MA: MIT Press.

Greenspan, S.L. (1986). Semantic flexibility and referential specificity of concrete nouns. *Journal of Memory and Language, 25*, 539–557.

Halff, H.M., Ortony, A., & Anderson, R.C. (1976). A context-sensitive representation of word meanings. *Memory and Cognition, 4*, 378–383.

Hoffman, J.E., & MacMillan, F.W. (1985). Is semantic priming automatic? In R. Parasuraman & D.R. Davies (Eds.), *Varieties of attention*. New York: Academic Press.

Jacoby, L.L., Craik, F.I.M., & Begg, I. (1979). Effects of decision difficulty on recognition and recall. *Journal of Verbal Learning and Verbal Behavior, 18*, 585–600.

Johnson-Laird, P.N. (1975). Meaning and the mental lexicon. In A. Kennedy & A. Wilkes (Eds.), *Studies in long term memory*. London: Wiley.

Johnson-Laird, P.N. (1983). *Mental models*. Cambridge, MA: Harvard University Press.

Johnson-Laird, P.N. (1994). Mental models and probabilistic reasoning. *Cognition, 50*, 189–209.

Keil, F.C. (1987). Conceptual development and category structure. In U. Neisser (Ed.), *Concepts and conceptual development*. Cambridge: Cambridge University Press.

Kintsch, W. (1974). *The representation of meaning in memory*. Hillsdale, NJ: Lawrence Erlbaum Associates Inc.

Legrenzi, P., Girotto, V., & Johnson-Laird, P.N. (1993). Focusing in reasoning and decision making. *Cognition, 49*, 37–66.

Martin, A., & Fedio, P. (1983). Word production and comprehension in Alzheimer's disease: The break-down of semantic knowledge. *Brain and Language, 19*, 121–141.

McClelland, J.L. (1987). The case for interactionism in language processing. In M. Coltheart (Ed.), *Attention and performance, 12. The psychology of reading*. London: Lawrence Erlbaum Associates Ltd.

McKoon, G., & Ratcliff, R. (1992). Inference during reading. *Psychological Review, 99*, 440–466.

Miller, G.A, & Johnson-Laird, P.N. (1976). *Language and perception*. Cambridge: Cambridge University Press.

Murphy, G.L., & Medin, D.L. (1985). The role of theories in conceptual coherence. *Psychological Review, 92*, 289–316.

Nelson, K. (1973). Some evidence for the cognitive basis of categorization and its functional basis. *Merrill-Palmer Quarterly, 29*, 387–394.

Olson, D.R. (1970). Language and thought: Aspects of a cognitive theory of semantics. *Psychological Review, 77*, 257–273.

Onifer, W., & Swinney, D.A. (1981). Accessing lexical ambiguity during sentence comprehension: Effects of frequency of meaning and contextual bias. *Memory and Cognition, 9*, 225–236.

Potter, M.C., & Faulconer, B.A. (1979). Understanding noun phrases. *Journal of Verbal Learning and Verbal Behavior, 18*, 509–521.

Prinzmetal, W., Presti, D.E., & Posner, M.I. (1986). Does attention affect feature integration? *Journal of Experimental Psychology: Human Perception and Performance, 12*, 361–369.

Rumelhart, D.E., & McClelland, J.L. (1986). *Parallel distributed processing: Explorations in the microstructure of cognition* (Vol. 1). Cambridge, MA: MIT Press.

Schwanenflugel, P., & LaCount, K.L. (1988). Semantic relatedness and scope of facilitation for upcoming words in sentences. *Journal of Experimental Psychology: Learning, Memory, and Cognition, 14*, 344–354.

Shallice, T. (1988). *From neuropsychology to mental structure*. Cambridge: Cambridge University Press.

Silveri, M.C., & Gainotti, G.B. (1988). Interaction between vision and language in category specific impairments. *Cognitive Neuropsychology, 5*, 677–709.

Simpson, G.B., & Burgess, C. (1985). Activation and solution processes in the recognition of ambiguous words. *Journal of Experimental Psychology: Human Perception and Performance, 11*, 28–39.

Simpson, G.B., Peterson, R.R., Casteel, M.A., & Burgess, C. (1989). Lexical and sentence context effects in word recognition. *Journal of Experimental Psychology: Learning, Memory, and Cognition, 15*, 88–97.

Swinney, D.A. (1979). Lexical access during sentence comprehension: (Re)consideration of context effects. *Journal of Verbal Learning and Verbal Behavior, 18*, 645–660.

Tabossi, P. (1988a). Effects of context on the immediate interpretation of unambiguous words. *Journal of Experimental Psychology: Learning, Memory, and Cognition, 14*, 153–162.

Tabossi, P. (1988b). Accessing lexical ambiguity in different types of sentential context. *Journal of Memory and Language, 27*, 324–340.

Tabossi, P., Colombo, L., & Job, R. (1987). Accessing lexical ambiguity: Effects of context and dominance. *Psychological Research, 49*, 161–167.

Tabossi, P., & Johnson-Laird, P.N. (1980). Linguistic context and the priming of semantic information. *Quarterly Journal of Experimental Psychology, 32*, 595–603.

Tabossi, P., & Zardon, F. (1993). Processing ambiguous words in context. *Journal of Memory and Language, 32*, 359–372.

Tanenhaus, M.K., Dell, G.S., & Carlson, G. (1987). Context effects in lexical processing: A connectionist approach to modularity. In J. Garfield (Ed.), *Modularity in knowledge representation and natural language processing*. Cambridge, MA: MIT Press.

Warrington, E.K. (1975). The semantic impairment of semantic memory. *Quarterly Journal of Experimental Psychology, 27*, 635–657.

Warrington, E.K., & Shallice, T. (1984). Category specific semantic impairments. *Brain, 107*, 829–853.

Whitney, P., McKay, T., Kellas, G., & Emerson, W.A., Jr. (1985). Semantic activation of noun concepts in context. *Journal of Experimental Psychology: Learning, Memory, and Cognition, 11*, 126–135.

3

The Other Side of Mental Models: Theories of Language Comprehension

Alan Garnham
Laboratory of Experimental Psychology, University of Sussex, UK

MENTAL MODELS AND LANGUAGE: SOME BEGINNINGS

In 1977 I was preparing for my final undergraduate examinations in Oxford, and considering various possibilities for postgraduate study. One topic that had particularly captured my interest was the analysis of motivation using the ideas of control system theory (MacFarland, 1971, 1974), and most of my options focused on the application of these ideas to the development of mother–infant interaction. Another strong interest was the later philosophy of Wittgenstein. However, the prospects for philosophy graduates in the UK in the late 1970s were particularly grim. It was partly for these reasons that I wanted to include among my options at least one that would allow me to work on the psychology of language. On the advice of my college tutor, Peter Bryant, this option took the form of an application to work with Phil Johnson-Laird in the Laboratory of Experimental Psychology at Sussex. Following an instinct that told me I had a deeper interest in questions about language than in questions about mother–infant interaction, I accepted an offer from Sussex. The rest is history. At least it is my personal history.

When I went there, the Laboratory of Experimental Psychology was positively buzzing with research on language. Kate Ehrlich, Til Wykes, and Mick Power were graduate students with Phil, and other members of the lab included Tony Ades, Anne Cutler, Steve Isard, Christopher Longuet-Higgins, Dennis Norris, and Kim Plunkett, not to mention the speech and hearing group! Phil suggested that I should consider investigating the psychological reality of selectional restrictions. However, his own attempts to address this issue were resulting in frustration, and I was not convinced that I should continue this line of research. An extensive review of the literature led me to, among other things, Richard Anderson's work on the instantiation of general terms (Anderson et al., 1977), and to studies of my own on instantiation (Garnham, 1979).

Reference and Mental Models

Instantiation is a type of inference. If someone is told that there is a container holding apples, they can infer that it is more likely to be a basket than a bottle. So work on instantiation links into a large body of research on language understanding both in psychology and in artificial intelligence (AI). Much of what was written about meaning and inference in psychology and AI in the 1970s was unsatisfactory. The term "semantic representation" was used as a catch-all, and different aspects of meaning were conflated. Anderson argued that a word such as "container" had infinitely many different meanings, one for each context in which it could be used—an idea that was clearly incompatible with the principles of lexicography. Phil had hinted at the notion of a mental model of a text in his chapter in *New horizons in linguistics* (Johnson-Laird, 1970), and he now suggested more specifically that reference was the key aspect of meaning that could explain the results on instantiation (see e.g. Johnson-Laird, 1983, pp.237–239, for his arguments). The crucial distinction, glossed over by Anderson, is that between sense and reference. "Container" does not have different *senses* in "The container held the apples" and "The container held the cola". But when these sentences are used felicitously, the noun phrase "the container" will almost certainly *refer* to objects of different kinds at the next level down in the classification hierarchy (in these cases, Anderson showed, quite probably a basket and a bottle).

In retrospect this idea seems an obvious one. But when it is thought through, it leads inexorably to a fully fledged mental models theory of language processing. If we forget, for the moment, about psycholinguistic experiments in which people read sentences without knowing who or what they are about, and think of how people use language in their everyday lives, we immediately realise that they talk about people, things, places, events, states, processes, and properties, and usually ones with which they are well acquainted. To understand everyday conversations—to extract the information that the contributors to those conversations are trying to convey—it is necessary to work out what particular people, things, places, events, states, processes, and properties are being talked about. Listeners must compute reference, and they must represent mentally the situations, real or imaginary, that are described or otherwise alluded to. To call these representations "semantic" is misleading. People don't convey meaning to each other, they convey information.

This idea was recognised, in the early 1980s, in the naming of one of the most important centres for the study of language, CSLI, the Center for the Study of Language and Information at Stanford University. It is no coincidence that the founders of CSLI share some of the concerns of the mental models theory of language comprehension. Phil's ideas about language, and indirectly my own, were strongly influenced by his attendance at a series of Cognitive Science conferences, which were part of the lead-in to the Sloan Foundation's Cognitive Science Program of the late 1970s and early 1980s. Among others attending these conferences were those who went on to found CSLI, including Stanley Peters and Jon Barwise.

Mutual Knowledge and the Use of Definite Descriptions

Reference is widely recognised as a central concern of mental models theory. The use of knowledge about other participants in a linguistic interchange, another topic that Phil and I puzzled over (Johnson-Laird & Garnham, 1980), is still largely neglected, at least in the mainstream mental models literature, which tends to be based on experiments using written, rather than spoken language. Nevertheless, it remains crucial to an account of how people understand each other, and has received some attention from people studying interactive dialogue (e.g. Clark & Wilkes-Gibbs, 1986; Garrod & Anderson, 1987).

Clark and Marshall (1981), in a paper originally presented at one of the Sloan conferences, considered the relation between definite reference and mutual knowledge. Although mutual knowledge, or some related concept, is important for theories of language understanding, there are problems with the particular account presented by Clark and Marshall (see Perner & Garnham, 1989). Phil and I, however, examined in more detail the implications of their ideas, together with the distinction drawn by the philosopher Keith Donnellan (1966) between referential and attributive uses of definite descriptions, for a proper account of how such descriptions are used in dialogue. In particular, we emphasised that it is lack of mutual knowledge, and hence an asymmetry between speaker/writer and listener/ reader, that typically prompts a linguistic interchange. Thus, both the speaker/writer's and the hearer/reader's knowledge (and their knowledge of each other's knowledge) determine how individuals ought to be described, and how descriptions will be understood. These considerations led to the idea of a mental model of discourse, which represents not only the content of what was said, but information about the participants in the discourse, and about who knows what about whom.

Towards a Mental Models Theory of Language Understanding

The "cognitive science" dimension of the mental models theory, which our work on definite descriptions introduced, is not an incidental aspect of the theory. To work in the mental models framework is to recognise that the niceties and complexities of language should not be ignored, or regarded as a nuisance, in constructing theories of language processing. They must directly inform the details of those theories. It is also to recognise that computing the information that a speaker or writer is trying to convey from linguistic input may be a complex process, but it is one that can be modelled in detail using techniques from AI and computer science. Although there has been some scepticism about the notion of cognitive science, and a tendency to think of it as a political convenience rather than a genuine meeting of minds, the mental models view is that a proper understanding of language processing cannot be developed from a narrow cognitive psychology perspective. It must be informed by the other disciplines of cognitive science.

For my own part, I am deeply grateful to Phil for suggesting that I spend a year as a Sloan postgraduate fellow at the newly founded Center for Cognitive Science at the University of Texas at Austin. In my thesis (Garnham, 1981, later published in a revised form as Garnham, 1987), I used ideas from the various cognitive sciences, and in particular from discourse representation theory (Kamp, 1981) and related ideas about the semantics of discourse, in presenting a mental models framework for thinking about language understanding in particular, and language processing more generally. What was perhaps not so clear at the time, but has become more apparent since, is that in the domain of language understanding mental models notions do, indeed, provide a *framework* for thinking about language understanding, and not a specific *theory* of language understanding or its subprocesses. In the remaining part of this chapter, I will consider this idea in more detail, as it is at the basis of many misunderstandings about what the notion of mental models does and does not have to offer to psycholinguistics.

MENTAL MODELS AS A FRAMEWORK

In the domain of reasoning, there is not only the mental models framework. There are also, on the one hand, theories of particular types of reasoning couched within that framework and, on the other hand, an alternative framework in which (alternative) specific theories can be couched. In the mental models framework, specific theories include a theory of syllogistic reasoning (Johnson-Laird & Bara, 1984), a theory of propositional reasoning (Johnson-Laird & Byrne, 1991), a theory of inductive reasoning (Johnson-Laird, 1994a), and a theory of probabilistic reasoning (Johnson-Laird, 1994b). The alternative framework, or perhaps the most important of two alternative frameworks, is that of mental logic. An example of a specific theory couched within that framework is the PSYCOP theory of deductive reasoning (Rips, 1994). Mental models theorists believe that mental logic is the wrong framework for thinking about human reasoning. They hold that belief chiefly because they consider the specific accounts of reasoning in the mental models framework are better supported empirically, and more coherent conceptually, than those in the mental logic framework. They do not, however, believe that mental logic is really mental models in disguise. Furthermore, although it is sometimes argued that reasoning with mental models is really a form of reasoning with a mental logic (Stenning & Oaksford, 1993), this argument is about a different matter. The claim is not that a mental models theory of, say, propositional reasoning proposes the same mental operations, or makes the same empirical predictions, as one based on a mental natural deduction system. Rather, it is that, despite the allegedly semantic, as opposed to syntactic, flavour of the mental models theory, the operations postulated in that theory are defined syntactically, and the theory is, in a sense, a proof theory for propositional calculus, albeit a nonstandard one.

On both counts, alternative framework and specific subtheories, the situation in language processing is different from that in reasoning. Before mental models, most experiments on the processing of meaning were presented in a loose theoretical framework, in which every aspect of meaning was dubbed "semantic" (or sometimes "semantic" and "pragmatic"). The important thing was to show that syntax could not account for all the empirical results, and that meaning played a role in comprehension. The exception to this general rule was the idea that the meaning could be captured in "propositions", and that the mental representation of the meaning of a text was, therefore, a propositional representation. This idea echoed various proposals for representing text meaning in AI, and became particularly influential in psychology following the publication of Kintsch's (1974) book, *The representation of meaning in memory*. Mental models have sometimes been regarded as an alternative to propositional representations, although Johnson-Laird (1982) suggests that they are derived from propositional representations. Furthermore, Kintsch later suggested (e.g. van Dijk & Kintsch, 1983) that situation models, which are in many respects similar to mental models, could be encoded as sets of propositions.

Are Propositional Representations an Alternative to Mental Models?

I will argue that there is no clear sense in which propositional representations provide an alternative to mental models. However, because of the way the term "propositional representation" has been used in the psychology of language, the issue is a complex one. In particular, the contrast between mental models and propositional representations appears initially to be a difference in the form of the proposed representation. However, questions about the form of mental representations are notoriously hard to answer, because answering them usually requires assumptions about the processes that build and manipulate those representations, and it can be difficult to justify assumptions about processes independently from assumptions about representation. In fact, propositional theories in the psychological literature tend to fail because they do not represent the *content* of texts correctly. Once their representational inadequacies are remedied, they are difficult to distinguish from mental model theories.

At their most general, "propositions" simply provide a way of writing down, or encoding, information. In the psychology of language, however, it has usually been assumed that a propositional representation closely reflects the way information is presented in a text. Thus, on this account, the propositional representation of a text describing a simple spatial layout, for example, will be different from a mental model of the same layout. If the text is:

The lamp is to the left of the candle.
The candle is in front of the cruet.
The cruet is to the left of the jug.

the propositional representation might be:

LEFT-OF(LAMP,CANDLE)
IN-FRONT-OF(CANDLE,CRUET)
LEFT-OF(CRUET,JUG)

whereas the mental model might be:

	cruet	jug
lamp	candle	

There is, however, no principled reason why representations that can be called propositional should be so closely linked to linguistic structure. Indeed, there is no reason why representations encoding information conveyed by text should directly reflect that structure (mental models don't). What is at issue here is in what sense the structure of a text reflects the structure of the information it conveys. If representations of the content of text reflect linguistic structure fairly directly, as propositional theorists in the psychology of language claim they do, the processes that construct them from linguistic input will be comparatively straightforward. If they do not, those processes must be more complex. Furthermore, the added complexity reflects the complexity in the relation between the information conveyed and the linguistic means of conveying it. Whatever format is used to represent that information mentally, there must be processes that derive the information from the text.

In fact, the idea that the meaning of texts might be encoded only in sets of propositions that closely reflect linguistic structure is easily dismissed, for example by the early experiments of Potts (e.g. 1972) on one-dimensional spatial arrays, and by later work on more complex arrays (e.g. Ehrlich & Johnson-Laird, 1982). Thus, any realistic theory of language processing based on the notion of a propositional representation would have to take a relatively sophisticated view of such representations.

Another potential problem for propositional theories arises in the domain of reference, which, as we have seen, was important in the genesis of the mental models theory. For example, in the propositional representation given earlier, the token of CANDLE in LEFT-OF(LAMP,CANDLE) is intended to represent the same object as the different token of CANDLE in IN-FRONT-OF(CANDLE,CRUET). However, it cannot in general be assumed that different tokens of a name of a category of objects refer to the same individual object. Otherwise it would be impossible to use propositional representations to represent situations in which there are, for example, two candles.

Many AI programs that used something akin to the propositional representations of psychologists solved the representational problem by appending numerical suffixes to tokens when they were intended to represent particular objects. Identity of suffix (for example, CANDLE63 and CANDLE63 in two different propositions) indicated a reference to the same object, different suffixes meant different objects. Further complications arose when representing, for example, people's beliefs, because people can believe that a single object seen in two different circumstances is two distinct objects (the morning star and the evening star, which are both the planet Venus) or, conversely, that two objects are one (for example, mistaking identical twins for a single person). Solving these representational problems does not, however, solve the language processing problem, as Garnham, Oakhill, and Johnson-Laird (1982) pointed out. Different linguistic expressions (e.g. "John", "the man I met last night", "him") can be used to refer to the same person or object, or to different people or objects. Thus, if propositional representations are too close to the linguistic form of text, so that they preserve information about the referring expressions used, constructing a propositional representation does not solve the problem of establishing co-reference (or nonco-reference). Hence, it does not solve the problem of reference itself. Alternatively, if "John", "the man I met last night", and "him" all get translated to tokens of JOHN15 or MAN326, it is the translation process that solves the problems of reference and co-reference, not the postulation of propositional representations. Thus, it is vital that a theory of comprehension should specify the details of this translation process.

Other representational problems that arise from the use of propositions can similarly be fixed. For example, some proposals about the representation of statements containing quantifiers in the propositional framework were unsatisfactory. These problems are, however, comparatively easily rectified, provided that the notion of a propositional representation is extended somewhat (see e.g. Hendrix, 1979). However, the changes that are necessary to rectify these representational problems all have the same effects. On the one hand they make propositional representations adequate to the task of encoding the information that texts and discourse convey. They do so by recognising that the structure of this information does not correspond in any simple way to the structure of texts. Hence, they lead to a notion of propositional representation in which such representations do not closely mirror the surface form of the texts whose information they encode. On the other hand, they make it increasingly hard to see how such representations can be derived from texts using the simple translational methods that proponents of propositional representations appear to have in mind. Such representations can only be constructed by using detailed knowledge of linguistic structure and detailed knowledge about the world— the kind of information thought to be essential in the construction of mental models. On this view there is no need to posit propositional representations of a particular kind as a halfway house between an encoding of the superficial form of a text and the construction of a mental model. We know that superficial representations *are* constructed, both from empirical evidence, and from the *a priori* consideration that there must be a mental representation of this information for the model-building processes to work on, particularly in the case of spoken language, where the linguistic signal itself is transient. We do not know exactly what superficial information is encoded from text, but we can be sure that the major content words, and their clausal relations are. Furthermore, the existence of these superficial representations can explain most or all of the facts that propositional representations, *qua* representations close to the surface form of texts, have been used to explain.

The preceding argument can be summarised as follows. The mental models theory captures an essential truth about representations of the *content* of texts. If propositional representations are to be taken seriously as representations of text content, they must be modified so that they capture the content we know (from considerations that are prior to psychological experimentation) that texts convey—information about people and things, their properties, and the relations between them. Thus, the argument is about the content of representations of content, and not specifically about their form, even though the contrast between mental models and propositional representations appears to be one about form.

It has, nevertheless, often been suggested that questions about the form of such representations can be addressed. The most general of these questions is whether "mental models", particularly those of spatial layouts, are in some sense analogue or imaginal. As the debate between proponents of imaginal and propositional (in the broad sense) representations has not led to a useful resolution, I will say only a few words on this issue.

Anderson (1978) showed that, in any particular case, the explanation of a psychological phenomenon could be attributed arbitrarily to assumptions about representations or assumptions about processes. One type of representation might appear to make some types of information readily available and others difficult to extract. But how available the information is depends on the processes responsible for extracting it. It might, for example, be natural to think of some types of mental model as analogue rather than propositional. Indeed, empirical evidence might appear compatible with the assumption that the representations are analogue (for example, it is easier to read off relations between objects that are far apart than relations between objects that are close, no matter which relations were explicit in the corresponding text, as in Potts' experiments referred to earlier). However, the apparent compatibility between evidence and theory depends not only on assumptions about representation, but also on assumptions about processes. One set of assumptions may be more plausible than another, and this is particularly likely when there is converging evidence about both representations and processes from different cognitive domains. But unfortunately this converging evidence is rarely strong enough to force a particular conclusion about the form of a representation. Nevertheless, it seems natural, when working at the abstract level of cognitive psychology, and not considering the mapping from, say, abstract processes to brain processes, to place the explanatory power largely in the form of the proposed representations and to assume straightforward (abstract) processes for manipulating those representations.

The Mental Models Theory as a Computational Theory

The conclusion of the previous section was already hinted at in my thesis (Garnham, 1981): there is no real alternative to mental models as a framework for studying language processing. This conclusion also follows from the assumption that the mental models theory is best considered as a computational theory of language processing, in the sense of David Marr (1982). Marr argued that the study of a complex cognitive system should start with a high-level *task analysis* of what the system does (what mathematical function it computes) and why. When this question is addressed seriously, it should receive a definitive answer. Thus, Marr argued that at least one of the functions of the human visual system is to provide a representation of the 3-D structure of the surrounding world, so that the viewer can move around in it, avoiding obstacles, and reaching desired objects. Of course, the computational theory does not tell us how this function is achieved, but it does guide the search for correct descriptions of the mechanisms, at both the algorithmic and the implementational level. A computational theory of language understanding must say that one of the functions of the language understanding system is to develop representations of those parts of the world, real or imaginary, concrete or abstract, that are under discussion. If those representations are propositional, in some sense, they are nevertheless representations of parts of the world.

MENTAL MODELS OF REASONING VS. MENTAL MODELS OF LANGUAGE

The idea that the mental models theory is a computational theory in the domain of language processing raises two questions, both hinted at by the earlier claims that there is no serious rival to mental models theory in the domain of language, but that there is in the domain of reasoning. The first question is: what is the status of mental models theory in the domain of reasoning? If there is a viable alternative, it seems unlikely that the mental models theory can be the computational theory. The second question is: if there is no alternative to mental models theory in language comprehension, what are the substantive questions about language processing that need to be addressed? I will consider these questions in turn.

The Status of Mental Models Theories of Reasoning

The questions that a computational theory of human reasoning must address are: what are people doing when they are reasoning, and why? One answer might be that they are trying (if not always succeeding) to draw conclusions that follow (in a broad sense, not necessarily restricted to deductive validity) from what they already know. They try to draw correct conclusions, because those conclusions reflect how the world is, or most probably is, (if the premises on which the reasoning is based are true) and they can be used to guide successful action in the world. On this view the various logics provide the broad ("computational") framework for describing what people are trying to do when they reason. Logic grew out of the attempt to describe and formalise valid arguments, and it provides a high-level characterisation of which arguments are valid. On this view, the mental models theory of (say) syllogistic reasoning is a theory at Marr's second level of analysis—that of algorithm and representation. Mental models provide one mechanism for solving syllogisms. It is a method that can be shown to work (i.e. syllogisms can be solved correctly using a mental model mechanism), and it is also a method that, with certain additional assumptions, can provide a plausible account of the mistakes people make, and the difficulties they have, in solving syllogisms.

There are, however, alternative methods for solving syllogisms, for example the set of rules formulated by Aristotle (see Garnham & Oakhill, 1994, pp.97–98), which could, at least in principle, form the basis of a psychological theory of syllogistic reasoning. More generally, logical inference can be performed by the syntactic manipulation of sentences of the language used to convey information, using standard proof-theoretic methods. Even though, from the point of view of language comprehension, these sentences must be taken to be about situations in the real or an imaginary world, inferences could be performed by what would, from a cognitive point of view, be the manipulation of superficial representations of the sentences, rather than by direct manipulation of mental models. In other words, there can be an account of human reasoning based on the notion of mental logic as a mental natural deduction system. There is, however, no sense in which the construction of these superficial representations could count as understanding the sentences from which conclusions are drawn, or of sentences expressing those conclusions. Moreover, because comprehension requires the construction of these models, and because there is a plausible account of reasoning as the manipulation of those models (the mental models theory), the principle of parsimony suggests that that account should be given precedence over its rivals.

As was mentioned earlier, the manipulation of mental models for the purposes of reasoning may be based on their "syntax", that is the rules for what counts as a well-formed mental model. Reasoning with mental models is proof-theoretic in this sense. But a theory of human reasoning based on the notion of manipulating mental models makes different predictions from a theory based on mental natural deduction. The two are not empirically equivalent.

The status of the mental models theory can, therefore, be summarised as follows. In the domain of language comprehension, the computational theory says that people try to extract the information that texts and discourse convey to them, and that (part of) this information is information about situations in the world. Thus, the most general mental models principles are part of the computational theory. In the domain of reasoning, the computational theory says that people try to draw valid (or justified, since "valid" is not intended in the sense of deductively valid) conclusions. One way to achieve this goal would be to manipulate mental models, but another would be to manipulate mental representations of sentences. Thus, much of the mental models theory is not part of the computational theory in this domain. It is one version of an algorithm for implementing the computational theory. It might, however, be argued that some of the most general considerations in mental models theory, those of situations in the world and recurring elements in those situations, determine which are the valid inferences that the logics of our computational theories of reasoning have to model.

This last point aside, a general principle—one of parsimony and not one of computational theory in Marr's sense—suggests that, other things being equal, there should be a "unified theory of cognition" (Newell, 1990), which provides accounts of language processing and reasoning that have as much in common as possible. This general principle justifies a mental models theory of reasoning, because there is no alternative to the mental models theory in the domain of language processing. This argument is different in nature from arguments suggesting that the theory is empirically superior to rivals in the domain of reasoning, but it relies on those arguments to underwrite its "other things being equal" clause.

Specific Theories in the Domain of Language Processing

The second main contrast between the mental models theory of language processing and the mental models theory of reasoning is that the latter appears to be better worked out than the former. Part of the reason is that there are mental models accounts of subspecies of reasoning: syllogistic reasoning, propositional reasoning, inductive reasoning, probabilistic reasoning. There are, however, no specific mental models theories of types of language understanding. The explanation of this fact is that there are no types of language understanding in the sense that there are types of reasoning. There is little reason to suppose, for example, that different types of text (e.g. novels, news reports, and technical writing) are processed in ways that are different in any sense that is relevant to the fundamental assumptions of the mental models theory. There are, however, questions about how the notion of a mental model applies to abstract texts (see Garnham & Oakhill, 1996, for discussion). In addition, there are different ways of reading: skimming, "ordinary reading", and detailed study, for example. It may well be that these types of reading call for different processing theories.

In theories of language processing, the natural division is not into types of language processing, but into *subcomponents* of language processing. At the broadest level, there are word-level, syntactic, and message-level processes. Of these three sets of processes, it is the third that is most intimately connected with the construction of mental models. The issue, therefore, is how the message-level processes divide up, and what repercussions that division has for the mental models theory. Message-level processing is highly complex, and a natural strategy in trying to understand it, suggested by general scientific principles, is that it should be divided into smaller subproblems. Furthermore, an attempt should be made to distinguish subproblems that can be tackled in a relatively contained way from those that cannot, and which should perhaps be set aside for the time being. One reason for thinking that there may be subproblems of the second type in message-level processing is that text interpretation depends on knowledge about the world. We have relatively little idea about how this knowledge is accessed and mobilised for text comprehension, and aspects of comprehension that can only be explained by making detailed assumptions about knowledge use, and not in terms of other more constrained processes, are likely to be difficult to tackle.

Our ignorance about how knowledge is used should not be confused with ignorance about what knowledge people have. Much of that knowledge is mundane knowledge, which is by definition public property. However, research that primarily sets out what that knowledge is, such as the writing of scripts in the sense of Schank and Abelson (1977), should not be confused with the development of a theory of how knowledge is organised and mobilised (although script theory is not entirely silent on that issue).

I would identify two subdomains of message-level processing that can be fruitfully studied with current tools, and which need, if they are to be discussed in an illuminating way, to be considered in the overall framework of the mental models theory of language processing. These two subdomains, which cannot be considered in isolation from one another, are inference and anaphora.

Inference. Considerations about inference led John Bransford (Bransford, Barclay, & Franks, 1972) to claim that comprehension was a *constructive* process, and Garnham and Oakhill (1996) have argued that Bransford's ideas were a direct precursor of the mental models theory of comprehension. Bransford's empirical claim, which may or may not be correct, was that a reader who learns, for example, that a delicate glass pitcher fell on a hard floor will infer that it breaks. A natural way of thinking about such inferences is that, in a representation that models the described situation, the information that the pitcher broke is encoded in the same way as the information that the pitcher was dropped. Thus, it may be impossible to determine, from examining the representation, which information was implicit in a text, and which has been inferred. The mental models theory provides a framework in which this process of inference is readily described. A model constructed from the explicit information in the text (about the pitcher being dropped) is a model of a (specific) situation. Background knowledge about delicate objects breaking when they are dropped on hard floors is information about a (generic) situation. The two fit readily together, with specific details being added to a copy of the generic information, which is integrated with the mental model of the specific situation to produce a new and more detailed model of a broader, but still specific, situation.

It is now believed that Bransford postulated too much undirected (or *merely elaborative*) inference-making, and that inferences he thought were made during initial comprehension were only made when questions were later presented. Nevertheless, some inferences have to be made to link information in different parts of a text together. These *bridging* inferences are thought to occur during reading, and many of them require constructive processing (Garnham, 1992). The mental models theory provides a framework for describing what happens when such inferences are made, a framework for specifying, for example, what it is, in analytic terms, to make an inference. It does not, however, answer detailed empirical questions about the circumstances under which such bridging inferences are made, or the time course of the processes that produce them.

Many difficult questions about inference-making remain to be answered. One is whether inferencing is all or none (the inferred information is either explicitly encoded in the mental model or it is not encoded at all). This question arises, in part, from attempts to interpret the results of the word-priming experiments that have become increasingly popular in investigating inference-making. If someone reads that a delicate glass pitcher fell on a hard floor, and then responds more quickly to the word "break" than they might otherwise have done, is that evidence that they have inferred that the pitcher broke? The answer is that it need not be. Activation models have long been popular in cognitive psychology, first semantic networks, and now connectionist models. Reading about a pitcher being dropped might activate knowledge about breaking, without leading to a direct encoding of the information that a specific pitcher broke. It might be this activation that produces speeded responding to "break". The question of when and how increased activation turns into a completed inference is a difficult one. Even if activation models remain important in language processing, and it seems likely that hybrid symbolic/connectionist models will become increasingly important, they do not of themselves answer such questions. Indeed, it is not possible to formulate such questions properly without an analytic understanding of the purpose of language processing, an understanding such as that provided by the mental models theory.

Inferences depend on background knowledge, which makes them potentially difficult to study. However, they are often triggered by specific elements in, or properties of, a text. It is this aspect of inferences that makes their investigation tractable. For example, the word "because" can signal a causal, intentional, or evidential link between the information in two clauses of a text. More generally, it is almost always necessary to make links between adjacent parts of a text, and there are many types of signal as to what those links might be. Sequences of tenses, for example, indicate types of relations between the events described. However, knowing that a particular type of link holds between two pieces of information is not the same as knowing what real-world relation underlies the link. Fleshing out such links almost always requires constructive, inferential, processes.

Anaphora.   Anaphoric expressions, such as pronouns and ellipses, provide another indication that links need to be made between parts of a text. Furthermore, the making of many of these links requires inferences, as for example in:

Mary lent her umbrella to Sue because she had to stay at home all day.

Understanding how anaphoric expressions are processed is an area of language research that has greatly benefitted from the mental models framework. In particular, it is within this framework that the incorrectness of the standard view of anaphoric reference has become apparent. On this view, anaphoric references depend directly on a link between the anaphor and a preceding piece of text (or occasionally a subsequent one)—the anaphor's *antecedent.* However, while this view is approximately correct for some of the verbal ellipses, which can crudely be regarded as ways of avoiding unnecessary repetition, it is not correct for pronouns and other examples of what have come to be called *deep* or *model-interpretive* anaphors (Sag & Hankamer, 1984). These anaphors refer to things that are represented in mental models, but which need not have been introduced into those models by expressions that are co-referential with the anaphoric expressions. The details are complex. Only some items that have been introduced indirectly in the preceding text can be referred to using pronouns. Others require full noun phrases. For example, one *can* say:

I need a plate. Where do you keep them?

(Gernsbacher, 1991). In this pair of sentences "them" refers to a set of plates that the addressee is assumed to have. These plates have only been introduced indirectly by the nonspecific reference to a wanted plate in the first sentence (plus, presumably, some assumptions about the likely context of the interchange). However, although one can say:

I've bought a secondhand car and I must check the tread on the tyres.

One cannot say:

I've bought a secondhand car and I must check the tread on them.

In the first of these sentences there is a definite reference to a particular set of tyres, whose existence is implied by the mention of a car. However, the attempt to refer to the tyres pronominally, in the second sentence, does not succeed, even though they are, presumably, part of the car that has been mentioned.

In addition, although deep anaphors refer to elements represented in mental models, the processes that link the anaphors to their referents may be mediated by a representation of the preceding text, though not necessarily in the way that the traditional theory of anaphora assumed (see e.g. Garnham, Oakhill, Ehrlich, & Carreiras, 1995; Murphy, 1985). The simple idea suggested by Sag and Hankamer (1984), that the search for referents of deep anaphors takes place only in mental models, is incorrect.

Thus, there are many issues about anaphoric reference, which is, both linguistically and psychologically, a complex phenomenon, that must be investigated empirically. The mental models framework poses comparatively few constraints on the outcome of these investigations. But at a high level of description it does say what sorts of interpretation anaphoric expressions will turn out to have, and hence what the result of the process of interpreting them correctly must be.

CONCLUDING REMARKS

I dedicated the published version of my thesis (Garnham, 1987) to Phil Johnson-Laird as "my psycholinguistic mentor". I chose to study language with him, because of his reputation, and because of what I knew of his work—I must have been one of the few undergraduates to read the whole of *Language and perception* (Miller & Johnson-Laird, 1976). And, like Phil (see Wason, this volume), I also read Kneale and Kneale's (1962) *The development of logic* as an undergraduate. I believe I also persuaded Phil that there might be something of value, and even of relevance to psychology, in the later writings of Wittgenstein (see Wason, this volume, for Phil's earlier dislike of Wittgenstein). I could never have become interested in psycholinguistic investigations that were not informed by linguistic and philosophical concerns—that were not, in short, part of cognitive science. The mental models theory is firmly located in cognitive science. However, particularly in the domain of language processing, we need to dispel the idea that because the theory is couched at a high level, and because in one sense what it says appears incontrovertible, that it has no content. Like the theory of evolution by natural selection, the mental models theory can be superficially dismissed in this way. However, if we are to think about language processing in a coherent way, we must continue to study mental models. Indeed, we must continue to study mental models in cognitive science.

REFERENCES

Anderson, J.R. (1978). Arguments concerning representations for mental imagery. *Psychological Review, 85*, 249–277.

Anderson, R.C., Pichert, J.W., Goetz, E.T., Schallert, D.L., Stevens, K.V., & Trollip, S.R. (1977). Instantiation of general terms. *Journal of Verbal Learning and Verbal Behavior, 15*, 667–679.

Bransford, J.D., Barclay, J.R., & Franks, J.J. (1972). Sentence comprehension: A constructive versus interpretive approach. *Cognitive Psychology, 3*, 193–209.

Clark, H.H., & Marshall, C.R. (1981). Definite reference and mutual knowledge. In A.K. Joshi, B. Webber, & I.A. Sag (Eds.), *Elements of discourse understanding* (pp.10–63). Cambridge: Cambridge University Press.

Clark, H.H., & Wilkes-Gibbs, D. (1986). Referring as a collaborative process. *Cognition, 22*, 1–39.

Donnellan, K.S. (1966). Reference and definite descriptions. *Philosophical Review, 75*, 281–304.

Ehrlich, K., & Johnson-Laird, P.N. (1982). Spatial descriptions and referential continuity. *Journal of Verbal Learning and Verbal Behavior, 21*, 296–306.

Garnham, A. (1979). Instantiation of verbs. *Quarterly Journal of Experimental Psychology, 31*, 207–214.

Garnham, A. (1981). *Mental models as representations of discourse and text*. Unpublished D.Phil thesis, University of Sussex, UK.

Garnham, A. (1987). *Mental models as representations of discourse and text*. Chichester, UK: Ellis Horwood.

Garnham, A. (1992). Minimalism versus constructionism: A false dichotomy in theories of inference during reading. *PSYCOLOQUY, 3*(63), reading-inference–1.1.

Garnham, A., & Oakhill, J.V. (1994). *Thinking and reasoning*. Oxford: Basil Blackwell.

Garnham, A., & Oakhill, J.V. (1996). The mental models theory of language comprehension. In B.K. Britton & A.C. Graesser (Eds.), *Models of understanding text* (pp.313–339). Hillsdale, NJ: Lawrence Erlbaum Associates Inc.

Garnham, A., Oakhill, J.V., Ehrlich, M-F., & Carreiras, M. (1995). Representations and processes in the interpretation of pronouns: New evidence from Spanish and French. *Journal of Memory and Language, 34*, 41–62.

Garnham, A., Oakhill, J.V., & Johnson-Laird, P.N. (1982). Referential continuity and the coherence of discourse. *Cognition, 11*, 29–46.

Garrod S.C., & Anderson, A. (1987). Saying what you mean in dialogue: A study in conceptual and semantic co-ordination. *Cognition, 27*, 181–218.
Gernsbacher, M.A. (1991). Comprehending conceptual pronouns. *Language and Cognitive Processes, 6*, 81–105.
Hendrix, G.G. (1979). Encoding knowledge in partitioned networks. In N.V. Findler (Ed.), *Associative networks: Representation and use of knowledge by computers* (pp.51–92). New York: Academic Press.
Johnson-Laird, P.N. (1970). The perception and memory of sentences. In J. Lyons (Ed.), *New horizons in linguistics* (pp.261–270). Harmondsworth, UK: Penguin.
Johnson-Laird, P.N. (1982). Propositional representations, procedural semantics and mental models. In J. Mehler, E.C.T. Walker, & M.F. Garrett (Eds.), *Perspectives on mental representation: Experimental and theoretical studies of cognitive processes and capacities* (pp.111–131). Hillsdale, NJ: Lawrence Erlbaum Associates Inc.
Johnson-Laird, P.N. (1983). *Mental models: Towards a cognitive science of language, inference, and consciousness.* Cambridge: Cambridge University Press.
Johnson-Laird, P.N. (1994a). A model theory of induction. *International Studies in the Philosophy of Science, 8*, 5–29.
Johnson-Laird, P.N. (1994b). Mental models and probabilistic thinking. *Cognition, 50*, 189–209.
Johnson-Laird, P.N., & Bara, B. (1984). Syllogistic inference. *Cognition, 16*, 1–61.
Johnson-Laird, P.N., & Byrne, R.M.J. (1991). *Deduction.* Hove, UK: Lawrence Erlbaum Associates Ltd.
Johnson-Laird, P.N., & Garnham, A. (1980). Descriptions and discourse models. *Linguistics and Philosophy, 3*, 371–393.
Kamp, H. (1981). A theory of truth and semantic representation. In J.A.G. Groenendijk, T.M.V. Janssen, & M.B.J. Stockhof (Eds.), *Formal methods in the study of language* (pp.227–322). Amsterdam: Mathematical Centre Tracts.
Kintsch, W. (1974). *The representation of meaning in memory.* Hillsdale, NJ: Lawrence Erlbaum Associates Inc.
Kneale, W., & Kneale, M. (1962). *The development of logic.* Oxford: Clarendon Press.
MacFarland, D.J. (1971). *Feedback mechanisms in animal behaviour.* London: Academic Press.
MacFarland, D.J. (Ed.) (1974). *Motivational control systems analysis.* London: Academic Press.
Marr, D. (1982). *Vision: A computational investigation into the human representation and processing of visual information.* San Francisco: Freeman.
Miller, G.A., & Johnson-Laird, P.N. (1976). *Language and perception.* Cambridge: Cambridge University Press.
Murphy, G.L. (1985). Processes of understanding anaphora. *Journal of Memory and Language, 24*, 290–303.
Newell, A. (1990). *Unified theories of cognition: The 1987 William James Lectures.* Cambridge, MA: Harvard University Press.
Perner, J., & Garnham, A. (1989). Conditions for mutuality. *Journal of Semantics, 6*, 369–385.
Potts, G.R. (1972). Information strategies used in the encoding of linear orderings. *Journal of Verbal Learning and Verbal Behavior, 11*, 727–740.
Rips, L.J. (1994). *The psychology of proof.* Cambridge MA: MIT Press/Bradford Books.
Sag, I.A., & Hankamer, J. (1984). Toward a theory of anaphoric processing. *Linguistics and Philosophy, 7*, 325–345.
Schank, R.C., & Abelson, R.P. (1977). *Scripts, goals, plans and understanding.* Hillsdale, NJ: Lawrence Erlbaum Associates Inc.
Stenning, K., & Oaksford, M. (1993). Rational reasoning and human implementations of logic. In K.I. Manktelow & D.E. Over (Eds.), *Rationality: Psychological and philosophical perspectives* (pp.136–176). London: Routledge.
van Dijk, T. A., & Kintsch, W. (1983). *Strategies of discourse comprehension.* Hillsdale, NJ: Lawrence Erlbaum Associates Inc.

4

Mental Models, Propositions, and the Comprehension of Pronouns

Rosemary J. Stevenson
Human Communication Research Centre, University of Durham, UK

A major problem for models of pronoun comprehension is to explain how pronouns are understood so readily despite the fact that they contain little information to assist in their interpretation and that they are frequently ambiguous. In tackling this problem, researchers have conceptualised pronoun comprehension as involving either a search process (e.g. Clark & Sengul, 1979) or a slot-filling process (Sanford & Garrod, 1981). According to the search model, a pronoun triggers a search for its referent in the mind of the reader or listener; according to the slot-filling model, the referent of the pronoun fills the slot identified by the pronoun. In more recent versions of this latter view, slot-filling is made possible because the pronoun is said to act as a cue to the retrieval of the referent (Greene, McKoon & Ratcliff, 1992). In this chapter, I will suggest that both search and slot-filling processes are used during pronoun comprehension. In order to do so, I will make use of Johnson-Laird's theory of mental models.

The format of the chapter will be as follows. First, I will introduce Johnson-Laird's theory of mental models as it relates to language comprehension. In the course of this introduction, I will consider the relation between mental models and propositional representations of discourse, and I will highlight the importance of mental models for an understanding of reference. Then I will focus on the comprehension of reference more specifically by discussing the comprehension of pronouns. I introduce the notion of top-down and bottom-up processes in comprehension, identifying them with processes triggered by mental models and

53

processes triggered by propositions respectively. I also identify slot-filling as an example of top-down processing and search as an example of bottom-up processing. After giving examples of these top-down and bottom-up processes, I go on to discuss the focusing of entities in a mental model, since focusing is the major factor underlying slot-filling accounts of pronoun comprehension. I outline two different types of focusing—structural and semantic/pragmatic focusing—and examine the relation between them. I conclude that focusing depends crucially on a dynamic interaction between top-down and bottom-up processes; that is, between processes triggered by mental models and processes triggered by propositions. Thus slot-filling models need to be supplemented with an account of how bottom-up processes maintain or shift the focus as a discourse proceeds.

THE THEORY OF MENTAL MODELS

Background: Propositions and Abstract Ideas

When Johnson-Laird first introduced the idea of mental models, two views of language comprehension were prevalent. One view proposed that the end-product of comprehension is a propositional representation while the other proposed that the end-product of comprehension is an underlying conceptual representation.

The Propositional View. This holds that a sentence is represented as a set of propositions that encode the linguistic meaning of the sentence, together with a minimal set of inferences (e.g. Fodor, Bever, & Garrett, 1974; Fodor, Fodor, & Garrett, 1975; Kintsch, 1974; Kintsch & van Dijk, 1978). Of course, no-one denies that a full interpretation of a discourse may require additional inferences, but these were not thought to be part of comprehension. Instead, they were said to be part of a separate and optional inference process that constructs a mental model of the text if necessary.

Certain problems with the propositional view have been emphasised by Johnson-Laird (1983). One problem is that it only considers the meaning of a sentence and not its reference. Fodor et al. (1975) proposed that the meanings of the words in a proposition are represented by meaning postulates. Others have argued that they are represented by lists of semantic features (e.g. Rips, Shoben, & Smith, 1973) or by nodes in a semantic network (e.g. Anderson & Bower, 1973; Quillian, 1968). However, Johnson-Laird has argued that, regardless of the particular system of representation, propositional accounts all fail to consider how language relates to the world. That is, the meanings of propositions only specify intensional relations: the relations between the meanings of the words. They do not specify extensional relations: the relations between the words and the things they refer to in the world. The following two phrases, for example, have different meanings:

The tallest man in the room.
The heaviest man in the room.

One concerns height and the other weight, and so each would have a different propositional representation. Yet in an appropriate context, they could refer to the same individual. In such circumstances, it would make sense to represent them in a single representation that contains a unique entity standing for the individual, something that is not possible with propositional representations. In contrast, Fodor et al. (1975) have argued that the meaning of an expression must be grasped before its referent can be identified. Thus they maintain that the end-product of comprehension is a propositional representation and so does not contain additional information inferred from general knowledge.

Johnson-Laird (1983), on the other hand, claims that meaning and reference interact during comprehension and cites examples to support his claim. In the following sentence, for example, the word *they* is ambiguous between two possible meanings:

They are very rich.

This ambiguity can be resolved either by identifying the referent of *they* or by establishing the meaning of *rich*. If you know that *they* refers to people, you can infer that *rich* means wealthy. If you know that *they* refers to cakes you can infer that *rich* means fruity. Conversely, if you know that *rich* means wealthy, you can infer that *they* refers to a set of people. And if you know that *rich* means fruity you can infer that *they* refers to cakes. Theories that only account for meaning cannot explain how sentences like this one are understood. In fact, people are very good at identifying the referents of a discourse (e.g. Ehrlich & Johnson-Laird, 1982) and comprehension suffers if the text makes identification impossible (Bransford & Johnson, 1972).

Johnson-Laird also argues that the propositional view fails to take account of the way an interpretation of an expression is constrained by general knowledge of the situation being described. A propositional representation only contains the information in the sentence, not any additional information that can be inferred from general knowledge of the described situation. As we shall see when presenting evidence for abstract conceptual representations, people routinely make inferences based on general knowledge in order to interpret sentences. Hence they represent and remember more than is contained in the linguistic input.

Abstract Conceptual Representations.   The idea of abstract conceptual representations was proposed by Bransford and his colleagues (e.g. Bransford, Barclay, & Franks, 1972; Bransford & Franks, 1971; Bransford

& Johnson, 1972). In an elegant series of experiments, Bransford et al. showed that people make inferences to integrate information from different sentences (Bransford & Franks, 1971) and to integrate information in the discourse with general background knowledge (Bransford & Johnson, 1972; Johnson, Bransford, & Solomon, 1973). The result, according to Bransford et al., is a single integrated representation of the underlying idea expressed by the discourse, not a propositional representation.

Although the idea that sentences are represented in terms of their underlying concepts is broadly compatible with the notion of mental models, it does have drawbacks. One is that the notion of an underlying conceptual representation is not well specified and so it is unclear how to describe its structure. The second is that Bransford et al. assume that propositional representations are not involved in remembering sentences at all. The difficulty with this assumption is that the experimental designs were such that the likelihood of remembering the propositional forms of the sentences was very low. In addition, there is evidence to suggest that a propositional representation is recovered during comprehension, as shown by the studies of Kintsch and his colleagues (e.g. Kintsch & Keenan, 1973). What is needed, therefore, is a model of comprehension that shows how both meaning (as exemplified by propositions) and reference (as exemplified by the underlying ideas) are represented during the processing of discourse.

Mental Models

Johnson-Laird (1983) proposed that there are two kinds of representations for discourse, a superficial propositional representation and a mental model. The propositional representation is structurally similar to the linguistic input, and it represents the meaning of a sentence. A mental model is a non-linguistic representation of the situation described by the sentence. It is structurally similar to part of the world rather than to any linguistic structure, as it represents the state of affairs described by the discourse, not the discourse itself. Information that is not explicitly mentioned in a discourse can be included in a mental model by means of inferences from general knowledge acting in conjunction with the propositional representation. A particular feature of the notion of a mental model is that it makes precise the ideas of Bransford et al. that the end-product of language comprehension is an abstract conceptual representation. This abstract conceptual representation can be thought of as a mental model of the described situation.

A study by Mani and Johnson-Laird (1982) supports the idea that there are two kinds of representations—propositions and mental models. They showed that a mental model is only constructed if the discourse describes a unique spatial layout. In these circumstances, subjects recall the gist of the discourse, that is, the situation represented in the mental model. If the discourse is compatible with more than one model, then the construction of a mental model is not possible and the original propositions are stored instead, resulting in verbatim recall.[1]

Mental Models and the Importance of Reference

Reference is a crucial component of mental models. Whenever a new individual is introduced into a discourse, a corresponding entity is introduced into the mental model. And whenever an individual is mentioned again in a discourse, then the entity standing for that individual is located in the model and the new information is integrated with the representation of that individual. Thus, according to Johnson-Laird, there are procedures for introducing new entities into the model and for adding new information to entities already in the model. There are also procedures for integrating two separate models if a proposition contains entities in both of them; for verifying that the asserted properties or relations hold if all the entities are in the current model; and for adding the property or relation to the model if it cannot be verified by the previous procedure. In other words, each sentence in a discourse must refer, implicitly or explicitly, to an entity mentioned or introduced in another sentence, as this is the only way that sentences can be represented in a single integrated model (Johnson-Laird, 1983).

Studies by Garnham (1987) and by Ehrlich and Johnson-Laird (1982) support this idea. Garnham exploited the fact that the representation of a text by means of propositions, and the representation of the described situation by means of mental models, do not always coincide. He pointed out that two statements such as:

The man standing by the window shouted to the host.
The man with the martini shouted to the host.

have different meanings, hence they are represented by different propositions. However, if they both refer to the same individual, the individual can be represented by a single entity in a mental model. Garnham asked subjects to listen to short texts containing sentences like these two, and then presented the subjects with a recognition memory test. He found that when the subjects were trying to understand the text rather than memorise it, they frequently confused the two sentences that described the same referent.

Ehrlich and Johnson-Laird presented subjects with three-sentence texts that described spatial arrays and measured the time it took to read each sentence. They found that reading times were facilitated if information in the incoming sentence could be added to the current mental model. This was the case when the sentence referred to an entity already in the model. They also found that reading times were slowed if two existing mental models had to be integrated into a single model so that information in the incoming sentence could be added to it. This was the case when the first two sentences of a text had no individuals in common and so were represented in separate mental models, while the incoming sentence had individuals in common with both models. Taking these two experiments together, the results suggest that mental models are crucial for understanding reference.

The procedures that introduce or locate an entity in a model make use of the semantics of referring expressions (Johnson-Laird, 1977). When an indefinite description is encountered, its semantic function is executed. The semantics of indefinite descriptions indicate that something new is being introduced and so a new memory location is set up to accept the incoming new information contained in the description. Thus, an indefinite description introduces an entity into the model. The semantics of definite descriptions indicate (among other things) that someone or something familiar is being referred to. Thus a definite description triggers an instruction to look in the mental model for an entity that was previously introduced. In the case of definite noun phrases, the referent can be identified by means of the semantic content of the noun. But in the case of pronouns, inferences are required to identify the referent, as pronouns contain very little semantic content to aid their interpretation. In the following sentence, for example, we interpret the pronoun *he* as referring to John because we use our general knowledge of the world to infer that the person who borrows a book is likely to be the person who wants to read it:

Bill lent the book to John because he wanted to read it.

In summary, the theory of mental models subsumes and makes explicit earlier models of discourse, based on propositions and underlying concepts. It also places reference at the heart of comprehension and argues that reference as well as meaning is needed to interpret discourse. While propositions enable the meaning of a sentence to be grasped, mental models establish the reference of the sentence and of the expressions the sentence contains. The remainder of this chapter will focus specifically on pronominal reference, and discuss how mental models and propositions interact during the course of comprehension.

THE COMPREHENSION OF PRONOUNS

In this section I discuss top-down and bottom-up processes. Top-down processes originate in mental models and underlie slot-filling models of pronoun comprehension. Bottom-up processes arise from propositions and underlie search models.

Top-down and Bottom-up Constraints on Comprehension

Top-down processes are responsible for the way in which the structure of the current mental model affects the interpretation of an incoming clause or sentence. Bottom-up processes are specialised processes specific to the particular linguistic input and they are triggered by the input. They are responsible for the way that the information in the input initiates, updates and modifies the accessibility of entities in the mental model.

Top-down Processes. With top-down processes, the structure of the mental model can be said to act as a context in which to interpret the incoming sentence. Gernsbacher's Structure Building Framework (Gernsbacher & Hargreaves, 1989) can be seen as an example of such processes. The structure building framework proposes that the first mentioned individual in a sentence is the most accessible entity in a mental model.

According to the structure-building framework, the first mentioned individual forms the foundation for a sentence-level representation onto which subsequent information is mapped. Thus the first mentioned individual is the most highly focused individual in the representation and so is readily accessed when a pronoun is encountered later in the sentence (Gernsbacher, 1989). The first mention effect can be regarded as a top-down effect, because the accessibility of the first mentioned individual is due to its pivotal role in the representation of the sentence. The first mention effect is also an example of the slot-filling model of pronoun comprehension. The first mentioned individual is readily available to fill the slot identified by a pronoun.

Bottom-up Processes. These depend on the specific semantic functions of the words in the discourse. For example, definite references, such as pronouns, trigger search processes designed to locate and identify the individual referred to by the pronoun. Yet other words, such as sentence connectives, trigger more complex semantic processes that direct attention to specific aspects of the represented event. As we will see, a common function of all these bottom-up processes is to maintain or modify and update the current top-down focus in the mental model.

The search processes triggered by pronouns are reflected in performance as pronoun assignment strategies. One such strategy is the parallel function strategy, according to which a pronoun is assigned to a preceding noun phrase occupying the same grammatical role as the pronoun (Sheldon, 1974; Smyth, 1994; Stevenson, Nelson, & Stenning, 1993). This strategy predicts that a subject pronoun would be assigned to a preceding subject noun phrase, and an object pronoun would be assigned to a preceding object noun phrase. Thus, John will be the preferred antecedent of *he* in the first sentence below while Bill will be the preferred antecedent of *him* in the second sentence:

John hit Bill and he ran away.
John hit Bill and Mary kicked him.

Empirical results support the idea of parallel function. Thus, referring to the two examples above, people assign *he* to John in the first sentence, while they assign *him* to Bill in the second sentence (Stevenson et al., 1993). The preference for Bill in the second sentence is less marked than the preference for John in the first, suggesting that the parallel function strategy is overlaid on a top-down first mention effect. However, the evidence for parallel function is quite strong, since no other strategy and no top-down process predicts a preference for assigning a non-subject pronoun to a non-subject and non-first mentioned antecedent.

Agnieszka Urbanowicz and I have recently investigated the parallel function strategy more closely. The assignment results of Stevenson et al. leave open the possibility that parallel function is only brought into play at a late stage in processing, perhaps only if there is no other information available to interpret the pronoun. We wished to see, therefore, if the strategy was triggered immediately the pronoun was encountered. To do this we used a probe recognition task with sentences that contained either a subject or an object pronoun, as in:

John chased Mike to retrieve a packet of sweets and
he attacked Liz to steal a bar of chocolate. (Subject pronoun)

John chased Mike to retrieve a packet of sweets and
Liz attacked him to steal a bar of chocolate. (Object pronoun)

Each sentence was presented on a computer screen one phrase at a time in a self-paced reading time task. At some point during the presentation of the sentence, instead of the next phrase being presented, a single capitalised name appeared in the center of the screen. This probe name occurred either immediately after the pronoun (the Early Position), or at the end of the sentence (the Late Position). In the experimental trials, the probe word was the name of either the subject or the object of the first clause of the sentence, and we measured the time taken for participants to decide that the name had already occurred in the sentence. Filler trials used probe names that had not occurred in the sentence. The results of the experiment are shown in Fig. 4.1.

As inspection of Fig. 4.1 indicates, object pronouns show a parallel function effect: the probe name is recognised more quickly when it is the object of the preceding clause than when it is the subject. Although this

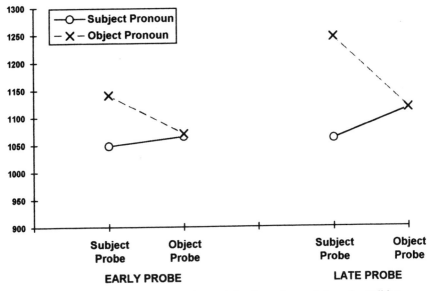

FIG. 4.1.   Mean recognition times (in msec) for the probe words in each condition.

effect is more pronounced when the probe appears in the late positions at the end of the sentence, it is also apparent when the probe word appears in the early position immediately after the pronoun. Subject pronouns are affected by parallelism to a lesser extent: when the probe is presented immediately after the pronoun, recognition times are relatively unaffected by the grammatical role of the probe word, but when the probe appears at the end of the sentence, it is recognised more slowly when it is the object of the preceding clause than when it is the subject.

Thus, the object pronouns demonstrate that a parallel function strategy is triggered as soon as an object pronoun is encountered. It is not clear why subject pronouns do not also show an immediate effect of parallelism. However, one possibility is that when the object was the probe name for subject pronouns, the object was still activated because the pronoun occurred so soon after the name. We deliberately inserted a six-word phrase between the object name and the subject pronoun to avoid such a recency effect, but it is possible that a longer interval than we had allowed is needed. Nevertheless, we feel confident that non-subject pronouns trigger a parallel function strategy as soon as they are encountered, as demonstrated by the probe recognition times with sentences containing object pronouns.

Bottom-up pronoun assignment strategies, like the parallel function strategy, are probably only used when top-down focusing is lacking. In the presence of top-down focusing, a bottom-up search for the referent is unnecessary, as the focused entity is readily available. It is likely, therefore, that such strategies are primarily evident either when there are no other strong constraints on assignment (e.g. gender cues or pragmatic constraints) or when the reader is unable to use the available pragmatic cues. This latter situation is probably more common than is usually supposed, particularly when novices are reading a difficult text on the subject to be learned. Consider, for example, people reading technical prose when they have no real knowledge of the subject matter. Broadbent (1977/1978) found that subject assignment is highly favoured in sentences such as:

(5)   The feedpipe lubricates the chain, and it should be adjusted to leave a gap half an inch between itself and the sprocket.

In this sentence, unless the reader has knowledge of the domain, he or she is unlikely to be able to make use of pragmatic inferences.

Nevertheless, the importance of bottom-up processes cannot be underestimated. The results of our probe recognition study show that the top-down focusing due to the first mention effect does not seem to hold for object pronouns. Instead, object pronouns seem to trigger specific bottom-up search processes.

THE FOCUSING OF ENTITIES IN A MENTAL MODEL

There have been a number of attempts to solve the problem of pronoun comprehension by means of focusing models. Such models are generally seen as special cases of slot-filling models of pronoun comprehension. In a focus-based account, entities in a mental model are not equally weighted. Instead, they are ranked according to their accessibility, with the most highly ranked entity being the most accessible as the referent of a pronoun. Focusing models differ in what they regard as the mechanism underlying focusing. Different researchers have argued for structural focusing (e.g. Grosz, Joshi, & Weinstein, 1983, 1995), semantic/pragmatic focusing (e.g. Stevenson, Crawley, & Kleinman, 1994) and focusing based on background knowledge of the topic of the discourse (e.g. Sanford & Garrod, 1981). In this chapter, I will concentrate on structural and semantic/pragmatic focusing, as I wish to examine the relation between propositions and mental models.

Structural Focusing: Centering Theory

Work on structural focusing can be found in the computational literature, with Grosz et al.'s centering theory giving the most explicit account (Grosz et al., 1983, 1995). Grosz et al. identify two kinds of local discourse centers:

a set of forward-looking centers (abbreviated here as Cfs) and a backward-looking center (abbreviated as Cb).

The Forward-looking Center. Each utterance in a discourse either introduces Cfs into the discourse model or refers to previously introduced Cfs. In the following sentence, three Cfs are introduced, John, book and Bill:

John gave the book to Bill
Cf = {John, book, Bill}

These forward looking centers can be said to correspond to the set of entities in a mental model from which the referent of a pronoun is chosen.

The Cfs are ranked according to their accessibility in the discourse model, the highest ranked Cf being the preferred referent of a subsequent pronoun. The factors that affect the ranking of Cfs are not completely determined, but in general, such structural features as surface position (Gordon, Grosz, & Gilliom, 1993), grammatical role (Walker, Iida, & Cote, 1994), being the Cb of the utterance (Grosz et al., 1983, 1995), and (in Japanese) empathy (Kameyama, 1986) are thought to interact to determine ranking (Brennan, Friedman, & Pollard, 1987; Kameyama, 1986; Walker et al., 1994). In the sentence above, therefore, John is the highest ranked Cf because John is mentioned first in the sentence and is also the subject of the sentence. I shall refer to the ranking of Cfs as a Focusing Effect.

The Backward-looking Center. For every utterance except the first in a discourse, the Cb is the preferred site for linking the current utterance to the previous one. According to Grosz et al. (1983), the Cb must refer to the highest-ranked Cf of the preceding utterance that is mentioned in the current utterance and must be realised as a pronoun if there is a pronoun in the sentence. Gordon et al. (1993) have recently added a further constraint that the Cb is typically the grammatical subject of the utterance. In the following discourse, the Cb of the second sentence is John, because a subject pronoun has been used to refer to the highest-ranked Cf of the preceding sentence:

John took the book from Bill. Cf = {John, book, Bill}

He had wanted to read it for ages. Cb = John. Cf = {John, book, Bill}

Hudson D'Zmura (1988) refers to the identification of the Cb as an Expectancy Effect, because it is concerned with the fact that people expect each utterance to contain a Cb with the aforementioned characteristics.

Empirical Studies of Centering. There is growing psychological evidence to support the main tenets of centering theory. First, as far as the focusing effect is concerned, subject pronouns referring to the highest-ranked Cf are interpreted more rapidly than subject pronouns referring to a lower-ranked Cf, where the ranking is determined by initial mention and being the grammatical subject (Hudson D'Zmura, 1988; Hudson, Tanenhaus, & Dell, 1986). (Grosz et al. assume that processing is from left to right and that initial assignments are made immediately. An assignment may need to be retracted later in the light of subsequent information in the sentence.) Hudson D'Zmura used materials like the following:

Context Sentence:
Jack apologised profusely to Josh.

Target Sentence:
He/Jack had been rude to Josh yesterday. (Anaphor refers to highest-ranked Cf)
He/Josh had been offended by Jack's comment. (Anaphor refers to lower-ranked Cf)

Hudson D'Zmura found that when the first target contained a pronoun it was judged to be more coherent and read more quickly than the second when the second also contained a pronoun. This can be attributed to a focusing effect because the pronoun in the first target refers to the highest-ranked Cf in the context sentence. In a recent series of studies, Gordon et al. (1993) tried to tease apart the effects of grammatical role and surface position on the ranking of Cfs and concluded that it is initial mention rather than subjecthood that determines ranking. Such a result is consistent with Gernsbacher's work on the first mention effect.

As far as the expectancy effect is concerned, studies show that a sentence is read more rapidly when the Cb is realised as a pronoun than when it is realised as a noun (Gordon et al., 1993; Hudson D'Zmura, 1988; Hudson et al., 1986). For example, referring again to the examples, Hudson D'Zmura found that with the first target sentence, in which the anaphor refers to the highest-ranked Cf, subjects judged it to be more coherent and read it more rapidly when it contained a pronoun than when it contained a repeated name.

Using three-sentence texts, Gordon et al. also found that, when a pronoun in the third sentence referred to the Cb of the second sentence, the reading time for the phrase containing the pronoun was facilitated. This supports Grosz et al.'s claim that the Cb of an utterance (that is, the referent of the pronoun in Cb position) is normally the highest-ranked element in the Cf of that sentence. In other words, pronoun assignment itself brings the referent into focus, at least when the pronoun is in Cb position.

Semantic/Pragmatic Focusing: Causal Bias and Thematic Roles

Causal Bias. Semantic/pragmatic focusing has long been recognised in psychological work showing that the causal bias of a verb affects the ease with which a pronoun is interpreted. For example, in a sentence continuation task using sentence fragments containing *because*, Garvey and Caramazza (1974) found consistent preferences for assigning a pronoun at the end of the fragment to either the first noun phrase of a sentence (NP1) or the second noun phrase (NP2) depending on the matrix clause verb. When the verb imputed the cause of the action to the first noun phrase, an NP1 bias was observed, but when the verb imputed the cause of the action to the second noun phrase, an NP2 bias was observed, as in the following examples:

John apologised to Bill because he regretted being so rude.
John scolded Bill because he was behaving very badly.

In the first example, apologise is an NP1 verb and so *he* refers to John. In the second example, scold is an NP2 verb and so *he* refers to Bill.

Further support for the idea that verbs affect the accessibility of an antecedent comes from studies of the time taken to make pronoun assignments (Caramazza, Grober, Garvey, & Yates, 1977; Ehrlich, 1980) and from probe recognition tasks (Stevenson, 1986). Caramazza and his colleagues attributed the effect to a semantic feature of the verb. However, Ehrlich used the connectives *but* and *and* as well as *because* and found that the verb bias varied as a function of the relation between the two actions. She argued, therefore, that the bias was due to inferences based on general knowledge of the actions being described.

Thematic Roles. More recently, Stevenson et al. (1994) have set these verb bias effects within a broader focusing framework. Specifically, they suggest that verb bias effects are components of more general focusing effects induced by the thematic roles of the nouns and by the particular connective used to combine the two clauses.

In three experiments, subjects were presented with clauses containing pairs of thematic roles followed by incomplete clauses containing pronouns. In each case, the two individuals occupying the two thematic roles were potential antecedents for the subsequent pronoun, and the position of the thematic roles in the clause (first or second) was also varied. Three different thematic role pairs were investigated: pairs containing goal and source thematic roles, pairs containing agent and patient thematic roles, and pairs containing experiencer and stimulus thematic roles[2]. Definitions of these thematic roles are given in Table 1. The definitions in the Table were gleaned from Andrews, (1985), Fillmore (1968), Jackendoff (1985) and Radford (1988).

In Experiment 1, the two clauses were in independent sentences, as in the following examples containing goal and source thematic roles:

John seized the comic from Bill. He ... (goal in first position)
John passed the comic to Bill. He ... (goal in second position)

The sentence continuations were then scrutinised to discover which thematic roles were chosen as antecedents for the pronouns.

Sentences like those above appeared in the Pronoun condition, as the fragment to be completed contained a pronoun. We also included a No Pronoun condition, in which the pronoun was omitted and subjects were instructed to write a second sentence. The number of references in the continuations to each thematic role was measured in this condition. The purpose of the Pronoun/No Pronoun manipulation was to determine whether thematic roles exert their influence in a top-down or bottom-up manner. If thematic role preferences appear only in continuations to fragments ending in pronouns, then we can conclude that the process is triggered by the pronoun. If, however, thematic role preferences also appear in continuations that do not end in pronouns, then we can conclude that the preferred thematic role is already more highly focused in a mental model and is thus exerting a top-down influence.

The results revealed clear thematic role preferences: goals were preferred to sources, patients were preferred to agents, and stimuli were preferred to experiencers. These preferences held for all continuations regardless of whether or not the original fragment contained a pronoun. Thus, we can attribute the preferences to a top-down effect. There was also a preference

TABLE 4.1
Definitions of Thematic Roles Used in the Experiments of Stevenson et al. (1994)

a. *Goal:* someone or something towards which something moves. Examples: "Mary" in *John gave the book to Mary.* "Peter" in *Peter took the book from Susan.*

b. *Source:* someone or something from which something moves. Examples: "John" in *John gave the book to Mary.* "Susan" in *Peter took the book from Susan.*

c. *Agent:* the instigator of an action. Examples: subjects of *kill, eat, smash, kick, wash.*

d. *Patient:* someone or something affected by an action. Examples: objects of *kill, eat, smash,* but not those of *watch, hear,* and *love.*

e. *Experiencer:* someone or something having a given experience. Examples: subject of *love,* object of *annoy.*

f. *Stimulus:* someone or something giving rise to a certain experience. Examples: object of *love,* subject of *annoy.*

for assigning the pronoun to the first mentioned (subject) antecedent, but only in the Pronoun condition. We can therefore attribute this finding to a bottom-up preference triggered by the pronoun.

The second experiment was designed to confirm the thematic role preferences found in Experiment 1. It used the same procedure as Experiment 1 except that the two clauses were in the same sentence, as in:

John seized the comic from Bill and he ... (goal in first position)
John passed the comic to Bill and he ... (goal in second position)

Clear thematic role preferences were observed, particularly in the Pronoun condition: goal was preferred to source and patient was preferred to agent. However, in contrast to the results of Experiment 1, the experiencer was preferred to the stimulus. The results also showed a marked preference for referring to the first mentioned individual when the fragments did not contain a pronoun. This was because in the No Pronoun condition, there was a predominance of conjoined verb phrases in the continuations. This prevalence of conjoined verb phrases is no doubt also responsible for there being a diminution of the thematic role preferences in this condition.

To explain this pattern of thematic role preferences, Stevenson et al. considered the way in which actions are represented in a mental model. Using Moens and Steedman's (1988) characterisation of the structure of actions, they argued that an action is represented in terms of three components: the initial conditions, the action itself, and the consequences of the action. They then suggested that the thematic role preferences reflect a preference for individuals associated with the consequences of the action. Thus, goals are preferred to sources and patients are preferred to agents. Only actions are represented in terms of the three components described, not states or processes. Consequently, we would not expect comparable preferences in the experiencer–stimulus sentences, because these sentences describe states rather than actions.

The observed thematic role preferences in the experiencer–stimulus sentences, therefore, must be attributable to something other than the structure that underlies actions. In fact, the preferences observed in the experiencer–stimulus sentences were not consistent across Experiments 1 and 2; instead they depended on whether the pronoun and its potential antecedents were in the same or different sentences. When they were in different sentences, the stimulus—the person giving rise to the experience— was preferred. But when they were in the same sentence and the two clauses were conjoined by *and*, the experiencer was preferred. Stevenson et al. suggested that these preferences were triggered by the full stop in the former case and by the *and* in the latter case. That is, the full stop acted as an implicit causal link between the two clauses, thus directing the subjects' attention to the cause of the described state. However, the *and* nullified this causal link and encouraged instead a focus on the consequences of the experience. Thus, Stevenson et al. argued that bottom-up processes triggered by the specific connection between the two clauses were most likely to be responsible for the observed preferences.

All of these proposals were tested in Experiment 3, where the two clauses were connected by either *because* or *so*. These connectives were used because they bring into focus either the consequences (*so*) or the cause (*because*) of the described action.

Recall that Stevenson et al. claimed that in goal–source sentences and agent–patient sentences, the representation of the action in the mental model focuses on the consequences of the action. As goal and patient are the roles associated with consequences, they are the focused entities in the model. Stevenson et al. also suggested that when a connective is encountered, it either reinforces or modifies the focusing that results from the action structure. That is, when *so* is encountered, the focus on the consequence will be reinforced, but when *because* is encountered, the focus on the consequence will be modified. Hence they predicted a clear preference for goal and patient with *so*, but a reduction in this preference with *because*. However, *because* should not result in outright preferences for source or agent (that is, for causes), as the focus on causes, arising from the connective, will interact with the focus on consequences, arising from the action structure in the mental model.

Stevenson et al. also claimed that with the experiencer–stimulus sentences, there is no focusing in the underlying representation, as no action structure is formed to represent sentences that describe states. Consequently, the only influence on what will be in focus is the type of connective: *so* or *because*. Thus, when the fragment ends in *so*, a preference for the experiencer is expected. When the fragment ends in *because*, a preference for the stimulus is expected.

The results of Experiment 3 confirmed these predictions. With goal–source and agent–patient sentences, the preference for goals and patients was reinforced by *so* and attenuated by *because*. (The attenuation with *because* was particularly marked in the goal–source sentences, where *because* seemed also to trigger a first mention effect.) With the experiencer–stimulus sentences, on the other hand, the only preferences to be observed were those that resulted from the type of connective. When the fragment ended in *so*, the experiencer was preferred; when the fragment ended in *because*, the stimulus was preferred, thus supporting the idea that the focusing is brought about by the connective and is absent from the representation of the state that is experienced.

Overall, therefore, our results favour the idea that the consequences of an action are psychologically salient. This causes the individual associated with the consequence to be more highly focused in the mental model of the described situation. However, this focusing is not all-or-none. Instead it will be reinforced or attenuated by later input, such as a connective.

Causal Bias Reconsidered. These findings seem to run counter to those observed by Garvey and her colleagues in the work on causal bias. The results of that work suggest that the cause of an action is psychologically salient, a suggestion that runs counter to our suggestion about the salience of consequences. However, we believe that these two conflicting suggestions can be reconciled because the causal bias effects only arise when the connective *because* is used.

In Stevenson et al.'s Experiment 3, where *because* was used as a connective, there was some shift of focus from consequences to causes, reducing the preference for patients and goals. (With goals, a first mention effect was also observed.) Thus, with materials used by Garvey and her colleagues, we would expect that sentences containing agents and patients would show an NP1 bias when the patient is mentioned first, and an NP2 bias when it is mentioned second. And we would expect an NP1 bias in goal–source sentences, regardless of the order of the thematic roles. Where no action is described, as in experiencer–stimulus sentences, the focusing properties of *because* lead to a straightforward preference for the stimulus. Thus, we would expect these sentences to show an NP1 bias when the stimulus is the first mentioned individual and an NP2 bias when it is mentioned second.

Stevenson et al. examined the verbs used by Caramazza et al. and found that, with one exception, these expectations were confirmed. Thus, the causal bias results seem to arise when the connective *because* is used. This connective modifies the focus on consequences in agent–patient and goal–source sentences, and it has a direct effect on bringing the cause into focus in experiencer–stimulus sentences, where thematic role focusing does not arise.

More recently Garnham and Oakhill (cited by Garnham, Oakhill, & Cruttenden, 1992) have found that with verbs of transfer (that is, verbs with source and goal thematic roles), the assignment of the pronoun in fragments containing *because* depends on the nature of the object transferred. This finding seems at odds with both the causal bias results and the thematic role results. Garnham et al. suggest that the nature of the object determines which protagonist is seen as the cause of the action. This is a plausible suggestion and it is also compatible with Stevenson et al.'s findings. As thematic role preferences are markedly attenuated when the connective is *because*, it seems likely that other features of the sentence, such as the nature of the described object, will interact with the connective to determine the degree of causal bias.

The Relationship between Structural Focusing and Thematic Role Focusing

In the Stevenson et al. study, first mention effects were observed in Experiments 1 and 2 and in the goal–source sentences with *because* in Experiment 3. Thus, the evidence suggests that structural focusing and thematic role focusing occur together. Stevenson and Urbanowicz (1995) conducted an experiment to examine more specifically the relationship between structural and thematic role focusing. In particular, they examined whether or not both thematic role preferences and surface position are responsible for the ranking of Cfs. They also sought to confirm the results obtained in continuation tasks in a reading time task.

In Stevenson and Urbanowicz's experiment, subjects were presented with two-clause sentences containing either *because* or *so*. The first clause contained goal and source thematic roles, while the subject of the second clause was a pronoun that referred to one of the two thematic roles[3]. The content of the second clause in each sentence biased the assignment of the pronoun to either the first mentioned or the second mentioned antecedent. Two examples follow, in which the content of the second clause biases the assignment of the pronoun to the first mentioned antecedent. In the first example, the first mentioned antecedent is the goal; in the second, it is the source:

Malcolm won some money from Stuart *so* he ended up feeling rich
Stuart lost some money to Malcolm *so* he ended up feeling poor

Our predictions concerned the focusing effect, that is, the ease of interpreting a clause containing a pronoun depending on whether or not it refers to the highest ranked Cf. On the basis of Stevenson et al.'s results, we expect that the reading times for the target clauses containing pronouns will be read more quickly when the pronoun refers to the goal as opposed to the source. We also expect the reading time facilitation to be mostly confined to *so* sentences, as Stevenson et al. found that the preference for goal was considerably attenuated with *because*. On the basis of Hudson D'Zmura's and Gordon et al.'s results, reading times should also be facilitated when the pronoun refers to the first mentioned antecedent rather than the second. However, this first mention effect may be modified by the thematic role focusing.

The results revealed a clear focusing effect of thematic roles: clauses were read more quickly when the pronoun referred to the goal rather than the source. This focusing effect was more pronounced with *so* than with *because*, as expected. The results also revealed a surface mention focusing effect, but only when the referent was the source rather than the goal. That is, surface mention only influenced focusing when the referent was the non-preferred thematic role, presumably because the presence of the preferred thematic role attenuated the focusing of the first mentioned noun phrase, while the non-preferred thematic role had no influence on focusing.

To summarise, evidence has been presented to show that focusing is influenced by both structural and semantic/pragmatic factors. Gordon et al., Hudson D'Zmura, and Hudson D'Zmura et al. have shown that the ranking of Cfs is influenced by surface position, while Stevenson et al. have shown that entities occupying thematic roles associated with the consequences of the described action are more highly focused than thematic roles associated with the cause of the action. Structural focusing and thematic role focusing both occur, with structural focusing being attenuated by later thematic role focusing (Stevenson & Urbanowicz, 1995).

TOWARDS A DYNAMIC MODEL OF FOCUSING

How can we account for the different focusing effects that have been discussed in this chapter? These different effects include top-down influences such as first mention and thematic role, as well as bottom-up influences such as those arising from pronoun assignment strategies like parallel function and from the focusing properties of connectives. The results of the second experiment in Stevenson et al.'s thematic roles study also suggest that a bottom-up subject assignment strategy may be triggered when the pronoun is the subject and first mentioned element in a sentence. That study found a first mention effect when a pronoun was included in the fragment to be completed but not when the pronoun was absent. Taken together, these results suggest a model of focusing in which an initial top-down effect of first mention is modified or changed by subsequent bottom-up input. The resulting shift in focus in turn becomes a top-down influence on the interpretation of subsequent input. In other words, what seems to be needed to explain these focusing effects is a dynamic model of focusing, in which top-down focusing is initiated, updated, and modified by bottom-up linguistic processes triggered by the input.

Traditionally, focusing models have been seen as arising from top-down influences and hence as representing slot-filling models of pronoun comprehension. By contrast, bottom-up processes in pronoun assignment, such as parallel function and subject assignment strategies, are regarded as search processes triggered by the pronoun. The evidence discussed in this chapter suggests, by contrast, that bottom-up processes not only trigger search strategies but also contribute to the maintenance or updating of the current focus. However, the bottom-up processes involved can be triggered by many different elements in a sentence and not just by a pronoun. While a pronoun triggers search strategies to find the antecedent, other elements trigger other processes that are determined by the semantic function of the element in question. Connectives, like *so* or *because*, for example, trigger processes designed to identify the consequence or cause of the described event.

Thus, Stevenson and Urbanowicz's study suggests that the focusing due to first mention is attenuated by the thematic roles encountered later in the utterance. This thematic role focusing is itself triggered by bottom-up information associated with the verb, because the verb identifies the argument structure of the utterance. Then, once the thematic role information is integrated into the mental model of the discourse, it can exert its top-down influence. This influence may in turn be modified by later bottom-up input, as shown by the way that the choice of connective either reinforces or modifies thematic role focusing[4]. Other evidence suggests that once a pronoun has been interpreted (at least a pronoun in subject or first mention position), the referent of the pronoun itself is brought more into focus (Gordon et al., 1993), thus indicating yet again the way that bottom-up processes, this time triggered by a pronoun, influence top-down processing. All in all, therefore, the picture that emerges is that the focused referent in a mental model of a discourse is initiated, updated, and modified as a function of top-down and bottom-up processes as the discourse proceeds.

SUMMARY

I began this chapter by discussing Johnson-Laird's theory of mental models in which the situation described by a discourse is represented. A mental model of a discourse is constructed from a propositional representation in conjunction with inferences based on general knowledge of the situation. A proposition represents the meaning of an utterance while a mental model represents its reference. Thus, mental models are crucial for understanding how reference is comprehended.

Against this background, the remainder of the chapter discussed the comprehension of pronouns. I introduced the distinction between top-down processes stemming from mental models and bottom-up processes stemming from propositions. I also noted that the two main models of pronoun comprehension, the slot-filling model and the search model, are thought of as instances of these two kinds of processes.

Focusing accounts of pronoun comprehension are regarded as slot-filling models because they claim that a particular entity in a model of the discourse is in focus at any given point and so is readily available to fill the slot identified by a pronoun. Structural focusing models assume that structural information, such as surface position, determines which entity will be in focus, or, in terms of centering theory, which will be the highest ranked

Cf in an utterance. Centering theory also identifies a Cb, the position in an utterance that normally refers to the highest ranked Cf of the preceding utterance. Semantic/pragmatic focusing models assume that semantic or pragmatic information, such as the thematic role of the entity, determines which entity will be in focus. I then described an experiment by Stevenson and Urbanowicz in which the relationship between structural and semantic/ pragmatic focusing was examined. The results showed that both thematic role information and structural information (surface mention) affected focusing, with thematic role focusing being the more prominent.

I concluded that, in general, bottom-up and top-down processes jointly help to maintain or to shift the current focus of a discourse. Bottom-up processes also have specific semantic functions that depend on the semantics of the element involved. Thus focusing is not simply an aspect of slot-filling, as the focusing properties of the bottom-up processes must also be taken into account. In short, although the structure of the mental model enables a single focused discourse entity to be established, such focusing is initiated, updated, and modified by bottom-up processes triggered by the linguistic input. All in all, the comprehension of discourse seems to depend crucially on the dynamic interaction of propositions and mental models.

ACKNOWLEDGEMENTS

The Human Communication Research Centre is funded by the Economic and Social Research Council of Great Britain. Thanks to Massimo Poesio for numerous stimulating discussions on centering theory, and to Jane Oakhill, Alan Garnham, and Elisabet Engdahl for constructive comments on an earlier version of this chapter.

NOTES

1. These results do not necessarily imply that mental models are stored in episodic memory. The results of Payne (1993) suggest that what may be stored are the mental operations by which mental models are constructed.
2. We also included what we called "agent–goal/source" sentences that contained verbs of motion with agent and goal or source thematic roles, for example:

   John ran towards Bill.
   John ran away from Bill.

   These sentences were included to assess the possibility that assignment in the goal–source sentences may be dependent on the transfer of the theme. However these sentences always showed a preference for the agent. As the agent role is confounded with the first mention effect, we do not discuss them here.
3. We also included conditions where names were used instead of pronouns. These conditions investigated a separate hypothesis and are not reported here.
4. We note here that this account does not help to explain why, in Stevenson et al.'s study, *because* also seems to trigger a first mention effect in goal–source sentences—a result that awaits a specific explanation.

REFERENCES

Anderson, J.R., & Bower, G.H. (1973). *Human associative memory*. New York: John Wiley & Sons.

Andrews, A. (1985). The major functions of the noun phrase. In , T. Shopen, (Ed.), *Language typology and syntactic description, Vol. 1: Clause structure*. Cambridge: Cambridge University Press.

Bransford, J.D., Barclay, J., & Franks, J. (1972). Sentence memory: A constructive versus interpretative approach. *Cognitive Psychology, 3*, 193–209.

Bransford, J.D., & Franks, J.J. (1971). The abstraction of linguistic ideas. *Cognitive Psychology, 2*, 331–350.

Bransford, J.D., & Johnson, M.K. (1972). Contextual prerequisites for understanding: Some investigations of comprehension and recall. *Journal of Verbal Learning and Verbal Behavior, 11*, 717–726.

Brennan, S.E., Friedman, M. W., & Pollard, C.J. (1987). A centering approach to pronouns. *Proceedings of the 25th Annual Meeting of the Association of Computational Linguistics* (pp.155–162). Stanford, CA: Association for Computational Linguistics.

Broadbent, D.E. (1977). Language and ergonomics. *Applied Ergonomics, 8*, 15–18. [Reprinted in *IEEE Transactions on Professional Communication, vol. PC–21*, No. 1, March, 1978.]

Caramazza , A., Grober, E.H., Garvey, C., & Yates, J.V. (1977). Comprehension of anaphoric pronouns. *Journal of Verbal Learning and Verbal Behavior, 16*, 601–609.

Clark, H.H., & C.J. Sengul. (1979). In search of referents for nouns and pronouns. *Memory and Cognition, 7*(1), 35–41.

Ehrlich, K. (1980). Comprehension of pronouns. *Quarterly Journal of Experimental Psychology, 32*, 247–255.

Ehrlich, K., & Johnson-Laird, P.N. (1982). Spatial descriptions and referential continuity. *Journal of Verbal Learning and Verbal Behavior, 21*, 296–306.

Fillmore, C. (1968). The case for case. In E. Bach & R.T. Harms (Eds.), *Universals in linguistic theory*. New York: Holt, Rinehart & Winston.

Fodor, J.A., Bever, T.G., & Garrett, M.F. (1974). *The psychology of language: An introduction to psycholinguistics and generative grammar*. New York: McGraw-Hill.

Fodor, J.A., Fodor, J.D., & Garrett, M.F. (1975). The psychological unreality of semantic representations. *Linguistic Inquiry, VI*, 515–531.

Garnham, A. (1987). *Mental models as representations of discourse and text*. Chichester, UK: Ellis Horwood Limited. [Also (1981), Unpublished PhD Thesis, University of Sussex.]

Garnham, A., Oakhill, J., & Cruttenden, H. (1992). The role of implicit causality and gender cue in the interpretation of pronouns. *Language and Cognitive Processes, 7*, 231–255.

Garvey, C., & Caramazza, A. (1974). Implicit causality in verbs. *Linguistic Inquiry, 5*, 459–464.

Gernsbacher, M.A. (1989). Mechanisms that improve referential access. *Cognition, 32*, 99–156.

Gernsbacher, M.A., & Hargreaves, D.J. (1989). Accessing sentence participants: The advantage of first mention. *Journal of Memory and Language, 27*, 699–717.

Gordon, P.C., Grosz, B.J., & Gilliom, L.A. (1993). Pronouns, names and the centering of attention in discourse. *Cognitive Science, 17*, 311–348.

Greene, S.B., McKoon, G, & Ratcliff, R. (1992). Pronoun resolution and discourse models. *Journal of Experimental Psychology: Learning, Memory and Cognition, 18* (2), 266–283.

Grosz, B.J., Joshi, A., & Weinstein, S. (1983). Providing a unified account of definite noun phrases in discourse. *Proceedings of the 21st Annual Meeting of the Association for Computational Linguistics*. Cambridge, MA: Association for Computational Linguistics.

Grosz, B.J., Joshi, A., & Weinstein, S. (1995). Centering: A framework for modelling the local coherence of discourse. *Computational Linguistics, 21*, 203–225.

Grosz, B.J., & Sidner, C.L. (1986). Attention, intentions and the structure of discourse. *Computational Linguistics*, *12*, 175–204.

Hobbs, J.R. (1976). *Pronoun resolution.* Research Report 76–1. Department of Computer Science, City College, City University of New York, NY.

Hudson D'Zmura, S.B. (1988). *The structure of discourse and anaphor resolution: The discourse center and the roles of nouns and pronouns.* PhD thesis, University of Rochester.

Hudson, S., Tanenhaus, M.K., & Dell, G. (1986). The effect of the discourse center on the local coherence of a discourse. In C. Clifton, Jr. (Ed.), *Proceedings of the 12th Annual Conference of the Cognitive Science Society* (pp.96–101). Hillsdale, NJ: Lawrence Erlbaum Associates Inc.

Jackendoff, R. (1985). The status of thematic relations in linguistic theory. *Linguistic Inquiry*, *18*, 369–411.

Johnson, M.K., Bransford, J.D., & Solomon, S. (1973). Memory for tacit implications of sentences. *Journal of Experimental Psychology*, *98*, 203–205.

Johnson-Laird, P.N. (1977). Psycholinguistics without linguistics. In N.S. Sutherland (Ed.), *Tutorial essays in psychology, Vol. 1.* Hillsdale, NJ: Lawrence Erlbaum Associates Inc.

Johnson-Laird, P.N. (1983). *Mental models.* Cambridge, MA: Harvard University Press.

Kameyama, M. (1986). A property-sharing constraint in centering. *Proceedings of the 24th Annual Meeting of the Association for Computational Linguistics* (pp.200–206). New York: Association for Computational Linguistics.

Kintsch, W. (1974). *The representation of meaning in memory.* Hillsdale, NJ: Lawrence Erlbaum Associates Inc.

Kintsch, W., & Keenan, J.M. (1973). Reading rate and retention as a function of the number of propositions in the base structure of sentences. *Cognitive Psychology*, *5*, 257–274.

Kintsch, W., & van Dijk, T.A. (1978). Toward a model of text comprehension and production. *Psychological Review*, *85*, 363–394.

Mani, K., & Johnson-Laird, P.N. (1982). The mental representation of spatial descriptions. *Memory and Cognition*, *10*, 181–187.

Moens, M., & Steedman, M.J. (1988). Temporal ontology and temporal reference. *Computational Linguistics*, *14*, 15–28.

Payne, S.J. (1993). Memory for mental models of spatial descriptions: An episodic construction-trace hypothesis. *Memory and Cognition*, *21*, 591–603.

Quillian, M.R. (1968). Semantic memory. In M. Minsky (Ed.), *Semantic information processing.* Cambridge, MA: MIT Press.

Radford, A. (1988). *Transformational grammar: A first course.* Cambridge: Cambridge University Press.

Rips, L.J., Shoben, E.J., & Smith, E.E. (1973). Semantic distance and the verification of semantic relations. *Journal of Verbal Learning and Verbal Behavior*, *12*, 1–20.

Sanford, A.J., & Garrod, S.C. (1981). *Understanding written language.* Chichester, UK: Wiley.

Sheldon, A. (1974). The role of parallel function in the acquisition of relative clauses in English. *Journal of Verbal Learning and Verbal Behavior*, *13*, 272–281.

Smyth, R. (1994). Grammatical determinants of ambiguous pronoun resolution. *Journal of Psycholinguistic Research*, *23*, 197–229.

Stevenson, R.J. (1986). The time course of pronoun comprehension. In C. Clifton, Jr. (Ed.), *Proceedings of the 12th Annual Conference of the Cognitive Science Society* (pp.102–109). Hillsdale, NJ: Lawrence Erlbaum Associates Inc.

Stevenson, R.J., Crawley, R.A., & Kleinman, D. (1994). Thematic roles, focus and the representation of actions. *Language and Cognitive Processes*, *9*, 519–548.

Stevenson, R.J., Nelson, A.W.R., & Stenning, K. (1993). Strategies in pronoun comprehension. *Proceedings of the 15th Annual Conference of the Cognitive Science Society* (pp.976–981). Hillsdale, NJ: Lawrence Erlbaum Associates Inc.

Stevenson, R.J., & Urbanowicz, A. (1995). Structural focusing, thematic role focusing and the comprehension of pronouns. *Proceedings of the 17th Annual Conference of the Cognitive Science Society*. Hillsdale, NJ: Lawrence Erlbaum Associates Inc.

Walker, M., Ilda, M., & Cote, S. (1994). Japanese discourse and the process of centering. *Computational Linguistics, 20*, 193–231.

5

Mental Models in Children's Text Comprehension

Jane Oakhill
Laboratory of Experimental Psychology, University of Sussex, UK

MENTAL MODELS IN SKILLED READING

To fully comprehend a text, we need to do much more than just understanding the individual words and sentences. In order to adequately understand a text, the skilled reader has to derive a mental representation of the state of affairs that the text describes: an integrated mental model of the whole (Johnson-Laird, 1983). To derive such a model, the reader will need to engage in a number of processes, and here I consider the main ones.

First, the reader has to integrate the meanings of individual sentences and paragraphs (a process that may involve inferences). Second, the reader needs to identify the structure and main ideas in the text. In the case of stories, they need to identify the main character(s) and their motives, follow the plot, etc. In the case of expository texts, they need to ascertain the topic of the text, distinguish important from less important information, follow a line of argument, etc. Third, the reader needs to go beyond what is stated explicitly, both by linking up ideas in the text to form a coherent overall model, and by bringing their general knowledge to bear on their understanding of it. Authors necessarily leave some of the links and expansions in a text implicit. A fully explicit text would not only be very long and boring, but it would disallow the possibility of the reader imposing their own meaning on the text—making it "their own". A short text, adapted from Charniak (1972), serves to illustrate how both background knowledge and inferences are needed to understand even a short, and apparently simple, text:

Jane was invited to Jack's birthday party.
She wondered if he would like a kite.
She went to her room and shook her piggy bank.
It made no sound.

To understand this text, one needs knowledge about birthday parties: the convention of taking presents, saving money, and the need for money to buy presents. Someone (perhaps from a different culture) who did not understand the nature of birthday parties, piggy banks, or money would find this simple story impossible to understand. Furthermore, a skilled reader will infer that Jane is not simply "wondering" if Jack would like a kite, she is thinking about buying him one for his birthday, and that the purpose of shaking her piggy bank is to find out if it contains any money. If such inferences are not made, then the text will be little more than a list of unrelated sentences. Similarly, the implications of the lack of sound in the final sentence are not explicit, but the skilled reader will immediately infer that Jane has no savings and they will, perhaps, give some thought to how Jane might resolve the situation. However, in the case of inferences, it is obviously not a question of "the more the merrier". Skilled readers have to make enough inferences to understand the text, but their inferential processing also has to be limited in some way: the number of inferences that could be made from a text is potentially infinite! Which inferences are made is a controversial issue in adult text processing, and one that will not be addressed here (see e.g. Garnham, 1992; McKoon & Ratcliff, 1992).

Readers also need to engage in "meta-level" processing, to monitor the success, or otherwise, of their comprehension processes, and need to know what to do if their understanding breaks down.

WHY MIGHT MODEL BUILDING GO WRONG?

One possible source of problems in higher-level comprehension processes is the efficiency with which lower-level processes are executed. If the processes of accessing the meanings of individual words and parsing sentences is a time-consuming and attention-demanding process, then higher-level processes (such as inference making, text integration, structure derivation, and comprehension monitoring) are likely to suffer.

Perfetti (e.g. 1985, 1988) has suggested that comprehension difficulties arise, in the main, because certain processes that can potentially become relatively automatic (e.g. word recognition) fail to become so. Perfetti has identified, in particular, two likely sources of comprehension problems: lexical processes and working memory limitations. An association between speed and automaticity of lexical processing and comprehension ability has been found in both children and adults. For example, Perfetti and

Hogaboam (1975) found large differences in word naming time between good and poor comprehenders in the third and fifth grades. These differences were evident even for common words, which all of the children were able to read without errors. Further work showed that such differences between good and poor comprehenders are specific to word reading: the children did not differ in the time they took to name colours, pictures, and numbers.

However, although decoding facility and comprehension skill tend to go together, there is no evidence for a direct causal link between the two. Groups of children can be found who differ in comprehension skill, even when they are matched for word recognition speed and automaticity (Cromer, 1970; Oakan, Wiener, & Cromer, 1971; Oakhill, 1981). In addition, if there were a direct causal link between decoding facility and comprehension, one would expect training in decoding to improve comprehension skill. However, such training studies have not met with success. For example, Fleischer, Jenkins, and Pany (1979) trained fourth- and fifth-grade poor comprehenders until they were able to recognise a set of words as rapidly as the good comprehenders. The children improved their decoding speed on the trained words to equal that of the good comprehenders, but did not improve their comprehension, even though the passages on which they were tested consisted entirely of the words on which they had been trained. Thus, it seems that speedy decoding probably does not have a direct causal influence on comprehension ability.

Furthermore, children with reading comprehension problems frequently also have listening comprehension problems (Stothard & Hulme, 1992), so decoding speed and automaticity can, at best, be the problem only in some children. It is certainly the case that the ability to read single words and comprehension skill are highly correlated in the population as a whole and, thus, many poor comprehenders may also have problems at the level of single words. However, it is clear that by no means all problems in text comprehension can be explained by difficulties at the level of single words.

A second, and not unrelated, view is that model building is highly dependent on the efficient use of working memory. There is now clear evidence that skilled comprehenders have more efficient working memories than less-skilled ones (e.g. Daneman & Carpenter, 1980; Perfetti & Goldman, 1976; Yuill, Oakhill, & Parkin, 1989). The working memory system is supposed to be implicated in text comprehension because of its capacity for simultaneous storage and processing of information. During text comprehension these simultaneous capabilities will be needed because of the requirement to recognise words, retrieve their meanings, and parse sentences, while simultaneously integrating the current sentence with what has gone before, and deriving an integrated model of the text as a whole.

I return to the two areas outlined earlier in the discussion of the particular problems of the children we have identified as poor comprehenders. In the next section, I describe some of the work that has been conducted by myself and colleagues at Sussex, on children who have a specific comprehension problem, and suggest how their difficulties relate to the processes that are needed for efficient comprehension.

INADEQUATE MODEL BUILDING BY POOR COMPREHENDERS

A small proportion of children in the early junior-school years (7–10 years old) are adequate or good at single-word reading but, nevertheless, have difficulty understanding the core content of a text they have read. In research conducted at Sussex, we have found that around 10% of children in mainstream schools can be classed as having a comprehension problem— that is, comprehension that is significantly behind what would be expected from their general reading ability. The children we have studied have a *specific* comprehension problem, in that their single-word reading and vocabulary is at least average for their age, but their ability to understand a text they have just read is considerably behind what would be predicted from their chronological age and word reading accuracy. We have compared the performance of such children with that of skilled comprehenders of the same age and word recognition ability. The two groups are selected using the Neale Analysis of Reading Ability and the Gates-MacGinitie Vocabulary Test. The Neale Analysis provides measures both of reading accuracy (word recognition in context) and comprehension (assessed by ability to answer a series of questions about short passages). The Gates-MacGinitie test requires the child to select one of four written words to go with a picture. Thus, it acts as a measure of silent word recognition, out of context, and provides an index of the child's reading vocabulary. In all our studies, the groups of skilled and less-skilled comprehenders are matched for word recognition ability (Neale Accuracy and Gates-MacGinitie) and chronological age, but differ in Neale Comprehension scores. In summary, the children who participated in our experiments were all at or above average at word recognition; one group were also good comprehenders, while the other group were poor comprehenders, particularly with respect to their ability to recognise words.

Lower-level Skills

Although it is possible, as outlined earlier, that comprehension is limited by the inefficient execution of lower-level processes, in my own studies I have excluded children who might have comprehension difficulties associated with word recognition problems. This procedure has been used because I was interested in looking at children who have a specific comprehension problem, rather than some more general reading deficit. Therefore, the children in these studies were matched for word recognition ability. Furthermore, I have found no differences between groups thus selected in decoding speed or automaticity (Oakhill, 1981).

It is also possible that poor comprehenders have difficulties at the sentence level, failing to understand certain syntactic constructions. Cromer and his colleagues explored extensively the idea that poor comprehenders fail to make use of the syntactic constraints in text (Cromer, 1970; Oakan et al., 1971; Steiner, Weiner, & Cromer, 1971). They found that poor comprehenders tend to read word-by-word, rather than using the syntactic and semantic groupings in text. One of the groups of poor comprehenders in Cromer's studies had similar characteristics to the poor comprehenders discussed here, in that they had comprehension difficulties even though their vocabulary and decoding skills were commensurate with those of good comprehenders of the same age. However, when we tested the children's syntactic abilities using the Test for Reception of Grammar (Bishop, 1982), we found no differences between the groups.

Recently, Shankweiler (e.g. 1989) has suggested that comprehension suffers because of parsing problems which are, in turn, related to poor phonological skills. However, we have found no evidence to support this hypothesis when the poor comprehenders are selected as described (Oakhill, Yuill, & Parkin, 1986; Cain, 1994). Of course, we must be careful when interpreting null results: it is possible that the tests we used were simply lacking in sensitivity, and failed to discriminate between the good and poor comprehenders. However, we have now conducted a number of studies, using a variety of paradigms, which converge on the same conclusion: that the main source of poor comprehenders' difficulties is not at the level of words or sentences.

Higher-level Processing: Inferences and Anaphora

One of the more reliable findings is that poor comprehenders have difficulties in making inferences. An early concern was to assess whether less-skilled comprehenders' poorer performance when they are asked questions about a text is simply a memory problem. To explore this issue, I asked children questions about short stories under two conditions (Oakhill, 1984). First, the children had to answer a series of questions about a story from memory. Second, they could re-read and look back over the story to find, or check, their responses to the questions. The questions were of two types: some were "literal" in that they simply asked about information that was explicitly stated in the text; the others were "inferential" in that they required the children to go beyond what was explicitly stated, to make simple inferences from it. In general, less-skilled comprehenders performed more poorly, and inference questions were harder for both groups. However, the particularly interesting aspect of these results was that, although the good and poor comprehenders were equally able to answer the literal questions when the text was available for them to re-read, the less-skilled comprehenders performed significantly more poorly on questions that required an inference. These findings indicate that the poor comprehenders' difficulties cannot simply be attributed to poor memory: even when the text was available for them to look over, they were still unable to answer a high proportion of the questions that required them to infer information that was not explicit in the text.

There are several possible explanations for this result, some of which will be taken up later. First, poor comprehenders might simply lack the general knowledge to make the required inferences. Such an explanation seems unlikely given the nature of the knowledge that the questions tapped (we would expect a 7-year-old to know that if someone is "pedalling" they are likely to be riding a bike). Indeed, this explanation has been ruled out in a later study by Kate Cain in which similar differences were shown, even though the poor comprehenders had the relevant knowledge (Cain & Oakhill, in press a). Second, poor comprehenders might not realise that inferences are necessary or even permissible—perhaps they focus on extracting the literal meaning from the text at the expense of inferential processing. Third, poor comprehenders may realise that inferences are legitimate, but may have difficulty accessing relevant knowledge, and integrating it with what is in the text, because of processing limitations. This last possibility relates to the earlier suggestion that comprehension processes may be limited by working memory. Later in this chapter I consider this third possibility, in particular, in more detail.

An experiment in which the children were not required to bring any additional knowledge to their understanding of short texts also revealed differences between good and poor comprehenders in their propensity to make inferences to connect up ideas in a text (Oakhill, 1982). This study showed that poor comprehenders make fewer constructive inferences when they listen to short texts, even though all the information on which the inferences could be based is given in the texts. These data are consistent with the idea that the good comprehenders are more likely to make integrative inferences, to bring together the ideas in the text as a whole, whereas the poor comprehenders tend to derive a more superficial, literal interpretation of the text.

Another procedure in skilled text comprehension is the use of anaphoric expressions to guide text integration. In several studies (Oakhill & Yuill, 1986; Yuill & Oakhill, 1988) we found that poor comprehenders have considerable trouble in understanding anaphoric expressions, such as pronouns and verb-phrase ellipses. In the first of those studies, the less-skilled comprehenders had difficulty in supplying an appropriate pronoun (*he* or *she*) in short sentences, such as:

Sally gave her shoes to Ben because ... needed them.

In other texts, where the link between the clauses of the sentence was less straightforward, the poor comprehenders had even greater difficulties, making almost twice as many errors as the good comprehenders:

Steven gave his umbrella to Penny because ... wanted to keep dry.

In the later experiment (Yuill & Oakhill, 1988) we used a short story to explore children's understanding of a wider range of anaphoric links. The children read the text through once, and were then asked about particular anaphoric expressions in a different version of the text, in which these expressions were underlined. First, the children were asked what these expressions "stood for" or "pointed back to" and then, if they did not answer correctly, they were asked a more direct question. For instance, for the portion of text: "Bill went fishing. *He* carried his rod to the bus stop", the child was asked, "Who carried his rod to the bus stop?". The good and poor comprehenders differed on all types of anaphor, and on both tasks. Even when asked direct questions, and when the text was available for them to refer to, the less-skilled comprehenders got only 72% correct, compared with 90% for the good group. These studies show that poor comprehenders have problems in using common cohesive devices to aid their text integration, particularly when the anaphoric link is not straightforward and requires an inference. However, the substantial numbers of errors made by the less-skilled comprehenders in these experiments suggest that they lack fundamental knowledge about anaphoric expressions. Such problems will obviously not be conducive to efficient text integration and model building.

WHAT GOES WRONG WITH POOR COMPREHENDERS' TEXT MODELS?

There is evidence (from some of the studies cited here, and elsewhere, see Yuill & Oakhill, 1991), that poor comprehenders' difficulties do not, in the main, lie at the level of understanding sentences, or recalling literal information from text but, rather, that it is their overall representations of texts that are inadequate. One possibility is that poor comprehenders are able to build partial, rather fragmentary models of text—perhaps integrating information locally—but are not able to build a coherent model of the text as a whole. Several recent studies conducted at Sussex suggest that this hypothesis is a viable one. These studies are discussed next.

Comprehension Monitoring and Comprehension Repair

One way to investigate the quality of a reader's text representation is to require them to test incoming information against information that should already be represented in the text model. If their model is adequate, then they should have no problem, either in rejecting information as inconsistent with the model so far, or in integrating the information and adjusting their model.

In an experiment to investigate this issue (Yuill et al., 1989) we used an anomaly detection task (adapted from Ackerman, 1984). In this study, the children listened to short stories describing an adult's response to a child's action, which was, apparently, inconsistent with their knowledge of social norms. Somewhere else within the story there was information to resolve the inconsistency. For example, in one story a mother praises her son for refusing to share his sweets with his little brother.

The apparent inconsistency was either preceded or followed by the resolving information (in the example, that the brother was on a diet, and was not allowed sweets). The ease with which the resolving information could be used was manipulated by varying the distance between the apparent anomaly and its resolution: these pieces of information were either in adjacent sentences, or were separated by a few sentences in the text. After each story had been read, the children were asked three types of questions. First they were asked about whether the adult in the story should have acted as he or she did, and why. This question could only be answered correctly if the anomaly had been correctly resolved. Second, they were asked a question to test their memory for crucial information from the story on which the anomaly was based. Third, they were asked a question about the rule on which the inconsistency was based, e.g. in this case, "Would someone usually be praised or blamed for not sharing their sweets with their little brother?". If children answered this question wrongly, their response can be taken as an indication that they did not agree with the behavioural norms, and should not find the story inconsistent. Very few children answered either the memory or the rule questions wrongly.

The result of particular interest from this study was the differential effects that the memory demands of the task had on the two skill groups. Good and poor comprehenders were equally good at resolving inconsistencies when the inconsistency and the resolving information were in adjacent sentences, but the poor comprehenders were much worse when the two pieces of information were separated in the text. This finding demonstrates that the poor comprehenders do not have any general deficit in this aspect of comprehension monitoring: they are competent at the task when the memory demands are small, but have considerable difficulties when the memory load intrinsic to the task is increased.

The experiment just described tested for ability to integrate new information within a current mental model, but did not test comprehension monitoring directly. The traditional test of comprehension monitoring uses an error-detection paradigm (see, e.g. Markman, 1977). In a further study (Oakhill, Hartt, & Samols, 1995), slightly older children (9- to 10-year-olds), were selected in the same way as described earlier. Older children were used as subjects because error-detection tasks are notoriously difficult, and we felt that older children would not only be better able to detect the errors, but would also be better able to comment on them sensibly. The errors were internal inconsistencies within the text—i.e. contradictory statements. This procedure had the advantage of allowing us, once again, to manipulate the intrinsic memory load of the task: the inconsistencies were either in adjacent sentences, or were separated by several sentences. An example passage is:

Gorillas are clever animals that live together in groups in Africa.
Gorillas sleep on the ground on a bed of leaves and they like to eat different types of fruit.
They are shy and gentle and they hardly ever fight with each other.
Gorillas have flat noses and a very poor sense of smell but their eyesight is very good.
They move about the ground on their hands and feet.
*
Gorillas sleep in trees and they often build a shelter out of leaves above them, to keep the rain out.

_____ This passage makes sense, it does not need to be changed.
_____ This passage does not make sense, it needs to be changed.

*Note: in the adjacent condition, the italicised sentence occurred in this position.

The children were presented with two passages in each of the two memory load conditions. They were also asked to read and make judgements about two passages without any inconsistencies, so that we could make sure that they really could discriminate between passages with problems and those without.

The children read the passages aloud, and were then asked to identify any problems with them ("something that doesn't make sense") by underlining. They were shown an example of the sort of blatant inconsistency that occurred in the test passages. At the end of each passage, they were asked to indicate their overall assessment of the passage. If they had indicated a problem, they were asked to explain it. In the case of passages with inconsistencies, if the child did not immediately identify a problem, they were given another chance to do so, and were asked more direct questions if they still failed. For each passage, the child was given a score between 0 and 3, depending on how much help they required to identify the problem. An analysis of these scores showed that the skilled comprehenders were better overall, and the inconsistencies that were separated by several sentences were harder to detect. However, of particular interest was the interaction between the distance and the skill variables: the good comprehenders were not affected by the distance manipulation, but the less-skilled comprehenders found the inconsistencies more difficult to detect in the distant than in the near condition. Performance on the non-problematic passages was uniformly high. Thus, the pattern of results was very similar to that observed in the previous experiment.

Taken together, the results of these two experiments suggest that less-skilled comprehenders do not have any difficulty in integrating incoming information with their mental model of the text so far, but that they are only successful in this integration if the memory demands are not too great. Thus, the processing ability of less-skilled comprehenders may permit them to integrate information over short segments of text, but not over the text as a whole. They could, therefore, be characterised as being able to build partial, but not complete, models of a text. This view will be taken up again in the next section.

Understanding Text Structure: Story Production

As outlined earlier, readers need to understand the structure of a text in order to see how the information they are currently reading fits into the text's overall organisation. It is a reasonable hypothesis that children's knowledge about story structure and coherence will aid their understanding of stories that they read or hear. There are several studies showing how a child's concept of a story becomes refined with age (e.g. Applebee, 1978; Peterson & McCabe, 1983; Stein & Glenn, 1979; 1982). However, little is known about how comprehension skill relates to such knowledge.

Children who have problems in seeing how the different parts of a text interrelate when they are trying to understand it would also be likely to have problems in producing a coherent and well-structured text. We decided to explore children's story production because it could be a useful tool to investigate their spontaneous use of anaphoric and other cohesive devices. Our previous work (see Yuill & Oakhill, 1991) has shown that skilled and less-skilled comprehenders differ in important ways in their story-telling abilities. In an experiment that required the children to plan and narrate their own stories prompted only by picture sequences, we found that the poor comprehenders were less consistent in their use of causal connectives, and were more likely to use referential ties (such as pronouns) ambiguously or repetitiously. However, this study was not designed to investigate specific aspects of story knowledge, such as how stories are structured, and whether stereotypical conventions are used. Thus, we do not know whether the differences arise primarily because of differences in ability to understand the use of cohesive links, and how they might be utilised in the production of a well-structured story, or whether differences in knowledge about story conventions and story concepts underlie differences in the quality of children's productions.

For these reasons, we conducted a further study (Cain & Oakhill, in press b) which had two aims. First, we wanted to see whether comprehension skill is related to story knowledge and, if so, how. A production task was used to assess how the concept of a story as a sequence of linked events is related to comprehension ability. The second aim was to explore the relation between comprehension and story knowledge: does story knowledge promote good comprehension skills, or is it a by-product of being a good comprehender? This issue was addressed by using a *Comprehension–Age Match (CAM)* design in which we compared the performance of poor comprehenders with that of two control groups: same-age skilled comprehenders (as in the studies outlined earlier) and younger children whose comprehension skill was similar to that of the older poor comprehenders, but was commensurate with the younger children's age and word reading ability (the Comprehension–Age Match). The CAM can help to address the issue of whether the poor comprehenders are just experiencing a developmental lag, or whether their comprehension skills are qualitatively different from those of other children. It can also help to rule out certain causal possibilities. If poor comprehenders are worse on certain measures than younger children with the same comprehension skill (the CAM group), we can infer that the differences do not arise from less experience of reading, because it is the younger children who would be expected to have less experience than older poor comprehenders. Thus, a causal link is a possibility, although not, of course, proven. One possibility is that the younger children, although they have less experience of reading, have better quality reading experiences than the older poor comprehenders.

In this study, two different types of prompt were used to elicit stories. One was a sequence of six pictures that "told a story" and the other was a title, e.g. "Pirates", about which the children were asked to tell a story (children told three stories in response to each type of prompt, in a blocked design, with order of prompt type counterbalanced). We expected that poor comprehenders might produce more poorly structured stories in general, and that the topic prompts might lead to poorer stories than the picture prompts, because the story structure and plot is, essentially, provided in the picture condition, providing that the sequence of pictures can be understood! We also expected that there might be a larger difference between the skill groups in the topic than in the picture prompt condition, with the poor comprehenders performing particularly poorly in the topic prompt condition. If the ability to produce well-structured and coherent stories is more than simply a by-product of being good at comprehension, then we might expect the older poor comprehenders to produce worse stories than the younger CAM group

The children's productions were tape-recorded and transcribed. Each story was scored in two ways: for the occurrence of story conventions and for the clarity of its event structure. Scoring was by two independent raters, who agreed in over 90% of instances (any disagreements were resolved by discussion).

We analysed the stories for four classes of story convention: typical openings and endings, such as *"Once upon a time"*, *"one day"*, *"the end"*, *"and they all lived happily ever after"*; character setting information, such as: *"There was a mum, a dad and a little girl"* and scene-setting information, such as *"this boy was at the circus"*. An analysis of these data showed no differences between the groups in their use of any of these conventional features: the conventions were used frequently by the children in all three groups.

Each story was categorised into one of three classes, to reflect the extent to which causality between events was signalled, and the story as a whole cohered. The three categories, with an example from each, were:

1. *Non-stories:* these narratives were either totally incoherent, or lacked any obvious sequence of events. Some such non-stories comprised only an opening and character and/or scene setting information, but nothing else. For example: *"Once upon a time there was a girl and she went on holiday"* (topic prompt: The Holiday).

2. *Intermediate stories:* these narratives contained a sequence of events, but the main events were not causally linked to each other. For example: *"It was a lovely day. The family decided to go down to the seaside. They saw lots of people there. The baby was making a sandcastle, the older children were playing in the sea, the mum and dad had their last swim before they went home"* (topic prompt: The Seaside).

3. *Complete stories:* narratives that related an integrated sequence of events, with the main events causally related. For example: *"There was once a girl who had scruffy hair. Her mum said she had to have her hair cut, but she didn't like to have her hair cut, she thought she might have the wrong haircut. So she went in mum's . . . her mum's room and got her hair scissors and she cut her hair short so . . . and she looked in the mirror and she didn't like the hair cut she did, so her mum came in the room and gave her a hat, so it didn't show her fringe. The end."* (Picture sequence prompt: The Haircut.)

The stories were scored by awarding points from 0–2 depending on the category to which the story was allocated. Thus, each child obtained a score out of 6 for each prompt type.

It is interesting to note that the stories produced by the less-skilled comprehenders tended to be longer than those produced by the skilled group, particularly in the title prompt condition, where the less-skilled groups' stories were, on average 45% longer. Thus, it was not the case that the poorer comprehenders were simply producing short stories that necessarily received the lowest rating for structure. Analysis of the structure scores showed that, overall, the poorer comprehenders produced less well-structured stories and, as predicted, the picture prompts elicited better-structured stories than the topic prompts. In the topic prompt condition, the skilled comprehenders and the CAM group produced significantly better-structured stories than did the less-skilled group. In the picture prompt condition, the skilled comprehenders were, once more, better than the less-skilled group, but there was no significant difference between the less-skilled group and the CAM group. Performance of the skilled comprehenders and the CAM group did not differ significantly in either prompt condition.

The results of this study provide no evidence of a relation between comprehension skill and the knowledge of conventional, formulaic features of stories. It seems that even poorer comprehenders and younger readers have this *knowledge* about story conventions. There were, however, differences among the groups in their ability to produce internally well-structured stories. In particular, the poor comprehenders needed the picture sequence in order to produce stories with a coherent event structure. The group differences were particularly marked in the more difficult topic prompt condition where the poor comprehenders performed more poorly than either of the control groups. This result is especially interesting because it rules out the possibility that the ability to produce a well-structured story is simply the result of extensive experience of reading (because we would expect the older children, and the older good comprehenders in particular, to have had more reading experience) and suggests, instead, an alternative explanation: that such knowledge might be causally linked to comprehension skill. There are two main reasons for coming to this conclusion. First, the less-skilled comprehenders produced less well-structured stories than the CAM group in the generally more difficult topic prompt condition (i.e. two groups of equivalent comprehension skill performed differently on this task, and, importantly, the older children were *worse*). Thus, as the two groups were matched for comprehension ability, the results suggest that the ability to produce well-structured stories is not simply a consequence of reading comprehension skill. Second, the less-skilled comprehenders produced stories of equivalent quality to those of the CAM group when a picture sequence was provided as a prompt. This suggests that it was this structural framework that the poor comprehenders were lacking in the topic prompt condition, and that one of the reasons for poor story production and comprehension might be lack of ability to keep track of the event structure of a text. We are not suggesting that what is being tapped in this experiment is necessarily a skill that is specific to story production. Rather, it is probably something more general, such as a "drive for coherence" which affects both comprehension and production. This inability to produce a well-structured and coherent event structure and the inability to use coherence links when trying to understand a text, may be related to the children's working memory skill—a point to which we return in the next section.

WORKING MEMORY IN TEXT COMPREHENSION

The work on comprehension monitoring, and that on anomaly detection and inferences, suggests that the integration of information from different parts of a text is much harder for poor comprehenders than for good comprehenders. Such problems may well be related to working memory. There is extensive work in adults showing that tests of working memory span are correlated with text comprehension (for a review, see Daneman, 1987). Daneman and Carpenter (e.g. 1980, 1983) have shown that various aspects of skilled comprehension (remembering facts, detecting inconsistencies, resolving pronouns) are related to a verbal test of working memory (the *sentence span* task). This task requires the subjects to read and understand a series of sentences (the processing requirement) while simultaneously trying to remember the final word in each (the storage requirement).

Although we have demonstrated that good and poor comprehenders do not differ in their performance on traditional short-term memory tasks, such as digit span and word span (see Oakhill, Yuill, & Parkin, 1986), and do not differ in their ability to recall short texts verbatim, we have consistently found that they do differ on tasks that require concurrent storage and processing of information in a temporary memory—so-called working memory tasks. Because Daneman and Carpenter's sentence span task requires subjects to read and understand sentences—a task at which the skilled comprehenders might be at an advantage—Nicola Yuill and I developed an analogous task using digits, rather than words. The children were presented with lists of numbers to read aloud (the processing requirement) and had to remember the final digit in each group (storage requirement). The memory load was varied by increasing the number of sets of digits (and, therefore, the number of final digits to be recalled): 2, 3, or 4. So, for example, in a two-digit case, the child might read the sets 7–4–2 and 1–3–9 and then have to recall 2 and 9. Although there was no difference between the groups in the easiest version (two-digit recall), there were differences in the harder, three- and four-digit, versions of the task. We have replicated this finding several times, with both 7- to 8-year-olds and 9- to 10-year-olds. In some recent work (Yuill, Oakhill, Garnham, & O'Donovan, in preparation) we have shown that, although verbal tests of working memory predict reading comprehension better than do numerical ones, both verbal and numerical tasks are predictors of comprehension skill, though not of reading ability more generally (i.e. single word reading accuracy).

So it is tempting to conclude, from the results of the studies on working memory, that skilled comprehenders are better at making inferences, monitoring their understanding, interpreting anaphors, and deriving the structure of stories *because* they have more efficient working memories. The idea of an underlying working memory deficit fits neatly with the results of the studies of anomaly detection and comprehension monitoring, described earlier, where we showed that it was *only* when the crucial pieces of information were non-adjacent in the text that the less-skilled comprehenders had difficulties.

This pattern of results—that the poor comprehenders are able to integrate information and detect inconsistencies at short distances, but not over longer distances—indicates that they are able to connect up information in text to some extent. The findings are consistent with the hypothesis that poor comprehenders are able to build adequate representations of parts of a text, but fail to relate and integrate these partial models to produce a coherent model of the text as a whole. Such a hypothesis would explain why they are able to appreciate anomalies and inconsistencies when the information on which this appreciation depends is not close together in the text. It can also explain why they have difficulty in making inferences that depend on the integration of information from different parts of a text, and perhaps the combination of that information with relevant background knowledge as well. We suggest that the poor comprehenders' more limited working memories are sufficient to support some local integration of text, but that they cannot support the integration of the text as a whole.

Furthermore, this interpretation could also explain poor comprehenders' problems in text production. It was evident from the lower scores of the less-skilled comprehenders in the story production experiment that they were able to produce locally coherent stories, but not ones that have a globally coherent causal structure. Once again, limited working memory provides a plausible explanation: the capacity of the poor comprehenders may be sufficient to allow them to keep track of their production over two or three sentences, so that their productions cohere in that each sentence follows on from the last, but not sufficient to permit them to plan and keep track of their overall production so that the text is coherent overall.

CONCLUSIONS

The picture that emerges of poor comprehenders from the studies we have presented here is of children who are able to integrate information locally in a text, but who are not able to produce a coherent mental model of the text as a whole. Such problems are apparent in both their understanding and their production of stories—they do not seem to be able to plan a globally coherent story, but can produce locally coherent text. We have suggested that many of the poor comprehenders' problems in text comprehension might be explained in terms of the efficiency of their working memory processes. There are two major problems with this analysis, however. First, as yet, we have no data that address the issue of the direction of the link. It may be the case, as Tunmer (1989) has suggested, that practice at reading with understanding increases working memory capacity, rather than the reverse.

Second, even if working memory were found to be causally linked to comprehension skill, it is unlikely to be a complete explanation of individual differences in skill. We have found that even brief periods of training to raise children's awareness of the need to make inferences, and to go beyond the literal information in a text, were successful in improving the poor group's performance on a standardised comprehension test, at least in the short term (for a review, see Oakhill & Yuill, 1991). It is highly unlikely that an incidental outcome of such training was that it also improved the children's working memory *capacity*. However, the two sets of findings—that the poor comprehenders have deficient working memories and that their comprehension can be improved by short periods of training—are not entirely incompatible. It may be that the training we gave the children provided them with strategies that helped them to circumvent their memory problems, rather than enabling them to process text as good comprehenders do. Perhaps the training strategies enabled them to link up the ideas in the texts and, thus, to utilise their available working memory resources more *efficiently*.

We are currently exploring the role of working memory in children's text comprehension in a longitudinal study, in which we will explore both how well early working memory ability predicts later comprehension in general and specific comprehension sub-skills (such as the ability to make inferences) and, conversely, how well early comprehension ability predicts later working memory skills. This investigation will enable us to disentangle causal issues in the development of comprehension skill, and assess whether working memory is fundamental to the development of the ability to build coherent text models.

ACKNOWLEDGEMENTS

I should particularly like to thank my DPhil supervisor, Phil Johnson-Laird, for his support and encouragement at the beginning of my research career. Many of the experiments reported here have resulted from collaborations with Nicola Yuill and

Kate Cain, whose contribution is gratefully acknowledged. Some of this work was supported by a Social Science Research Council postgraduate award, and subsequently by an Economic and Social Research Council project grant (COO 232053). I am also grateful to Alan Garnham and Ted Ruffman for comments on earlier drafts of this chapter.

REFERENCES

Ackerman, B.P. (1984). The effects of storage and processing complexity on comprehension repair in children and adults. *Journal of Experimental Child Psychology, 37*, 303–334.

Applebee, A.N. (1978). *The child's concept of story: Ages two to seventeen.* Chicago: University of Chicago Press.

Bishop, D. (1983). *Test for reception of grammar.* Department of Psychology, University of Manchester.

Cain, K. (1994). *An investigation into comprehension difficulties in young children.* Unpublished D. Phil. Thesis: University of Sussex, UK.

Cain, K., & Oakhill, J.V. (in press a). Comprehension skill and inference making ability: Issues of causality. In C. Hulme & R.M. Joshi (Eds.), *Reading and spelling: Development and disorder.*

Cain, K., & Oakhill, J.V. (in press b) The nature of the relationship between comprehension skill and the ability to tell a story. *British Journal of Developmental Psychology.*

Charniak, E. (1972). *Toward a model of children's story comprehension.* Technical Report A1-TR-266. Boston, MA: MIT Press.

Cromer, W. (1970). The difference model: A new explanation for some reading difficulties. *Journal of Educational Psychology, 61*, 471–483.

Daneman, M. (1987). Reading and working memory. In J.R. Beech & A.M. Colley (Eds.), *Cognitive approaches to reading.* Chichester, UK: Wiley.

Daneman, M., & Carpenter, P. (1980). Individual differences in working memory and reading. *Journal of Verbal Learning and Verbal Behavior, 19*, 450–466.

Daneman, M., & Carpenter, P.A. (1983). Individual differences in integrating information between and within sentences. *Journal of Experimental Psychology: Learning Memory and Cognition, 9*, 561–584.

Fleischer, L.S, Jenkins, J.R., & Pany, D. (1979). Effects on poor readers' comprehension of training in rapid decoding. *Reading Research Quarterly, 15*, 30–48.

Garnham, A. (1992). Minimalism versus constructionism: A false dichotomy in theories of inference during reading. *PSYCOLOQUY, 3*(63), reading-inference–1.1.

Johnson-Laird, P.N. (1983). *Mental models.* Cambridge: Cambridge University Press.

Markman, E. (1977). Realizing that you don't understand: A preliminary investigation. *Child Development, 48*, 986–992.

McKoon, G., & Ratcliff, R. (1992). Inference during reading. *Psychological Review, 99*, 440–466

Oakan, R., Wiener, M., & Cromer, W. (1971). Identification, organization and reading comprehension in good and poor readers. *Journal of Educational Psychology, 62*, 71–78.

Oakhill, J.V. (1981). *Children's reading comprehension.* Unpublished D.Phil. Thesis: University of Sussex, UK.

Oakhill, J.V. (1982). Constructive processes in skilled and less-skilled comprehenders. *British Journal of Psychology, 73*, 13–20.

Oakhill, J.V. (1984). Inferential and memory skills in children's comprehension of stories. *British Journal of Educational Psychology, 54*, 31–9.

Oakhill, J.V., Hartt, J., & Samols, D. (1995). *Comprehension monitoring and working memory in good and poor comprehenders.* Paper presented at the Experimental Psychology Society meeting, Cambridge, April 1995.

Oakhill, J.V., & Yuill, N.M. (1986). Pronoun resolution in skilled and less-skilled comprehenders: Effects of memory load and inferential complexity. *Language and Speech*, *29*, 25–37.

Oakhill, J.V., & Yuill, N.M. (1991). The remediation of reading comprehension difficulties. In M.J. Snowling & M. Thomson (Eds.), *Dyslexia: Integrating theory and practice*. London: Whurr Publishers Ltd.

Oakhill, J.V., Yuill, N.M., & Parkin, A.J. (1986). On the nature of the difference between skilled and less-skilled comprehenders. *Journal of Research in Reading*, *9*, 80–91.

Perfetti, C.A. (1985). *Reading ability*. Oxford: Oxford University Press.

Perfetti, C.A. (1988). Verbal efficiency in reading ability. In M. Daneman, G. MacKinnon, & T.G. Waller (Eds.), *Reading research: Advances in theory and practice*. San Diego, CA: Academic Press.

Perfetti, C.A., & Goldman, S.R. (1976). Discourse memory and reading comprehension skill. *Journal of Verbal Learning and Verbal Behavior*, *15*, 33–42.

Perfetti, C.A., & Hogaboam, T. (1975). Relationship between single word decoding and reading comprehension skill. *Journal of Educational Psychology*, *67*, 461–469.

Peterson, C., & McCabe, A. (1983). *Developmental psycholinguistics: Three ways of looking at a child's narrative*. New York: Plenum Press.

Shankweiler, D. (1989). How problems of comprehension are related to difficulties in decoding. In D. Shankweiler & I.Y. Liberman (Eds.), *Phonology and reading disability: Solving the reading puzzle*. Ann Arbor: University of Michigan Press.

Stein, N.L., & Glenn, C.G. (1979). An analysis of story comprehension in elementary school children. In R.O. Freedle (Ed.), *New directions in discourse processing*, vol 2, (pp. 53–120). Norwood, NJ: Ablex.

Stein, N.L., & Glenn, C.G. (1982). Children's concept of time: The development of a story schema. In W.J. Friedman (Ed.), *The developmenal psychology of time*. New York: Academic Press.

Steiner, R., Wiener, M., & Cromer, W. (1971). Comprehension training and identification for good and poor readers. *Journal of Educational Psychology*, *62*, 506–513.

Stothard, S., & Hulme, C. (1992). Reading comprehension difficulties in children: The role of language comprehension and working memory skills. *Reading and Writing*, *4*, 245–256.

Tunmer, W. (1989). The role of language-related factors in reading disability. In D. Shankweiler & I.Y. Liberman (Eds.), *Phonology and reading disability: Solving the reading puzzle*. Ann Arbor: University of Michigan Press.

Yuill, N., & Oakhill, J. (1988). Understanding of anaphoric relations in skilled and less skilled comprehenders. *British Journal of Psychology*, *79*, 173–186.

Yuill, N.M., & Oakhill, J.V. (1991). *Children's problems in text comprehension: An experimental investigation*. Cambridge: Cambridge University Press.

Yuill, N.M., Oakhill, J.V., Garnham, A., & O'Donovan, D. (in preparation). The relation between working memory abilities and children's reading.

Yuill, N.M., Oakhill, J.V., & Parkin, A.J. (1989). Working memory, comprehension ability and the resolution of text anomaly. *British Journal of Psychology*, *80*, 351–61.

6 Mental Models in Reasoning and Decision-making Processes

Paolo Legrenzi and Vittorio Girotto
CREPCO, Université de Provence, France

The purpose of this chapter is to show the importance of some recent developments of mental model theory (henceforth MMT) for the study of decision-making processes. MMT was originally developed by Phil Johnson-Laird (see Johnson-Laird, 1983) and later by Johnson-Laird and Byrne (1991) mainly to account for deductive inferences. However, in contrast with other theories of reasoning, MMT can be extended in such a way as to explain various domains of human thinking, including judgement and choice.

Our analysis will concentrate on two main phenomena that are present in both reasoning and decision-making processes and that are predicted by MMT. The first class of phenomena involves the tendency to focus on the initial representation of a situation, the second one concerns the difficulties in reasoning and making a choice under uncertainty.

After a brief outline of MMT, we will discuss the nature of focusing effects in information-seeking before deciding. These effects and related de-focusing procedures will be discussed in relation to the evidence provided by Legrenzi, Girotto, and Johnson-Laird (1993). In addition, the so-called pseudo-diagnosticity bias elicited with various tasks requiring information-seeking will be interpreted as a specific case of focusing. New evidence of this bias has been provided by Mynatt, Doherty, and Dragan (1993). We will show how it is possible to eliminate it, by reporting some new experimental results that corroborate the predictions derived from MMT.

MMT predicts other effects than those of focusing on decision-making. In particular, the disjunction effects in decision-making discovered by Tversky and Shafir (1992) can be interpreted as cases of erroneous preference patterns due to the difficulty of holding in mind disjunctive alternatives and of assessing their consequences. This interpretation will also be applied to the erroneous performance elicited by a hypothetico-deductive task. In both cases, successful results have been obtained by some de-biasing procedures which help people to separate and to hold in mind a disjunction of alternatives. This set of findings is clearly in line with the predictions of MMT.

Finally, an illusory inference recently discovered by Johnson-Laird and Savary (in press) will be interpreted as new evidence of the presence of disjunction effects in deductive reasoning. We will also report the results obtained by Girotto (1995) who has shown that it is possible to de-bias people on this illusion as predicted by MMT.

THE MODEL THEORY OF DEDUCTION

According to MMT (Johnson-Laird, 1983; Johnson-Laird & Byrne, 1991), people reason by building some initial models of the content of the premises or, more generally, models of a situation. On the basis of the initial set of models, reasoners draw a putative conclusion and evaluate it by searching for alternative models that might falsify it.

In order to illustrate how MMT explains deduction, we will use some examples of propositional reasoning. Given the following conditional statement concerning a hand of cards:

If there is a King, then there is an Ace,

people will probably build a mental representation (model) containing the contingencies indicated:

King   Ace

A conditional assertion refers to only one possibility, i.e. that there is a King. If reasoners are not concerned with the alternative possibilities in which the King does not occur, they represent them in an implicit model that has no initial content and thus reduce the load on working memory. By convention, the implicit model is indicated by three dots:

King   Ace
. . .

If reasoners do worry about the hands in which the King does not occur, they can indicate that the King element is exhaustively represented in the explicit model. In other words, they represent the information that there are no alternative models in which the King is present. By convention, a type of item that is exhaustively represented is indicated by square brackets:

[King]   Ace
    ...

Reasoners can represent the information about the hands in which the King is not present in another way; that is, they can add a mental footnote to the implicit model (Johnson-Laird, 1995a). The explicit model represents the hands containing the King, and so the footnote (symbolised by parentheses) represents the hands in which the King is not present:

King   Ace
{-King} ...

where "-" signifies negation.

Suppose that reasoners who have built this representation of the conditional statement, are given the following categorical assertion:

There is a King.

It is likely that virtually all of them will draw the following conclusion:

There is an Ace.

This assertion corresponds to the valid conclusion that can be drawn by using the modus ponens inferential schema (If p then q, p, therefore q). However, according to MMT, in order to draw it, people do not need to apply this schema, neither do they need to flesh out the implicit model of the conditional premises. All they have to do is to ignore the implicit alternatives and to eliminate from the explicit model the redundant contingency

There is a King.

So far, we have considered a simple deduction. Suppose instead that along with the conditional premise

If there is a King, then there is an Ace,

reasoners were given the following categorical assertion:

There is not an Ace.

In this case, it is likely that some reasoners will draw the conclusion:

Nothing follows.

According to MMT, individuals who have to reason from the given premises are likely to base their conclusion on the explicit model of the conditional assertion. Given that this model represents a hand in which there is an Ace, nothing seems to follow about the hands in which the Ace is not present. However, this conclusion is not correct. In order to draw the valid conclusion, reasoners should flesh out the implicit models of the conditional. That is, they should consider all the possible cases, including the alternative possibilities which do not contain the King:

```
King     Ace
-King    Ace
-King    -Ace
```

With such wholly explicit models, reasoners should not have difficulty in drawing the valid conclusion

There is not a King,

by eliminating the models in which the Ace occurs. In other words, according to MMT, reasoners have difficulties in drawing such a valid conclusion (which corresponds to modus tollens: If p then q, not-q, therefore not-p) because they are *focused* on the initial models of the conditional and concomitantly fail to consider other models[1]. Individuals who cease focusing, by making explicit the alternative models, can draw the valid conclusion (see Girotto, Mazzocco, & Tasso, in press).

We can summarise the MMT of deduction on the basis of two main predictions: (1) Deductions that require one explicit model only (e.g. modus ponens) are easier to draw than deductions that require multiple models (e.g. modus tollens). More generally, the difficulty of a deduction is a function of the number of disjunctive models that have to be constructed

---

[1] There is an interesting convergence between the concept of focusing with other notions which similarly explain reasoning and/or decision-making performances on the basis of a selective representation of the problem information, in particular the notions of "relevance" (cf. Evans, 1995; Sperber, Cara, & Girotto, 1995) and "focalisation" (Klar, 1990; see also empirical data provided by Love & Kessler, 1995).

(we will see later the difficulties of solving "double disjunctive" problems). (2) Erroneous deductions are due to people's tendency to focus on one of the possible models of the premises. Johnson-Laird and Byrne (1991) have tested these predictions in various domains of deduction, including propositional, quantified, and relational reasoning. The evidence they have found appears to support MMT and run counter to alternative views of deductive reasoning.

In the remaining part of this chapter, we will show how these predictions can be applied to decision-making processes. First, we will describe the presence of focusing effects in tasks requiring information-seeking before choosing among alternatives. These effects will be interpreted as a result of an initial representation of only one model, i.e. in the same way as MMT explains erroneous deductive inferences. Second, we will discuss how erroneous inferential and choice patterns can be elicited in problems in which people have to build models of a disjunction of alternatives and to assess their consequences. For both focusing and disjunctive effects we will also report results that show how it is possible to de-bias people.

FOCUSING AND DE-FOCUSING IN INFORMATION SELECTION

Individuals who make a choice have to use various reasoning abilities. For example, they make inferences about the hypothetical outcomes of the options that they have to consider. Hence, phenomena that occur in reasoning should also occur in decision-making. For this reason, the successful account of reasoning provided by MMT could be used to understand the mental processes underlying choice. In collaboration with Johnson-Laird, we have tried to make such an application of MMT to the study of decision-making, by extending the notion of focusing (Legrenzi et al., 1993). In particular, we have investigated how individuals seek information in order to make a decision or a judgement under uncertainty.

Participants in our experiment were asked to make some simple decisions, such as whether to go to the cinema. Before making the decision, they could request any information that they needed, and the experimenter provided it. The instructions read as follows:

> You have to decide whether or not to go to see a certain film. I will give you any information you want until you can make the decision.

The result was that participants asked on average three questions focusing on the given action (e.g. "going to the cinema") and never asked questions about the possible alternatives to it. Despite the absolute lack of information about the alternatives, they made a mean of 2.25 positive decisions (e.g. "I will go to see the film"), out of five trials.

According to rational choice theory (see Lindley, 1971), as well as our intuition, in order to make a rational decision it is necessary to take into consideration alternative courses of action. Obviously, if one knows nothing about the alternatives to a particular course of action, one can neither assess their utility nor compare it with that of the action. This intuition seems obvious, perhaps trivial. It is incorporated into any model of decision-making, particularly economic decision-making. However, the pattern of information-seeking and decision-making elicited in our experiment represents a clear violation of this principle.

As indicated, MMT predicted and explained this effect as a form of focusing[2]. The choice between, say, going to the cinema or not going to the cinema is represented by two models. The first model is explicit and exhaustive, and so the other model, which corresponds to not going to the cinema, can be left implicit:

$$[c]$$
$$\ldots$$

where "c" denotes a model of going to the cinema and the three dots denote the implicit model. This mental representation explains why the task for the decision-maker appears to be limited to searching for information about "c". However, as indicated, MMT predicts both the presence of focusing effects in decision-making and the possibility of reducing them. In order to de-focus people one has to devise a scenario that activates the representation of other courses of action, i.e. a scenario that will force the decision-makers to flesh out the implicit model. In a second condition of our experiment, the instructions read as follows:

> Imagine that you are visiting Rome for the first time, but only for one day; and imagine that I have lived in Rome for a long time and have an excellent knowledge of the tourist attractions of the town. Your task is to decide whether or not to go to see a certain film. I will give you any information you want until you can make the decision.

As in the previous (uncontextualised) condition, we found that the majority of questions were related to the action (in this example, to see a certain film). However, all but one of the participants presented with this kind of scenario asked at least one question about the alternatives to the action (vs. none of the participants in the previous condition). In other words, our results demonstrate that there are some contexts that make the alternatives

---

[2] Friedman and Neumann (1980) have also shown that people tend to neglect alternative options and their costs when they are unstated, i.e. people violate a cornerstone of micro-economics: the "opportunity cost principle".

available for fleshing out the implicit model . In sum, on the basis of MMT, it has been possible to predict a new phenomenon in the domain of decision-making, and to relate it to a more general tendency exhibited by reasoners: focusing on what is explicitly represented in their models and neglecting other possibilities.

The interpretation of focusing effects offered by MMT can be extended to other phenomena about information-seeking reported in the literature. In particular, the so-called "pseudo-diagnosticity bias" can be considered as a case of focusing. Consider the following problem:

> Your sister has a car she bought a couple of years ago. It's either a car X or a car Y, but you can't remember which. You do remember that her car does over 25 miles per gallon and has not had any major mechanical probems in the two years she's owned it.
>
> You have the following piece of information:
>
> 1. 65% of car Xs do over 25 miles per gallon.
>
> Three additional pieces of information are also available:
>
> 2. The percentage of car Ys that do over 25 miles per gallon.
> 3. The percentage of car Xs that have had no major mechanical problems for the first two years of ownership.
> 4. The percentage of car Ys that have had no major mechanical problems for the first two years of ownership.
>
> Assuming you could find out only *one* of these three pieces of information (2, 3, or 4), which would you want in order to help you decide what car your sister owns?

When people are presented with this scenario and forced to ask for just one piece of information beyond the information given, their reasoning might be expected to be something like:

> I know the petrol consumption of car Xs. I could ask for the reliability of car Xs. Afterwards, I could check the corresponding data of car Ys, so that I could compare the two types of car. But I can ask for only one piece of information. In this case, I will ask for the consumption of car Ys. At least, I could compare car Xs and car Ys along this dimension.

Contrary to this ideal and rational line of reasoning, the majority of individuals presented with this problem by Mynatt et al. (1993) selected the piece of information about the mechanical reliability of Xs. In other words, they preferred additional information about Xs over information about the alternative Ys, even if they knew that they were allowed to gather just one more item of information.

This effect corresponds to a difficulty in computing the likelihood ratio of two hypotheses: $P(D_1/H_1)/P(D_1/H_2)$. (In our example, D_1 corresponds to the datum about petrol consumption, H_1 corresponds to the hypothesis that your sister's car is X and H_2 corresponds to the hypothesis that your sister's car is Y.) This effect was discovered and labelled "pseudo-diagnosticity" by Doherty, Mynatt, Tweney, and Schiavo (1979; see also Beyth-Marom & Fischhoff, 1983). In a more recent work, Mynatt et al. (1993, p.760) have related this effect to "one of the most fundamental limitations of human cognition. That limitation is the number of things that we can think about at a given time—more specifically, the number of alternatives that can be operated upon in working memory at a given time. We posit that that number is *one*, and we argue further that from this limitation there flow interesting, and relatively unexamined, consequences". From this general assumption, Mynatt and colleagues have derived an interesting difference between two types of problems. They defined "inference problems" as scenarios such as the previous one, in which people have to select data in order to make an inference (e.g. indicate which car your sister owns), whereas they called "action problems" the scenarios in which people have to select information in order to carry out an action (e.g. to buy a car). Consider the following case:

You're thinking of buying a car. You've narrowed it down to either car X or car Y. Two of the things you are concerned about are petrol consumption and mechanical reliability.

You have the following piece of information:

1. 65% of car Xs do over 25 miles per gallon.

Three additional pieces of information are also available:

2. The percentage of car Xs that have had no major mechanical problems for the first two years of ownership.
3. The percentage of car Ys that do over 25 miles per gallon.
4. The percentage of car Ys that have had no major mechanical problems for the first two years of ownership.

Assuming you could find out only *one* of these three pieces of information (2, 3, or 4), which would you want in order to help you decide which car to buy?

Presented with this scenario, the majority of people selected the piece of information about the petrol consumption of car Ys, while only a minority of them selected the item corresponding to the mechanical reliability of car Xs. In general, with action problems 51% of the participants selected the piece of information that makes it possible to compare the two alternatives (e.g. compare the petrol consumption of car Xs and car Ys; see Table 6.1).

TABLE 6.1
Percentage of Data Selection

	Focus on One Object		Focus on Two Dimensions	
Study/Problem	Inference	Action	Inference	Action
Mynatt et al.	28	–	–	51
Our study	20	20	55	65

Percentage of data selection relevant to both characteristics as a function of the focus (one object vs. two dimensions) and type (inference vs. action) of problem, in Mynatt et al.'s (1993) and our studies.

According to Mynatt et al., action problems do not require a comparison of two alternative hypotheses. That is, in contrast to inference problems, action problems do not require a comparison in working memory between different hypotheses, so that people are less likely to reason in a pseudo-diagnostic manner. Moreover, they claim that the explanation they have provided for pseudo-diagnosticity and "hypothesis testing more broadly, is indirectly related to Johnson-Laird's (1983) theorizing about other reasoning problems in that we also focus on limitations on working memory as the key *explanans*" (Mynatt et al., 1993, p.775).

We accept this connection with MMT as well as the proposed account of pseudo-diagnosticity in terms of an attentional bias. However, as we have indicated in our study of focusing, "we would go further: the underlying mechanism is once again a consequence of models that represent only certain information in an explicit way" (Legrenzi et al., 1993, p.52). From this viewpoint, the failure to select information about both alternatives in the inference problems depends on the initial model of the situation in which a given datum (e.g. about petrol consumption) and a given hypothesis (e.g. the car is X) co-occur. The subsequent search for information is guided by this model, so that the cases in which the datum is present but the hypothesis is absent (e.g. the car is Y) are not considered. How can we explain, then, the reported differences in performance elicited by inference vs. action problems? In other words, is it possibile to find a general explanation for these findings, based on MMT, rather than to attribute them to an intrinsic difference between the two kinds of problems? Among the "major determinant[s] of what is explicit in mental models" we have listed "the verbal description of a problem" (Legrenzi et al. 1993, p. 59). Hence, if we are right, it should be possible to find the source of the reported differences between problems in the way in which they are verbally framed.

A similar interpretation has been recently advanced by Evans and Over (1996) who have analysed the texts of the problems used by Mynatt et al., on the basis of their relevance theory. As they have noted, the preamble of the inference problem gives specific information about the sister's car ("You do remember that her car does over 25 miles per gallon and has not had any major mechanical problems in the two years she's owned it"). So that readers tend "to form a concrete mental model of the car in question". Consequently, they are likely to ask for information only about X cars. By contrast, in the action version, the preamble gives pragmatic relevance to the two dimensions (petrol consumption and reliability: "Two of the things you are concerned about are petrol consumption and mechanical reliability"). Thus, when information 1 (about petrol consumption of cars Xs) is given, it is likely that readers focus attention on it. Therefore, they will ask for information about this dimension for both kinds of car.

This relevance-based interpretation of the pseudo-diagnosticity findings is compatible with the MMT interpretation of focusing phenomena. As stated by Evans and Over, performance depends on factors that "induce selective attention or focusing on certain aspects of the available information". If this interpretation is correct, then it should be possible to frame an inference problem so as to de-focus individuals from the explicit model of the sister's car. Moreover, it should be possible to frame an action problem so as to force individuals to make explicit only one model.

These predictions have been empirically tested in a series of experiments that we have conducted in collaboration with Jonathan Evans (Girotto, Evans, & Legrenzi, 1996). In one of these experiments, participants have to solve an inference problem in which the scenario, instructions, and task are identical to those used by Mynatt et al. (1993), except that the preamble reads as follows:

> Your sister has a car she bought a couple of years ago. It's either a car X or a car Y, but you can't remember which. However, you do remember that the two things she was most concerned about were petrol consumption and mechanical reliability.

In another condition, participants have to solve an action problem in which the preamble was:

> You're thinking of buying a car. You've narrowed it down to either car X or car Y. You have not taken your decision, but you want your car to do over 25 miles per gallon and not to have any major mechanical probems in the first two years.

In other words, compared to Mynatt et al.'s study, we exchanged the preambles of inference and action versions, so as to reduce focusing in the former and to increase it in the latter. Two control conditions which replicated those used by Mynatt et al. (inference problem with focus on one object vs. action problem with focus on two dimensions) completed the design.

The results corroborated our predictions (see Table 1). Although in the control conditions performance was similar to that elicited in the original study (20% of data selection relevant to both alternatives in the inference version vs. 65% in the action one), in the other conditions the pattern of results was reversed. The majority of participants (55%) selected the datum concerning the second hypothesis in the inference problem, whereas only 20% of them made the same selection in the action problem.

In sum, these and other experimental results that we have obtained demonstrate that an inference content is not sufficient to determine biased data selections in hypothesis testing problems. In addition, they show that action problems can elicit pseudo-diagnostic choices. In both cases, the crucial factor for determining people's selections seems to be the wording of the text problem, which can focus or de-focus individuals on a specific representation of the situation. More generally, these findings corroborate MMT, by showing how focusing and pseudo-diagnosticity phenomena can be viewed as cases of a more general tendency which has been previously discovered in the study of deductive reasoning.

DISJUNCTIVE EFFECTS IN CHOICE AND REASONING UNDER UNCERTAINTY

In this section, we consider another prediction about decision making processes which stems from MMT. In the reasoning literature, it has been shown that the difficulty of deductive inferences is a function of the number of disjunctive models they require in order to reach a conclusion (see Johnson-Laird & Byrne, 1991). Similarly, one should expect that people will exhibit more difficulties when they have to make decisions requiring the representation of multiple options.

Let us consider first an example from reasoning literature. Johnson-Laird, Byrne, and Schaeken (1992) have demonstrated that there is a breakdown in deductive performance as the number of models to be constructed increases. They have used problems based on double disjunctions, such as:

Raphael is in Tacoma or Julia is in Atlanta, or both.
Julia is in Atlanta or Paul is in Philadelphia, or both.
What, if anything, follows from these premises?

These two disjunctive premises support five possible states of affairs corresponding to five alternative models:

```
T    A    P
T    A
T         P
     A    P
     A
```

where T denotes Raphael in Tacoma, A denotes Julia in Atlanta, and P denotes Paul in Philadelphia.
According to MMT, the construction of all these models exceeds the capacity of working memory, so that very few individuals are able to draw a valid conclusion, such as:
Raphael is in Tacoma and Paul is in Philadelphia, or Julia is in Atlanta, or both.
Indeed, Johnson-Laird and colleagues found that only 21% of reasoners were able to make a valid deduction from the indicated premises.
However, as predicted by MMT, it is possible to improve performance in these tasks, provided that the alternative possibilities are made more explicit. Bauer and Johnson-Laird (1993) were able to show that people are both faster and able to draw more valid conclusions in double disjunctive problems, by using spatial analogues in the form of diagrams. These visual analogues, bypassing the representation of the meaning of verbal premises, appear to reduce the load on working memory and to speed up the process of inference. In sum, MMT can both explain the well known difficulties of solving problems involving disjunctive possibilities and provide some antidote to de-bias reasoners.
As indicated, MMT also predicts cognitive difficulties in decisions involving disjunctive models. In this case, situations in which the decision-makers are in front of a fork with just two branches, each representing a different state of the world, can elicit non-normative choices. "Indeed, like deduction, there can be a breakdown in rationality as soon as there are two explicit alternatives to choose from" (Legrenzi et al., 1993, p.64). Consider a minimal disjunction in which either the state of the world X or the complementary state not-X can occur. Imagine that for both possible branches, individuals are asked to choose between option A and option B. Suppose that in both cases they prefer option A to B. Now, what would be their preference when they do not know whether X or not-X occurs? One of the fundamental principles of the rational choice theory predicts that, once again, they would prefer option A to B, for, if they choose option A for both possible branches of the fork, they should choose it also when they are ignorant of which event occurs. This normative prediction, which has a strong intuitive appeal, is based on the "sure-thing principle" defined by Savage (1954).

If considered from the viewpoint of MMT, a decision between two alternatives requires individuals to build two explicit models and to assess both of them. Consequently, as in deductive reasoning tasks, they will exhibit difficulties in some choice tasks of this kind. Indeed, as predicted by MMT but contrary to the normative account, individuals who prefer option A for both states of the world (X vs. not-X) change their mind under uncertainty, that is they appear to violate the "sure-thing principle". The best illustration of this preference pattern has been provided by Tversky and Shafir (1992). Participants had to imagine they had just played a game of chance that gave them equal chances of winning $200 or of losing $100. On the supposition that the coin was tossed and they won $200, they had to decide whether or not to play the same gamble a second time. The majority of them (69%) accepted the second gamble. A week later a different version of the problem was presented, one in which they had to suppose that they had lost the first gamble. Once again, the majority of them (59%) accepted the second gamble. Finally, ten days later, a further version was presented in which the outcome of the first gamble was unknown. In this case the majority of them (64%) rejected the second gamble. In other words, a substantial proportion of the respondents exhibited a pattern of preferences that clearly violate Savage's sure-thing principle, because having accepted the second gamble both after having won and lost the first, they should have accepted the second gamble even when the outcome of the first was unknown (see Fig. 6.1). This pattern of preferences was called the *disjunction effect* by Tversky and Shafir, who also found examples of it in problems requiring inter-individual decisions, such as a one-shot prisoner's dilemma game. Contrary to the sure-thing principle, many players defected when they knew their opponent's choice, be it cooperation or defection, but cooperated when their opponent's choice was unknown (Shafir & Tversky, 1992; see also Morris, Sim, & Girotto, 1995).

According to Tversky and Shafir, disjunction effects depend on a loss of acuity induced by uncertainty. Thinking through a disjunctive condition requires decision makers to "assume momentarily as true something that may in fact be false". Of course, if the structure of the task is made salient, people will exhibit more normative preference patterns. For example, Tversky and Shafir presented the double-gamble task without temporal intervals, so that participants had to solve the three versions one after the other ("you know that you won … you know that you lost … you ignore the result of the first gamble"). In this condition, disjunction patterns diminished significantly. The majority of individuals who chose the same option for each possible outcome of the first gamble also chose that option under uncertainty.

These findings and the explanation provided by Tversky and Shafir are clearly consistent with an MMT account of people's difficulties in dealing

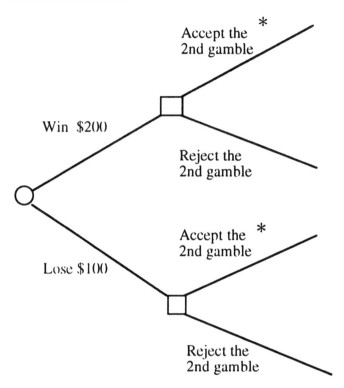

Fig. 6.1.   A tree diagram from the double-gamble problem (Adapted from Tversky & Shafir, 1992) (Note: the circle denotes the change node; the squares denote the decision nodes; * denotes the preferred option under each possible state).

with disjunctive models. Moreover, the improvement of double-gamble performance elicited in the sequential presentation condition is similar to the results obtained by Bauer and Johnson-Laird (1993) with the diagrammatic presentation of the double disjunction problems. In both cases, a better representation of the alternative models produced an increase in normative answers.

One might argue that the double-disjunction problems used in the reasoning literature are computationally too difficult (see Bonatti, 1994), so that it is not appropriate to compare them with the single-disjunction choice problems used by Tversky and Shafir. However, as noted by Johnson-Laird, Byrne, and Schaeken (1994), the diagram studies show that people can solve such inferential problems. More importantly, there are at least two sets of results concerning hypothetico-deductive reasoning that fit very well with the disjunction effects obtained in simple contexts involving a single disjunction[3]. In all these cases, a disjunction of alternatives is sufficient to elicit non-normative performance, as predicted by MMT.

Let us start with a reasoning problem devised by Wason (1978). In front of you there are four designs: a black diamond, a white circle, a black circle, and a white diamond, as in Fig. 6.2. You are told that the experimenter has written down one of the colours (black or white) and one of the shapes (a circle or a diamond). Then the experimenter gives you an exclusive disjunctive rule relating an arbitrary name (THOG) to the designs: "If, and only if, one of the designs includes either the colour I have written down or the shape I have written down, but not both, then it is called a THOG." Knowing for sure that the black diamond is a THOG, you have to say whether each of the three remaining designs is a THOG. Before answering this question, you have to indicate only *one* of the two possible combinations of features written down by the experimenter, by writing down a particular shape and a particular colour.

Suppose that you have indicated the combination "black and circle". What is the anwer to the first question? The solution does not seem to be too difficult (see Fig. 6.3): The black circle is not a THOG given that it contains both properties; the white diamond is not a THOG given that it contains neither of the properties; only the white circle is a THOG given that it contains just one of the indicated properties (the shape). Of course, if you had proposed the other combination (i.e. "white and diamond"), the same solution would have followed: the white diamond could not be a THOG because it contains both properties; the black circle could not because it contains neither of the properties; and the white circle is a THOG because it contains just one of the indicated properties (the colour). Wason and Brooks (1979), who have used this version of the THOG problem, found that most participants had no difficulty in individuating one combination of features and solving the subsequent request to find the other THOG.

Suppose that you had *not* been requested to write down one of the colours and one of the shapes, what would your answer have been to the THOG problem? Despite the fact that the correct solution is the same as for

FIG. 6.2.   Designs used in the THOG problem.

---

[3] It should be noted that an early demonstration of disjunction effects in deductive reasoning can be found in a study conducted by Johnson-Laird and Wason (1970). However, they did use complex disjunctive statements (see also Oakhill & Johnson-Laird, 1985).

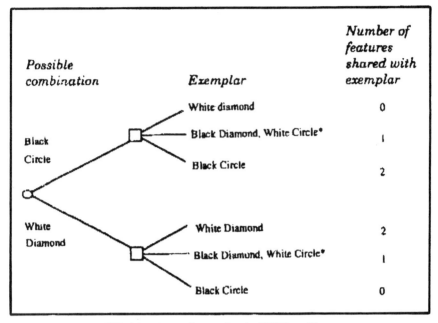

FIG. 6.3.   A tree diagram for the THOG problem.

the previous version (the white circle is the second THOG design), it is likely that your answer would be different from the previous one. Indeed, several experimental results show that individuals requested to find *one* combination of properties do solve the THOG problem presented subsequently, but they fail to solve it when presented without the former request (Girotto & Legrenzi, 1989/Experiment 1; Wason & Brooks, 1979/Experiment 1). In other words, reasoners who are able to identify *one* particular hypothetical combination ("the experimenter has written down: colour X and shape Y") and to assess its consequences ("the other THOG design is the white circle"), are not able to assess the consequences of *two* hypothetical combinations ("the experimenter has written down: colour X and shape Y *or* colour Y and shape X"). In this case, the typical erroneous solution is the mirror image of the correct one: "the white circle is not a THOG, the other two designs are THOGs or it is impossible to decide whether or not they are THOGs". As we have suggested (Girotto & Legrenzi, 1993; see also Newstead, Girotto, & Legrenzi, 1995), this pattern of responses corresponds to the disjunction effects found in decision making. A visual inspection of Figs. 6.1 and 6.3 will reveal the structural equivalence of choice problems such as the double gamble task and reasoning problems such as THOG. In both cases, individuals appear to be unable to find the normative solution when they have to hold in mind the two branches of the tree and to assess their consequences, despite the fact that they are able to test each hypothetical branch. Wason and Brooks (1979, p.88) envisaged a similar interpretation, by stressing how individuals who are able to assess a *particular* hypothesis are not able to assess the consequences of *real* hypotheses when "it is not known which one corresponds to reality. It may be peculiarly difficult to reason about hypothetical possibilities to reach determinate conclusions".

Given the hypothesised equivalence between the two problems, one might wonder whether it is possible to de-bias people on the THOG problem as has been done on the double-gamble one. The answer is that the difficulties in both kinds of task are due to a similar necessity of considering a disjunction of alternatives, but the solution of the THOG problem requires an additional effort. Reasoners have to distinguish properties of the data (the actual designs) and those of the hypothetical combinations. Indeed, strategies of de-biasing similar to those that have proved successful for the double-gamble task (i.e. strategies that make the logic of the task salient) are not effective for the THOG problem when presented without additional help to avoid the confusion of data and hypotheses. For example, the explicit request to generate *both* combinations of properties does not improve performance in the standard THOG problem (Wason & Brooks, 1979/Experiment 2). By contrast, versions of the problem that make clear the structure of the problem as well as reducing the load required by the separation of data and hypotheses, do facilitate performance. This has been proved both with realistic versions in which reasoners were explicitly requested to find the hypothetical combinations but could not confuse them with the properties of the data (Girotto & Legrenzi, 1989; Newstead & Griggs, 1992), and with a standard version in which the request to find the hypotheses corresponded to a search of exemplars whose label differed from the label of the THOG items (Girotto & Legrenzi, 1993).

In sum, a set of results about hypothetico-deductive reasoning appear to corroborate MMT. They have shown that the necessity of holding multiple models in working memory can hinder the assessment of a disjunction of hypotheses. In what follows, we will present some new experimental results about disjunctive reasoning which have been predicted on the basis of MMT.

Johnson-Laird & Savary (in press) have recently discovered a new phenomenon in deductive reasoning which is a further illustration of the difficulty of holding multiple models in mind. The interest of this phenomenon is twofold. First, it has been predicted by a computer program implementing the MMT. Second, it is a real illusion: virtually everyone draws a conclusion that seems obvious, but is opposite to the correct one. Consider the following instructions:

Only one of the following assertions is true about a specific hand of cards:

If there is a King in the hand, then there is a Seven
If there is a Queen in the hand, then there is a Seven

What can you deduce about the hand of cards?

The answer seems straightforward: "In the hand there is a Seven". The point is that the presence of a Seven in the hand is logically impossible, for if the first assertion is true, then the second is false, hence in the hand there is a Queen and there is not a Seven. Alternatively, if the second assertion is true, then the first is false, hence in the hand there is a King and there is not a Seven. Therefore, in neither case, can a Seven occur in the hand.

This and other inferential problems devised by Johnson-Laird and colleagues[4] have elicited a very robust result: the great majority of individuals (including some distinguished psychologists) draw illusory inferences such as the one indicated. We will briefly see how MMT predicts them.

Consider the two premises of the reported problem. The initial models of the first premise are as follows:

[King]   Seven
. . .

and the initial models of the second premise are as follows:

[Queen]   Seven
. . .

The assertion that only one of the two premises is true requires the representation of an exclusive disjunction of them. When two propositions, P and Q, are related by an exclusive disjunction, they are represented as follows:

P
Q

Therefore, the initial models of the two premises are:

[King]   Seven
          [Queen]   Seven
. . .

---

[4] In addition to the study outlined, Johnson-Laird and his colleagues have conducted several experiments which have revealed the existence of the illusion in a set of problems containing different connectives, as well as in problems requiring probabilistic judgements (see Johnson-Laird, 1995b).

From this representation, it is tempting to derive the conclusion that there is a Seven in the hand, for in both explicit models built so far a Seven is present. However, given that only one conditional is true, reasoners have to consider the false contingencies. When the first conditional is false, then there is a King but not a Seven:

King   -Seven

When the second conditional is false, then there is a Queen but not a Seven:

Queen   -Seven

Either way, there is not a Seven:

King   -Seven
Queen   -Seven

But reasoners do not draw this conclusion, their answer is "there is a Seven". In other words, as in other deductive problems, reasoners tend to draw the conclusion that is supported by the initial set of models, and in special cases such as this one, they draw conclusions that seem obvious but are totally wrong.

Girotto (1995) has proposed an interpretation of these illusions that is based on MMT, but which considers them as strictly related to the disjunction effects and the aforementioned difficulties in dealing with uncertainty. The two premises of the illusory problems are related by an exclusive disjunction of the kind previously analysed: reasoners have to derive a conclusion by evaluating each premise separately (i.e. representing its counterexample) but ignoring which one is true. That is, they have to do what is required by the problems that elicit the disjunction pattern of choice: "assume momentarily as true something that may in fact be false".

If this analysis is correct, then it should be possible to find an antidote to the illusory inferences, by using some of the strategies that have proved successful in the research on disjunction effects. Indeed, Girotto (1995) has demonstrated that it is possible to de-bias people. In a first attempt, as had been done with the double-gamble choice, the logic of the task was made clear. Participants had to indicate the possible counterexample for each premise, and subsequently they were requested to derive a conclusion. The two premises were presented as two statements of two different characters who were describing a pair of cards (a court-card and a number-card) chosen from a deck. Paolo's statement was:

In this pair, if there is a King, then there is a Seven

Maria's statement was:

In this pair, if there is a Queen, then there is a Seven

Participants have to suppose that each of them, in turn, was wrong, and to indicate their actual cards ("Suppose you know that ... is wrong. What would be the actual cards?"). Finally, ignoring who was really wrong, they have to draw a conclusion about the number-card ("You don't know who is really telling the truth. However, what could you deduce about the number-card?").

This attempt was not successful. That is, the clarification of the logic of the task was not sufficient to eliminate the illusion. Although the request to construct the counterexample for each assertion was correctly complied with by most of the participants (88%), the majority of them (76%) failed to draw the valid conclusion. The most typical pattern of response was similar to the disjunction choice pattern and, in particular, to the erroneous performance elicited in the THOG problem. That is, people who found the correct solution for each branch of the disjunction (i.e. the statement of each character) were not able to see that in both cases the hand contained the same card (i.e. the number-card was the same whoever was wrong), so that the conclusion should have been the same even when they ignored what branch was actually occurring (i.e. who was really telling the truth).

As we discussed previously, a successful procedure for facilitating THOG performance required both a clarification of the structure of the problem (the elicitation of the hypothetical combinations of features) and a simplification of the evaluation of the consequences, by a reduction of load on working memory (for example by labelling data and hypotheses differently). On this basis, Girotto devised a successful procedure for reducing the illusory inferences. In a second experiment, participants were given a two-character version of the problem in which the initial set contained only four cards: two court-cards (a King and a Queen) and two-number-cards (a Seven and a Two). From this set, two cards (a court-card and a number-card) were chosen. Consequently, the representation of the counterexample for each character's statement was much easier. In both cases ("If there is the King, then there is the Seven" vs. "If there is the Queen, then there is the Seven") the negation of the number-card mentioned in the assertions (Seven) is necessarily the Two, so that for each assertion there is only one counterexample: King and Two, Queen and Two, respectively. Therefore, whatever court-card is actually present in the pair, the number-card will be Two. Indeed, 65% of participants turned out to be able to draw this deduction (vs. 5% in the control condition). In other words, a combination of clarification of the problem and reduction of working memory load has reduced the illusion[5].

In sum, a new and promising line of investigation has so far contributed to the corroboration of MMT, by showing: (1) the existence of previously unknown illusions in the domain of deduction; and (2) the possibility of finding an antidote to them, based on an MMT interpretation of the phenomena.

CONCLUSIONS

In this chapter we have examined some developments of MMT. On the basis of the MMT account of deductive reasoning (Johnson-Laird & Byrne, 1991), we have seen how it has been possible to investigate other areas of human thinking, in particular the processes underlying judgement and decision making. Well-known and new phenomena in these domains of research appear to corroborate the two principal predictions of MMT of reasoning. On the one hand, people's tendency to focus on only one model of the content of the premises has been found in information-seeking before deciding (Legrenzi et al., 1993). A non-normative consideration of only one branch of the decision tree (i.e. the branch corresponding to the mentioned option), is the picture that has emerged from the studies under review, including the research on pseudo-diagnosticity (Mynatt et al., 1993). Factors related to the verbal description of the problem and to the contextual availability of knowledge seem to determine what is explicit in the focused representation of a problem (Girotto et al., 1996). Experimental manipulations of these factors have reduced focusing phenomena (Legrenzi et al., 1993). On the other hand, people exhibit poor deductive performance when they have to draw a conclusion from premises requiring the representation of disjunctive models (Johnson-Laird et al., 1992). Similarly, they make decisions that violate some fundamental principles of the normative theory of rational choice when they have to consider a disjunction of alternatives (Shafir & Tversky, 1992; Tversky & Shafir, 1992). However, as with the focusing phenomena, MMT predicts that it is possible to de-bias people, provided that they can form a clearer representation of the problem—that is they can separate and hold in mind the disjunction of models, both in deduction (Bauer & Johnson-Laird, 1993; Girotto & Legrenzi, 1993) and in decision-making (Tversky & Shafir, 1992). Finally, on the basis of MMT it has been possible both to predict that reasoning about disjunctive models produces illusory inferences (Johnson-

---

[5] For similar demonstrations of the combined effect of a clearer structure of the problem and a easier representation of the counterexamples in eliciting correct performance in otherwise difficult reasoning problems, see Green (1995) and Sperber et al. (1995).

Laird & Savary, in press), and to devise a procedure for reducing such non-normative answers (Girotto, 1995). In conclusion, we hope to have contributed to demonstrating the importance of MMT for the construction of a unified explanation of reasoning and decision-making processes, in line with some recent developments in the two domains of research (Johnson-Laird and Shafir have edited a special issue of Cognition with various contributions on the relationships between reasoning and choice; see Johnson-Laird & Shafir, 1993). Controversies with the proponents of rival theories are still open. However, the success of MMT in increasing our understanding of human reasoning seems undoubted. The developments we have illustrated indicate how the theory can evolve towards a general explanation of thinking (see Johnson-Laird, 1993). Whether or not these developments will succeed is a question we cannot answer. In any case, they clearly demonstrate the productivity of the theory proposed by Phil Johnson-Laird.

Finally a personal note. Paolo Legrenzi belongs to a generation in which psychology of reasoning essentially did not exist in Italy. When Paolo met Phil in a summer conference at Brixen in 1969, his expertise was minimal in the psychology of reasoning and non-existent in English. So he learned both from Phil, or, to be more precise, he learned about reasoning from Phil whereas Phil learned a new language, Italiano-English, thanks to Paolo. After Paolo's stay in England in the 1970s, a steady flow of Italian students went to learn about the psychology of reasoning in Phil's laboratory, where they benefited both from his intellectual insight and from his human generosity. The chapters of this book written by Italian scholars are the fruit of such contact. Vittorio Girotto belongs to the third generation of the same tradition, and he has worked with Phil since Phil moved to Princeton. In the last 20 years, Phil's writings have been translated into Italian, and he has become quite well known in Italy, both inside the psychology community and outside. For all these reasons, we wish to express our gratitude to Phil Johnson-Laird.

ACKNOWLEDGEMENTS

Preparation of this chapter has been supported by a grant from CNR. We wish to thank Simonetta Fabrizio, Alan Garnham, and Jane Oakhill for their comments on a first version of the chapter.

REFERENCES

Bauer, M.I., & Johnson-Laird, P.N. (1993). How diagrams can improve reasoning. *Psychological Science, 4,* 372–378.

Beyth-Marom, R.B., & Fischhoff, B. (1983). Diagnosticity and pseudodiagnosticity. *Journal of Personality and Social Psychology, 45,* 1185–1195.

Bonatti, L. (1994). Propositional reasoning by models? *Psychological Review, 101,* 725–733.

Doherty, M.E., Mynatt, C.R., Tweney, R.D., & Schiavo, M.D. (1979). Pseudodiagnosticity. *Acta Psychologica, 43,* 111–121.

Evans, J.St.B.T. (1995). Relevance and reasoning. In S.E. Newstead & J.St.B.T. Evans (Eds.), *Perspectives on thinking and reasoning.* Hove, UK: Lawrence Erlbaum Associates Ltd.

Evans, J. St.B.T., & Over, D. (1996). *Rationality and reasoning.* Hove, UK: Lawrence Erlbaum Associates Ltd.

Friedman, L.A., & Neumann, B.R. (1980). The effects of opportunity costs on project investment decisions: A replication and extention. *Journal of Accounting Research, 18,* 407–419.

Girotto, V. (1995). *Reasoning about what is impossible.* Paper presented at the workshop on Reasoning and Decision Making, University of Sienna, Italy, July.

Girotto, V., Evans, J.St.B.T., & Legrenzi, P. (1996). *Relevance of information and consideration of alternatives. Pseudo-diagnosticity as a focusing phenomenon.* Paper presented at the 3rd International Conference on Thinking, University College London, August.

Girotto, V., & Legrenzi, P. (1989). Mental representation and hypothetico-deductive problem: The case of the THOG problem. *Psychological Research, 51,* 129–135.

Girotto, V., & Legrenzi, P. (1993). Naming the parents of the THOG: Mental representation and reasoning. *Quarterly Journal of Experimental Psychology, 46A,* 701–713.

Girotto, V., Mazzocco, A., & Tasso, A. (in press). *The effect of premise order in conditional reasoning: A test of the mental model theory.* Manuscript submitted for publication.

Green, D.W. (1995). Externalization, counter-examples, and the abstract selection task. *Quarterly Journal of Experimental Psychology, 48A,* 424–446.

Johnson-Laird, P.N. (1983). *Mental models.* Cambridge: Cambridge University Press.

Johnson-Laird, P.N. (1993). *Human and machine thinking.* Hillsdale, NJ: Lawrence Erlbaum Associates Inc.

Johnson-Laird, P.N. (1995a). Inference and mental models. In S.E. Newstead & J.St.B.T. Evans (Eds.), *Perspectives on thinking and reasoning.* Hove, UK: Lawrence Erlbaum Associates Ltd.

Johnson-Laird, P.N. (1995b). *Reasoning about what is possible, probable and necessary.* Paper presented at the workshop on Reasoning and Decision Making. University of Sienna, Italy, July.

Johnson-Laird, P.N., & Byrne, R.M.J. (1991). *Deduction.* Hillsdale, NJ: Lawrence Erlbaum Associates Inc.

Johnson-Laird, P.N., Byrne, R.M.J., & Schaeken, W. (1992). Propositional reasoning by models. *Psychological Review, 99,* 418–439.

Johnson-Laird, P.N., Byrne, R.M.J., & Schaeken, W. (1994). Why models rather than rules give a better account of propositional reasoning: A reply to Bonatti and to O'Brien, Braine, and Yang. *Psychological Review, 101,* 734–739.

Johnson-Laird, P.N., & Savary, F. (in press). Illusory inferences about probabilities. *Acta Psychologica.*

Johnson-Laird, P.N., & Shafir, E. (1993). The integration between reasoning and decision-making: An introduction, *Cognition, 39,* 1–9.

Johnson-Laird, P.N., & Wason, P.C. (1970). Insight into a logical relation. *Quarterly Journal of Experimental Psychology, 22,* 49–61.

Klar, Y. (1990). Logical, statistical, and causal reasoning: Compartmentalized or generic process? In W. Stroebe & M. Hewstone (Eds.), *European Review of Social Psychology, Volume 2.* London: Wiley.

Legrenzi, P., Girotto, V., & Johnson-Laird, P.N. (1993). Focusing in reasoning and decision-making. *Cognition, 49,* 37–66.

Lindley, D.V. (1971). *Making decisions.* London: Wiley.

Love, R.B., & Kessler, C.M. (1995). Focusing in Wason's selection task: Content and instruction effects. *Thinking and Reasoning, 1*, 153–182.

Morris, M., Sim, D., & Girotto, V. (1995). Time of decision, ethical obligation and causal illusion: Temporal cues and social heuristics in the prisoner's dilemma. In R.M. Kramer & D.M. Messick (Eds.), *Negotiation as a social process*. Newbury Park, CA: Sage.

Mynatt, C.R., Doherty, M.E., & Dragan, W. (1993). Information relevance, working memory and the consideration of alternatives. *Quarterly Journal of Experimental Psychology, 46A*, 759–778.

Newstead, S.E., Girotto, V., & Legrenzi, P. (1995). The THOG problem and its implication for human reasoning. In S.E. Newstead & J.St.B.T. Evans (Eds.), *Perspectives on thinking and reasoning*. Hove, UK: Lawrence Erlbaum Associates Ltd.

Newstead, S.E., & Griggs, R.A. (1992). Thinking about THOG: Sources of error in a deductive reasoning task. *Psychological Research, 54*, 299–305.

Oakhill, J., & Johnson-Laird, P.N. (1985). Rationality, memory and the search for counter-examples, *Cognition, 39*, 85–105.

Savage, L.J. (1954). *The foundations of statistics*. New York: Wiley.

Shafir, E., & Tversky, A. (1992). Thinking through uncertainty: Nonconsequential reasoning and choice. *Cognitive Psychology, 24*, 449–474.

Sperber, D., Cara, F., & Girotto, V. (1995). Relevance theory explains the selection task. *Cognition, 52*, 3–39.

Tversky, A., & Shafir, E. (1992). The disjunction effect in choice under uncertainty. *Psychological Science, 3*, 305–309.

Wason, P.C. (1978). *Hypothesis testing and reasoning. [Unit 25, Block 4, Cognitive Psychology.]* Milton Keynes, UK: Open University.

Wason, P.C., & Brooks, P.G. (1979). THOG: The anatomy of a problem. *Psychological Research, 41*, 79–90.

7

Models, Arguments, and Decisions

David W. Green
Centre for Cognitive Science, University College London

One function of mind is to create models of reality so as to allow effective action and decision-making (Craik, 1943). A mental model symbolises a situation or entity in the world by letting mental tokens, their properties and relations correspond to actual entities and their properties and relations (e.g. Johnson-Laird, 1983, 1993). Such models may be constructed from perceptual information or from verbal descriptions.

The theory of mental models has been applied successfully to the various domains of deduction such as relational inference (including spatial descriptions) and syllogisms (e.g. Johnson-Laird & Byrne, 1991; Johnson-Laird, Byrne, & Schaeken, 1992). Essentially, the more models needed for a deduction the more difficult individuals find it. More recently it has been applied to induction (Johnson-Laird, 1994). Here addition of information to a model covers a variety of operations of linguistic generalisation. In this paper I propose a type of mental model in which the tokens are arguments for decisions or actions. I also discuss some research bearing on the proposal.

The paper opens with a rationale for the proposal based on the fact that human beings must be able to argue in order to fulfil their roles as social agents. It then discusses the nature of informal argument and describes Toulmin's data argumentation scheme. This scheme distinguishes the data relevant to a claim from the warrant for the claim which states why a person feels the claim follows from the data. After briefly considering some research on argument, an adapted version of Toulmin's scheme is related to the theory of mental models. This section also discusses the connection between argument models and causal models. A processing scheme is proposed in which constructing arguments is distinguished from resolving arguments. In addition, a higher-level process is identified which constrains the operation of these two processes. Next, a decision problem is described which requires individuals to decide on the level of fine a restaurant should pay given an incident of food-poisoning. As expected, fines depend on warrants and on how alternatives are resolved. Such results are consistent with the claim of model theory that decisions depend on what is explicitly represented. A final section discusses the nature of the control processes involved in constructing and resolving arguments.

THE COGNITION OF SOCIAL AGENTS

The ability to model the social world is important to us. We need to understand how our close relations, friends, and peers think and feel and might respond. Byrne and Whiten (1988) supposed that pressures to understand and to predict the behaviour of others in the social group was critical to the evolution of the human mind. Similarly, Humphrey (1984) supposed that intelligence evolved to allow social agents to take advantage of living in a community (see also Cosmides, Tooby, & Barkow, 1992; Dunbar, 1993). One well-researched ability is the ability to recognise the beliefs of others. As research on autism attests, this is important to negotiating and participating fully in the social world (e.g. Baron-Cohen, Leslie, & Frith, 1985). We are embedded in social settings and the biological bases of our cognitive and affective worlds reflect this (Brothers, 1990).

Another critical ability is the ability to argue. Groups reach decisions by arguing the merits of different courses of action in terms of what is plausible, probable, and desirable. Different positions may be voiced by different people. In order to participate in such discussions individuals need to be able to represent the various arguments, keep track of them, and be able to contribute to them. Further, when advocating a particular course of action, individuals may take account of the likely objections that others may propose. Mental models need to represent social situations and the way in which actions are achieved through talk (Green, 1994a). But because we are born into a social group we learn its practices (Vygotsky, 1960). How we think may then be usefully viewed as a process of internal argumentation (Billig, 1987). Thinking as internal argument provides a natural way in which to link the individual to the social context.

INFORMAL ARGUMENT AND TOULMIN'S ARGUMENT SCHEME

An informal argument may be deductively valid. Consider the following exchange:

A: I'll need a coat if it's going to snow
B: You'll need a coat

In this exchange the minor premise, "It's going to snow", is understood. But a critical feature of informal arguments in everyday talk is that they are geared to reaching a conclusion (claim or decision) which is more or less probable given some piece of data. The move from data or premise to claim is no longer determined by whether it follows logically. Consider an example:

Jack has normal blood cholesterol
Therefore, other things being equal he is unlikely to die of a heart attack

Here, the claim or conclusion follows to the extent that normal blood cholesterol is consistent with a healthy heart. But this claim is hedged—other things may not be equal for various reasons.

Toulmin proposed that individuals establish certain claims (e.g. Jack is a British citizen) on the basis of certain *data* (Jack was born in Bermuda) and a *warrant*—a man born in Bermuda may be taken to be a British citizen though this claim may be qualified (presumably). However, this claim may be *rebutted* if both parents were aliens or Jack has become a naturalised American. If a person attacks the warrant then its backing can be put in: this will record the dates of enactment of the Acts of Parliament and other legal provisions governing the nationality of persons born in British colonies (Toulmin, 1958, p.104). In fact, a backing is just another argument which can be used to certify or legitimate. In Toulmin's scheme, data refer to what the arguer has to go on: these may be factual claims (scientific findings) or claims from other arguments. Warrants can be of a number of different types. They might refer to rules or to principles or causal mechanisms (see below). Various pieces of data and types of warrants may *support* a particular claim rather than render it logically necessary.

In the heart disease example, the datum is that Jack has normal blood cholesterol and the warrant is that normal cholesterol is consistent with a healthy heart. The claim that Jack is not at risk can be challenged. For instance, the data that Jack has normal cholesterol might be disputed. Alternatively, the warrant could be challenged. An argument to support the warrant might then refer to various pieces of medical evidence or to some causal mechanism. But the claim can be challenged in another way. It ignores other relevant pieces of information. It may turn out that Jack smokes, takes little exercise, and has high blood pressure. These data are consistent with an alternative claim that Jack may get heart disease. This argument would *rebut* the earlier claim.

Consider, a further example. Baron (1995) captures one line of argument in the abortion debate in the following way:

Pro-abortion warrant: Americans have the right to make their own decisions

As Baron notes, this warrant is relatively weak and can be attacked: if abortion is murder, as the anti-abortion group contends, then the government is no more denying rights than it is when it declares that murder is illegal. Americans should not have the right to make decisions that cause harm to others.

Consider next an anti-abortion warrant:

Anti-abortion warrant: The fetus has rights

This counter-argument rebuts by proposing rights for the unborn rather than denying the warrant that women have rights. It too might be considered weak because it assumes that a fetus is a person.

Warrants can be of different types. The range is captured by one typology proposed by Mason and Mitroff (1981, see also Huff, 1991). They distinguished substantive, authoritative, and motivational warrants. *Substantive warrants* appeal to a listener's sense of reason. These include warrants where a conclusion follows deductively. But this type of warrant also includes instances where a claim is made because a datum is a sign of some symptom or because it evokes a parallel or analogous case. *Authoritative warrants* warrant a claim because the source of the claim is trustworthy, reliable, and believable. So the claim itself is likely to be true. *Motivational warrants* warrant some claim according to a value system which might include how an individual feels about some decision or claim.

PRIOR RESEARCH ON ARGUMENT

The concept of argument using Toulmin's scheme as a point of departure has been used to analyse strategic decisions in business (e.g. Mason & Mitroff, 1981; see also Weick & Browning, 1986) and policy formulation (see Voss, Tyler, & Yengo, 1983). Antaki (1988, 1994) has used the scheme to look at the kinds of arguments individuals use in everyday talk. Such research shows that individuals do not always mention relevant data and establishes that the kinds of things individuals say depends on what effects they are trying to achieve (see also Edwards & Potter, 1993). A particular kind of argument will be developed with a view to countering particular objections.

Kuhn (1991) has carried out extensive work looking at the extent to which individuals can expound, criticise, and defend their views on important social issues. This ability is often quite limited and is affected by educational attainment. On social and political issues, individuals tend to construct arguments in favour of just one side ("myside bias", Perkins, 1989), although they may know of arguments on the other side. Baron (1995) found that most individuals rate texts with arguments on only one side of an issue more highly than those presenting arguments on both sides of an issue. But a critical factor according to Baron is the extent to which individuals consider that open-mindedness is a virtue. This affects how many other-side arguments they give. Such research does not of course imply that individuals only consider one kind of argument when they make decisions.

Toulmin's scheme has also been applied to the protocols of individuals estimating probabilities (Curley, Browne, Smith, & Benson, 1995). So, for example, when asked to estimate the probability that the price of a share will rise or fall, a person might warrant their probability assessment on the basis of earnings per share. The price of a share and earnings per share tend to covary so that anticipating a change in earnings per share warrants anticipating a change in share price. The concept of argument has also been fruitfully recruited in the AI literature on risk and probability (see, for example, Fox, 1994).

Of present relevance is the work of Shafir, Simonson, and Tversky (1993). They proposed that individuals would defer taking a decision if they lacked a definite reason for doing so. In one study individuals read a scenario in which they were presented with an opportunity to buy a very attractive holiday package to Hawaii at an exceptionally low price. One group was told that they had just passed an exam, another group was told that they had just failed the exam (which could be retaken in two months) and a third group (the don't know group) was told that their results would not be known until the day after tomorrow. Individuals could decide to buy, not to buy, or to pay a small amount of money to defer the choice for two days (after the exam results would be known for those in the don't know group) and still be able to buy the package at the same price.

They obtained the following results: of the subjects in the pass group and the fail group, half chose to buy the vacation package. In contrast, two-thirds deferred the decision in the don't know group. Shafir et al. explained their results in the following way: once the outcome of the exam is known the student has a good reason for buying the package. If the exam was passed, the holiday is a reward: if the exam was failed, the holiday is a consolation and a time for recuperation. Not knowing the outcome, the students lacked a definite reason. On the supposition that a person would tend to buy the package either way, it seems that a disjunction of different reasons (for the don't know group) is less compelling than either of the definite reasons alone. This account is consistent with the claim that arguments are vital to decisions, but perhaps individuals who defer do have a specific reason in mind. The account can be checked by requiring individuals to provide reasons.

I adapted the material to the UK context and required individuals (applicants for places in the Psychology Department, University College London) to give a reason for their decision. Just over half the applicants in the pass and fail groups decided to buy the package (52%; 31/60) and, as expected on the basis of Shafir et al.'s results, significantly more subjects deferred in the don't know group. Just over half deferred in this group (52%; 17/33) compared to 32% (19/60) in the other two groups. My concern was the warrants they gave for their decisions. Table 7.1 summarises the main warrants for each decision.

As expected those who were informed that they had passed the exam bought the package as a reward and/or to recuperate; those informed that they had failed bought the package as a consolation and/or to recuperate. Those who purchased in the don't know group (46%; 15/33) did so because they would have gone on holiday whether they passed the exam or failed it, and so there was no warrant for paying to defer. Having more than one reason for a decision was no impediment for them.

For other subjects, however, a purchase decision is not to be made hastily. The defer option buys time for these people so that they can

TABLE 7.1
Grounds for Decisions in the Holiday Scenario

Decision	Data	Grounds Warrant
Buy	Low price attractive package (stated)	Reward or consolation/ recuperation
Not buy	Ditto	Costs money/ prefer to stay at home/ get on with revision
Defer	Ditto	Make sure it's what I want/ consider alternatives/ await outcome not go if fail/ decide when I know—can't tell how I will feel

really think things through and thereby avoid the feeling of regret if they decide not to go. All subjects (19/19) who deferred in the pass group and in the fail group gave this type of warrant. Only a few subjects (18%; 3/17) deferred for this reason in the don't know group. Some 35% (6/17) stated that they would not go if they failed, just as some subjects in the fail group decided not to go. A further 35% stated that they would decide when they knew the outcome because they did not know how they would feel. A further 12% (2/17) stated that they would go either way but wanted to know the results before leaving (they assumed that the holiday had to be taken immediately).

These results indicate that decisions, even the decision to defer, are based on specific reasons. The warrants for a decision reflect not simply the decision context but the person's belief about the benefits of a holiday and their personal circumstances. Individuals seek grounds (data and warrants) that make sense to them.

In the literature, reasons have sometimes been taken to be "rationalisations" for decisions taken on some other basis. For instance, in the four card selection task (Wason, 1968) it has been supposed that selections are based on preconscious judgements of relevance (Evans, 1989; Evans & Wason, 1976; Wason & Evans, 1975) and the reasons individuals provide for their decisions are the result of a subsequent analytic process that rationalises the decision. This proposal predicts that reasons are simply consistent with decisions.

However, the same decision can be warranted in various ways and this fact provides a way to test the proposal. For instance, suppose the conditional claim was "If there is an A on one side of the card then there is a 4 on the other side of the card" and individuals are presented with four cards with the symbols A, K, 4, and 7 on their facing sides. In order to determine whether the claim is true or false a person might select a card for a number of different reasons. For example, a card could be selected to see what was on the other side, or because the letter or number on the card was mentioned in the claim or because turning the card might help to prove the claim true or false. Green (1994b) found that the latter logically apposite reason figured much more frequently when individuals selected the correct cards (the true antecedent, A and the false consequent, 7) than when individuals selected incorrectly (A and 4). Yet such a difference is inexplicable on the rationalisation proposal: informational and relevance reasons should have figured to the same extent for both correct and incorrect selections, as they may also be consistent with the choices made. Green (1995) proposed instead that selections reflect an internal process of argumentation: a process of considering alternative warrants and resolving them. Selections and reasons arise from the same cognitive basis.

TOULMIN'S SCHEME AND MENTAL MODELS

Toulmin's scheme has been applied to texts and to discourses. The present proposal is that attending to such material individuals may establish a mental argument-model in which a mental token comprises a possible claim, decision, or action, relevant data and a warrant. Tokens are conceptual-intentional objects and are interlinked in various ways. For instance, an argument may support or rebut another argument. The structure of the argument-model represents the structure of the debate or discussion. Conversely, when individuals are faced with a decision they may construct an argument-model. Where do warrants come from?

In some cases warrants derive from prior knowledge or belief. For instance, in selecting between two foods a person might recall that they had an allergic reaction to one of them. In other cases a warrant must be actively constructed. For instance, faced (again) with a choice between two foods a person might consider the levels of fat they contain or the likely delay before the food is ready to eat. In some cases they might imagine themselves eating the food. Think of eating soup on a rocky boat trip. They might construct a model of the situation in order to determine a warrant: easy to eat or not easy to eat (see also Kahneman & Tversky, 1982).

Beach (1992) provides another instance. He imagines a weather forecaster. The forecaster might use conditional probability data in order to determine the probability of rain. Alternatively, the forecaster might use satellite photographs and a kind of "mental projection" of how the weather fronts might move and affect a particular area. The outcome of the mental simulation of the weather model warrants the forecast. Such simulations also warrant claims in other areas. In the history of science, thought experiments pinpoint the need for conceptual change (see, for instance, Nersessian, 1991). The need for change is warranted by the mental simulation.

The relationship between argument-models and other kinds of mental model is not just one-way. Consider cases where the decision context is more complex. Arguments can be used to construct links or connections in a causal model. For instance, individuals may use arguments to construct a cognitive model of the factors that affect the risk of coronary heart disease (Green & McManus, 1995) or to represent how different factors affect an individual's prospects of employment (Green, McManus, & Derrick, in preparation). So, by way of example, what warrant is there that "increased effort" affects a person's prospects of employment? One subject gave the warrant for a direct link between this factor and a person's prospects of employment as "looking and spending more time increases opportunities". Another gave a warrant for an indirect link via education: "will help secure better grades and enhance employment prospects". If a warrant is available then a causal connection can be mentally constructed. Having constructed a mental causal model, decisions can be based on it. We have shown for both the heart disease example and the employment example that the nature of an individual's model affects their decisions about the effectiveness of different actions designed to reduce the risks of coronary heart disease in the first case and increase a person's prospects of employment in the second case.

Pennington and Hastie (1993) have developed a similar approach in the context of juror decision-making. They supposed that individuals used a variety of inference forms to construct a story accounting for the evidence. Jurors who construct different stories chose different verdicts. Both approaches concur that the nature of the arguments used and the type of causal model constructed depend on the person's knowledge of the domain (see, for example, Axelrod, 1976, for a diplomat's political model of forces in the Middle East, and Bostrom, Fischhoff, & Morgan, 1992 for an expert's model of the effects of radon on health).

PROCESSING SCHEME FOR ARGUMENT

The present proposal is that in order to reach a decision about a novel but relatively simple problem, individuals engage in an internal process of argumentation and build an argument-model. We can distinguish between the process of constructing the argument-model and the process of resolving the argument-model. This contrast is an instance of a general distinction between model-forming and model-using proposed by Gilhooly (1987). For instance, in the selection task, the process of constructing the argument-model involves identifying possible warrants for selecting or for not selecting each card. The decision is an outcome of resolving these warrants. Green (1995) proposed a process of weighing the warrants for and against selecting each card. The ones selected are those with the highest weights.

In addition to these processes of construction and resolution, we must envisage a further process (a meta-process) that constrains the activity of these two. For instance, in accordance with the task, different construction and resolution processes may be required. In addition, as noted earlier, the extent to which individuals deliberate may be a function of the issue they are considering or their level of education.

WARRANTS AND DECISIONS: MODEL THEORY PREDICTIONS

The notion of a mental token is general and so we can use existing properties of model theory to derive predictions about argument-models. A fundamental property of model theory is that individuals minimise what is explicitly represented mentally. Decisions may then be based on what is initially represented. However, precisely what decision is reached will depend on the extent to which alternatives have been considered and on the extent to which the relationship between these alternatives has been made explicit. Evidence that individuals consider alternative possibilities may be more forthcoming in circumstances where a decision can be expressed on a scale. The presence of an alternative may bias the decision. This section describes some of our current research using a decision problem that allows subjects to express a decision as a scale value (Green, McClelland, & Muckli, in preparation; Green, Muckli, & McClelland, 1995). This problem is useful too because it exemplifies an important property of informal argument. In everyday life, practical reasoning often concerns what we should do (see Over & Manktelow, 1993).

We adapted a scenario from Macrae (1992). Individuals are told about Lucy who normally eats in a particular restaurant. On the Saturday in question she follows her habit, but gets food-poisoning and is ill in hospital for four days. Individuals are asked to decide the amount of fine the restaurant should pay by circling one figure on a 9-point scale which ranges from £0 to £4000 in steps of £500.

Macrae surmised that individuals make their judgements by imagining how they would feel about it. He assumed that this outcome would affect their ratings of sympathy for Lucy. In fact he did show that their ratings of sympathy for Lucy predicted their fines. In the present context, we can see the sympathy rating as expressing an affective warrant for the decision—an instance of a motivational warrant in the earlier typology. However, in this situation cognitive warrants might be even more important. One could feel sympathy for Lucy without thinking the restaurant was at fault. Conversely, one might feel the restaurant was at fault and yet feel little sympathy for the unfortunate Lucy. Unlike Macrae we also asked our sample about the reasons for their decision on the amount of the fine. In our studies, where individuals are free to provide a cognitive warrant, we have found that sympathy is a relatively weak predictor, and so I will not consider it further here although the relationship between cognitive and affective warrants is well worth further study.

The basic idea underlying these experiments is that individuals reach a decision by considering one or more arguments, i.e. by considering the data and warrants relevant to possible decisions. They construct an argument-model. The nature of this argument-model affects the amount of fine selected. Where there is more than one argument token in the model then individuals must weight or endorse one of the tokens in order to resolve the model—in other words a further act of model construction is needed. We concentrate here on warrants because the data are provided. Now although a single figure for the fine must be selected, any other active warrant will bias the decision unless the process of resolution involves the explicit rebuttal of the argument of which it is part. For purposes of visualising the argument-model, imagine that rebuttal involves an inhibitory connection between one token and another and that this blocks or reduces the biasing effect of that token on the decision.

Empirical Studies

In all the studies we anticipated that the warrant selected or generated would be critical to the decision, as the data part of the argument within any one condition was constant. Our subjects were applicants for places in the Psychology Department, UCL who were fully debriefed as to the purpose of the studies.

Our first study sought to establish that cognitive warrants were indeed predictive of the amount of the fine. Table 7.2 details the type of warrants and the relation to the amount of the fine. The warrants were independently coded by two judges with a high level of inter-judge agreement. In what follows we relate fines to warrants but it should be borne in mind that warrants are part of an argument and that the theoretical entity is an argument token.

Overall, the mean level of fine increased across the three warrants. It averaged £532 for those generating the one-off accident warrant, £1728 for those wishing to encourage the restaurant, and £2806 for those generating the duty of care warrant.

It would be expected that the frequency with which individuals generate a particular warrant would depend on the circumstances of the food-poisoning. Clearly if it was Lucy's normal restaurant she would not keep going back if she got food-poisoning each time! Individuals might then be more willing to treat the event as a one-off accident. In contrast, if they read that on the Saturday in question Lucy decided to eat elsewhere and got food-poisoning they might be less likely to make this inference.

In order to examine this expectation, the first study in fact compared the performance of subjects presented with the routine scenario with those

TABLE 7.2
Grounds for Decisions in the Food-poisoning Scenario

		Grounds
Level of fine	Data	Warrant
Low	Lucy ill for four days	One-off accident
Moderate	Ditto	Not regular, encourage to improve standards
High	Ditto	Duty of care (Lucy could have died)—should be punished to deter others

presented with the exception scenario in which Lucy ate in a restaurant that was new to her. Overall, we expected that individuals might fine the restaurant less in the routine condition because they might be more likely to see the food-poisoning as a one-off accident. We confirmed Macrae's earlier finding that fines were higher in the exception condition and showed that this derives in part from a much greater tendency for subjects in the routine condition to generate the one-off accident warrant. Of the 37 subjects, 13 (35%) in that condition generated this warrant whereas 3 of the 43 subjects (7%) in the exception condition did so. This study confirms that warrants are an important predictor of fine ratings. It also shows that the context of judgement affects the frequency with which individuals generate different kinds of warrants.

Given that individuals generate rather a small number of different warrants for their decisions what is the consequence of giving subjects a warrant? In our next study each subject, in either the routine or the exception condition, was presented with all three warrants: it was a *one-off accident*; *encourage* the restaurant to be more careful; the restaurant broke the law—it has a *duty of care* and should be punished to discourage others. They were free to tick one of these if it fitted their view or to write down another warrant that better expressed their view.

In this task individuals must resolve the argument-model by endorsing one of the presented warrants. But in this case, the other warrants are still mentally represented and so may affect the decision.

As expected, fines were higher in the exception condition (£1715) than in the routine condition (£1216) and as previously, fine levels were strongly related to warrants. Again, the nature of the warrant selected helps to explain why fines were lower on average in the routine condition, as the one-off accident warrant was selected by significantly more subjects in the routine condition. However, the actual amount of fine associated with the duty of care warrant was also affected by the condition. It was higher by £914 in the exception condition. Conceivably, the one-off accident warrant remained relatively more salient for those selecting the duty of care warrant in the routine condition and so biased the decision. It is worth noting too that the difference in the amount of fine for the one-off accident warrant and the duty of care warrant was £1321 in this study compared to £2274 in the first study. This suggests that the presented warrants, although not selected, exerted an effect. There was, of course, nothing in the instructions to say that these alternative warrants, and so the arguments of which they are part, should be explicitly rebutted.

If individuals need an argument for a decision as we have supposed, then presenting them with a warrant should lead many to adopt it—if it is at least plausible. In the routine condition an equal number of individuals consider the event to be a one-off accident as consider that the restaurant has a duty of care and should be punished. We predicted then that after reading the routine scenario, and presented with one of these two warrants, individuals would tend to select whichever warrant was presented. In terms of the theory of mental model we predicted a focus effect (Legrenzi, Girotto, & Johnson-Laird, 1993). As before, our subjects were free to construct an alternative warrant which was judged by two independent raters. Ten subjects were excluded either because they awarded compensation to Lucy rather than fined the restaurant, or gave no reason.

There was a significant focus effect. Of the subjects presented with the one-off accident warrant, 75% (19/24) selected it. The remainder generated the duty of care warrant. Of the subjects presented with the duty of care warrant, 73% (19/26) selected it. The remainder generated the one-off accident warrant. As previously, there was a significant effect of the warrant on the level of fine.

Interestingly the difference in the amount of the fine as a function of these two warrants was not affected by whether subjects selected the presented warrant—that is, agreed with it, or disagreed with it and gave a new one (either the one-off accident warrant or the duty of care warrant). The difference in the agree case was £1079 and in the disagree case it was £871. Clearly when subjects construct an alternative warrant, the presented warrant was mentally represented. It is therefore capable of biasing the decision. The fact that the difference in fines between the one-off accident warrant and the duty of care warrant is the same when subjects select the presented warrant suggests that these individuals, too, mentally considered an alternative warrant. So, according to these data, the presence of a focus effect, in which subjects select the presented warrant, does not mean that they did not consider an alternative warrant. Apparently they did and this biased their decision.

However, the last experiment did not require individuals who wished to give an alternative warrant to *rebut* the presented warrant *explicitly*. Model theory leads to the expectation that the influence of an already represented warrant depends on whether it is explicitly rebutted or not.

In order to examine this question we asked subjects as previously to read the routine scenario and presented them with either the one-off accident warrant or the duty of care warrant. However, if they did write down an alternative they had to write down why they rejected the presented warrant: that is, they had to rebut it explicitly. We expected to find a focus effect, but now we predicted that the difference in the amount of fine between the one-off accident warrant and the duty of care warrant would be greater for those subjects who wrote down the alternative warrant and explicitly rebutted the one presented. Again alternative warrants were assessed independently by two judges. Four subjects awarded Lucy compensation and twelve subjects generated other warrants (e.g. "allergic reaction"; "supplier's fault") which were assigned to a category "other"; the remaining responses were readily categorised into either the one-off accident warrant or the duty of care warrant.

As before, the focus effect was highly significant with 61% (25/41) of subjects selecting the one-off warrant when presented with it and 73% (30/ 41) of subjects selecting the duty of care warrant when presented with it. Also, fines were lower for those choosing or generating the one-off accident warrant than the duty of care warrant. However, in contrast to the previous study and in line with our predictions, the difference in the amount of fine for these two warrants was greater for those subjects who explicitly rebutted the presented warrant/argument. For those ticking the presented warrants the difference was £923 whereas for those generating the warrants the difference was £2446. The overall difference between the two warrants for those who explicitly rebutted the presented warrant is comparable to that found in the study where subjects generated their own warrants uncued in the routine condition (£2738). It is a moot point as to whether subjects in the uncued case effectively rebutted some envisaged alternative argument or merely entertained just one argument.

In rebutting the one-off accident warrant, subjects generally stated that restaurants have obligations (e.g. "Ultimately, restaurants have an obligation to their customers and food-poisoning is usually caused by negligence"; "Restaurants should have immaculate standards of hygiene"). In rebutting the duty of care warrant, individuals generally proposed that it could have been a one-off accident ("As Lucy has visited the restaurant numerous times before, then it could have been a one-off occurrence because she has not been ill before"). One subject, though, disputed the attribution of blame: "the illness was traced back to the meal, but nothing proved the restaurant's guilt in the poisoned meal".

What can we conclude so far? These studies provide some evidence for the role of argumentation: (a) warrants (i.e. arguments) determine fines; (b) individuals frequently select the presented warrant—there is a focus effect. Individuals tend to select the presented warrant despite entertaining an unmentioned alternative—prompted by the format perhaps which gives individuals the option of writing down an alternative warrant; (c) when individuals do generate an alternative warrant they are affected by the presented warrant unless they explicitly rebut it.

All three studies are based on a single scenario. Can we generalise? Certainly we expect the grounds (the data and warrants) that individuals offer for their decisions to be decisive. Where plausible alternative warrants come readily to mind we would expect to find no focus effect. We have carried out some preliminary work consistent with this idea. We used the scenario of a mugging, reported in Macrae, Milne, and Griffiths (1993). The warrants for a decision showed a strong relationship with the level of punishment recommended. What of the focus effect? In deciding the severity of punishment for a mugging, individuals consider a wide range of warrants (these include how great the crime is relative to other crimes; the prior behaviour of the offender, and the effects of prison life on rehabilitation) and in these circumstances there is no focus effect.

LEVELS OF CONTROL IN ARGUMENTATION

We have distinguished three processes in this proposal on thinking as internal argument: an argument-construction process, an argument-resolution process, and a meta-level process that constrains the other two processes. In general, the nature of the model-construction and model-resolution processes used in reaching a decision depends on an individual's recognition of the relevance of argument and on the nature of the task they are asked to perform (the meta-level).

Kuhn (1991) identified three distinct views of the relevance of argument to contentious issues; for some, knowledge was certain and absolute, so once the facts were declared there was no room for debate; for others everyone was entitled to an opinion and none was better than others. Again for such relativists there was no point in debate. Others valued argument because through it one could reach a provisional but justified view. As noted earlier, individuals who consider that good thinking involves active open-mindedness produce more arguments in favour of both sides of an issue and appraise arguments that are two-sided more highly (Baron, 1988, 1995).

The meta-level constrains the nature and richness of the argument-model and the nature of the process for resolving the model where a decision is required. In addition, it is also clear that in some cases reaching a decision requires the mental construction of a causal model. Arguments in this case concern the nature of the causal model. This model then becomes critical either in reaching a single decision such as a verdict (Pennington & Hastie, 1993) or in a variety of effectiveness decisions (Green & McManus, 1995). In yet other decision contexts other decision processes may be involved (e.g. Einhorn & Hogarth, 1986).

In addition to meta-level control, the ability to form arguments of various types depends on a person's capacity to make use of what they know (the strategic level of control) and on their knowledge (the knowledge level). A strategic level of control is needed to explain individuals' ability to actually explore different alternatives, to use different kinds of warrants (e.g. analogies or mental simulations) or different kinds of argument (e.g. rebuttal), and their ability to keep track of the structure of argument.

A number of consequences follow from this proposal. First, meta-level considerations are general across domains: this suggests, as others have noted, that it should be possible to teach skills of argument and that individual differences should be consistent across domains. Second, expertise may play a crucial role in the fleshing-out of a mental model. Expertise may furnish elaborate structures of argument. Third, in the case of novel decisions, the effectiveness of a decision will depend on the extent to which individuals have strategic control over their knowledge. In the absence of such control, warrants for decisions will be based solely on what happened in the past or on what is currently prepotent. The kind of computational model proposed by Norman and Shallice may be useful here in developing a process model (see Shallice, 1988, 1994). We expect that any impairment in the ability to regulate the knowledge level (either because of competing task demands or constraints on working memory, or because of brain-damage, e.g. executive dysfunction) will allow decisions based on inappropriate warrants. In such circumstances, there may be a dissociation between the verbally expressed warrant for an action or a decision and what actually controlled the behaviour.

CONCLUSION

In the course of this chapter I have proposed that in situations of uncertainty individuals may set up a type of mental model in which the tokens in the model correspond to arguments for different courses of action. As used here, an argument consists of a potential claim or potential decision and the ground for that decision or claim. In turn, the ground comprises any data relevant to the claim and the warrant for it, i.e. the reason as far as the individual is concerned that the claim follows. The proposal is that there is a single cognitive basis mediating the process of reaching decisions and providing reasons or warrants for those decisions. A decision is the outcome of a process of internal argumentation. However, the process of argumentation can be complex. It can lead to the mental construction of a causal model.

One of the virtues of this proposal is that a decision can be warranted in many different ways: a logical warrant is just one possibility. Another kind of warrant might be based on the person's theory of human motivation. The proposal allows the theory of mental models to extend to informal reasoning in which claims and decisions are warranted in diverse ways. At the same time, we can retain a key property of the theory of mental models, namely that decisions are based on what is explicitly represented.

Four studies were discussed that tested some predictions from the proposal in a relatively simple decision context. In these studies, individuals had to decide on the level of fine for a restaurant in a case of food-poisoning. Individuals tend to select the presented warrant and this warrant is a major determinant of the level of fine. When they generate an alternative warrant, the presented warrant continues to exert an effect unless it is explicitly rebutted. Moreover, these data suggest that selection of a presented warrant does not mean that no other warrant was considered. It seems rather that individuals alerted to the possibility of alternative warrants by the task do consider them and their influence is detectable in their decisions.

The final section of this chapter outlined the nature of some of the control processes. Much remains to be spelled out: for instance, what factors determine the nature of the resolution process? How are arguments in support or against a claim aggregated? What properties of the context call forth different kinds of model-building activity?

A model-based theory of argumentation should also be able to account for decision-making in social groups such as the family, as well as business and governmental groups concerned with policy-making and strategy. In such groups, data and warrants may be widely distributed but effective decision-making requires that they be brought together, and arguments for alternative decisions and courses of action constructed and resolved. Effective decisions are made more likely by considering arguments for alternative options as Janis' (1982) analysis of the Bay of Pigs disaster reminds us. However, commitment to a course of action may require something more: a feeling of its rightness. If argumentation provides a basis for decision, mental simulation may provide the experiential basis for commitment.

ACKNOWLEDGEMENTS

I thank the editors Jane Oakhill and Alan Garnham for helpful comments on an earlier draft of this chapter.

REFERENCES

Antaki, C. (1988). Structures of belief and justification. In C. Antaki (Ed.), *Analyzing everyday explanation*. London: Sage Publications.

Antaki, C (1994). *Explaining and arguing: The social organization of accounts*. London: Sage Publications.

Axelrod, R. (Ed.) (1976). *Structure of decisions: The cognitive maps of political elites*. Princeton: Princeton University Press.

Baron, J. (1988). *Thinking and deciding*. Cambridge: Cambridge University Press.

Baron, J. (1995). Myside bias in thinking about abortion. *Thinking and Reasoning, 1*, 221–235.

Baron-Cohen, S., Leslie, A., & Frith, U. (1985). Does the autistic child have a "theory of mind"? *Cognition, 21*, 37–46.

Beach, L.P. (1992). Epistemic strategies: Causal thinking in expert and non-expert judgement. In G.Wright & F. Bolger (Eds.), *Expertise and decision support* (pp.107–127). New York: Plenum Press.

Billig, M.(1987). *Arguing and thinking: A rhetorical approach to social psychology*. Cambridge: Cambridge University Press.

Bostrom, A., Fischhoff, B., & Morgan, M.G. (1992). Characterizing mental models of hazardous processes: A methodology and an application to radon. *Journal of Social Issues, 48*, 85–100.

Brothers, L. (1990). The social brain: A project for integrating primate behavior and neurophysiology in a new domain. *Concepts in NeuroScience, 1,* 27–51.

Byrne, R., & Whiten, A. (1988). *Machiavellian intelligence: Social expertise and the evolution of intellect in monkeys, apes and humans.* Oxford: Oxford University Press.

Cosmides, L., Tooby, J., & Barkow, J. (1992). Introduction: Evolutionary psychology and conceptual integration. In J.H. Barkow, L. Cosmides & J. Tooby (Eds.), *The adapted mind.* Oxford: Oxford University Press.

Craik, K. (1943). *The nature of explanation.* Cambridge, UK: Cambridge University Press.

Curley, S.P., Browne, G.J., Smith, G.F., & Benson, P.G. (1995). Arguments in practical reasoning underlying constructed probability responses. *Journal of Behavioral Decision-Making, 8,* 1–20.

Dunbar, R. (1993). Coevolution of neocortical size, group size, and language in humans. *Behavioral and Brain Sciences, 16,* 681–735.

Edwards, D., & Potter, J. (1993). Language and causation: A discursive action model of description and attribution. *Psychological Review, 100,* 23–41.

Einhorn, H.J., & Hogarth, R.M. (1986). Judging probable cause. *Psychological Bulletin, 99,* 3–19.

Evans, J.St.B.T. (1989). *Bias in human reasoning: Causes and consequences.* Hove, UK: Lawrence Erlbaum Associates Ltd.

Evans, J.St.B.T. (1991). Theories of human reasoning: The fragmented state of the art. *Theory and Psychology, 1,* 83–105.

Evans, J.St.B.T., & Wason, P.C. (1976). Rationalization in a reasoning task. *British Journal of Psychology, 63,* 205–212.

Fox, J. (1994). On the necessity of probability: Reasons to believe and grounds for doubt. In G. Wright & P. Ayton (Eds.), *Subjective probability.* Chichester, UK: John Wiley & Sons.

Gilhooly, K. (1987). Mental modelling: A framework for the study of thinking. In D.N. Perkins, J. Lochhead, & J.C. Bishop (Eds.), *Thinking.* Hillsdale, NJ: Lawrence Erlbaum Associates Inc.

Green, D.W. (1994a). Induction: Representation, strategy and argument. *International Studies in the Philosophy of Science, 8,* 45–50.

Green, D.W. (1994b). *Externalizing performance in the selection task: Reasoning as argumentation.* Paper presented to the Seventh Conference of the European Society for Cognitive Psychology, Lisbon, 10–14 September, 1994. [*Abstracts,* p.32.]

Green, D.W. (1995). The abstract selection task: Thesis, antithesis and synthesis. In S. Newstead & J.St.B.T. Evans (Eds.), *Perspectives on thinking and reasoning.* Hove, UK and London: Lawrence Erlbaum Associates Ltd.

Green, D.W., McClelland, A., & Muckli, L. (in preparation). *Warranting decisions.*

Green, D.W., & McManus, I.C. (1995). Cognitive structural models: The perception of risk and prevention in coronary heart disease. *British Journal of Psychology, 86,* 321–336.

Green, D.W., McManus, I.C., & Derrick, B. (in preparation). *Cognitive structural models of employment and unemployment.*

Green, D.W., Muckli, L., & McClelland, A. (1995). *Argument and decision.* Paper presented to the British Psychological Society Cognitive Psychology Section Meeting, Bristol, September 7–9, 1995. *Proceedings of the British Psychological Society, 1996, 4,* 42.

Huff, A.S. (Ed.) (1991) *Mapping strategic thought.* New York: John Wiley & Sons.

Humphrey, N. (1984). *Consciousness regained.* Oxford: Oxford University Press.

Janis, I.L. (1982). *Victims of groupthink.* (2nd Edn.) Boston: Houghton Mifflin.

Johnson-Laird, P.N. (1983). *Mental models: Towards a cognitive science of language, inference and consciousness.* Cambridge, MA: Harvard University Press.

Johnson-Laird, P.N. (1993). *Human and machine thinking.* Hillsdale, NJ: Lawrence Erlbaum Associates Inc.

Johnson-Laird, P.N. (1994). A model theory of induction. *International Studies in the Philosophy of Science, 8,* 5–29.

Johnson-Laird, P.N., & Byrne, R.M.J. (1991). *Deduction.* Hillsdale, NJ: Lawrence Erlbaum Associates Inc.

Johnson-Laird, P.N., Byrne, R.M.J., & Schaeken, W. (1992). Propositional reasoning by model. *Psychological Review, 99,* 418–439.

Kahneman, D., & Tversky, A. (1982). The simulation heuristic. In D.Kahneman, P. Slovic, & A. Tversky (Eds.), *Judgement under uncertainty: Heuristics and biases* (pp.201–208). New York: Cambridge University Press.

Kuhn, D. (1991). *The skills of argument.* Cambridge, UK: Cambridge University Press.

Legrenzi, P., Girotto, V., & Johnson-Laird, P.N. (1993). Focusing in reasoning and decision-making. *Cognition, 49,* 37–66.

Macrae, C.N. (1992). A tale of two curries: Counter-factual thinking and accident-related judgements. *Personality and Social Psychology Bulletin, 18,* 84–87.

Macrae, C.N., Milne, A.B., & Griffiths, R.J. (1993). Counterfactual thinking and the perception of criminal behaviour. *British Journal of Psychology, 84,* 221–226.

Mason, R.O., & Mitroff, I.I. (1981). *Challenging strategic planning assumptions: Theory, cases and techniques.* New York: John Wiley & Sons.

Nersessian, N.J. (1991). Why do thought experiments work? *Thirteenth Annual Conference of Cognitive Science Society Chicago.* Hillsdale, NJ: Lawrence Erlbaum Associates Inc.

Over, D.E., & Manktelow, K.I. (1993). Rationality, utility and deontic reasoning. In K.I. Manktelow & D.E. Over (Eds.), *Rationality: Psychological and philosophical perspectives.* London: Routledge.

Pennington, N., & Hastie, R. (1993). Reasoning in explanation-based decision-making. *Cognition, 49,* 123–163.

Perkins, D.N. (1989). Reasoning as it is and could be: An empirical perspective. In D.M. Topping, D.C. Crowell, & V.N. Kobayashi (Eds.), *Thinking across cultures: The third international conference on thinking.* Hillsdale, NJ: Lawrence Erlbaum Associates Inc. [Cited in Baron (1995).]

Shafir, E., Simonson, I., & Tversky, A. (1993). Reason-based choice. *Cognition, 49,* 11–36.

Shallice, T. (1988). *From neuropsychology to mental structure.* Cambridge, UK: Cambridge University Press

Shallice, T. (1994). Multiple levels of control processes. In C. Umilta, & M. Moscovitch (Eds.), *Attention and performance XV: Conscious and nonconscious information processing* (pp.395–420). Cambridge, MA: MIT Press.

Toulmin, S. (1958). *The uses of argument.* Cambridge: Cambridge University Press.

Voss, J.F., Tyler, S.W., & Yengo, L.A. (1983). Individual differences in the solving of social science problems. In R.F. Dillon & R.R. Schmeck (Eds.), *Individual differences in cognition* (Vol. 1, pp.205–232). New York: Academic Press.

Vygotsky, L.S. (1960). The development of higher mental functions. [Quoted in J.V. Wertsch (1985) *Vygotsky and the social formation of mind.* Cambridge, MA: Harvard University Press.]

Wason, P.C. (1968). Reasoning about a rule. *Quarterly Journal of Experimental Psychology, 20,* 273–281.

Wason, P.C., & Evans, J.St.B.T. (1975). Dual processes in reasoning? *Cognition, 3,* 141–154.

Weick, K.E., & Browning, L.D. (1986). Argument and narration in organizational communication. *Journal of Management, 12,* 243–249.

8

Compatibility in Decisions and in Models

Eldar Shafir
Princeton University, USA

INTRODUCTION

It is a pleasure to contribute to a volume honouring the work of Phil Johnson-Laird. My undergraduate thesis at the Center for Cognitive Science at Brown University was heavily based on Johnson-Laird's then recently published book, *Mental models* (1983). Since then, Johnson-Laird has not only continued to be a mentor, but has become a cherished colleague and a dear friend. Ten years after my foray into the cognitive sciences, Johnson-Laird and I edited a volume dedicated to the interaction between research in reasoning and in decision making (Johnson-Laird & Shafir, 1993). Of particular interest were empirical findings and psychological principles that were shared by these two domains of inquiry, or that originated in one but could shed light on the other. It is on one such principle, the principle of compatibility, that I focus in what follows.

An important feature shared by scholarship on reasoning, judgement, and choice, is the existence of a rich normative analysis in each of these domains. In the case of reasoning, the normative treatment stems from formal logic; in the case of probability judgement, it derives from classical probability theory; and in the case of choice, the normative account is expected utility theory. These analyses provide general frameworks that specify what ought to count as rational inferences, expectations, and decisions, and many theorists have argued that these analyses indeed provide faithful, if somewhat idealised, accounts of human competence in each of these domains.

On the empirical side, however, an increasing body of work has documented systematic and predictable ways in which the descriptive analyses of human behaviour systematically depart from the classical, normative analyses. Studies of intuitive judgement have shown that people are not intuitive Bayesians (see e.g. Kahneman, Slovic, & Tversky, 1982; Osherson, 1995); studies of decision making have shown that people are not intuitive utility maximisers (see e.g. Bell, Raiffa, & Tversky, 1988; Camerer, 1995; Dawes, 1988); and studies of deductive and inductive reasoning have shown that people are not intuitive logicians (Evans, 1989; Johnson-Laird and Byrne, 1991; Osherson et al., 1989; Rips, 1994). In principle, there could be a number of reasons for the systematic divergence of reasoning and decision behaviour from the normative account. First, people might not be persuaded by the normative arguments and, as a result, might act intentionally in ways that are discrepant with the requirements of the normative analyses. Second, people might try to conform to the normative ideals but find the task too hard to carry out; among other things, this may be due to a limited attention span, limited memory capacity, or "bounded" computational power.

Interestingly, some of the better-known and systematic violations of normative behaviour, both in reasoning and in decision making, cannot be attributed to the causes outlined above. First, many of the classical violations involve remarkably simple tasks that are unlikely to make major computational demands. Second, it has been repeatedly observed that normative principles that are often violated in non-transparent situations are generally satisfied when their application is transparent. Furthermore, when confronted with the fact that their actions violate some normative principle of deduction or of choice, people typically wish to modify their behaviour to conform with the normative principles. It thus appears that people's systematic violation of compelling normative principles stems largely from their failure to detect the principles' relevance and applicability; it is often not the result either of computational limitations, or of a failure to appreciate the principles' normative appeal.

The reason why the applicability of normative principles often goes undetected, even in contexts where they would otherwise prove easy to apply, is inherent to the psychology of reasoning and decision making. The normative analyses rely on extensional considerations, formal principles, and systematic rules, whereas actual reasoning and decision making are conducted at the level of scenarios, mental models, schemata, and intuitive heuristics. Compare the syntactic structure of a linguistic utterance with the logical structure of a deductive argument, or the extensional representation of a decision problem. Whereas the underlying structure of a linguistic utterance is systematically represented and practically impossible for the hearer to avoid, the logical structure of a deductive argument, or the future outcomes of a decision problem, do not get represented in some standard, canonical form. Instead, slight variations in the formulation of a reasoning or decision problem often lead to different representations and, consequently, to discrepant choices and conclusions.

In contrast with the classical theory of choice, which assumes clear values and well-ordered preferences, work in behavioural decision making has shown that people often do not have well-established values, and that preferences are actually constructed—not merely revealed—during the elicitation process. In a similar development in the study of reasoning, Johnson-Laird and his colleagues have conducted an extensive research programme demonstrating that people do not systematically apply clear logical rules, and have argued that conclusions are actually tested and explored—not merely deduced—via the construction of mental models. As a result of this form of reasoning, minor and logically irrelevant differences in the formulation of inferential problems can be shown to lead to discrepant conclusions on the part of subjects (e.g. Evans, 1989; Girotto, 1993; see also Garnham & Oakhill, 1994, for review).

The classical view presupposes a mental apparatus that gauges worth, estimates likelihoods, and deduces conclusions in a normative, rule-following fashion. Instead, the picture that emerges is of a rich, on the fly, context dependent, frame dependent, constructive mental life. The normative principles are endorsed upon reflection, but they often do not predict the behaviours that result from the constructive and contingent processes that guide reasoning and decision making. Behavioural research in these domains tries to understand the psychological principles that guide the representation of problems, the factors that determine how these representations are then manipulated, and the behavioural phenomena that arise from these processes.

In what follows, I discuss the principle of compatibility, which has emerged in research on decision making and which seems relevant to, and very much in line with, the work on reasoning conducted by Johnson-Laird and many colleagues. The principle of compatibility plays an important role in how decisions are represented and evaluated, and it figures prominently in various other areas of the cognitive sciences, including visual attention, social judgement, and motor control. The following section provides a brief review (for a more extensive review, see Shafir, 1995, and references therein). In the third and final section it is proposed that compatibility might play a role in the construction and manipulation of mental models, and thus may prove an interesting dimension to explore in the study of these processes.

COMPATIBILITY

The principle of compatibility relates the characteristics of an input to the ways in which people code the information, construct a representation, and produce a response. This principle states that, when stimuli and responses are mentally represented, the weight of a stimulus attribute is enhanced to the extent that it is compatible with the required response. In the realm of perceptual–motor performance, for example, stimulus–response compatibility predicts that some tasks will be easier or more difficult than others because of the particular stimuli and responses that are used, and because of the ways in which these stimuli and responses interact. Thus, responses to visual displays of information, such as an instrument panel, are faster and more accurate if the response-structure is compatible with the arrangement of the stimuli (Fitts & Seeger, 1953; Wickens, 1984). A square array of four burners on a stove, for example, is easier to control with a corresponding square array of knobs than with a linear array. Similarly, the response to a pair of lights is faster and more accurate if the left light is assigned to the left key and the right light to the right key than if the assignment of sides is reversed.

Although spatial compatibility is the most prevalent in the experimental literature, stimulus–response compatibility can also be observed among stimuli and responses that share no physical spatial dimensions. Stimulus–response compatibility has been evoked, for example, to account for the fact that a pointing response is faster than a vocal response when the stimulus is visual, whereas a vocal response is faster than pointing when the stimulus is presented in an auditory mode (Brainard, Irby, Fitts, & Alluisi, 1962). Another example is that of compatibility effects based on phonetic features (Gordon & Meyer, 1984), wherein responses were faster when a speech stimulus and a speech response shared a voicing feature (e.g. "tuh" and "puh", both unvoiced) than when they did not (e.g. "duh" and "puh", the former voiced, the latter unvoiced). Similarly, reaction times are shorter when stimuli such as the written words *left* and *right*, or left- and right-pointing arrows, are assigned to left and right physical responses; or when "left" and "right" vocal responses are assigned to corresponding stimulus locations (Magliero, Bashore, Coles, & Donchin, 1984; Weeks & Proctor, 1990).

Compatibility implies that some stimulus components will be more salient and more likely to be explicitly represented than others, and that some tasks will be easier to perform than others because of the particular sets of stimuli and responses that are being considered, and the ways in which these stimuli and responses interact. The significance of compatibility between input and output has recently been evoked by cognitive psychologists and by students of judgement and decision making to account for a series of surprising yet systematic patterns of behaviour. In what follows, I consider the compatibility hypothesis as it relates to recent findings in judgement and decision making, and illustrate how it helps explain systematic patterns of decision behaviour that are puzzling from a normative perspective. That leads to the suggestion that considerations of compatibility may enter into the investigation and analysis of deductive reasoning in general, and of mental models in particular, in ways that have so far not been extensively explored.

Scale Compatibility

Work in judgement and decision making has extended the notion of compatibility and proposed that the weight of certain stimulus attributes in judgement or in choice is enhanced by their compatibility with the particular scale that is being used to provide the response (Slovic, Griffin, & Tversky, 1990; Tversky, Sattath, & Slovic, 1988; see also Mellers, Ordoñez, & Birnbaum, 1992). The rationale for this is that the specific nature of the response scale tends to focus attention on the compatible features of the stimulus. Thus, setting the price of a gamble, for example, is likely to emphasise payoffs more than probabilities because both the price and the payoffs are in monetary units (e.g. dollars). When a stimulus attribute and the response scale do not match, additional steps are presumably required to map one into the other. As with the spatial mapping between stimulus and response ensembles, noncompatibility between a stimulus attribute and the response scale requires additional mental operations, which often increase effort and error, and reduce impact on judgement or choice.

Scale compatibility accounts for one of the better-known and more extensively investigated counter-normative phenomena in the study of decision behaviour, known as the "preference reversal phenomenon". The preference reversal phenomenon was first demonstrated by Lichtenstein and Slovic (1971, 1973), who presented subjects with two prospects of similar expected value. One typical prospect, the H bet, offers a high chance to win a relatively small payoff (e.g. 8 chances in 9 to win $4) whereas the other prospect, the L bet, offers a lower chance to win a larger payoff (e.g. a 1 in 9 chance to win $40). Subjects are asked to choose between these prospects and, on a separate occasion, they are also asked to price each prospect by indicating the smallest amount of money for which they would be willing to sell the prospect if they owned it. When asked to choose between these prospects, most subjects choose the H bet over the L bet; however, when asked to price the two prospects most subjects assign a higher price to the L bet than to the H bet. In a recent study that used the pair of bets mentioned here, for example, 71% of the subjects chose the H bet over the L bet, while 67% priced L above H (Tversky, Slovic, & Kahneman, 1990).

Preference reversal typically occurs when subjects choose a lottery that offers a greater chance to win over another that offers a higher payoff, but assign a higher price to the lottery offering the higher payoff than to the one with the greater chance to win. This pattern of preferences has been observed in numerous experiments using a variety of prospects and incentive schemes, including a version conducted in the Peoples' Republic of China for real payoffs equivalent to months' worth of the subjects' salary (Kachelmeier & Shehata, 1992). It has also been observed among professional gamblers in a study conducted on the floor of the Four Queens Casino in Las Vegas (Lichtenstein & Slovic, 1973).

Although most replications of the preference reversal phenomenon involve risky prospects, note that the compatibility hypothesis does not depend on the presence of risk. Indeed, it implies a similar discrepancy between pricing and choice in the context of riskless options that have a monetary component. Consider a long-term prospect L, which pays $2,500 five years from now, and a short-term prospect S, which pays $1,600 in one and a half years. Tversky, Slovic, and Kahneman (1990) asked subjects to choose between L and S and to price them, by stating the smallest immediate cash payment for which they would be willing to exchange each prospect. As before, because the payoffs and the prices are expressed in the same units, compatibility suggests that the long-term prospect (which offers the higher payoff) will be overvalued in pricing relative to choice. In accord with compatibility, subjects chose the short-term prospect 74% of the time but priced the long-term prospect above the short-term prospect 75% of the time.

The classical analysis of choice assumes that people's preferences can be elicited through any of a number of normatively equivalent methods. People can be asked to indicate which option they prefer; alternatively, they can be asked to price each option. The standard assumption of *procedure invariance* requires that normatively equivalent elicitation procedures give rise to the same preference order: if an option is chosen over another, it should also be priced higher. Studies specifically designed to discriminate between alternative causes of the preference reversal phenomenon (e.g. intransitivity of choices versus a discrepancy between choice and pricing) have shown that a great majority of preference reversals are in fact due to violations of procedure invariance. In particular, the most common violation in this context consists of the overpricing of the L bets (i.e. those offering the greater payoff, the attribute most compatible with pricing) relative to choice (for a detailed discussion, see Tversky et al., 1990; Tversky & Thaler, 1990). Further evidence for the role of scale compatibility in preference reversals is provided by Schkade and Johnson (1989) who, using a computer-controlled experiment, were able to show that subjects spend more time on, thereby presumably focusing more attention on, the stimulus components that are most compatible with the scale of the response mode.

Preference reversal phenomena are thus instances of compatibility-induced weighting, not some peculiar phenomena limited to choice between options. The major cause of preference reversal is the compatibility between the response mode and certain attributes of the options, which are weighted differentially depending on the response. Naturally, compatibility effects have only a limited influence on decision. If one option is overwhelmingly preferred over another, then a differential weighting of dimensions is unlikely to alter a person's choice. However, in many instances, when the decision is difficult and the options are of otherwise comparable worth, compatibility can have a decisive effect on the formation of preference.

Semantic Compatibility

Compatibility effects can also be induced by the semantic correspondence between instructions given to subjects and particular features of the stimuli under consideration; features of a stimulus that are more compatible with the given instructions will be weighted more heavily than features of the stimulus that are less compatible.

Similarity Judgements.   An early example of semantic compatibility was provided in the context of similarity judgements. In his contrast model of similarity, Tversky (1977) presents a set-theoretical approach to similarity, in which objects are represented as collections of features, and similarity between objects is expressed as an increasing function of the features that they have in common and a decreasing function of their distinctive features; that is, the features that each object has and the other does not. Judgements of dissimilarity, or difference, are commonly assumed to be complementary to similarity judgements: dissimilarity is an increasing function of distinctive features and a decreasing function of common features.

Tversky suggests, however, that due to a change in focus induced by the task, judgements of similarity and dissimilarity may not be mirror images. In the assessment of similarity between stimuli, the subject—as suggested by semantic compatibility—is expected to attend more to their common features, whereas in the assessment of difference, the subject will attend more to their distinctive features. As a result of semantic compatibility, common features are predicted to loom larger in judgements of similarity than in judgements of dissimilarity, whereas distinctive features are predicted to loom larger in judgements of dissimilarity than in judgements of similarity. This leads to a straightforward but surprising prediction, namely that a pair of objects with many common and many distinctive features could be judged more similar, as well as more dissimilar, than another pair of objects with fewer common and fewer distinctive features.

Tversky and Gati (1978) observed this pattern in the comparison of pairs of well-known (i.e. "prominent") countries with pairs of countries that were less well-known. They had one group of subjects—the similarity group—select between each two pairs of countries the pair that were more similar. The second group of subjects—the difference group—selected between each two pairs of countries the pair of countries that they thought were more different.

If similarity and difference are complementary, then the percentage of subjects who select the prominent pair in the similarity task plus the percentage who select it in the difference task should equal 100. On the other hand, if common features are weighted more in judgements of similarity, and distinctive features loom relatively larger in difference judgements, then the prominent pair should be selected more often and this sum should exceed 100. Indeed, in line with semantic compatibility, the average share obtained by Tversky and Gati for the more prominent pairs (113.5) was significantly greater than 100. For example, most subjects in the similarity condition selected East Germany and West Germany (the prominent pair) as more similar to each other than Ceylon and Nepal (the nonprominent pair), whereas most subjects in the dissimilarity condition selected East Germany and West Germany as more different from each other than Ceylon and Nepal. Related findings are reported in Medin, Goldstone, and Gentner (1990; see also Medin, Goldstone, & Markman, 1995, for discussion). The results demonstrate that, in line with compatibility, the relative weight of common and distinctive features varies with the nature of the task. Common features, which contribute to the perceived similarity between objects, are weighted more heavily when judging similarity, and distinctive features, which contribute to perceived difference, are weighted relatively more heavily when the task focuses on differences.

Choice and Rejection.   Semantic compatibility has also been documented in decisions to choose and to reject options, specifically due to the compatibility between the positive and negative features of those options and the particular task at hand. The advantages of an option provide compelling reasons for choosing it, whereas disadvantages are more compatible with rejection. Thus, compatibility suggests that positive dimensions will be given more weight when choosing than when rejecting, whereas negative dimensions will loom relatively larger when rejecting than when choosing.

Imagine having to choose one of two options or, alternatively, having to reject one of two options. Logically, the tasks are identical. According to the assumption of procedure invariance, in a binary choice situation it should not matter whether people are asked which option they prefer, or which they would rather reject. If people prefer the first they will reject the second, and vice versa. Instead, consider a situation in which one option—the *enriched* option—contains both more positive and more negative features than another—*impoverished*—option. If, in line with compatibility, positive features weigh more heavily when choosing and negative features loom relatively larger when rejecting, then the enriched option could be chosen over, and also rejected in favour of, the impoverished alternative.

Shafir (1993) presented subjects with descriptions of two hypothetical vacation spots. One spot, the enriched option, was described as having lots of sunshine, lovely beaches, an ultra-modern hotel, but very cold water, strong winds, and no nightlife. The second, impoverished, alternative was said to have average weather and beaches, average nightlife, medium-temperature water, and a medium-quality hotel. One half of the subjects were asked to indicate which vacation spot they preferred; the other half were asked to suppose that they had reservations in both that could no longer be retained, and asked to indicate which of the two they would rather cancel. The impoverished option is unremarkable yet unobjectionable on all counts. The enriched alternative, on the other hand, has certain features—the lovely beaches, the sunshine, the modern hotel—that render it preferable to many subjects, and other features—cold water, winds, and no nightlife—that make many subjects decide to reject it. Indeed, whether subjects were engaged in selecting or in cancelling had a significant effect on which vacation they chose: the lovely beaches are more compatible with selecting and the strong winds are more compatible with rejecting a vacation. As a result, subjects were more likely to end up in the enriched location when they were asked which vacation they preferred than when they contemplated which to cancel. Whereas two-thirds of the subjects expressed a preference for the enriched spot when asked to choose, nearly half the subjects opted to forego that same spot when asked which they would rather cancel. Because it presents more compatible reasons for being selected and for being rejected, subjects are relatively more likely to select and to cancel the enriched option over its impoverished alternative. As predicted, the enriched spot's share of being chosen and rejected (which totalled 115%) significantly exceeded the 100 that we would expect if choosing and rejecting were complementary.

Semantic compatibility effects stemming from the differential weighting of features of enriched and impoverished alternatives can also be observed in social judgement tasks. Downs and Shafir (1996) presented subjects with two personality descriptions; one—the enriched personality—was ascribed behaviours characteristic of moral and of immoral behaviour (e.g. giving to charity and flirting with employees), while the description of the other—impoverished personality—consisted of behaviours largely irrelevant on the morality dimension. Half the subjects were asked which of the two people they considered more moral; the others were asked which of the two they considered more immoral. In line with compatibility, subjects were inclined to judge the enriched personality, who presented instances of both types of behaviours, as both more moral (52%) and more immoral (72%) than the impoverished personality, who presented fewer instances of either.

Visual Estimation. A recently documented "region salience" bias in a visual estimation task presents another interesting example of semantic compatibility. Goldstone (1993) presented subjects with two displays composed of a mixture of 60 black and white squares. In one display the squares were randomly distributed, whereas the second "clustered" display was designed to have clusters of black and white squares. Half the subjects were asked to choose the display with a higher percentage of black squares; the others were asked to choose the display with a higher percentage of white squares. The clustered display was judged to have a higher percentage of both kinds of squares: when subjects were asked to select the display with a greater percentage of white squares, the clustered display was chosen 56% of the time, and when asked to select the display with the greater percentage of black squares, the clustered display was again chosen about 56% of the time. This is consistent with the hypothesis that subjects selectively focus on areas that have a high concentration of instruction-compatible features. Because the percentage of instruction-compatible features in these salient areas is high, the prevalence of those features tends to be overestimated.

Along similar lines, it may be interesting to explore the possibility that elements that are more frequent or salient in the initial representation of a mental model will increase the likelihood that compatible elements will figure prominently in the conclusions that are drawn and in the model that evolves after further manipulation. This could be related to the notions of "mood" and "atmosphere" that characterise the premises of syllogisms (see e.g. Garnham & Oakhill, 1994). Thus, the structure of premises, e.g. whether they are positive or negative, existential or universal, may—via compatibility—influence the nature of the conclusions that follow.

CONCLUDING REMARKS

The tendency to focus on features of a stimulus that are compatible with the instructions has been observed in the behaviour of young children. Falk (1983) presented children (6 years old) with two urns containing different proportions of blue and yellow beads, with one urn containing more of both coloured beads than the other (e.g. one urn with six blue and four yellow beads; the other with two blue and one yellow). In each round, the children were told which colour (blue or yellow) was the winning colour and were invited to draw from either urn at random. The more frequent error that characterised the children's choices was to select the urn with the greater number of beads of the winning colour. Thus, whether told that the winning colour was blue or yellow, the children reached into the same urn, namely, the one containing the larger absolute number of winning-colour beads (see also Falk, Falk, & Levin, 1980; Piaget & Inhelder, 1975).

Selective focusing on compatible instances has also been shown to occur in memory search. Subjects in Snyder and Cantor's (1979) study, for example, read a story about a woman who behaved in ways that could be characterised as "extroverted" and in other ways that could be characterized as "introverted". Two days later, these subjects were asked to assess the woman's suitability for an "extroverted" occupation (estate agent) or for an "introverted" occupation (librarian). Subjects considering the extrovert occupation recalled more extrovert items, whereas those considering the introvert occupation recalled more introvert items, each group recalling with greater ease those items that were compatible with its hypothesis. Along similar lines, mood-induced focusing on compatible instances has been documented, wherein people's good or bad moods increase the availability of "mood-congruent" thoughts and information, thus biasing retrievability and affecting judgements of subjective well-being (Bower, 1981; Isen, Shalker, Clark, & Karp, 1978; although see Schwarz & Clore, 1983, for an alternative interpretation). The tendency to focus selectively on compatible instances can result in a bias towards confirming hypotheses and detecting covariation, as it is always possible to encounter compatible (i.e. positive) instances, thus detecting relationships between things even when, in fact, there is no relationship between them (see e.g. Gilovich, 1991).

Selective focusing on features that are compatible with a hypothesis or with the instructions has been observed in numerous studies, reporting what have variously been called congruence biases (Baron, 1994), confirmatory biases (Barsalou, 1992; Skov & Sherman, 1986; Snyder & Swann, 1978), verification biases (Johnson-Laird & Wason, 1970), focusing effects (Legrenzi, Girotto, & Johnson-Laird, 1993), and matching biases (Evans, 1984; 1989; Evans & Lynch, 1973). In this vein, Pollard (1982) has borrowed the term "availability" to suggest that responses in reasoning tasks are often mediated by available cues, rather than deeper reasoning. In most of these cases, performance that violates the normative principles of reasoning is not simply attributed to a lack of understanding of these normative principles. As with decision making, subjects appear to understand the logical principles, but then fail to apply them in the context of specific problems. Instead, biases arise out of people's tendency to focus selectively on "confirming", "matching", "congruent", or "available" instances, usually those that are more *compatible* with the terms that appear in the instructions or with the hypotheses being considered. Further empirical and conceptual analyses may help to clarify the extent to which these biases are manifestations of the compatibility principle.

According to Johnson-Laird's theory of mental models, when people think about some situation in the world, they create a representation in the form of a mental model intended to reflect the structure of the relevant situation. Models are constructed using world knowledge, the premises, and other available information, and are then mentally manipulated to depict changes and reflect possible implications. Everyday reasoning is charac-terised not in terms of rules of inference, but in terms of the construction and manipulation of plausible models. This is a highly constructive process, one that depends heavily on the particular pieces of information that are brought to bear, and the particular order, format, and number of the models that are mentally represented.

In the context of the analysis of choice, the experimental evidence suggests that preferences are often constructed during the elicitation procedure, and that these constructions depend on the context of decision, the framing of the problem, and the method of elicitation, among other factors (see e.g. Payne, 1982; Shafir & Tversky, 1995; and Tversky & Kahneman, 1986, for further discussion). Similarly, the factors that guide the construction of mental models will form an integral part of our understanding of this form of reasoning. One factor worthy of investigation is the principle of compatibility. As we have seen, compatibility figures prominently in tasks ranging from visual attention and perception to a selective retrieval from memory, and the weighing of features in predictive and evaluative judgements. Because the construction and manipulation of mental models incorporates essentially these types of mental activity, it is possible that considerations of compatibility may add insight to the theory of mental models. Consider, for example, the fact that people are consistently observed to "scan models in the direction in which they construct them" (Johnson-Laird, 1988, p.230). This, after all, is not an obvious feature of a model that is intended to capture the structure of a specific situation in the real world. Could it be that this effect is due to the compatibility between the direction of construction and that of scanning a model, much like that between physically pointing left and a left-pointing arrow?

Johnson-Laird (1994) has recently suggested a mental model account of the inductive strength of everyday arguments. According to this proposal, the strength of an inference depends on the relative proportion of two sorts of possible states of affairs consistent with the premises: those in which the conclusion is true and those in which it is false. The construction of candidate states of affairs, however, is likely to be highly contingent: it may be interesting to explore whether considerations of compatibility can illuminate what sort of states of affairs are represented and, consequently, the probability estimates that result.

As mentioned earlier, perhaps the most basic assumption of the rational theory of choice is the principle of procedure invariance, which requires strategically equivalent methods of elicitation to yield the same preference order. Compatibility was seen to lead to violations of procedure invariance in systematic and predictable ways. Because invariance is normatively indispensable, no normative theory of decision making can be reconciled with these findings. More importantly, perhaps, these findings may not be easily reconcilable with people's own intuitions. Although compatibility can have a powerful effect on performance, people are generally unaware of its influence, operating as it does at an elementary level of information processing (see Slovic et al., 1990, for discussion). Diverse aspects of stimuli and responses may enhance their compatibility. These include spatial and perceptual organisation, the use of similar units on a scale, an evaluation in qualitative versus quantitative terms, a reliance on shared versus distinctive attributes, the specific instructions that guide the decision, and the particular hypothesis or perspective that motivates the evaluation. Because there is neither a formal definition of compatibility nor a general procedure for its assessment, an analysis in terms of compatibility must remain informal and incomplete. It is evident, however, that some stimulus–response configurations are more compatible than others. Just as a control panel is clearly more compatible with some information displays than others, and the disadvantages of options are more compatible with rejection than with choice, so may the compatibility ranking in the context of constructing mental models be sufficiently clear to allow experimental investigation and insight.

ACKNOWLEDGEMENT

This work was supported by US Public Health Service Grant No. 1-R29-MH46885 from the National Institute of Mental Health.

REFERENCES

Baron, J. (1994). *Thinking and deciding: Second edition.* New York: Cambridge University Press.

Barsalou, L.W. (1992). *Cognitive psychology: An overview for cognitive scientists.* Hillsdale, NJ: Lawrence Erlbaum Associates Inc.

Bell, D.E., Raiffa, H., & Tversky, A. (Eds.). (1988). *Decision making: Descriptive, normative, and prescriptive interactions.* New York: Cambridge University Press.

Bower, G.H. (1981). Mood and memory. *American Psychologist, 36,* 129–148.

Brainard, R.W., Irby, T.S., Fitts, P.M., & Alluisi, E. (1962). Some variables influencing the rate of gain of information. *Journal of Experimental Psychology, 63,* 105–110.

Camerer, C.F. (1995). Individual decision making. In J.H. Kagel & A.E. Roth (Eds.), *Handbook of experimental economics,* Princeton, NJ: Princeton University Press.

Dawes, R.M. (1988). *Rational choice in an uncertain world.* New York: Harcourt Brace Jovanovich.

Downs, J., & Shafir, E. (1996). Why Ronald Reagan is more confident and more insecure than John Major: Enriched and impoverished options in social judgment. Manuscript, Princeton University.

Evans, J.St.B.T. (1984). Heuristic and analytic processes in reasoning. *British Journal of Psychology, 75,* 451–468.

Evans, J.St.B.T. (1989). *Bias in human reasoning: Causes and consequences.* Hillsdale, NJ: Lawrence Erlbaum Associates Inc.

Evans, J.St.B.T., & Lynch, J.S. (1973). Matching bias in the selection task. *British Journal of Psychology, 64,* 391–397.

Falk, R. (1983). Children's choice behavior in probabilistic situations. *Proceedings of the First International Conference on Teaching Statistics, University of Sheffield, Vol. II,* 714–726.

Falk, R., Falk, R., & Levin, I. (1980). A potential for learning probability in young children. *Educational Studies in Mathematics*, *11*, 181–204.

Fitts, P.M., & Seeger, C.M. (1953). S–R compatibility: Spatial characteristics of stimulus and response codes. *Journal of Experimental Psychology*, *46*, 199–210.

Garnham, A., & Oakhill, J. (1994). *Thinking and reasoning*. Oxford: Blackwell Publishers.

Gilovich, T. (1991). *How we know what isn't so: The fallibility of human reason in everyday life*. New York: The Free Press.

Girotto, V. (1993). Modèles mentaux et raisonnement. In M.-F. Ehrlich, H. Tardieu, & M. Cavazza (Eds.), *Les modèles mentaux: Approche cognitive des représentations* (pp.101–119). Paris: Masson.

Goldstone, R.L. (1993). Feature distribution and biased estimation of visual displays. *Journal of Experimental Psychology: Human Perception and Performance*, *19*, 564–579.

Gordon, P.C., & Meyer, D.E. (1984). Perceptual-motor processing of phonetic features in speech. *Journal of Experimental Psychology: Human Perception and Performance*, *10*, 153–178.

Isen, A.M., Shalker, T.E., Clark, M., & Karp, L. (1978). Affect, accessibility of material in memory, and behavior: A cognitive loop? *Journal of Personality and Social Psychology*, *36*, 1–12.

Johnson-Laird, P.N. (1983). *Mental models*. Cambridge, MA: Harvard University Press.

Johnson-Laird, P.N. (1988). *The computer and the mind*. Cambridge, MA: Harvard University Press.

Johnson-Laird, P.N. (1994). Mental models and probabilistic thinking. *Cognition*, *50*, 189–209.

Johnson-Laird, P.N., & Byrne, R.M.J. (1991). *Deduction*. Hillsdale, NJ: Lawrence Erlbaum Associates Inc.

Johnson-Laird, P.N., & Shafir, E. (Eds.) (1993). *Reasoning and decision making*. A special issue of *Cognition: International Journal of Cognitive Science*. [Reprinted by Blackwell Publishers, Oxford, 1994.]

Johnson-Laird, P.N., & Wason, P.C. (1970). A theoretical analysis of insight into a reasoning task. *Cognitive Psychology*, *1*, 134–148.

Kachelmeier, S.J., & Shehata, M. (1992). Examining risk preferences under high monetary incentives: Experimental evidence from the People's Republic of China. *American Economic Review*, *82*, 1120–1141.

Kahneman, D., Slovic, P., & Tversky, A. (Eds.) (1982). *Judgment under uncertainty: Heuristics and biases*. New York: Cambridge University Press.

Legrenzi, P., Girotto, V., & Johnson-Laird, P.N. (1993). Focusing in reasoning and decision making. *Cognition*, *49*, 1–2, 37–66.

Lichtenstein, S., & Slovic, P. (1971). Reversals of preference between bids and choices in gambling decisions. *Journal of Experimental Psychology*, *89*, 46–55.

Lichtenstein, S., & Slovic, P. (1973). Response-induced reversals of preference in gambling: An extended replication in Las Vegas. *Journal of Experimental Psychology*, *101*, 16–20.

Magliero, A., Bashore, T.R., Coles, M.T.H., & Donchin, E. (1984). On the dependence of P300 latency on stimulus evaluation processes. *Psychophysiology*, *21*, 171–186.

Medin, D.L., Goldstone, R.L., & Gentner, D. (1990). Similarity involving attributes and relations: Judgments of similarity and difference are not inverses. *Psychological Science*, *1*, 64–69.

Medin, D.L., Goldstone, R.L., & Markman, A.B. (1995). Comparison and choice: Relations between similarity processes and decision processes. *Psychonomic Bulletin and Review*, *2*(1), 1–19.

Mellers, B.A., Ordóñez, L.D., & Birnbaum, M.H. (1992). A change-of-process theory for contextual effects and preference reversals in risky decision making. *Organizational Behavior and Human Decision Processes*, *52*, 331–369.

Osherson, D.N. (1995). Probability judgment. In E.E. Smith & D.N. Osherson (Eds.), *An invitation to cognitive science, Second Edition (Volume 3: Thinking)*. Cambridge, MA: MIT Press.

Osherson, D.N., Smith, E.E., Wilke, A., Lopez, A., & Shafir, E. (1990). Category based induction. *Psychological Review, 97*, 185–200.

Payne, J.W. (1982). Contingent decision behavior. *Psychological Bulletin, 92*, 382–402.

Piaget, J., & Inhelder, B. (1975). *The origin of the idea of chance in children*, L. Peake Jr., P. Burrell, & H.D. Fishbein, Trans. New York: Norton. [Originally published 1951.]

Pollard, P. (1982). Human reasoning: Some possible effects of availability. *Cognition, 12*, 65–96.

Rips, L.J. (1994). *The psychology of proof: Deductive reasoning in human thinking*. Cambridge, MA: MIT Press.

Schkade, D.A., & Johnson, E.J. (1989). Cognitive processes in preference reversals. *Organizational Behavior and Human Decision Processes, 44*, 203–231.

Schwarz, N., & Clore, G.L. (1983). Mood, misattribution, and judgments of well-being: Informative and directive functions of affective states. *Journal of Personality and Social Psychology, 45*, 513–523.

Shafir, E. (1993). Choosing versus rejecting: Why some options are both better and worse than others. *Memory & Cognition, 21*, 546–556.

Shafir, E. (1995). Compatibility in cognition and decision. In J.R. Busemeyer, R. Hastie, & D.L. Medin (Eds.), *Decision making from the perspective of cognitive psychology*. New York: Academic Press.

Shafir, E., & Tversky, A. (1995). Decision making. In E.E. Smith & D.N. Osherson (Eds.), *An invitation to cognitive science, Second Edition (Volume 3: Thinking)* (pp.77–100). Cambridge, MA: MIT Press.

Skov, R.B., & Sherman, S.J. (1986). Information-gathering processes: Diagnosticity, hypothesis-confirmatory strategies, and perceived hypothesis confirmation. *Journal of Experimental Social Psychology, 22*, 93–121.

Slovic, P., Griffin, D., & Tversky, A. (1990). Compatibility effects in judgment and choice. In R. Hogarth (Ed.), *Insights in decision making: Theory and applications* (pp.5–27). Chicago: University of Chicago Press.

Snyder, M., & Cantor, N. (1979). Testing hypotheses about other people: The use of historical knowledge. *Journal of Experimental Social Psychology, 15*, 330–342.

Snyder, M., & Swann, W.B. (1978). Behavioral confirmation in social interaction: From social perception to social reality. *Journal of Experimental Social Psychology, 14*, 148–162.

Tversky, A. (1977). Features of similarity. *Psychological Review, 84*, 327–352.

Tversky, A., & Gati, I. (1978). Studies of similarity. In E. Rosch & B. Lloyd (Eds.), *Cognition and categorization* (pp.79–98). Hillsdale, NJ: Lawrence Erlbaum Associates Inc.

Tversky, A., & Kahneman, D. (1986). Rational choice and the framing of decisions. *Journal of Business, 59*, 251–278.

Tversky, A., Sattath, S., & Slovic, P. (1988). Contingent weighting in judgment and choice. *Psychological Review, 95*, 371–384.

Tversky, A., Slovic, P., & Kahneman, D. (1990). The causes of preference reversal. *American Economic Review, 80*, 204–217.

Tversky, A., & Thaler, R.H. (1990). Preference reversals. *Journal of Economic Perspectives, 4*, 201–211.

Weeks, D.J., & Proctor, R.W. (1990). Compatibility effects for orthogonal stimulus–response dimensions. *Journal of Experimental Psychology: General, 119*, 355–366.

Wickens, C.D. (1984). *Engineering psychology and human performance*. Columbus, OH: Merrill.

9 Towards a Model Theory of Imaginary Thinking

Ruth M.J. Byrne
University of Dublin, Trinity College, Ireland

MENTAL MODELS: FROM DEDUCTION TO IMAGINARY THOUGHT

We use our imagination in many ways, for example when we think about what might have been, that is, when we think *counterfactually*, especially when we compare a situation to an imaginary alternative in which events turned out differently. For example, if your friend is seriously injured in a car crash, you might mull over the events that led to the tragic outcome and wish, "If only she hadn't been speeding". Thinking about imaginary alternatives plays an important role in many aspects of cognition, for example, in establishing causal relations by considering what might happen in cases where the cause does not occur, and in carrying out the search for counterexamples in deductive reasoning by considering that a putative conclusion is not the case and imagining situations consistent with this possibility (e.g. Chisholm, 1946; Ginsberg, 1986; Hofstadter, 1985; Isard, 1974; Johnson-Laird, 1986; McGill & Klein, 1993; Wells & Gavanski, 1989). Counterfactual thinking is also one of the interfaces between cognition and emotion, underlying feelings of regret and disappointment, as well as hope and relief (e.g. Johnson, 1986; Kahneman & Miller, 1986; Landman, 1987). Arguably, you could not experience an emotion such as regret if you did not keep in mind the way a situation turned out and did not compare it to an imaginary alternative in which events turned out differently. One key issue in understanding counterfactual thinking is to discover how people generate

155

imaginary alternatives to a situation and in this chapter I will try to sketch part of an answer to this question.

The answer I will outline is based on the conjecture that imaginary thinking and logical inference have more in common than has been envisaged previously. To develop this idea, I will begin by outlining the model theory of conditional inference that Phil Johnson-Laird and I developed in our book *Deduction* in 1991. Then I will discuss the similarities and differences between deductions from factual conditionals and deductions from counterfactual conditionals, based on the results of experiments that I have carried out with Alessandra Tasso from the University of Padua in Italy. Next, I will move beyond inferences from counterfactual scenarios, to the *generation* of counterfactual scenarios and I will describe the results of experiments that I have carried out with Susana Segura from the University of Malaga in Spain and Ronan Culhane from the University of Dublin, Trinity College in Ireland. I will conclude with some remarks on the extension of the mental model theory beyond an account of deductive reasoning to become a general account of thinking.

THE MODEL THEORY OF CONDITIONALS

During the three years from 1986 to 1989 when I had the good fortune to work with Phil Johnson-Laird at the MRC Applied Psychology Unit at Cambridge in England we tried to develop and test a general theory of deduction. Based on the ideas that Phil advanced in his 1983 book *Mental models*, we developed a theory of reasoning that spanned propositional deduction, quantificational deduction, relational deduction, and meta-deduction; we carried out experiments in these domains to test the theory, and we wrote computer programs to simulate it. I will illustrate the model theory of deduction with reference to just one aspect of one of those domains: conditional inference (e.g. Johnson-Laird, Byrne, & Schaeken, 1992). Conditional inference is central to our ability to think hypothetically (e.g. Byrne, 1989a, b), and as we will see, it provides a crucial link between logical deduction and imaginary thought. Consider the following conditional:

1.   If she drove within the speed limit, then she arrived home safely.

Phil and I suggested that reasoners understand conditionals by constructing an initial model that contains some information represented in an explicit manner, and maintains other information implicitly (Johnson-Laird & Byrne, 1991). The conditional is understood by constructing a mental model, that is, a representation that corresponds to the way the world would be if the assertion were true. We suggested that this representation contains explicitly the information that the assertion is true in the situation where she drove within the speed limit and arrived home safely, and it contains implicitly the information that the assertion may also be true in alternative situations, and we captured this representation in the following sort of diagram:

2.   l   h
      . . .

where "l" represents the information that she drove within the speed limit, "h" represents the information that she arrived home safely, separate models are represented on separate lines, and the three dots in the implicit model represents the idea that there may be alternatives to the first model. The set of models can be fleshed-out to be fully explicit, and in fact, the models must contain other annotations to provide information about the appropriate way in which the models can be fleshed-out:

3.   [l]   h
      . . .

The square brackets around the "l" indicate that the information that she drove within the speed limit has been represented exhaustively, that is, it cannot occur in any other model unless it occurs with the information that she arrived home safely. The information that she arrived home safely, represented by the "h" has not been exhaustively represented, that is, it may occur in other models with or without the information that she drove within the speed limit (for further details see Johnson-Laird & Byrne, 1991). Thus, this initial set of models may be fleshed-out in just one way, and it is consistent with a strict conditional interpretation:

4.   l   h
      not-l not-h
      not-l h

where "not" is a propositional-like tag to represent negation and "not-l" represents the information that she did not drive within the speed limit (for a defence of propositional-like tags within models, see Johnson-Laird & Byrne, 1989, 1991). The first model represents the situation in which she drove within the speed limit and arrived home safely, the second model represents the situation in which she did not drive within the speed limit and did not arrive home safely, and the third model represents the situation in which she did not drive within the speed limit but she nonetheless arrived home safely. The assertion is true in each of these situations according to a strict conditional or "material implication" interpretation of "if". A

reasoner who reaches a biconditional or "material equivalence" interpretation will consider the assertion to be true in only the first two models:

5.   l   h
      not-l   not-h

The model theory of propositional reasoning specifies the number of models
required for both the initial representation and the fully fleshed-out
representation for each of the main propositional connectives, "and",
"or", "if", and "not", as Table 9.1 shows (reproduced from Johnson-Laird
& Byrne, 1991, Table 3.1, p.51).

TABLE 9.1
Models for the propositional connectives. Each line
represents an alternative model, and the square brackets
indicate that the set of contingencies has been
exhaustively represented

1. p and q

Implicit model:	p	q		
Explicit model:	[p]	[q]		

2. p or q

Implicit models:	p			
		q		

	Inclusive		Exclusive	
Explicit models:	[p]	[-q]	[p]	[-q]
	[-p]	[q]	[-p]	[q]
	[p]	[q]		

3. If p then q

Implicit models:	p	q		
	...			

	Conditional		Biconditional	
Explicit models:	[p]	[q]	[p]	[q]
	[-p]	[q]	[-p]	[-q]
	[-p]	[-q]		

4. p only if q

Implicit models:	[p]	q		
	-p	[-q]		
	...			

	Conditional		Biconditional	
Explicit models:	[p]	[q]	[p]	[q]
	[-p]	[-q]	[-p]	[-q]
	[-p]	[q]		

Reasoners make conditional inferences by constructing and revising models of the premises (for details of the principles by which models are manipulated and a description of one of the computer implementations of an algorithm, see Chapter 9 in Johnson-Laird & Byrne, 1991). For example, consider the following modus ponens premises:

6.   If she drove within the speed limit then she arrived home safely.
     She drove within the speed limit.
     What, if anything, follows?

The majority of subjects in experiments assert readily the following conclusion:

7.   She arrived home safely.

(for a review of the phenomena of conditional inference, see Evans, Newstead, & Byrne, 1993). We suggested that the inference is easy to make because it can be based on the initial set of models of the conditional. The first premise is represented as indicated by the diagram in 3 earlier, and the second premise rules out any alternatives to the first model in the set:

8.   l   h

The conclusion can be reached without any need to flesh-out the initial set of models.

In contrast, the following modus tollens inference is more difficult than the modus ponens one:

9.   If she drove within the speed limit then she arrived home safely.
     She did not arrive home safely.
     What, if anything, follows?

Many subjects conclude erroneously that nothing follows from these premises (see Evans et al., 1993). The representation of the information from the second premise:

10.   not-h

is not readily integrated with the initial set of models for the first premise illustrated in the diagram in 3 earlier. Instead, it requires reasoners to flesh-out their models to be explicit, illustrated in the diagram in 4 earlier. The information in the second premise can be integrated with the information in this fully explicit set of models and it rules out all but one of the models:

11.   not-l   not-h

and so the conclusion that she did not drive within the speed limit is valid. The inference is difficult because it requires multiple models to be kept in mind, and so it places a burden on working memory. We have found that inferences that can be based on the initial set of models are easier than those that require models to be fleshed-out and that single model inferences are easier than multiple models inferences in a variety of domains (see Byrne & Johnson-Laird, 1989, 1992; Byrne, Handley, & Johnson-Laird, 1995; Byrne & Handley, in press; Johnson-Laird & Byrne, 1989; Johnson-Laird et al., 1992; Johnson-Laird, Byrne, & Tabossi, 1989).

The theory explains the established phenomena of conditional inference such as the difference in difficulty between the modus ponens and modus tollens inferences and it also makes novel predictions, some of which we have tested experimentally (see Johnson-Laird et al., 1992). One such prediction concerns the relative difficulty of inferences based on a conditional "if" which requires three models in its fully fleshed-out set as illustrated in 4 earlier, and inferences based on a biconditional "if and only if" which requires only two models in its fully fleshed-out set illustrated in 5 earlier. We accordingly predicted that the modus tollens inference—which requires reasoners to flesh-out their models to be explicit—would be easier from a biconditional than from a conditional, whereas the modus ponens inference—which can be based on the initial set of models—should be equally easy from both sorts of assertions. In collaboration with Walter Schaeken of the University of Leuven in Belgium we corroborated this prediction: reasoners made the modus tollens inference more often from the biconditional (59%) than from the conditional (37%), and they made the modus ponens inference on 97% of trials from both sorts of premises (see Johnson-Laird et al., 1992). The difference in difficulty of the modus tollens inference from the biconditional and the conditional is problematic for other theories of deduction. For example, formal inference rule theories propose that exactly the same cognitive processes are required to make a modus tollens inference from a conditional and from a biconditional: the process depends on accessing the same type of inference rules and constructing the same number and type of inference steps in a mental derivation for the modus tollens inference from both sorts of premises, and so they predict no difference between them (e.g. Braine & O'Brien, 1991; Rips, 1994).

When we developed the model theory of conditional inference we also considered the nature of the models that reasoners construct to understand a counterfactual conditional such as:

12.   If she had driven within the speed limit then she would have arrived home safely.

(Johnson-Laird & Byrne, 1991, Chapter 4). We turn now to a comparison of the similarities and differences between factual conditionals such as described in 1 earlier and counterfactual conditionals such as described in 12.

THE MODEL THEORY OF COUNTERFACTUAL CONDITIONALS

Counterfactual conditionals bring to mind not only the hypothetical situation that they describe but also the presupposed factual alternative to it. A counterfactual conditional such as 12 concerns matters that once were possible but are so no longer. The counterfactual conditional suggests that had she driven within the speed limit she would have arrived home safely, but it also conveys the presupposition that in fact she did not drive within the speed limit and she did not arrive home safely. As a result, part of the problem of counterfactual conditionals is that they seem to mean the opposite of what they assert.

Philosophers have long considered the difficulties that counterfactual conditionals pose for a general theory of conditionals (e.g. Adams, 1970; Ayers, 1965; Barwise, 1986; Chisholm, 1946). The problem is that it is not clear in what circumstances a counterfactual conditional could ever be false. First, consider a factual conditional: there are clear-cut circumstances in which a factual conditional is true and in which it is false, as the truth table in Table 9.2 illustrates. A factual conditional is true in the situation in which the antecedent is true—she drove within the speed limit, and the consequent is also true—she arrived home safely. It is equally clearly false in the situation where the antecedent is true—she drove within the speed limit, and the consequent is false—she did not arrive home safely. In the remaining two situations where she did not drive within the speed limit, the factual conditional is true (on a strict conditional interpretation). But for the

TABLE 9.2
Truth Table

She drove within the speed limit	She arrived home safely	If she drove within the speed limit then she arrived home safely
True	True	True
True	False	False
False	True	True
False	False	True

A truth table for the factual conditional "If she drove within the speed limit then she arrived home safely".

counterfactual conditional the situation is not so clear-cut. The counter-factual carries the presupposition that the antecedent is false, that is, she did not drive within the speed limit, and so it rules out the first two rows of the truth table immediately. As a result, there seem to be no situations in which the counterfactual could be false. Yet people clearly view some counter-factuals as plausible and others as less so (e.g. Miyamoto & Dibble, 1986; Miyamoto, Lundell, & Tu, 1989).

One of the most influential views of counterfactuals has been that they are understood by assessing whether the consequent is inferable from the antecedent together with relevant facts indicated by the context, by adding the antecedent hypothetically to your stock of knowledge (Ramsey, 1931). From this initial starting point, two alternative views of the meaning of counterfactuals have been developed in philosophy and psychology. Some philosophers (e.g. Chisholm, 1946; Goodman, 1973) have suggested that we understand counterfactuals by assessing whether the consequent follows from the antecedent taken together with any relevant premises. This position has been adopted by some psychologists (e.g. Braine & O'Brien, 1991) and the problem then is to specify the set of relevant premises. Other philosophers (e.g. Lewis, 1973; Pollock, 1986; Stalnaker, 1968) have suggested that we understand counterfactuals by assessing whether the consequent is true in the scenarios constructed by adding the false antecedent to the set of beliefs it recruits about the actual world, and making any necessary adjustments to accommodate the antecedent, and the problem then is to specify the most similar, minimally changed scenario in which to evaluate the consequent. The model theory of counterfactual conditionals is essentially a psychologically constrained version of this latter position (Johnson-Laird, 1986; Johnson-Laird & Byrne, 1991).

We suggested that people construct a more explicit initial set of models for a counterfactual than for a factual conditional (Johnson-Laird & Byrne, 1991). The initial set of models for a counterfactual conditional makes explicit not only the hypothesised counterfactual situation, but also the factual situation. The initial set of models for a counterfactual conditional such as:

13.   If Linda had been in Dublin then Cathy would have been in Galway.

can be captured by the following diagram:

14.   factual: not-d not-g
      counterfactual   d   g
                        ...

where "d" represents Linda is in Dublin, "g" represents Cathy is in Galway, and the models may be annotated to keep track of their epistemic status (we omit the square brackets for ease of exposition, see Johnson-Laird & Byrne, 1991, for details). The subjunctive mood and past tense of the counterfactual conditional help to convey that the hypothesised situation is no longer possible. The subjunctive mood can also be used with the present tense to convey matters that may still be possible, however remote, e.g:

15.   If the ozone layer were replenished then there would be a decrease in the incidence of cancers.

(e.g. Dudman, 1988). The same sort of models as in 14 hold for such a *semi-counterfactual* conditional, in which the hypothesised situation may still be possible.

Based on this suggested representation, Alessandra Tasso and I derived novel predictions from the model theory about the relative difficulty of inferences from factual conditionals, such as:

16.   If Linda is in Dublin then Cathy is in Galway.
       Linda is in Dublin.
       What, if anything, follows?

and semi-counterfactual conditionals, e.g:

17.   If Linda were in Dublin then Cathy would be in Galway.
       Linda is in Dublin.
       What, if anything, follows?

We predicted that certain inferences should be made with equivalent frequency from a factual conditional and a semi-counterfactual one— inferences that can be based on the initial set of models. This condition holds for the modus ponens inferences illustrated in 16 and 17 (and it also holds for the related *affirmation of the consequent* inference, which is fallacious on a conditional interpretation, see Byrne & Tasso, 1994, for details) and so we predicted no difference between factual and semi-counterfactual conditionals for these sorts of inferences. We predicted that other sorts of inferences should be made more readily from a semi-counterfactual conditional than from a factual conditional—inferences that require the more explicit representation. For example, given the premises:

18.   If Linda were in Dublin then Cathy would be in Galway.
       Cathy is not in Galway.
       What, if anything, follows?

the first premise is represented as:

19.   factual: not-d   not-g
       hypothetical: d   g
                       . . .

and the information from the second premise:

20.   factual: not-g

can be added immediately to the initial set of models. It requires that the hypothetical models be eliminated and it rules out all but the factual model:

21.   factual: not-g   not-d

There is no need to flesh-out the models to be more explicit. In contrast the modus tollens inference from a factual conditional:

22.   If Linda is in Dublin then Cathy is in Galway.
       Cathy is not in Galway.
       What, if anything, follows?

requires the initial set of models to be fleshed-out. The initial models of the factual conditional are:

23.   d   g
               . . .

and the information from the second premise:

24.   not-g

cannot be integrated readily with them. They need to be made more explicit, e.g.

25.   d   g
       not-d   not-g
       not-d   g

before the inference can be made. The more explicit representation is available in the initial set of models for the semi-counterfactual but it requires the initial set of models to be fleshed-out for the factual conditional. This condition holds for the modus tollens inference (and for the related *denial of the antecedent* inference, which is fallacious on a conditional interpretation) and so we predicted that reasoners should make more of these inferences from the semi-counterfactual than from the factual conditional.

We carried out the first psychological experiments on counterfactual deductions to test these predictions, and the results of the experiments corroborated our predictions (Byrne & Tasso, submitted). In one experiment, 80 subjects from the University of Dublin, Trinity College, each carried out a single inference based either on a factual or a semi-counterfactual conditional, and on one of the four types of inference: modus ponens, modus tollens, denial of the antecedent, or affirmation of the consequent. As Table 9.3 shows they made more modus tollens inferences— twice as many—from the semi-counterfactual than from the factual conditional, whereas they made the same frequency of modus ponens inferences from both types of conditional (see Byrne & Tasso, 1994, submitted, for details).

According to the model theory, a general theory of factual conditionals can be extended to encompass counterfactual and semi-counterfactual conditionals as well. Counterfactuals seem to mean something very different from their corresponding factual conditionals because they contain more information represented explicitly in their initial set of models. But as the results of our experiments corroborate, deductions about factual matters and deductions about imaginary possibilities may arise from the same cognitive mechanism: the ability to construct and revise mental models of the situations described. In the next section I will try to show that the initial generation of an imaginary alternative may also be guided by this same mechanism.

TOWARDS A MODEL THEORY OF THE GENERATION OF COUNTERFACTUAL SCENARIOS

When we think counterfactually in our everyday consideration of how an outcome could be undone, we mutate some aspect of the events that led to the outcome. For example, a family mourning the death of their father in a

TABLE 9.3
Percentages of four sorts of inferences made for factual and semi-counterfactual inferences (from Byrne & Tasso, 1994).

	MP	AC	MT	DA
Factual	100	30	40	40
Semi-counterfactual	90	50	80	80

MP = modus ponens, MT = modus tollens,
DA = denial of the antecedent, AC = affirmation of the consequent.

car accident may think "if only..." and complete this thought by imagining their father hadn't gone to work that day, or the other driver hadn't been on the road at the same time as him, and so on (e.g. Kahneman & Tversky, 1982). The purpose of counterfactual thinking ultimately may be to enable us to learn from our mistakes or our good fortune (e.g. Kahneman & Varey, 1990; Markman, Gavanski, Sherman, & McMullen, 1993; Roese, 1994).

When we consider *what* the mind is doing when it computes a counterfactual comparison, that is, when we try to formulate a theory at Marr's (1982) computational level, we can discern at least two major *informational* constraints (e.g. Keane, Ledgeway, & Duff, 1994). One primary constraint seems to be that counterfactual thinking is *goal-driven*, that is, people aim to construct a counterfactual scenario that is effective—events are changed in order that they will effectively undo the outcome (e.g. Wells & Gavanski, 1989). People do not consider a counterfactual scenario to be satisfactory when a change to an event nonetheless results in the occurrence of the same outcome. The second major constraint is that people construct counterfactual scenarios in which the factual situation is *recoverable* from the counterfactual one. As philosophers such as Stalnaker (1968), Lewis (1973), and Pollock (1986) have suggested, counterfactuals contain minimal mutations, that is, mutations to reality result in an imaginary scenario that is similar to or accessible from the actual situation. The most minimal mutation of a situation may be to alter the most mutable element, and so the question becomes, what are the mutable aspects of reality?

An answer to that question begins to emerge when we consider *how* people generate counterfactual alternatives to reality, that is, when we try to formulate a theory at Marr's algorithmic level. It is clear that the most mutable aspect in the mental representation of a scenario is one for which it is easy to think of alternatives (e.g. Kahneman & Miller, 1986; Kahneman & Tversky, 1982). What determines how easy it is to think of alternatives to an aspect may depend on heuristics such as the availability heuristic (Kahneman & Tversky, 1982). The availability heuristic reflects the tendency that individuals exhibit to base their judgements on the ease with which instances come to mind, not only on the retrieval of instances but also on the construction of scenarios to simulate a situation. As a result, Kahneman and Tversky (1982) have observed a differential ease of mutations: downhill changes that delete unlikely events are made more readily than uphill changes that add unlikely events, or horizontal changes that alter the value of an arbitrary variable (e.g. changing 10 minutes to 20 minutes). Why is it easier to delete aspects from a representation than to add them? Perhaps because aspects in a representation, in particular exceptional aspects, can spontaneously recruit their own norms, that is, the normal or typical value comes to mind (Kahneman & Miller, 1986; Miller & McFarland, 1986).

The sorts of mutations that reasoners make tell us about the underlying mechanism, and the mutations are principled and clear. For example, people tend to undo exceptional events rather than normal ones (e.g. Bouts, Spears, & Van der Plight, 1992; Gavanski & Wells, 1989; Kahneman & Tversky, 1982); they change the first event in a causal sequence rather than subsequent events (e.g. Wells, Taylor, & Turtle, 1987); they change events under voluntary control rather than outside it (e.g. Girotto, Legrenzi, & Rizzo, 1991); and they change actions rather than inactions (e.g. Gilovich & Medvec, 1994; Kahneman & Tversky, 1982; Landman, 1987). One effect of particular cognitive consequence is the temporality effect: people tend to undo the most recent event in a sequence of independent events. I will focus on the temporality effect for the remainder of the chapter so let me illustrate it with the following scenario from Miller and Gunasegaram (1990, p.1111):

26.   Imagine two individuals (Jones and Cooper) who are offered the following very attractive proposition. Each individual is asked to toss a coin. If the two coins come up the same (both heads or both tails), each individual wins £1,000. However, if the two coins do not come up the same, neither individual wins anything. Jones goes first and tosses a head; Cooper goes next and tosses a tail. Thus, the outcome is that neither individual wins anything.

The majority of their subjects—over 80%—judged that it was easier to undo the outcome by the alternative of Cooper tossing a head, rather than Jones tossing a tail. And as is regularly observed in studies of counterfactual thinking, a similar pattern of emotional amplification was observed: the more mutable the event, the greater its emotional impact (e.g. Landman & Manis, 1992; Gleicher et al., 1990). The subjects believed that Cooper would experience more guilt than Jones, and would be blamed more by Jones. Logically of course, neither event should be considered more mutable than the other because the scenario concerns matters of chance. Miller and Gunasegaram showed that people tended to find the more recent event more mutable in everyday situations as well, for example, when they considered how a student who failed an examination might have passed. Miller and Gunasegaram suggest that early events tend to be presupposed or taken for granted more than later events, and they argue that the temporality tendency may play a role in many everyday judgements, such as the tendency for teams to sport their faster runner last in a relay race, or for blackjack players to be averse to playing on the last box.

Why do people undo recent events? One possibility is that the temporality effect arises because of working memory constraints. People may undo the more recent event because it is more available in working memory, or it is readily accessed through a backward search through the entries to working memory. In other words, the more recent event may be "fresh" in mind. An alternative hypothesis, which I wish to advance, is that the temporality effect arises because of the nature of the mental representations that reasoners construct. In the coin-toss scenario earlier, reasoners construct a model in which they explicitly represent the situation that is described:

27.   jones -head   cooper -tail

where each individual and their coin-toss outcome is represented in the model. When they must think of ways in which the outcome could have been different they consider the counterfactual possibilities that are implicit in their models:

28.   factual: jones -head   cooper -tail
      counterfactual: . . .

They may be able to flesh them out to be fully explicit, if need be:

29.   factual: jones -head   cooper -tail
      counterfactual: jones -head   cooper -head
                        jones -tail   cooper -tail
                        jones -tail   cooper -head

They may even annotate their models to indicate the outcomes that follow from each alternative situation:

30.   factual: jones -head   cooper -tail   *lose*
      counterfactual: jones -head   cooper -head   *win*
                        jones -tail   cooper -tail   *win*
                        jones -tail   cooper -head   *lose*

The temporality tendency indicates that individuals tend to flesh-out their models to be consistent with just one of the options:

31.   factual: jones -head   cooper -tail
      counterfactual: jones -head   cooper -head
                              . . .

and the remaining counterfactual models are represented implicitly only. We suggest that people do not consider the counterfactual alternative in which the players both lose (the last in the fully fleshed-out set here) because it is not an effective counterfactual alternative—it does not undo the outcome of losing the game and so it does not satisfy the goal-driven constraint on counterfactual thinking. There are two counterfactual alternatives that do succeed in undoing the outcome:

32.	factual:	jones -head	cooper -tail
	counterfactual:	jones -head	cooper -head
		jones -tail	cooper -tail

. . .

What guides subjects' preference for the first instead of the second counterfactual alternative? The guiding principle cannot be exceptionality or norms, because there is nothing more exceptional or normal about both players picking heads rather than tails, and a toss of one sort by the first individual is unlikely to make a toss of the same sort by the second individual more "normal" or a toss of a different sort "exceptional" in the usual sense. Complementary to the recruitment of norms (e.g. Kahneman & Miller, 1986), some additional mechanism is required to explain the local allocation of mutability—the interpretation that the game is now "about" heads once the first player has tossed heads—that seems to mediate the integration of the subsequent play into the model. Nor can the guiding principle hinge solely on what is explicitly represented or focused on in the model. Complementary to focusing on aspects of the situation explicitly represented in the foreground against others in the background (e.g. Kahneman & Tversky, 1982; Legrenzi, Girotto, & Johnson-Laird, 1993), some additional mechanism is required to explain which of the two possible counterfactual alternatives is preferred.

The guiding principle underlying their preference may be that the earlier event provides the essential context for the interpretation of the subsequent events, that is, reasoners *initialise* their model by the first event. The model is defined as being about heads, say, if heads is the first toss in the game. Just as models in numerical domains are "anchored" by the earlier information—demonstrated for example by the observation that reasoners asked to estimate quickly the answer to $8 \times 7 \times 6 \times 5 \times 4 \times 3 \times 2 \times 1$ produce larger estimates than those asked to estimate the answer to $1 \times 2 \times 3 \times 4 \times 5 \times 6 \times 7 \times 8$ (Tversky & Kahneman, 1982)—a similar anchoring may occur in non-numerical domains. The initialising role of the earlier event aids the integration of information in the representation, and the construction of a coherent unified representation is critical for reasoning (see e.g. Evans et al., 1993, Chapter 6). Because reasoners construct minimal models that represent explicitly as little information as possible, some events are conferred the status of contextualising the model to constrain the interpretation of subsequent information inserted into the model. The earlier event is immutable because of its critical initialising role. The immutability of the first event ensures that the recoverability constraint is met, that is, mutations to the model of the factual situation do not damage its coherence. The immutability of the first event also results in a preference for the counterfactual alternative in which the earlier event is left untouched over the alternative in which it is mutated. The temporality effect arises because of constraints on the integration of knowledge in models.

Ronan Culhane, Alessandra Tasso, and I tested this suggestion by de-coupling the initialising or anchoring role of the first event from its position in the target sequence (Byrne, Culhane, & Tasso, 1995). Our scenarios were based on the following sort of content:

33.   Imagine two individuals (Jones and Brady) who take part in a television game show, on which they are offered the following very attractive proposition. Each individual is given a shuffled deck of cards, and each one picks a card from their own deck. If the two cards they pick are of the same colour (i.e. both from black suits or both from red suits) each individual wins £1,000. However, if the two cards are not the same colour, neither individual wins anything. Jones goes first and picks a black card from his deck. At this point, the game-show host has to stop the game because of a technical difficulty. After a few minutes, the technical problem is solved and the game can be restarted. Jones goes first again, and this time the card that he draws is a red card. Brady goes next and the card that he draws is a black card. Thus, the outcome is that neither individual wins anything.

The technical hitch device enables us to de-couple the contextualising role of the first (pre-hitch) event, and its (post-hitch) role in the target plays. In the different-context version shown in 33, the pre-hitch and post-hitch plays differ, and so we expected the temporality effect to be eliminated. In a second version, the pre-hitch and post-hitch plays were the same and we expected to observe the standard temporality effect. We corroborated these predictions in an experiment in which we gave 75 subjects from the University of Dublin, Trinity College, one scenario each based on either the different-context version or the same-context version of the story in 33, and they completed the sentence "Jones and Brady could each have won £1,000 if only one of them had picked a different card, for instance if . . ." as well as some questions about the emotions of the players (for details see Byrne, Culhane, & Tasso, submitted). As Table 9.4 shows, people exhibited the standard temporal order effect for the same-context version of the story—more subjects undid the second target event overall, by saying for example, "If only Brady had picked red" (59%) rather than the first target event, by saying for example, "If only Jones had picked black" (23%), and this effect was eliminated for the different-context version (44% vs. 42%).

These results rule out an alternative explanation of the temporality effect in terms of the event being "fresh" in working memory—if "freshness" were responsible for the effect, the temporality effect should be observed in the different-context version as well as the same-context version. It also rules out an explanation based on setting up expectations about how the game

TABLE 9.4
Counterfactual Undoing Task

	Description of cards	
Undoing choice	Black ... hitch Black ... Red (same-context)	Black ... hitch Red ... Black (different-context)
Overall second event	59	44
Overall first event	23	42

The percentages of mutations of the first event and the second for a counterfactual undoing task (from Byrne, Culhane, & Tasso, 1995).

can be won: if the mutability of the second player arose from expectations set up by the first player's choice, the temporality effect should also continue even in the different-context version. Likewise, it rules out an explanation based on the salience of counterfactual alternatives: if individuals mutate the event for which a counterfactual alternative has been made available, then the temporality effect should be reversed when the first player's post-hitch choice differs from the pre-hitch one, rather than eliminated. The temporality effect arises because the first event in an independent sequence is immutable as a result of the information-integrating function it plays in the construction of a model. Moreover, people mutate the recent *event* in the sequence regardless of the order of mention of events in the description of the sequence (Byrne, Segura, McAlinney, & Berrocal, submitted). We have implemented these processes in a computer program called IMP (for Imaginary Models Production), and we have shown experimentally that decoupling the representation-integration role of an event from its temporal order by the provision of a separate context eliminates the temporality effect. We suggest that temporal mutability emerges from a representation-integration mechanism central to the construction of minimal models.

CONCLUSIONS

An important current development in research on thinking is the attempt to extend the model theory from its base as a theory of deduction to account for other aspects of thinking, such as prediction (e.g. Rodrigo, de Vega, & Castañeda, 1992), probabilistic inference (e.g. Johnson-Laird, 1994), as well as counterfactual thinking (e.g. Byrne & Tasso, 1994; Byrne, Culhane, & Tasso, 1995). In this chapter I have tried to trace some of the links between the logical skills we engage when we make deductive inferences and the imaginative skills we engage when we create alternative realities. The model theory of conditional inference that Phil Johnson-Laird and I developed provides a general account of conditionals that encompasses not only inferences about matters of fact but also inferences about matters of possibility. The generation of imaginary counterfactual alternatives may also depend on a mechanism designed to construct and revise minimal models.

REFERENCES

Adams, E.W. (1970). Subjunctive and indicative conditionals. *Foundations of Language, 6,* 89–94.

Ayers, M. R. (1965). Counterfactuals and subjunctive conditionals. *Mind,* 347–364.

Barwise, J. (1986). Conditionals and conditional information. In E.C. Traugott, A. ter Meulen, J.S. Reilly, & C. Ferguson (Eds.), *On conditionals.* Cambridge: Cambridge University Press.

Bouts, P., Spears, R., & van der Plight, J. (1992). Counterfactual processing and the correspondence between events and outcomes: Normality versus value. *European Journal of Social Psychology, 22,* 387–396.

Braine, M.D.S., & O'Brien, D.P. (1991). A theory of IF: A lexical entry, reasoning program, and pragmatic principles. *Psychological Review, 98,* 182–203.

Byrne, R.M.J. (1989a). Suppressing valid inferences with conditionals. *Cognition, 31,* 61–83.

Byrne, R.M.J. (1989b). Everyday reasoning with conditional sequences. *Quarterly Journal of Experimental Psychology, 41A,* 141–166.

Byrne, R.M.J., Culhane, R., & Tasso, A. (1995a) The temporality effect in thinking about what might have been. In J. Moore & J. Lehman (Eds.), *Proceedings of the Seventeenth Annual Conference of the Cognitive Science Society.* Hillsdale, NJ: Lawrence Erlbaum Associates Inc.

Byrne, R.M.J., Culhane, R., & Tasso, A. (1995b). *Representational integration alters temporal mutability in imaginary counterfactual thinking.* Manuscript submitted for publication.

Byrne, R.M.J., Handley, S.J., & Johnson-Laird, P.N. (1995). Reasoning with suppositions. *Quarterly Journal of Experimental Psychology, 48A,* 915–944.

Byrne, R.M.J., & Handley, S.J. (in press). Reasoning strategies for suppositional deductions. *Cognition,* ???.

Byrne, R.M.J., & Johnson-Laird, P.N. (1989). Spatial reasoning. *Journal of Memory and Language, 28,* 564–575.

Byrne, R.M.J., & Johnson-Laird, P.N. (1992). The spontaneous use of propositional connectives. *Quarterly Journal of Experimental Psychology, 44A,* 89–110.

Byrne, R.M.J., Segura, S., McAlinney, P.H., & Berrocal, P. (1995). *Event order and temporal mutability in thinking about what might have been.* Manuscript submitted for publication.

Byrne, R.M.J., & Tasso, A. (1994). Counterfactual reasoning: Inferences from hypothetical conditionals. In A. Ram & K. Eiselt (Eds.), *Proceedings of the Sixteenth Annual Conference of the Cognitive Science Society.* Hillsdale, NJ: Lawrence Erlbaum Associates Inc.

Byrne, R.M.J., & Tasso, A. (1995). *Counterfactual conditionals: Deductive reasoning in imaginary scenarios.* Manuscript submitted for publication.

Chisholm, R.M. (1946). The contrary-to-fact conditional. *Mind, LV,* 289–307.

Dudman, V. H. (1988). Indicative and subjunctive. *Analysis, 48,* 113–122.

Evans, J.St.B.T., Newstead, S., & Byrne, R.M.J. (1993). *Human reasoning: The psychology of deduction.* Hillsdale, NJ: Lawrence Erlbaum Associates Inc.

Gavanski, I., & Wells, G.L. (1989). Counterfactual processing of normal and exceptional events. *Journal of Experimental Social Psychology, 25,* 314–325.

Gilovich, T., & Medvec, V.H. (1994). The temporal pattern to the experience of regret. *Journal of Personality and Social Psychology, 67,* 357–365.

Ginsberg, M. L. (1986). Counterfactuals. *Artificial Intelligence, 30*, 35–79.

Girotto, V., Legrenzi, P., & Rizzo, A. (1991). Event controllability in counterfactual thinking. *Acta Psychologica, 78*, 111–133.

Gleicher, F., Kost, K.A., Baker, S.M., Strathman, A.J., Richman, S.A., & Sherman, S.J. (1990). The role of counterfactual thinking in judgements of affect. *Personality and Social Psychology Bulletin, 16*, 284–295.

Goodman, N. (1973). *Fact, fiction and forecast.* (3rd Edn.), New York: Bobbs-Merrill.

Hofstadter, D.R. (1985). *Metamagical themas: Questing for the essence of mind and pattern.* London: Penguin.

Isard, S.D. (1974). What would you have done if . . .? *Journal of Theoretical Linguistics, 1*, 233–255.

Johnson, J. (1986). The knowledge of what might have been: Affective and attributional consequences of near outcomes. *Personality and Social Psychology Bulletin, 12*, 51–62.

Johnson-Laird, P.N. (1983). *Mental models.* Cambridge: Cambridge University Press.

Johnson-Laird, P.N. (1986). Conditionals and mental models. In E.C. Traugott, A. ter Meulen, J.S. Reilly, & C. Ferguson (Eds.), *On conditionals.* Cambridge: Cambridge University Press.

Johnson-Laird, P.N. (1994). Mental models and probabilistic thinking. *Cognition, 50*, 189–209.

Johnson-Laird, P.N., & Byrne, R.M.J. (1989). *Only* reasoning. *Journal of Memory and Language, 28*, 313–330.

Johnson-Laird, P.N., & Byrne, R.M.J. (1991). *Deduction.* Hove, UK and Hillsdale, NJ: Lawrence Erlbaum Associates.

Johnson-Laird, P.N., Byrne, R.M.J., & Schaeken, W. (1992). Propositional reasoning by model. *Psychological Review, 99*, 418–439.

Johnson-Laird, P.N., Byrne, R.M.J., & Tabossi, P. (1989). Reasoning by model: The case of multiple quantification. *Psychological Review, 96*, 658–673.

Kahneman, D. & Miller, D (1986). Norm theory: Comparing reality to its alternatives. *Psychological Review, 93*, 136–153.

Kahneman, D., & Tversky, A. (1982). The simulation heuristic. In D. Kahneman, P. Slovic, & A. Tversky (Eds.), *Judgement under uncertainty: Heuristics and biases* (pp.201–208). New York: Cambridge University Press.

Kahneman, D., & Varey, C.A. (1990). Propensities and counterfactuals: The loser that almost won. *Journal of Personality and Social Psychology, 59*, 1101–1110.

Keane, M.T., Ledgeway, T., & Duff, S. (1994). Constraints on analogical mapping: A comparison of three models. *Cognitive Science, 18*, 387–438.

Landman, J. (1987). Regret and elation following action and inaction: Affective responses to positive versus negative outcomes. *Personality and Social Psychology Bulletin, 13*, 524–536.

Landman, J., & Manis, J.D. (1992). What might have been: Counterfactual thought concerning personal decisions. *British Journal of Psychology, 83*, 473–477.

Legrenzi, P., Girotto, V., & Johnson-Laird, P.N. (1993). Focusing in reasoning and decision-making. *Cognition, 49*, 37–66.

Lewis, D. (1973). *Counterfactuals.* Oxford: Blackwell.

Lewis, D. (1979). Counterfactual dependence and time's arrow. *Nous, X111*, 455–476.

Markman, K.D., Gavanski, I., Sherman, S.J., & McMullen, M.N. (1993). The mental simulation of better and worse possible worlds. *Journal of Experimental Social Psychology, 29*, 87–109.

Marr, D. (1982). *Vision.* New York: Freeman.

McGill, A.L., & Klein, J.G. (1993). Contrastive and counterfactual reasoning in causal judgement. *Journal of Personality and Social Psychology, 64*, 897–905.

Miller, D.T., & Gunasegaram, S. (1990). Temporal order and the perceived mutability of events: Implications for blame assignment. *Journal of Personality and Social Psychology, 59,* 1111–1118.

Miller, D.T., & McFarland, C. (1986). Counterfactual thinking and victim compensation: A test of norm theory. *Personality and Social Psychology Bulletin, 12,* 513–519.

Miyamoto, J.M., & Dibble, E. (1986). Counterfactual conditionals and the conjunction fallacy. *Proceedings of the Eighth Annual Conference of the Cognitive Science Society.* Hillsdale, NJ: Lawrence Erlbaum Associates Inc.

Miyamoto, J.M., Lundell, J.W., & Tu, S. (1989). Anomalous conditional judgements and Ramsey's thought experiment. *Proceedings of the Eleventh Annual Conference of the Cognitive Science Society.* Hillsdale, NJ: Lawrence Erlbaum Associates Inc.

Pollock, J.L. (1986). *Subjunctive reasoning.* Dordrecht: Reidel.

Ramsey, F.P. (1931). *The foundations of mathematics and other logical essays.* London: Kegan Paul.

Rodrigo, M.J., de Vega, M., & Castañeda, J. (1993). Updating mental models in predictive reasoning. *European Journal of Cognitive Psychology, 4,* 141–157.

Roese, N.J. (1994). The functional basis of counterfactual thinking. *Journal of Personality and Social Psychology, 66,* 805–818.

Rips, L.J. (1994). *The psychology of proof.* Cambridge, MA: MIT Press.

Stalnaker, R.C. (1968). A theory of conditionals. In N. Rescher (Ed.), *Studies in logical theory.* Oxford: Basil Blackwell.

Tversky, A., & Kahneman, D. (1982). Judgement under uncertainty: Heuristics and biases. In D. Kahneman, P. Slovic, & A. Tversky (Eds.), *Judgement under uncertainty: Heuristics and biases* (pp.3–20). New York: Cambridge University Press.

Wells, G.L., & Gavanski, I. (1989). Mental simulation of causality. *Journal of Personality and Social Psychology, 55,* 161–169.

Wells, G.L., Taylor, B.R., & Turtle, J.W. (1987). The undoing of scenarios. *Journal of Personality and Social Psychology, 53,* 421–430

10 Emotions, Rationality, and Informal Reasoning

Keith G. Oatley
Ontario Institute for Studies in Education
and University of Toronto, Canada

INTRODUCTION

It is not right to pervert the judge by moving him to anger or envy or pity—one might as well warp a carpenter's rule before using it.

Aristotle, *Rhetoric*, 1354a, 24

Emotions have a bad name. We earthlings are liable to fall in love with unsuitable people, storing up misery for ourselves and our children. We visit upon others ancient psychological hurts that do not concern them. We bear disfiguring scars of warfare, products of anger and contempt.

The case against the emotions seems so overwhelming that to try and answer it may seem mischievous. Yet without denying any of the baleful effects of emotions, I will argue that there is something in emotions that is important for our humanity. Without emotions there would be no humanity and, I propose, no human ability to reason.

The Communicative Theory of Emotions

I first met Phil Johnson-Laird more than 20 years ago when he came to the Laboratory of Experimental Psychology at the University of Sussex. We were colleagues, we taught together a course on inference, we had lunches in which we talked about psychology, about language, about literature. We even played, for ourselves only, in a jazz quartet of which Phil, an accomplished pianist, was by far the most talented member—he led, wrote arrangements, and cheerfully tolerated the rest of us.

At that time, in that laboratory, we believed we were hacking out for British psychology the outlines of the new cognitive science based on computation and an understanding of inference. As Gardner (1985) correctly discerned in his history of cognitive science, emotions were eschewed in the analyses, by us and by other cognitive psychologists. Such apparently Dionysian elements seemed to have no place in the Apollonian structures of representations and inference.

When Phil left Sussex to take a position at the MRC Applied Psychology Unit in Cambridge, our friendship continued. Despite emotions being so marginal in the cognitive enterprise, he and I found ourselves viewing them from a cognitive perspective. Phil wanted to fill a gap left in his work on psychological semantics (with George Miller), and I had an aspiration, derived from theories of artificial intelligence and the problems of psychiatry, to understand the role of emotions in people's life plans.

So we started to work on what we now think of as the communicative theory of emotions. It is a cognitive theory which combines concerns for psychological semantics and planning. Its slogan is that emotions are communications to ourselves and others. Emotions are distinctive mental states that can be understood in terms of their cognitive functions. They arise from monitoring the progress of plans. People become aware of them in ways that allow significant correspondences between human intuitions about them and cognitive scientific accounts. During the last 10 years Phil and I have published together a series of papers including Oatley and Johnson-Laird (1987), Johnson-Laird and Oatley (1989), Johnson-Laird and Oatley (1992), and Oatley and Johnson-Laird (1996).

Although one of the central concerns of cognitive science is the understanding of inference, only recently has our theory come to make a contribution to this problem. In this chapter I lay out some of the directions of this contribution. I recount some steps that my colleagues and I have recently taken in applying the theory of emotions that Phil and I devised to a problem that Phil has spent most of his life on: the analysis of reasoning. In this work, and in this chapter, I concentrate only on informal reasoning, the reasoning that people do in ordinary life and in some specialised social situations (law, business communication, literature) in which there is no recourse to formal methods such as deductive logic, mathematics, or the like. I first present some issues concerning the psychology of informal reasoning, and then present two empirical studies that illuminate these issues.

REASON AND EMOTION

The emotions are all those feelings that so change men as to affect their judgments...

Aristotle, *Rhetoric*, 1378a, l. 21.

Plato and Aristotle can be thought of as beginning the study of reasoning in the Western history of ideas. Aristotle discovered the syllogism as a way of understanding valid reasoning (*Prior Analytics*), and also invented the practical syllogism as a way of conceptualising intentions to act, given a goal or value as the major premise, and a belief about some particular as the minor premise (*Nicomachean Ethics*). Phil Johnson-Laird has gone a long way in exploring both the properties of syllogistic reasoning and the psychological processes of mental models that underlie it (Johnson-Laird, 1983; Johnson-Laird & Byrne, 1991).

So where do we find work on informal reasoning? Aristotle began this too—in his book *Rhetoric*. It is no coincidence that this book contains his main account of emotions. As this work is no longer as familiar as hitherto, let me restate its central argument.

Wherever we appeal to truth there are two general cases. In the first we have an unequivocal demonstration. This is the realm of the syllogism, and of mathematics. If anyone does not accept certain demonstrable truths, then he or she had better do a bit more work on understanding logic or mathematics. In the second case, however, no unequivocal demonstration is possible, but we are still interested in the truth. So what do we do? We try to persuade ourselves and others. For Aristotle, persuasion was the means of approaching as closely to the truth as possible in those situations where exact demonstration was not possible.

So, asks Aristotle, what can we say about persuasion? First, it is essential to most practical situations, for instance in making political decisions. We can take these to include not just Political with a capital "P" as when considering whether the only alternative to socialism is barbarism, but also in politics with a small "p" as in considering whether we should hire a woman or a minority person in the next appointment in the Psychology Department. In fact the principles of persuasion are important for any practical decisions on which interested people might have more than one opinion. It is also important in certain semi-formal social situations, for instance in legal cases.

Aristotle argues that persuasion depends on just three issues (1356a). First, persuasion depends on the speaker. In general people believe a good person rather than a bad one, someone public-spirited rather than someone self-interested, and so forth. Second, persuasion depends on the frame of mind of the hearers, specifically on the emotions that any persuasive speech may set up in them: "our judgements when we are pleased and friendly are not the same as when we are pained and hostile" (1358a, l. 14). Third, persuasion depends on what is said, on the qualities of the argument to arrive at a truth, or an apparent truth. Notice three matters.

1. The Extent of the Imperfectly Knowable

As soon as we see Aristotle's setting out of the grounds of rhetoric, particularly if we compare it with the domain of logic, e.g. of syllogistic reasoning in the *Prior Analytics*, it is clear that the rhetorical is a large area as compared with the perfectly demonstrable. Let us put it like this. If an individual human life were a path a kilometre long, then even in the most favourable cases, beliefs and the decisions derived by unequivocal demonstrations may guide us—what?—a few centimetres along this way? A metre or two? There might be an endgame of chess here, a choice there to buy a product from this store rather than that one because exactly the same thing without any relevant side-effects was 10% cheaper, an occasional execution of a skill completely learned and with all the considerations exactly understood. For the most part, however, the matters we need to know are too many, too uncertain, too amorphous, to allow any complete and effective application of logic, be it Aristotle's, or anyone else's.

Artificial Intelligence can be thought of as the domain of fully rational solutions to knowledge-based problems. As a source of models of human inference it has tended to overestimate the number and pervasiveness of problems for which there are fully rational solutions in which we know enough or have enough resources to generate full demonstrations in advance of decision making.

2. The Role of Emotions in Rationality

A general assumption in Western thought has been that whereas thinking is rational, emotions are irrational. This idea was entertained by Plato, with influential results on subsequent Western intellectual history. Nearer our own time it was given a fillip by Darwin (1872) who, in writing the most important scientific book on emotions yet produced, characterised emotions as deriving from beasts and infants. Long ago, in our evolutionary history and in the history of our individual development, the expressions that we now recognise as emotional had functions. But in adulthood these expressions occur—for Darwin this was their very definition—"though they may not ... be of the least use" (p.28). In other words, although expressions of emotion are largely involuntary, as adults we should have grown out of them; they are interesting to students of evolution as indications of the difficulties of deleting once-useful procedures from the programmes of our behavioural repertoire.

Aristotle's approach to emotions is quite different. In the *Rhetoric*, he explains emotions, in a matter of fact way, as types of judgement. Anger, for instance, he defines as: "an impulse, accompanied by pain, to a conspicuous revenge for a conspicous slight directed without justification towards what concerns oneself or what concerns one's friends" (1378a, l. 31. This and other translations from *Rhetoric* in this chapter are by W. R. Roberts, taken from the Random House edition, 1954).

Aristotle's idea is that emotions are judgements about events that are "conspicuous" and relate to goals—"what concerns oneself or what concerns one's friends". The role of emotions in adult human life, in relation to goals, has begun to be explored in intelligent systems, human and computational (Simon, 1967).

The argument goes like this (Oatley, 1989, 1992). It is related to the considerations given under heading 1. When it comes to human decisions about action in the world, there are three impediments to making perfectly rational decisions:

(a) Limited knowledge and resources. In most parts of the environment humans simply do not know enough to predict what will happen following this or that action; our mental models are almost always incomplete and sometimes inaccurate, and our resources of time, materials, etc., are inevitably limited.

(b) Multiple goals. Wherever a human agent has several goals there may be no solution that will satisfy all or even several of them with full rationality. Oatley and Larocque, (1995) have recently found that people very frequently do have several goals when undertaking plans, and that the incompatibilities among them are associated with making errors.

(c) Distributed agency. Many human actions are performed not singly but in relation to others. The human species is one that compensates for limitations in individual resources by distributing planning and action among several agents. But in adopting this kind of solution to problems of limitation of resources, the problems of insufficient or inaccurate knowledge and of multiple goals increase, because for each agent part of the relevant knowledge and some of the goals that affect action will be held by other people.

It is possible to imagine various kinds of fully rational being—De Sousa (1987) has an argument similar to the one that follows, and I have been influenced by his analysis. One kind of intelligent being, a robot for instance, can be fully rational within a particular environment; the trick is to limit the world in which it works, and the aspects of the world that can impinge on it. Certain insects are a bit like robots. A female tick for instance, lives in a very simplified world. It responds like a computational production system made up of elements such as: "if event A, do action B". The female tick is equipped with specific responses to specific stimuli. So if a sensor detects butyric acid in the air, the tick lets go of the branch on which it is hanging. Butyric acid (the stimulus) occurs in the sweat of mammals and diffuses into the air. The response (letting go of the branch) therefore gives the tick a good chance of landing on a mammal passing under the tree or bush. Then another stimulus, increased temperature, triggers burrowing through the fur towards the skin. So the tick too is fully rational within its narrowly defined sensory and motor universe.

Similarly a god could be fully rational but in a more complex universe. We might say such a being would be omniscient (with perfect mental models) and omnipotent (with no limitations of resources).

But we human beings are neither ticks nor gods. We are somewhere in between. That is to say we do have mental models, and we do act with intentions, and we do have some resources to enable us to carry out these intentions. But the results of our actions are not always as expected. At the junctures of our plans, as we assess the effects of actions or of events bearing on our goals, emotions often occur. We feel happy at having achieved a subgoal, sad because a goal or a valued friend has been lost, angry at a frustration caused by some other agent occupying part of the area in which we are working, and so on.

Emotions, then, as Phil Johnson-Laird and I have postulated, arise from specific mechanisms that monitor the inner and outer worlds for events relevant to each goal–plan complex. Figure 10.1 illustrates the mechanism. The effects of the monitoring systems are to communicate to all parts of the cognitive system any "conspicuous" events related to "concerns".

It has been advantageous during evolution for events that impinge on goals to elicit attention. So the emotion signal is a bit like the sound of a burglar alarm, pervasive and attention-provoking. Something sets it off, but in itself it is without propositional information about what the event was. In the case of emotions, usually the non-propositional signal is accompanied by a signal carrying propositional information about what caused the emotion, and to what object the emotion is directed. So we feel the emotion and some of its effects on our cognitive structure, and we normally know what it is about.

In general, if a conspicous event (for instance, the outcome of an action) makes it discriminably more likely that a goal will be achieved (e.g. we take a step in reasoning towards a solution of a problem that concerns us) then a non-specific signal is propagated throughout the cognitive system. It sets the system into a mode to continue in that goal–plan complex, not backtracking, largely ignoring difficulties, using resources that are to

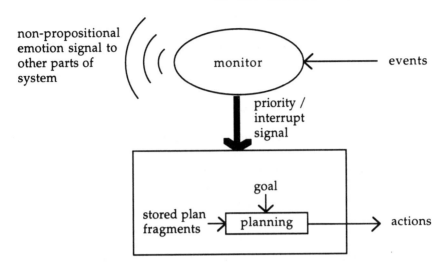

FIG. 10.1. Diagram of Oatley and Johnson-Laird's proposed system that monitors progress towards a goal, and transmits a non-propositional emotion signal on detecting any significant change of progress.

hand, and trying to assimilate future events to the plan. Phenomenologically we experience this as happiness and enthusiasm.

Where some event occurs that signals that a goal or plan is less likely to succeed than was expected, then the system is set into a different mode which we experience as a negative emotion: sadness when a goal is lost, anger when a plan is frustrated but can perhaps be reinstated (Stein, Trabasso, & Liwag, 1993), fear when any active or latent goal is threatened, or when a goal conflict is revealed.

Each of these modes—happiness, sadness, anger, fear, and a few others—is a configuration of the cognitive system that has evolved to meet the particular kind of event in relation to a goal (e.g. subgoals being achieved, goal loss, etc.). Fear, for instance, which occurs when any important goal is threatened, is the mode in which current actions are interrupted, a readiness occurs to escape or defend ourselves, attention is directed to monitoring the environment carefully for all signs of danger and avenues of safety, and results of recent actions are checked. It is a mode in which the cognitive system is specialised to respond to events of the dangerous kind. Notice that it is good for this purpose, but it tends to exclude other purposes, for instance creative problem solving, or productive social interaction.

Johnson-Laird and I have postulated that there have been recurrences of certain events in relation to important goals (achievements, losses, dangers, etc.) throughout mammalian evolution, and emotions have emerged as ways of dealing with such events.

Damasio (1994) has found that some patients with damaged frontal lobes suffer deficits both in emotions and in social planning, and proposed that these deficits have a common cause. He argues that when we plan our lives we do not consider decisions that would be socially punishing, because the emotion of fear blocks them off from consideration. By contrast, other directions are emotionally attractive. For Damasio, emotional events are experienced as bodily reactions. He calls them "somatic markers", which can be learned. So, for instance, in considering decisions, any outcome of a kind that has previously been bad occurs as a mental conditioned avoidance: "you experience as an unpleasant gut feeling" (Damasio, 1994, p.173).

Oatley and Jenkins (1996, p.123) have proposed a slight amendment to Damasio's idea, in terms of metaphor:

> Think of decision-making about your life as exploring within a landscape in which height indicates emotional difficulty. Mountains make progress in some directions hard: you might have to climb against steep gradients of fear, or potential loss. Fertile valleys are attractive and indicate easier going, helped by familiarity, by roads, by signposts, by people, and other aspects of culture.

So emotions are not as such irrational; they are heuristics that limit search space (one of the classical problems of cognitive science) and prompt classes of action when no fully rational solutions are available. It is our possession of emotions that allows us and other mammals to occupy the niches of complex environments, which include social interaction. We are somewhere between ticks and gods. Let me try to clarify this by giving two examples.

First, falling in love: in Western society falling in love is the event that signals the recognition of a person as a sexual partner, and acceptance to share economic resources for most of a lifetime. But of course we cannot foresee how lives will turn out, or what aspects of character certain events will develop. Nevertheless we have to choose. There is no rational method of making such choices; in Western culture the idea is that we make the choice by falling in love.

Second, anger: anger occurs typically between people who know each other. The typical event is when person X, let's say Xavier, does something that person Y, Yolande, finds hurtful. Here is an example from a corpus collected by Oatley and Larocque (1995). We asked people to keep structured diaries of incidents in which something went wrong in some plan or arrangement with another person. In this incident the subject keeping the diary, Yolande, waited in a restaurant for her colleague Xavier. She waited for half an hour. He did not arrive. She returned to her office, where she shortly afterwards received a phone call: it was Xavier asking where she was. He had been waiting for her for an hour—in a restaurant in the same chain as that in which Yolande had waited, but in a different location. He had forgotten that they had decided not to go to his preferred location in the suburbs, because her other appointments that day were downtown. Xavier apologised, and they rescheduled the appointment. Yolande was angry; she explained that she had never been stood up before. In this episode of anger Xavier and Yolande made a repair to the their plan, by rescheduling. More importantly, despite the repair to the plan, despite Xavier's phone call, despite his apology, despite his having waited for an hour, what the incident did for Yolande was to invoke a piece of schematic knowledge about being stood up. Into her model of him she compiled the attribute "untrustworthy".

What anger did in this example—a typical result of the effects of this emotion—was to prompt Yolande to focus not so much on the plan or the error, but on the ongoing relationship with the planning partner. She adjusted her model and expectations of him in the ongoing relationship. The emotion occurred because of ordinary human difficulties in coordinating plans with another person. Something imperfect happened. It is not clear whether there would be a fully rational response to the situation: if Xavier left after 30 minutes, she would not know whether he would turn up after 31 minutes, or whether he had had an accident, etc. Neither is full rationality easily possible in the aftermath, although Xavier and Yolande did effect a repair by rescheduling their lunch meeting.

Certainly it seems that the interpretation "being stood up" was not rational, as it imputes an intention to Xavier, and all the evidence was that no such intention was present. But we human animals can readily understand that for Yolande the juncture would be marked by anger, and that this emotion then constrained the repertoire of actions and interpretations of the event. We can appreciate how the incident and its emotional repercussions might have continuing effects on the relationship, the terms of which were (for Yolande at least) adjusted, so that they would constrain future decisions concerning Xavier.

3. The Social Nature of Most Informal Reasoning

Perhaps the most radical proposal of Aristotle about the nature of informal reasoning is that it is social. The cognitive revolution rode a wave of understanding of certain aspects of cognition. The focus was on mental representations and processes of an individual in relation to some object in the world. Considerable progress was made on the cognitive bases of language, vision, problem solving... Until recently the social nature of most cognition was rather neglected. This has begun to change, (Oatley, 1991; Solomon, 1993).

Aristotle was clear that most informal reasoning is done in situations where two or more agents, with different concerns, knowledge, and resources, strive to come to some common belief, or agree a common goal. Hence rhetoric—one person speaks to persuade others, then another speaks, in debate, until there is a resolution. The object is not to pervert anyone's judgement: "one might as well warp a carpenter's rule before using it" (Aristotle, *Rhetoric*, 1354a, 24), but to approach a truth, to come to a common judgement, to make a joint decision when exact demonstrations are not available. So we can say that rhetoric concerns the informal reasoning that we use most of the time.

The incident just described, between Yolande and Xavier, is typical of the domain of informal reasoning. It involved, as Aristotle stated in the *Rhetoric*, speakers and their attributes as compiled into mental models of recipients (good, trustworthy), emotions of recipients (anger, anxiety), and the arguments that could be put (apology, evidence of good faith in having waited in another restaurant, the making of a phone call).

The event of the bungled lunch meeting did not occur in a typical rhetorical situation such as a political debate or a law court. But this means merely that in confining his remarks to rhetorical situations such as political speeches and legal arguments Aristotle may have encircled a group of cognate events too narrowly. Had he included other kinds of everyday reasoning, his proposed analysis into speaker characteristics, emotions of recipients, and attributes of the argument would still be valid and useful.

The conclusion, then, is that to make a good start at understanding informal reasoning we must see it as primarily social. Neisser (1988) has described a set of psychological situations in which there are two people (and their relation to each other), plus some third person or thing which is an object of their attention and concern. Such situations, I believe, will provide subject matter for the cognitive psychology of the 21st century.

The person usually credited with seeing the importance of the social in thinking is Vygotsky (1962). His situations of two-persons-and-an-object were, classically, a child, a teacher, and something being learned. He argued that thinking is the inner enactment of dialogue first experienced between people in the course of early development, and then capable of being applied to objects by the individual.

Two further cases of distributed cognition were pointed out by Ed Hutchins, in a manuscript paper circulated in 1989 (cited by Oatley, 1991). In both situations there is very explicit a concern for truth. Both are, as it were, social inventions that offer a solution to the limitations of human rationality by means of distributed cognition—legal trials with prosecution and defence, and institutional science.

In the legal system, no-one now believes it likely that truth on which justice depends will be arrived at when one person is both prosecutor and judge. So, we have evolved a distributed system (there are certain national variations). One person appears for the prosecution, another for the defence, and a third person or group of people decide on a verdict. Liberal democratic societies believe it worth supporting such an elaborate and expensive system, because we think it more likely that truth and justice will be approached using such a system than with some other system. Here the extension of Aristotle's arguments by Quintillian is instructive, emotion is important in order for a judge, or jury, to appreciate events in their full impact. Quintillian (circa 90, p.393) a Roman expositor of Aristotle's rhetoric explains how to argue in a law court:

> Suppose we are complaining that our client has been beaten. We must first speak of the act itself; we shall then proceed to point out that the victim was an old man, a child, a magistrate ... and that the assailant was a worthless and contemptible fellow, or (to take the opposite case) was in a position of excessive power ... the hatred excited by the act will be enhanced if it was committed in the theatre, in a temple, or at a public assembly, and if the blow was given not in mistake or in a moment of passion or, if it was the result of passion was quite unjustifiable, being due to the fact that the victim had gone to the assistance of his father or....

The plaintiff's counsel must not only refer to what happened, but allow the judge to feel what it was like to be this victim with a vivid elicitation of the emotions of the incident. The defence make a different case—so the judge can feel that too. The judge's task is to reconcile these two partial mental models, in relation to the constraints of written law.

In science too, one person puts forward some evidence and a piece of rhetorical argument concerning it, another may present other evidence and perhaps a counterargument, and yet a third person, perhaps the editor of a journal or the writer of a textbook, decides what will have a chance of becoming influential. Again, because we do not know enough, we erect an elaborate system not for deciding the truth but for getting closer to it. Recently, moreover, Dunbar (1993) has shown how this distributed system works in practice in four top molecular biology laboratories that work on mechanisms of cancer, AIDS, etc. Dunbar found that much of the conceptual change that occurred was traceable to the regular laboratory meetings of seven to thirty people in which the scientists made presentations to the rest of the group. One of the processes that led to conceptual change Dunbar calls "regional analogy". When there was a result that was difficult to understand, some contradiction, then analogies to what was known in another biochemical system, or from some other related approach to research, or from some other organism were suggested by listeners to the presentation, and these analogies led to conceptual change.

Second, Dunbar found that confirmation bias, frequently found in studies of thinking, and linked, I believe, to the emotion of happiness and enthusiasm for one's own current beliefs and plans, was counteracted by other people at the laboratory meetings. An example, described by Dunbar in departmental colloquia, although not in detail in the only paper so far published on this work, occurred when a scientist presented some of his results and said there were aspects of them he could not understand. Another scientist, quickly joined by others, proposed an alternative interpretation. Dunbar says the new explanation became the basis of an important advance, but it took the original presenter, who as we might say was emotionally attached to his original view, two weeks before he could understand this alternative explanation, or accept it.

Science in general would not work with individual knowers and doers. Its cognition is necessarily distributed. Each of us has a role in this process of gradual approach to truth, and because our work is of concern to us, emotions, positive such as the excitement when we realise we are onto something, and negative as when we angrily seek to rebut alternative explanations. None of us embodies, let alone reaches, the truth as a whole. It is the social system with its rhetorical structures of informal reasoning, in science assisted by more formal means, that enables truths to be approached. Emotions are part of the process. The distributed system is such as to allow us to move beyond what Dyer (1987) correctly called the "local rationality" of emotions, to something more global, i.e. a generalised scientific truth.

There are many other forms of distributed cognition in Western society. Let me mention just one more: an author writes a story, play, or novel, and this is then read by a reader. Again, here is Neisser's structure of two cognitive agents and a shared object. Again, we have the joint possibility of both experiencing emotions (as Aristotle pointed out in *Poetics*), and also of approaching truths about ourselves and others.

TWO EMPIRICAL EXPLORATIONS

When people are feeling friendly and placable, they think one sort of thing; when they are feeling angry they think either something totally different or the same thing with a different intensity.
Aristotle, *Rhetoric*, (1377b, l. 31).

The conclusion from the consideration of the previous section is not that emotions are destructive of reason, rather they are its foundation—but they work best towards rationality in certain circumstances, notably in social settings when some degree of dialogue and reflection occurs. They are urgent, and because of the constraints they put on cognitive structure they are necessarily selective. What this means is that to contribute to rationality they are best set in a social relation, as when one person shares emotions by discussing them with another (emotions are typically shared, as Rimé, Mesquita, Philippot, & Boca, 1991, have found), when someone is moved by something he or she has read and reflects upon it, or in settings like institutional science or the law.

In order to understand such issues more fully we need to know empirically what the effects of emotions are on reasoning, social interaction, judgement, and so forth.

The area in which this issue has been most extensively explored recently is within social psychology. There has been a growing interest in effects of emotion (also referred to as mood) on judgement. Experiments have been conducted in which moods have been induced by music, by watching movies, and otherwise. Evidence supports the theoretical claim that in a positive mood, since one is attaining one's goals, there is little need to engage in cognitive effort unless required to do so by other currently active goals. Because events are going as planned, short-cuts are preferred to effortful judgemental strategies (Mackie & Worth, 1989). At the same time, as an aspect of making progress towards a goal, new procedures and possibilities are explored (Schwartz & Clore, 1988). When in a positive mood creative thinking is increased because one is willing to take risks (Isen & Geva, 1987; Isen, Johnson, Mertz, & Robinson, 1985), since the current situation is considered safe. Also more positive information is brought to mind and the emotion itself is used as input to the cognitive processing in use (Martin, Ward, Achee, & Wyer, 1993).

By contrast, negative emotional states occur when goals are not being approached or attained, or when threat is perceived. Motivation therefore shifts to changing the current situation. This involves being systematic and careful so that further loss or danger does not occur. In a negative mood, one is unlikely to take risks in a situation that is already perceived as problematic (Mathews, 1993). Negative moods increase the use of detail-oriented, analytical processing strategies. Like positive mood, information about negative mood can be used as input to the cognitive processing strategy being used (Clore & Parrott, 1991; Schwartz & Bless, 1991). An excellent review of this area and a theoretical proposal is by Forgas (1995).

Study of Juror Reasoning

Here is a brief account of a study of reasoning of the kind jurors undertake at criminal trials. The study was designed by Seema Nundy and myself, was carried out by Seema Nundy, and will be published shortly (Nundy & Oatley, in preparation). Juror reasoning takes place in a forum of distributed cognition, with the verdict and the sentence determined respectively by jury and judge. It involves participation of prosecution and defence counsels, and the evidence of witnesses. Juries and judges are therefore required to form and then integrate two competing incomplete mental models of a situation. Based on adversarial presentations, in which attempts are typically made on one side to ascribe intent and method to the defendant, and on the other side to deny the possibility of such intent and method, the jury is asked to render a verdict.

Research Questions. As the type of reasoning that a jury engages in uses both incomplete mental models and distributed cognition, and as legal reasoning was one of Aristotle's principal concerns in the *Rhetoric* it seemed that moods would play a role in jurors' reasoning. Based on previous research on effects of mood induction on reasoning about arguments (Mackie & Worth, 1991; Schwartz & Bless, 1991), therefore, we formed the following main hypothesis. Subjects in whom a happy mood had been induced would employ short-cut strategies to reach a verdict in a jury reasoning task, and subjects given a sad mood induction would be more systematic and analytic in their reasoning.

Method and Procedure. There were 44 subjects, 32 from a community college and 12 from a graduate school. They were randomly assigned to a mood induction condition: happy or sad.

Mood inductions. Moods were induced by taking subjects to a separate classroom, in small groups, and showing them a 10-minute video made up of scenes from a commercial movie. For the happy induction subjects were shown a 10-minute selection of scenes from *Splash*, and for the sad induction subjects were shown a 10-minute selection of scenes from *Sophie's Choice*.

Mood manipulation checks. Before viewing the movies subjects filled out a pre-induction questionnaire which asked for an indication of the intensity of current mood, on 11-point scales (0 = mood not noticeable, 10 = as intense as I have felt in my life), with separate scales for happiness, sadness, anger, fear, disgust, and "any other kind of emotion". After a distractor task of rating the movie they had seen, subjects completed a post-induction mood questionnaire similar to the pre-induction questionnaire. They then completed the juror reasoning task (see next para.), and finally they were given a post-task mood questionnaire.

Juror reasoning task. Subjects were given a condensed version of a trial transcript based on a real trial in which a female defendant was accused of murdering her husband by shooting him one night after a small party at the couple's house. The defendant claimed she shot her husband in self-defence. The transcript included expert testimony by a witness who described battered woman syndrome and its effects. After reading the transcript, subjects were given the judge's instructions which outlined the differences between possible verdicts, and the considerations affecting each verdict.

After reading the transcript and judge's instructions, the transcript but not the judges instructions was removed, and subjects were asked to do a reasoning task about the evidence. This consisted of giving a verdict, an explanation of how they chose it, and a rating of how certain they were that their verdict was correct. Then they were asked to complete a series of 9-point scales, only one of which I will discuss here—a scale in which subjects rated how much they identified with the accused in her actions. While completing the reasoning task and these scales, subjects could not refer back to the trial transcript; hence all responses were based on memory of the evidence.

Categorisation of reasoning and reliability check. The explanations of how subjects chose their verdicts were categorised as short-cut or analytic according to whether subjects were perfunctory in reaching the verdict—for instance paying attention only to how they perceived the accused—or reasoned analytically explaining the steps of their thinking and the considerations they had used. Responses in which the subject had analysed the situation, interpreted the judge's instructions, and used rather than merely repeated the facts of the case, were coded as analytic. Categorisations were also made independently by a second rater. The categorisations were reliable, with 40 out of 44 categorisations (91%) being the same between the two raters.

Results. The mood manipulation check was satisfactory: the happy induction produced a mean of 4.9 on the happiness scale as compared with 1.0 on the sadness scale. The sad induction a mean of 6.7 on the sad scale, and 2.8 on the happy scale.

In Table 10.1 you may see the main result: more subjects who received the happy induction reasoned analytically, and more subjects who received the sad induction reasoned using a short-cut. This difference was significant (χ^2 7.5, *df* 1, *P* < 0.01). There were no verdicts of murder in the first degree.

TABLE 10.1
Juror Reasoning Study

Reasoning style	Happy induction	Sad induction
Short-cut	5	17
Analytic	14	8
Totals	22	22

Numbers of subjects in Nundy and Oatley's study of juror reasoning showing different styles of reasoning (short-cut or analytic) following a mood manipulation (happy or sad).

Those who reasoned analytically were more likely than those who reasoned by means of a short-cut to render a verdict of murder in the second degree, as compared with self defence ($F=4.77$, $df=1$, $P<0.05$). The main result, an increase in analytic reasoning by those who received the happy induction, exactly contradicted our hypothesis based on the kinds of results found by social psychologists who have investigated judgements of the persuasiveness of arguments about, for instance, the advisability of legislation against the pollutants that cause acid rain (Mackie & Worth, 1989). So far as we know, the general results of such experiments have been that people who received happy inductions tended to reason by means of short-cuts, and those who received sad inductions tended to reason more analytically. Nundy and I have two comments and an explanation.

The first comment is that the social psychologists such as Mackie and Worth (1989) and Schwartz and Bless (1991) may have touched on only some aspects of the influence of mood on judgement. In other words, although effects of mood on social judgements are readily found, they are more sensitive to context than had been thought. Our results suggest that subjects who had the happy mood induction can perfectly well employ strategies that in the literature on social judgements are called "analytic". This suggests, perhaps, that the way in which emotions affect people may depend on the task at hand. Perhaps in the social psychological experiments where more short-cut reasoning has been found following happy inductions, the tasks had no particular meaning for the subjects (e.g. judgements about acid rain), and decisions are not consequential. In our study the subjects were quite highly involved.

The second comment is that our result may have been affected by the kind of induction used. Although our method, based on showing excerpts from the movies *Splash* and *Sophie's Choice* was the standard one in experiments on the effects of mood on judgement, it may have been that in our experiment the meaningful content of the movies, in particular the content of *Sophie's Choice*, in which a woman is subjected by a Nazi SS officer to a choice of saving one or other of her two children, may have induced thought as well as a mood. In inducing the mood, the excerpt we used was certainly effective: there was a large effect on our mood manipulation check scale for sadness. Personally I can vouch that I found myself feeling sad and reflective about the human condition for several hours after seeing this clip. But the mood was not content-free. It included (for me) a compelling consideration of the unfairness of a male world to women, and it seems likely that this kind of effect also occurred for others who saw the movie segment. It may be that this heightened the identification with the female defendant in the murder trial. In order to link our kind of result on reasoning specifically to mood (rather than, for instance to analogical semantic content) therefore, we would have to run a study in which mood was manipulated independently of any meaningful content, for instance by music, or by activating one side of the cortex rather than the other by muscular contractions (Schiff & Lamon, 1989).

Our explanation of the result is that people who had the sad induction (seeing *Sophie's Choice*) were more likely to identify with the woman defendant in the trial, and having done so, they were more likely to reason by means of a short-cut. On the 9-point scales that subjects completed in which we asked about identification, we found that those who reasoned by means of a short-cut were much more likely to have identified with the accused woman's actions ($F = 11.9$, $df\ 1$, $P < 0.01$). As Aristotle might put it, a state of mind had been induced, so that some subjects were more liable to identify with the accused and to think about the case in a certain way, which was more compelling and seemed more appropriate to them, than going more analytically through a legal argument.

Study of Emotions and Inference in Reading a Short Story

In the second study that I shall describe briefly, emotions and moods occurred not by means of an independent induction, but in what might be thought of as the ordinary way, during the reading of a short story. The study was conceived in association with Seema Nundy and Laurette Larocque. It was carried out by Seema Nundy, and will be published shortly (Oatley, Nundy, & Larocque, in preparation). The story, chosen by Laurette Larocque was Russell Banks's *Sarah Cole: A type of love story*. It is about a man called Ron who is a New England lawyer, who thinks himself good looking. At a bar one evening an unattractive woman, Sarah, comes to talk to him, on a dare from her friends. A sexual relationship begins, and lasts a few months. Ron tires of Sarah, and cruelly ends the relationship calling her degrading names. Years later Ron recognises that he loved Sarah, and feels in retrospect that he killed her on the evening when he broke up with her. The story is, in the words of its first-person narrator: "an attempt to understand what happened between [him] and Sarah Cole."

Method and Procedure. Subjects were 22 third-year undergraduates. They each completed a pre-reading emotion diary, to record the type, intensity, and duration, of any emotion or mood they were feeling before reading.

Questions about emotions and reasoning about the story. We asked subjects (individually) to read the Sarah Cole story, then at a certain point, just before the relationship between Sarah and Ron becomes explicitly sexual, we asked them to stop reading and answer two questionnaire items about their emotion: what emotion they were experiencing at that moment in the story, and to rate its intensity on a 0–10 scale. Subjects were asked to write what they thought would happen next in the story. Then they finished reading the story and, after they had done so, they filled out a post-reading emotion diary similar to the pre-reading diary, and answered three interpretive questions, as follows:

Question 1: From the narrator's point of view, why do you think the story says "she's transformed into the most beautiful woman he had ever seen"?
Question 2: From the narrator's point of view, why do you think the story says "It's not as if she has died, it's as if he has killed her"?
Question 3: What do you think the meaning of the story is from the narrator's point of view?

In this study induction of emotion and judgement were more closely bound together than in the traditional social psychological experiment. We chose the Sarah Cole story because it had been found in our previous studies to elicit strong emotions in the readers, including negative emotions such as anger, and sometimes disgust.

Categorisation of responses and reliability. Seema Nundy's idea was to categorise subjects' answers to each of the three interpretive questions as involving either forward chaining (reasoning forward from events towards a goal) or backward chaining (reasoning backwards from an effect towards its antecedents). Two raters, blind to what emotions the subject had experienced, categorised the interpretive answers in this way. There was 91% agreement.

Results. Our main result was that sadness was associated with backward chaining, and anger with forward chaining. This same association between the type of emotion experienced by the reader, and the type of reasoning in response was found for each of the three interpretive questions we asked: see Table 10.2. Chi-square analyses on responses these questions gave $P < 0.02$ for each question. We follow Camilli and Hopkins (1978) who have shown that chi-square analyses, without continuity correction, give accurate estimates of P values in 2×2 contingency tables, even with expected values as low as 1 in any cell.

Implications of the Study on Reasoning About the Sarah Cole Story. In empirically investigating readers' reasoning about stories, we have at our potential disposal the complete set of factors set out by Aristotle as influencing rhetorical persuasiveness: (a) effects of the speaker, author, or narrator, (b) effects of the emotions aroused in the recipient, and (c) effects of the argument itself. In this study we measured only the effects of emotions, arising directly from reading the story, on the subjects' reasoning, but there is no reason why other effects should not be sought within this

TABLE 10.2
Short Story Study

Type of emotion		Type of reasoning	
		Forward chaining	Backward chaining
Question 1.	Sadness	0	5
	Anger	4	0
Question 2.	Sadness	0	5
	Anger	4	1
Question 3.	Sadness	1	4
	Anger	4	0

The numbers of subjects in Oatley, Nundy, and Larocque's study who felt sad or angry after reading "Sarah Cole," cross tabulated with whether they engaged in forward or backward chaining in response to three questions about the story. (NB some of the 22 subjects had other emotions than sadness or anger, and some were classified as "not engaging in reasoning" in response to the questions.)

kind of paradigm, altering, for instance, the character of the narrator (a), and altering the material available to the reader (c). We also think that alongside independent manipulation of mood, it is worth studying emotions that are closely tied to the objects about which inferences are made, as when a person reads a story, and both feels an emotion while reading and then makes inferences about the story.

Our result fits very well with the kind of theory of emotions that Phil Johnson-Laird and I have proposed. Sadness is an emotion of loss. It involves thinking backwards about a result that cannot be altered, in order to try and make sense of its antecedents. By contrast anger is an emotion of frustration, and prompts attempts, as Aristotle pointed out, at revenge or at reinstating the goal or plan that has been interfered with. This in turn implies thinking forward from the present, constructing plans about what to do about the situation.

CONCLUSION

[people] choose their means with reference to their ends.
Aristotle, *Rhetoric*, 1366a, l. 9.

The study of informal reasoning is not new but, as compared with the study of formal reasoning within cognitive science, it is undeveloped. We have no doubt that some of the same apparatus that has been found so useful in studies of formal reasoning, for instance the theory of mental models as developed by Phil Johnson-Laird, will be useful in understanding informal reasoning.

The study of informal reasoning will, however, involve at least two further elements that have not been traditional in cognitive science. To avoid them will make the study of informal reasoning less satisfying and less accurate. The first is that informal reasoning is typically social: one person says things that affect the mental state of another. Sometimes (as in psychotherapy or in some kinds of confiding), in addition, what is said to another also affects how one thinks about an issue oneself. The second is that in the typical social interaction, not just truth values but goals are involved. Moreover the goals of more than one participant must be considered. Where goals are involved, so too are emotions, those states that, as Johnson-Laird and I have proposed, monitor events for their implications on goals.

Emotions are elements in reasoning that usefully limit the search space of a finite agent who has goals, preconceptions, and limited resources of time, abilities, and knowledge. Emotions bias thinking in this way or that. A godlike reasoner with an interest only in truth would not need emotions. But for we earthlings, in our limitations and aspirations, emotions are not in opposition to rationality. They are heuristics that help us to make occasional leaps in life where no rational structures have yet been built to bridge the ravines of our ignorance.

ACKNOWLEDGEMENT

My thanks to the Social Science and Humanities Research Council of Canada for a grant that partially supported this work.

REFERENCES

Aristotle *Complete works. Revised Oxford translation in 2 Volumes* (1984 edn.). Princeton, NJ: Princeton University Press.

Aristotle *Rhetoric and Poetics* (Trans. W.R. Roberts). (1954). New York: Random House.

Camilli, G., & Hopkins, K.D. (1978). Applicability of Chi-square to 2 × 2 contingency tables with small expected cell frequencies. *Psychological Bulletin, 85,* 163–167.

Clore, G.L., & Parrott, W.G. (1991). Moods and the vicissitudes: Thoughts and feelings as information. In J.P. Forgas (Ed.), *Emotion and social judgements* (pp.107–123). Oxford: Pergamon.

Damasio, A.R. (1994). *Descartes' error.* New York: Putnam.

Darwin, C. (1872). *The expression of the emotions in man and animals.* Chicago: University of Chigaco Press (1965).

De Sousa, R. (1987). *The rationality of emotions.* Cambridge, MA: MIT Press.

Dunbar, K. (1993). How scientists really reason: Scientific reasoning in real-world laboratories. In R.J. Sternberg & J. Davidson (Eds.), *Mechanisms of insight.* Cambridge, MA: MIT Press.

Dyer, M.G. (1987). Emotions and their computations: Three computer models. *Cognition and Emotion, 1,* 323–347.

Forgas, J. (1995). Mood and judgement: The affect infusion model (AIM). *Psychological Review, 117,* 39–66.

Gardner, H. (1985). *The mind's new science: A history of the cognitive revolution.* New York: Basic Books.

Isen, A.M., & Geva, N. (1987). The influence of positive affect on acceptable level of risk: The person with large canoe has large worry. *Organizational Behavior and Human Decision Processes, 39,* 145–154.

Isen, A.M., Johnson, M.M.S., Mertz, E., & Robinson, G.F. (1985). The influence of positive affect on the unusualness of word associations. *Journal of Personality and Social Psychology, 48,* 1413–1426.

Johnson-Laird, P.N. (1983). *Mental models: Towards a cognitive science of language, inference, and consciousness.* Cambridge: Cambridge University Press.

Johnson-Laird, P.N., & Byrne, R.M.J. (1991). *Deduction.* Hillsdale, NJ: Lawrence Erlbaum Associates Inc.

Johnson-Laird, P.N., & Oatley, K. (1989). The language of emotions: An analysis of a semantic field. *Cognition and Emotion, 3,* 81–123.

Mackie, D.M., & Worth, L.T. (1989). Processing deficits and the mediation of positive affect in persuasion. *Journal of Personality and Social Psychology, 57,* 27–40.

Mackie, D.M., & Worth, L.T. (1991). Feeling good, but not thinking straight: The impact of positive mood on persuasion. In J.P. Forgas (Ed.), *Emotion and social judgements* (pp.201–219). Oxford: Pergamon.

Martin, L.L., Ward, D.W., Achee, J.W., & Wyer, R.S. (1993). Mood as input: People have to interpret the motivational implications of their moods. *Journal of Personality and Social Psychology, 64,* 317–326.

Mathews, A. (1993). Biases in emotional processing. *The Psychologist: Bulletin of the British Psychological Society, 6,* 493–499.

Neisser, U. (1988). Five kinds of self-knowledge. *Philosophical Psychology, 1,* 35–59.

Oatley, K. (1989). Do emotional states produce irrational thinking? In K.J. Gilhooly, M.T.G. Keane, R.H. Logie, & G. Erdos (Eds.), *Lines of thinking, Volume 2* (pp.121–131). Chichester, UK: Wiley.

Oatley, K. (1991). Distributed cognition. In M.W. Eysenck (Ed.), *Dictionary of cognitive psychology* (pp.102–107). Oxford: Blackwell.

Oatley, K. (1992). *Best laid schemes: The psychology of emotions.* New York: Cambridge University Press.

Oatley, K., & Jenkins, J.M. (1996). *Understanding emotions: In psychology, psychiatry, and social science.* Cambridge, MA: Blackwell.

Oatley, K., & Johnson-Laird, P.N. (1987). Towards a cognitive theory of emotions. *Cognition and Emotion, 1,* 29–50.

Oatley, K., & Johnson-Laird, P.N. (1996). The communicative theory of emotions: Empirical tests, mental models, and implications for social interaction. In L.L. Martin & A. Tesser (Eds.) *Striving and feeling: Interactions among goals, affect, and self-regulation* (pp.363–393). Mahwah, NJ: Erlbaum.

Oatley, K., & Larocque, L. (1995). Everyday concepts of emotions following every-other-day errors in joint plans. In J. Russell, J.-M. Fernandez-Dols, A.S.R. Manstead, & J. Wellenkamp (Eds.), *Everyday conceptions of emotions: An introduction to the psychology, anthropology, and linguistics of emotion. NATO ASI Series D 81* (pp.145–165). Dordrecht: Kluwer.

Quintillian (circa 90). *Institutio Oratoria, VI, in Loeb Classical Library: Quintillian, II.* Cambridge, MA: Harvard University Press.

Rimé, B., Mesquita, B., Philippot, P., & Boca, S. (1991). Beyond the emotional event: Six studies on the social sharing of emotions. *Cognition and Emotion, 5*, 435–465.

Schiff, B.B., & Lamon, M. (1989). Inducing emotion by unilateral contraction of facial muscles: A new look at hemispheric specialization and the experience of emotion. *Neuropsychologia, 27*, 923–935.

Schwartz, N., & Bless, H. (1991). Happy and mindless, but sad and smart? The impact of affective states on analytic reasoning. In J. Forgas (Ed.), *Emotion and social judgment* (pp.55–71). Oxford: Pergamon.

Schwartz, N., & Clore, G.L. (1988). How do I feel about it? The informative function of affective states. In K. Fiedler & J.P. Forgas (Eds.), *Affect, cognition, and social behavior* (pp.44–62). Toronto: Hogrefe.

Simon, H.A. (1967). Motivational and emotional controls of cognition. *Psychological Review, 74*, 29–39.

Solomon, G. (Ed.) (1993). *Distributed cognitions: Psychological and educational considerations.* New York: Cambridge University Press.

Stein, N.L., Trabasso, T., & Liwag, M. (1993). The representation and organization of emotional experience: Unfolding the emotion episode. In M. Lewis & J.M. Haviland (Eds.), *Handbook of emotions* (pp.279–300). New York: Guilford Press.

Vygotsky, L. (1962). *Thought and language* (E. Hanfmann & G. Vakar, Trans.). Cambridge, MA: MIT Press.

11 The Mental Health of Mental Models and the Mental Models of Mental Health

Professor Mick Power
Department of Psychiatry, University of Edinburgh, UK
Dr Til Wykes
Department of Psychology, Institute of Psychiatry, London, UK

INTRODUCTION

Since the "birth" of the modern cognitive approach on 11 September 1956 at a symposium at the Massachusetts Institute of Technology (according to Bruner, 1983), academic psychology has no longer been governed by the behavioural approach, but has come to be dominated by modern cognitivism. There is, however, a tendency for applied areas of science to lag behind the developments in basic theoretical areas. So although modern cognitivism is a strapping forty-year-old, its application to psychopathology is in many ways still in its infancy and only now are many of the implications of the cognitive approach being examined or understood. In this chapter, we examine one area in which Phil Johnson-Laird has blazed a trail – that of reasoning. We consider some of the insights that Phil and others who have studied normal reasoning processes have offered us, and how these insights might be applied to the problems of depression and schizophrenia.

There is increasing interest in the application of cognitive models to the range of problems encountered in psychopathology. From the clinical point of view, Beck's (e.g. 1976) cognitive therapy approach has provided considerable impetus for this interest, both in the area of depression for which the approach was originally developed and, more recently, in the areas of anxiety disorders (Beck & Emery, 1985; Clark, 1986), personality disorders (Beck & Freeman, 1990), and schizophrenia (Fowler, Garety, &

Kuipers, 1995). However, the extant cognitive approaches to psychopathology typically have weak or inadequate conceptual bases (Power & Champion, 1986), a problem that has impeded the construction of a good cognitive theory of depression. One important problem centres on the assumptions made about reasoning in normal individuals. For example, in the area of schizophrenia there has been a long tradition of studying logical thinking; thus, a number of early researchers assumed that thinking obeys the rules of Aristotelian syllogism, and, furthermore, that these rules broke down in schizophrenia (Arieti, 1975; Matte-Blanco, 1976; von Domarus, 1944). For example, von Domarus (1944) proposed that in schizophrenia there is evidence of 'paralogical reasoning' with people suffering from schizophrenia being prone to errors, as in the invalid syllogism:

Socrates is mortal
Horses are mortal
Socrates is a horse

Unfortunately, however, the evidence did not turn out favourably for von Domarus' proposal (see later discussion on delusions) and the original theory was eventually dropped. The proposal that disordered reasoning plays a significant role in psychopathology resurfaced again in Beck's (1976) cognitive therapy which proposed that depressed individuals make logical errors that demonstrate a breakdown of normal logical thinking. This approach has also been adopted in another area of psychopathology, the psychoses, where it has now been proposed that psychotic individuals also make errors in reasoning. However, from the mental models viewpoint (Johnson-Laird, 1983) we shall argue that normal thinking is not based on the operation of formal logical rules, but, instead, is based on the construction of mental models from which conclusions may be drawn. Under many circumstances these conclusions will concur with the outcomes of reasoning with formal logical rules, but there are certain circumstances that reveal the limitations of reasoning and support the mental models approach instead (e.g. Garnham & Oakhill, 1994).

We will present some evidence from two areas of psychopathology to support the mental models argument. The areas we have chosen are our specialist subjects, depression and psychosis. In both diagnostic areas there is evidence that biases in information search and retrieval can not only make people more vulnerable to disorders but can also explain the maintenance of such disorders. These biases and changes in information retrieval can best be explained in the mental models framework. Our patients do reason incorrectly sometimes but we contend that this is more likely to be due to performance limitations (e.g. working memory capacity being used for purposes other than reasoning), and to the acceptance of conclusions that match mood and other related biases, rather than to problems in the use of incorrect logic.

The two areas of psychopathology will be described briefly to set the context. Then we will describe the cognitive approaches to each and consider the ways in which the mental models approach may contribute to both the study and the understanding of these disorders.

DEPRESSION

The Symptoms

One of the most famous ancient accounts of depression was presented in the Book of Job in which Satan robs Job of his children, his possessions, and his health. Following these losses there occurs a long monologue with considerable depressive content, for example:

My spirit is broken, my days are extinct,
the grave is ready for me...
He has made me a byword of the peoples,
and I am one before whom men spit.

These aspects of depression and a number of other symptoms have formed the basis of diagnostic and classification systems such as the World Health Organization's International Classification of Diseases (ICD-10, 1992) and the American Psychiatric Association's diagnostic and Statistical Manual (DSM-IV, 1994). The main symptoms that most systems focus on have been summarised by Champion (1992) and include:

1. dysphoric mood
2. sleep disturbance
3. appetite disturbance leading to weight loss or weight gain
4. loss of energy
5. decreased libido
6. slowness in thinking and, in extreme cases, slowness in movement (motor retardation)
7. feelings of self-condemnation
8. suicidal ideation
9. feelings of guilt
10. loss of interest in usual activities.

Specific symptoms have at various times provided the focus for different theories. For example, earlier behavioural theories focused on loss of usual activities and therefore structured their interventions accordingly (e.g. Lewinsohn, 1974). In contrast, in his classic paper *Mourning and melancholia*, Freud (1917) focused on the melancholic's feelings of self-condemnation which, he argued, were derived from anger turned inwards against the self. Biological models (e.g. Willner, 1985) have focused on the more supposedly biological symptoms such as sleep and appetite disturbance, and motor retardation. The cognitive approaches have, in the same way as the Freudian psychoanalytic approach, tended to focus on self-condemnation, though this may in part be explained by Bibring's (1953) classic ego psychology theory which presaged most of the recent cognitive accounts even down to the use of terms such as 'helplessness' and 'hopelessness'.

Cognitive Approaches to Depression

There have been three major cognitive approaches to depression. The first has been a series of formulations and reformulations by Seligman of his Learned Helplessness theory (1975), the focus of which has been on the proposal that the depressed individual perceives the causes of events to be uncontrollable. The initial theory was reformulated in 1978 (Abramson, Seligman, & Teasdale, 1978) in order to emphasise a wider range of attributional dimensions relevant to the perception of the causes of events (for example, whether the cause is perceived to be internal or external to the individual). More recently, Lyn Abramson has offered a further reformulation, now termed Hopelessness Theory (Abramson, Metalsky, & Alloy, 1989), in which the presumed uncontrollability of events has been dropped and replaced by hopelessness about the future. This group of theories does not provide an adequate cognitive model, but, rather, a set of testable hypotheses (Power & Champion, 1986). Of particular relevance is the proposal that biases may occur in the perception of events and their causes which, therefore, could lead to apparent distortions in thinking and reasoning. We will concentrate on one particular tradition within this line known as 'depressive realism' (Alloy & Abramson, 1979), in which it was suggested that depressed individuals might be more rather than less accurate than normal individuals on judgement and reasoning tasks. We will consider this proposal in more detail later, after briefly considering other cognitive approaches.

   The second main cognitive approach to emotional disorders was provided by Gordon Bower (1981) following his work on a range of cognitive biases associated with different mood states. Bower presented an associative network model in which emotions such as depression were represented as nodes connected via facilitatory and inhibitory links to a range of other conceptual, emotional, and physiological nodes. Spreading activation passing along the facilitatory links between the nodes led to a set of activated nodes that influenced thinking and behaviour. There are, however, a number of problems with associative network models, as summarised by Johnson-Laird, Hermann, and Chaffin (1984). Amongst a number of empirical and theoretical problems that have been noted, associative networks present frameworks in which a theory can be instantiated rather than presenting theories in themselves, and the output from a network needs to be interpreted semantically. Bower's network approach also predicted that a wide range of biases would be associated with different mood states, whereas more recent evidence suggests that only certain types of biases may be observable in particular mood states (see Power & Dalgleish, in press).

The third main cognitive approach, which we will deal with in most detail, is Beck's (e.g. 1976) cognitive therapy. Beck developed his approach in the clinic rather than in the experimental laboratory, so the approach reflects both the advantages and disadvantages of the clinical setting. The key advantage is that cognitive therapy provides a major therapeutic approach to depression, a therapy that will stand or fall separately from the theory on which it is based. The disadvantage is that Beck developed his theory in parallel to, rather than because of, developments in cognitive science: although terms such as 'schema' apparently provide the bridges between cognitive therapy and cognitive science, Beck uses such terms in a much looser and more clinical fashion so that the overlap with cognitive science is sometimes more apparent than real. Indeed, this problem is related to Beck's proposals about putative distortions of logic in the processes of thinking and reasoning in depressed individuals. Because of the importance of the theory and the clear predictions that it makes about reasoning in depression, we will consider cognitive therapy in more detail.

Beck's Cognitive Therapy

The basic cognitive therapy model of depression is presented in Fig. 11.1 (Beck, 1976; Beck, Rush, Shaw, & Emery, 1979). Relationships in early childhood are considered to lead to a set of dysfunctional schemata; for example, overly critical or overprotective parents may lead the child to develop excessively high standards or become overly dependent on others. These dysfunctional schemas are considered to lie dormant until later life when the occurrence of a matching negative event can cause their activation. In theory, therefore, a vulnerable individual might never experience a matching event, or might only experience one much later in life, as when for example a highly successful individual is forced to retire and then becomes depressed for the first time (e.g. Murphy, 1982).

Once the underlying schema has been activated, the cognitive therapy model states that individuals will then experience numerous negative automatic thoughts that lead to the lowering of mood seen in depression.

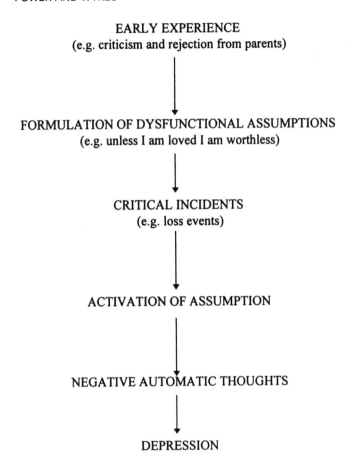

EARLY EXPERIENCE
(e.g. criticism and rejection from parents)

FORMULATION OF DYSFUNCTIONAL ASSUMPTIONS
(e.g. unless I am loved I am worthless)

CRITICAL INCIDENTS
(e.g. loss events)

ACTIVATION OF ASSUMPTION

NEGATIVE AUTOMATIC THOUGHTS

DEPRESSION

FIG. 11.1.   An outline of Beck's cognitive therapy model of depression.

Although Beck's early model presented this simple linear cognition–causes–emotion sequence, a number of more recent cognitive therapists have argued for a circular model in which the change in the emotional state may in turn give rise to further depressogenic thoughts (e.g. Clark, 1986; Teasdale, 1983).

The depressed individual is also prone to make a number of logical errors of thinking which serve to maintain the person in a state of depression. Beck et al. (1979) have listed a number of these typical logical errors as follows:

1. All-or-nothing Thinking: "If I can't do it perfectly, there's no point in doing it at all".
2. Overgeneralisation: "I always get things wrong".

3. Discounting the Positive (Selective Abstraction): "I finished my work today, but I should have done more".
4. Jumping to Conclusions (Mind-reading): "Everyone is fed up with me because I'm depressed again".
5. Catastrophising (Magnification and Minimisation): "It's all going to go wrong and I can't change it".
6. Emotional Reasoning: "I feel bad therefore I must have done something wrong".
7. Shoulds: "I should pull my socks up and get on with it".
8. Personalisation: "It always rains when I arrange to go out".

Hopefully by now most cognitive psychologists should be squirming at the arbitrary nature of this list and the fact that many examples can be generated that fall into two or more of the categories. The list was derived by Beck and his colleagues in an ad hoc fashion from clinical examples rather than from a systematic conceptual analysis of the nature of logical errors. Perhaps a more serious problem, however, is the fact that in his early work Beck seemed to suggest that these errors of thinking were the sole preserve of depressed individuals. But his recent views have clearly moved back from such a strong position with the acknowledgement tht normal non-depressed individuals also make errors of thinking (see Weishaar, 1993). As an illustration of the fact that normal non-depressed individuals may also be prone to similar thinking errors, we offer the following set of positive rather than negative examples of the logical errors listed above:

1. All-or-nothing Thinking: "This place would fall apart without me".
2. Overgeneralisation: "You know I'm always right".
3. Discounting the negative (Selective Abstraction): "I was just doing my duty and following orders".
4. Jumping to Conclusions (Mind-reading): "I feel happy and everyone thinks I'm wonderful".
5. Magnification and Minimisation: "If I were running the country, I'd soon sort the mess out".
6. Emotional Reasoning: "I feel so good I know I'm going to win the National Lottery".
7. Shoulds: "Other people should pay me more respect and recognise my talents".
8. Personalisation: "The sun always shines when I arrange to go out".

Before we consider how a cognitive science based approach to reasoning might inform some of these issues, one further aspect of reasoning in depression needs to be considered. In a challenging paper published in 1979,

Alloy and Abramson argued that, far from showing the range of depressive distortions predicted by cognitive therapy, mildly depressed students were often more accurate and realistic than their non-depressed counterparts. The particular task used was contingency judgement, in which subjects were required to estimate the degree of control they thought they had over an outcome in which they lost or gained small amounts of money. Whereas normal subjects overestimated the degree of control they had over positive outcomes, depressed subjects were more accurate in their estimations of control over negative outcomes. Alloy and Abramson termed this phenomenon 'depressive realism'. Their approach makes the opposite predictions to cognitive therapy, in that it is normal individuals who show positive biases. In depressed individuals these positive biases are absent so that depressed individuals are more realistic. Although later work has suggested a number of qualifications to Alloy and Abramson's strong position (e.g. see Vazquez, 1987), nevertheless, even the latest views state that under certain conditions depressed individuals may be more accurate and realistic than non-depressed individuals. This weaker version of the theory still contradicts the cognitive therapy approach and is not predicted anywhere within Beck's theory.

A Mental Models Approach to Depression

The mental models approach can form the basis of both an adequate cognitive theory and, therefore, an adequate theoretical starting point for a cognitive theory of depression (Champion & Power, 1995; Power & Champion, 1986). There are a number of important advantages of the mental models approach that can be highlighted for the development of such a theory including the following:

1. The emphasis in the mental models approach is on how useful the model is, rather than on whether it is true or valid. Most of our models of ourselves, of the world, and of other people are incomplete or imprecise, but, nevertheless, they are still useful. We may know enough about a car to spot that it sounds wrong, so we take it to someone with a more detailed model of cars than our own, in the hope that the car will run smoothly again. In the same way, we may know enough about ourselves to know that we do not feel right, and therefore take ourselves along to a psychotherapist in the hope that he or she might have a better model of psychic functioning than we have. The emphasis on usefulness therefore gives an alternative view of an apparently dysfunctional model that a patient or client brings to therapy; namely, the possibility that the model may have been useful under some other set of circumstances which presumably no longer

hold. Although there are therapeutic approaches that clearly recognise the equivalent of such expediency, mental models can provide a theoretical basis for these approaches.

2. The organisation of models, and of models within models, may also vary according to circumstances. The fact that models may be organised recursively, that is, in computational terms a model can call itself during processing, provides both computational power and a mechanism by which the self, and self-reflective aspects of the self, can be understood. Furthermore, unlike semantic networks the organisation of mental models need not be restricted to a rigid hierarchy of invariant superordinate–subordinate relationships, but could also include a more flexible heterarchical organisation in which, for example, the superordinate to subordinate relationships varied according to necessity and circumstances. An individual might for example be ruthlessly competitive in a work context, but very different in more personal or intimate contexts in which competitiveness was inappropriate; such changes in the individual could be modelled within a more flexible approach in which the dominant mental model could vary (Power, 1987).

3. A third advantage of mental models is that they capture both intensional and extensional aspects of meaning. One of the criticisms of a semantic network approach such as Bower's (1981) is that it captures only intensional aspects of meaning—that is, the way in which concepts relate to each other—but it fails to capture the extensional aspects of meaning such as how the representations refer to objects in the external world. Equally, purely referential theories of meaning fail to capture the important intensional relationships between concepts (Fodor, 1977). A theory of meaning therefore requires the combination of intensional and extensional relationships: a requirement for which mental models are ideal. Moreover, it is not only theories of meaning that require the combination of intensional and extensional information; thus, an adequate theory of depression needs to combine aspects of personal meaning with social reality, because depression most often lies at the intersection of the two (Champion & Power, 1995; Gotlib & Hammen, 1992).

4. The final advantage is that the mental models approach incorporates multiple levels of meaning. The fact that theories such as Beck's cognitive therapy have focused on a single level of meaning has been criticised as theoretically inadequate (Power & Champion, 1986; Teasdale & Barnard, 1993). There has also been a general trend in cognitive theories of emotion to consider multi-level representation systems (Leventhal & Scherer, 1987; Power & Dalgleish, in press; Teasdale & Barnard, 1993) which might include models, propositions,

and lower levels of representation. There are a number of advantages of multiple-level approaches over single-level ones through allowing for example different, potentially contradictory, outcomes from different levels. Why might someone feel happiness tinged with sadness as an apparent success? Perhaps different affective responses are the outcome of processes at different levels within the system. Again, a mental models approach has the major advantage of permitting such different outcomes.

In relation to depression therefore, if the depressed individual holds a negative self-model, one might expect negative beliefs to influence the process of reasoning, especially reasoning in relation to the self. The more general proposal that general knowledge influences the process of reasoning has been demonstrated in numerous studies. For example, Oakhill and Johnson-Laird (1985) showed that individuals will readily accept conclusions that match with pre-existing knowledge or beliefs, but continue to search for alternative conclusions if the initial conclusions are knowledge-contradictory. On this basis we could expect negative beliefs about the self to bias reasoning processes for appropriate material in certain ways, but such bias is not the same as the necessary distortion that cognitive therapy seems to predict (cf. Haaga, Dyck, & Ernst, 1991). To return to the opposite proposal by Alloy and Abramson (1979) that depressives are more realistic than normal controls, there should be some circumstances under which bias leads to greater distortion and other circumstances under which bias leads to greater accuracy (Power, 1991). Hence, we might predict that depressed individuals should be more accurate or 'realistic' when rejecting false positive information and accepting true negative information, but, in contrast, should be less accurate or 'unrealistic' because of problems with the acceptance of true positive information and a failure to reject false negative information. These predictions did in fact form the starting point for two studies that we have carried out in a preliminary exploration of these proposals. We will briefly describe these two studies before considering their more general implications for cognitive theories of depression and other types of psychopathology.

Two Studies

The purpose of the two studies was to test the application of a mental models approach to reasoning in depression. Based on the arguments presented, we were interested in designing a task that allowed the manipulation of whether or not the material referred to the self, and whether the material was positively or negatively valenced; thus, previous studies of the depression-related biases found in mnemonic tasks suggest that the biases may be restricted to self-related rather than other-related material (e.g. Bradley & Mathews, 1983) and there is empirical and clinical support for the fact that there is an overall negative bias found in depression (e.g. Haaga et al., 1991).

There were a number of possible reasoning tasks that we considered, but in the end we decided to modify the linear syllogism or three-term series task, because this allowed the most appropriate manipulation of the factors (Quelhas & Power, 1991). This task has fallen into disuse in recent years, in part because of an unresolved series of debates between Phil Johnson-Laird and Janellen Huttenlocher about modelling the empirical findings from the task (e.g. see Wason & Johnson-Laird, 1972). Nevertheless, we believe that the task has some applied usefulness despite its unclear theoretical basis; an analogous situation arises with the Stroop task which, despite its many years of use since Stroop first put paint to paper (Stroop, 1935), is not understood, yet is widely used in applied studies (Williams, Watts, MacLeod, & Mathews, 1988).

In the actual task, we constructed linear syllogisms of four different types including syllogisms that were knowledge-contradictory, emotionally neutral, emotionally positive, or emotionally negative in content (see Quelhas & Power, 1991, for further details). The knowledge-contradictory syllogisms were included to demonstrate the importance of belief-based biases in the task. In addition, some of the conclusions referred to the subjects themselves (the 'I' conclusions), whereas other conclusions did not refer to them (the 'not-I' conclusions). We also manipulated the complexity of the syllogism by using both the form A is greater than B, B is greater than C, followed by the question Who is greater? and the more complex form C is less than B, B is less than A, Who is greater? (see Wason & Johnson-Laird, 1972). To give some examples:

1. A > B, B > C, Self-reference Conclusion, Negative:

I am worse than my boss
My boss is worse than my colleagues

Who is worst?

2. A < B,   B > C,   Non-self-reference Conclusion,   Knowledge-contradictory:

The elephant is smaller than the mouse
The mouse is smaller than the ant

Who is smallest?

3. C < B, B < A, Self-reference Conclusion, Positive:

My colleagues are less happy than my boss
My boss is less happy than me

Who is happiest?

With many reasoning tasks there is a choice of dependent variable between measuring time to correct solution or looking at errors within a set time limit. Because we were interested in the predictions about circumstances under which individuals were more likely to make errors in reasoning, we opted for setting a time limit of ten seconds for each problem so as to keep the error rate moderately high.

In the first study that we carried out with these materials, a group of 182 introductory psychology students were tested as a class. In addition to a set of 24 linear syllogisms, the students also completed the Beck Depression Inventory (BDI; Beck et al., 1961) and Spielberger State-Trait Anxiety Inventory Form Y (STAI; Spielberger et al., 1970). The depression and anxiety measures were used to select those subjects that met the following criteria:

1. Normal Controls (BDI < 6, STAI < 30) N = 20
2. Anxious (BDI < 10, STAI > 46) N = 15
3. Depressed (BDI > 14) N = 22

A summary of the results from this first study is presented in Table 11.1. The key results showed that normal and anxious subjects showed a bias towards positive syllogisms with both groups obtaining the highest numbers correct in this condition (1.95 and 1.93, respectively). Moreover, the normal and anxious groups were significantly better at the positive syllogisms than they were at the negative $F(1,33) = 7.96$, $P < 0.01$. In contrast, the depressed group were even-handed in their responses to positive and negative syllogisms with almost identical levels of performance in the two conditions (1.89 versus 1.87 correct, respectively) which, needless to say, did not differ significantly from each other ($F < 1$). Other results confirmed that

TABLE 11.1
Results From the First Reasoning Study (Mean No. Correct, Max = 3)

	NEUTRAL	CONTRA.	POSITIVE	NEGATIVE
Group 1 Normal	1.78	1.83	1.95	1.83
Group 2 Anxious	1.60	1.90	1.93	1.73
Group 3 Depressed	1.64	1.64	1.89	1.87

the C < B < A syllogisms were harder than the A > B > C form. In addition, the neutral syllogisms were unexpectedly found to be relatively poorly performed. These were spatial syllogisms of the form 'to the left of' and 'to the right of', though it is unclear why these syllogisms should have proven to be more difficult.

In order to replicate the findings from the first study, we have recently repeated the task with a new set of introductory psychology students. The materials, instructions, and procedure were essentially the same as those used in the first study. The results from the second study are summarised in Table 11.2; the Table shows the results for the normal subjects and for the depressed subjects. Again, the normal subjects were found to show a bias for the positive syllogisms (1.68 correct) for which they were significantly more accurate than for the negative syllogisms (1.46 correct) $F(1,25) = 12.7$, $P < 0.01$. In contrast, the depressed group showed a slight numerical superiority for the positive syllogisms in comparison to the negative syllogisms, but this difference did not reach significance (F < 1). The depressed group in this second study also showed a tendency towards poorer performance overall when compared to the normal controls ($P = 0.078$), a tendency that had not been present in the first study. One might however predict such a tendency given the cognitive and motor slowing noted earlier that is characteristic of depressions.

Taken together, these two studies show that even in student samples the mood state of the individual may influence the type of conclusions that are drawn and whether or not these conclusions are compatible with the currently dominant model of the self. The mental models approach provides a powerful framework in which to understand such effects. However, before we consider the implications in more detail, we will review findings from studies of schizophrenia.

TABLE 11.2
Results From the Second Reasoning Study (Mean No. Correct, Max = 3)

	NEUTRAL	CONTRA.	POSITIVE	NEGATIVE
Group 1 Normal	1.40	1.58	1.68	1.46
Group 3 Depressed	1.12	1.40	1.43	1.36

SCHIZOPHRENIA

The Symptoms

There are a number of diagnostic classification systems for schizophrenia but the most useful and recent is contained in DSM-IV (APA 1994) which specifies that a person should display all of the following:

(a) Two or more characteristic symptoms e.g. delusions, hallucinations, disorganised speech, grossly disorganised behaviour and/or negative symptoms (for instance, affective flattening).
(b) Social or occupational functioning is affected.
(c) There are continuous signs of a disturbance for at least six months.

Bizarre delusions in this system are central to the diagnosis of schizophrenia, especially beliefs about control of the body, will, mind, mood or thought. Other types of delusions such as paranoid ones are in fact common to many conditions besides schizophrenia (Maher & Ross, 1984); others such as delusions of grandiosity, poverty or guilt, although they can occur with schizophrenia, are more common in affective psychoses. Delusions have long been considered a category of thought qualitatively different from both normal thinking and neurotic disorders such as depression, earlier considered.

The first description of delusions that influenced psychiatric nosology was given by Jaspers (1913). He describes delusions as beliefs that were held with extraordinary conviction against any counter evidence and that had impossible content. Jaspers also made a distinction between primary and secondary delusions. Primary delusions are linked directly to perception and are an immediately experienced change of meaning of a particular perception. For example, a man looking at a marble table-top became convinced that the end of the world was coming. Secondary delusions appear as sudden notions and new meanings of remembered life experiences. More modern explanations have built on this core description, although downgrading the primary/secondary distinction, adding only that their content is often fantastic and is not shared by those of a common social or cultural background (Mullen, 1979). These criteria all distinguish delusions from the sort of thoughts exhibited by patients with depression. However, we now know that delusions are not always held with absolute conviction but they can be described along a number of dimensions. For example, Buchanan et al. (1993) measured eight dimensions which include whether the delusions are acted on, and Garety and Hemsley (1987) describe 11 dimensions which include the distress or worry experienced by the person reporting them. All scales now have in common a measure of the intensity of the belief along a continuous scale in place of what was once thought to be a categorical scale.

Jaspers also emphasised the irrationality of the judgements made by the person and even the modern descriptions suggest 'disturbed judgements' (Mullen, 1979). The strongest of these irrationality criteria is in DSM-III-R (APA, 1987) in which they are described as 'incorrect inferences' about external reality. The irrationality is said to be in two stages both in the formation of the delusion and in its maintenance. There is no doubt that people can reason logically from false premises and that any set of premises may yield a vast number of valid conclusions. So, in drawing any specific conclusion we must be guided by more than logic, as Oakhill and Johnson-Laird (1985) have argued. What is still in dispute is whether people with schizophrenia reason invalidly because of problems with their use of normal rules of inference, whether they use the normal inferential rules on false premises, or a mixture of both. The next section will report studies of the reasoning processes of people with psychosis designed to unravel this problem.

Studies of Reasoning in People With Schizophrenia

Case study evidence (Johnson, Ross & Mastria, 1977; Maher & Ross, 1984) suggests that delusions are sometimes rational attempts to account for unpleasant or disturbing perceptions. But given that disturbed perceptions such as hallucinations do not always give rise to delusional explanations, it seems most unlikely the perceptual abnormalities alone are sufficient for the acquisition of abnormal beliefs. It is also clear that some patients are deluded in the absence of perceptual abnormalities (Chapman & Chapman, 1988). The remaining possibility is that patients with schizophrenia can draw incorrect inferences from normal perceptions.

Context Effects.   The argument about the 'irrationality' of delusions centres on studies either carried out by Williams (1964) or reported in that paper. These widely cited investigations into logical reasoning compared 50 hospitalised normal patients and about 50 patients with schizophrenia on syllogistic reasoning tasks. The syllogisms were varied in content but no differences were found between the groups, who both made a large number of errors. Much has been made of these results (e.g. Maher, 1973) but some comments in the original paper considerably weaken the conclusions. Williams commented (1964, p. 58) that most patients with schizophrenia had "recovered temporarily from the psychotic episode and were functioning normally with regard to intellectual functions at the time of testing". The study therefore did not test patients who were in a psychotic episode and there was no evidence that they had ever been deluded. A more recent study of three people with late onset schizophrenia has supported aspects of Williams' results. Phillips, Howard and David (1995) found that there were few differences in syllogistic reasoning between subjects with schizophrenia and normal subjects matched for age. For example, invalid but believable statements were endorsed to a greater extent than valid but unbelievable statements. However, reasoning on conditional tasks did sometimes differ between the groups. These differences depended on the type of conclusion (valid inferences vs fallacies), the inclusion of other premises in the simple task, and the emotional content of those premises.

Byrne (1989) argued that the provision of additional premises leads to the suppression of valid inferences but has no effect on fallacies, whereas the provision of alternative premises has no effect on valid inferences but reduces fallacies. This interaction was found in patients and healthy controls but was significant only for the schizophrenia group and only when the emotive content of the premises was high. Perceptual processing was also abnormal in these patients, suggesting that perceptual inputs may affect the formation of delusions. But it is also clear that the deluded subjects' reasoning about emotive subjects was more 'normal' (following Byrne, 1989), that is, the deluded subjects' reasoning pattern was more affected by the content of the premises even though the themes chosen were not necessarily congruent with the currently held delusions.

Further evidence of biases in reasoning depending on the content of the task is provided by a series of experiments by Bentall and colleagues. Kaney and Bentall (1989) compared deluded subjects with depressed and normal controls and found that, in contrast to depressed subjects, the deluded subjects made excessive external attributions for negatively valenced events and excessively internal attributions for positively valanced events. That is, the deluded subjects made the opposite attributions to depressed subjects who are biased to attribute negative events to themselves (see earlier). This result was substantially replicated by Candido and Romney (1990). Subsequent studies identified similar biases when deluded subjects were asked to reason about the behaviour of others (Bentall, Kaney, & Dewey, 1991); that is, they made excessive person attributions and were more certain about their judgements than were either depressed or normal subjects. These results seem to confirm that deluded subjects exhibit an abnormal self-serving bias towards accepting greater responsibility for positive outcomes than negative outcomes (Kaney & Bentall, 1992). It is argued by Bentall and colleagues that this bias in reasoning has a protective function (against depression) which would also explain the subjects' unwillingness to countenance the possibility of being wrong.

The effects of these biases when made from memory rather than from immediate experiences were further investigated by Lyon, Kaney, and Bentall (1994). They asked depressed and deluded subjects to read short texts in the first person and to answer questions based on their memory for the vignettes. The target questions were those that could be answered either by an internal or external attribution and these questions were divided into those with a positive and those with a negative outcome. The subjects were also asked to answer an attributional style questionnaire with questions such as "You win a competition—write down one major cause" and then were asked to rate whether the cause was internal vs external, stable vs unstable, and global vs specific on 7-point scales. The same results were found for the immediate attributional style questionnaire as in other studies; deluded and normal subjects gave more internal attributions for positive events and more external attributions for negative events whereas depressed patients showed an absence of this bias. But there was a change in the bias when subjects were asked to make attributions based on memory for the texts. In this condition both the depressed and deluded groups showed the same biases, both groups making fewer internal inferences for positive in comparison to negative events. The normal group, however, continued to show a positive bias as they had done in the previous attribution task. Why should there be this shift in responses when deluded subjects have to rely on memory for the events? It is possible that it depends on making explicit vs implicit judgements which are thought to be subserved by different cognitive mechanisms (e.g. Berry & Broadbent, 1988). Implicit knowledge is used in an automatic, fast, and effortless fashion which makes no demands on attention whereas explicit knowledge is sustained by a cognitive system that is controlled, effortful, and slow. Power and Dalgleish (in press) similarly have collated evidence that there are two routes to the generation of emotion. The first route is appraisal-based and draws on controlled processes and the second is a direct associative route; there are many situations under which a more self-serving appraisal can be made, even though this might be contrary to the outcomes of automatic processing of the same event or situation.

False Detection. These results may reflect only the preference for deluded subjects to make external attributions for unwelcome experiences. But there is an alternative explanation. Deluded subjects may falsely tend to detect covariation between randomly associated events. In other words coincidences may be perceived as significant. The tendency to perceive causal relationships inaccurately may make some people vulnerable to delusions. Others too have found such causal misperceptions. Brennan and Hemsley (1984) showed that patients with schizophrenia who were also paranoid were more likely than non-paranoid patients to judge two randomly associated events to be causally related (an illusory correlation) especially when the stimuli were relevant to the subjects with paranoid delusions. Even if this is not an explanation for the development of the initial delusion it might well be a circular disturbed thought process, which maintains the disorder as described previously by Clark (1986).

Perceptual Abnormalities. One further factor may predispose patients with schizophrenia to develop or maintain delusions is that they tend to 'jump to conclusions' when presented with ambiguous stimuli. Patients with schizophrenia have normal perceptual sensitivity but under conditions of uncertainty have a greater bias towards believing that an external stimulus is present (Bentall & Slade, 1985).

Probabilistic Reasoning and Hypothesis Testing.   All the aforementioned difficulties in reasoning would make a person vulnerable to the formation of delusions but their maintenance presumably depends on a lack of hypothesis testing. Deficits in hypothesis testing have mostly been tested with emotionally neutral material in the hope of detecting general reasoning deficits. In a study by Huq, Garety, and Hemsley (1988) people with schizophrenia were given a probabilistic reasoning task. They were shown two jars containing different proportions of coloured beads. They were asked to guess from which jar an experimenter was drawing the beads. Deluded patients requested less information than did either normals or a mixed psychiatric control group. They were also relatively over-confident about their judgements even though they were based on little information. Garety, Hemsley, and Wesseley (1991) repeated this experiment with similar results but also added a further experimental manipulation. After patients had made their decision about the jar from which the coloured beads had been taken, the experimenter then allowed more beads to be shown and the subjects were asked whether they would like to change the confidence ratings of their original choice. The results were similar to those of the initial study; deluded subjects chose a jar on little information but, surprisingly, they were also willing to reduce their confidence ratings in the face of potentially contradictory information. It seemed therefore that contrary to expectation a substantial number of deluded subjects did not hold on tenaciously to their hypotheses but, instead, they seemed all too eager to abandon one in favour of another. The results of reasoning with neutral stimuli seem to fit with theories about the abnormalities attributed to people with schizophrenia which state that they react to immediate environmental stimuli rather than to the effects of prior learning (Hemsley, 1987; Gray et al., 1991).

Social Reasoning.   Frith and Corcoran (1996) have shown some deficits in social reasoning when they presented various tasks that required the subject to represent the states of mind of another person. The tasks included hinting tasks, understanding of jokes, and inferring mental states in texts. People with schizophrenia were found to be deficient at these tasks. However, when the group was categorised in relation to three types of symptoms it was found that patients with passivity experiences (delusions of alien control or experiences of thoughts being inserted into your head) and those in remission were not very disabled on these tasks. However, people who had paranoid delusions and those with behavioural signs (poverty of speech, flattening of affect) were particularly affected even when they seemed to be able to recall the stories. It may be that the group showing passivity phenomena were unable to represent their own intentions and therefore misinterpret their own thoughts as those of others, but this problem does not seem to generalise to the interpretation of others' beliefs or intentions. For the paranoid group it is not clear how this deficit in reasoning about mental states relates to the biases in social attributions because the answers to the tasks in the Theory of Mind experiments are emotionally neutral and do not reflect on the self-esteem of the protagonists. However, it is possible that the paranoid patients develop delusional systems not only as a defence against depression (as suggested by Bentall et al., 1991) but also in order to provide a scheme for 'chunking' information in order to reduce the load on working memory.

Memory Effects. Working memory has been suggested as one explanation of the difficulties of some syllogistic reasoning tasks. Gilhooly, Logie, Wetherick, and Wynn (1993) have shown that when working memory, particularly the central executive component, is disrupted then syllogistic reasoning performance is also disrupted. There is now increasing interest in the role that deficits in working memory might play both in the development of psychosis and as a predictor of the future course of the disorder (Wykes, 1994). But there are few data relating reasoning performance and working memory either in normal or abnormal populations.

One study has investigated the effects of working memory on syllogistic reasoning studies in young and older adults (Gilinsky & Judd, 1994). Four different factors were investigated: the effect of changes in working memory capacity, belief biases with changes in content, number of models required to produce a valid conclusion, and whether the task was to evaluate or construct a conclusion. They found that, although there was some effect of individual differences in working memory, this was swamped by the tendency of older adults to be biased towards accepting conclusions consistent with belief. This acceptance bias was only noticeable in the evaluation tasks. In the construction tasks there was no conflict because no conclusions were provided and subjects had little difficulty in concluding that 'All cows speak French'. Performance on multiple model tasks declined for both the younger and older group. This may, however, be accounted for by different processes. Younger subjects were less affected by belief biases and therefore probably did carry out the task as suggested by using working memory and evaluating the incorrect but believable conclusions. For older adults the belief biases, especially towards the acceptance of invalid but believable statements were a potent predictor of syllogistic performance. Gilinsky and Judd (1994) suggested that these biases are stronger in older subjects who may in fact not use working memory but rely heavily on their knowledge of the world to carry out these tasks. The only adequate test of the working memory hypothesis would be to investigate the effect of dual tasks on syllogistic performance using abstract syllogisms eliminating the effects of knowledge of the world on task performance. As far as the authors are aware this test has not been carried out. Nevertheless, the older adults are acting in a similar way to patients with paranoid delusions, in that they accept invalid inferences that accord with their views of the world.

In summary, the evidence suggests that, apart from particular theory of mind problems, people with schizophrenia perform reasoning tasks in relatively normal ways with the exception that a proportion of them are likely to make (and change) decisions that are based on less information than normal subjects or people with other psychiatric diagnoses. Their reasoning ability is entirely consistent with a mental models approach. They follow all the three key predictions: the larger the number of models required, the harder the task; erroneous conclusions will tend to be consistent with the premises; and if the putative conclusion is unbelievable, subjects will tend to search for a more believable one (Johnson-Laird, 1994). However, people with schizophrenia are handicapped both by their cognitive abilities and their reasoning styles. The manipulation of mental models relies heavily on the ability of the subjects to represent such models in working memory, but it is now thought that people with schizophrenia have particular problems with working memory (Morice & Delahunty, 1996) which might prevent such manipulations from taking place. Evidence from brain imaging studies suggests that the area in which activation is most apparent when temporary information is needed to guide a response (that is when working memory is required for a task) lies within the prefrontal cortex. This is the area that seems most deficient in the same brain imaging studies of people with schizophrenia (Kotrla & Weinberger, 1995). If working memory capacity is reduced, the representation of models will be limited. The addition of further premises will reduce performance considerably (as shown by Phillips et al., 1995) but in the direction of normal biases in reasoning. If fewer models are represented by patients with schizophrenia, then it is more likely that further information would disconfirm any particular model and patients would therefore appear to 'jump to conclusions' or change hypotheses too readily (e.g. Garety et al., see later). Any new information would in effect only be compared to a reduced set of models in the case of patients with schizophrenia.

For delusional thinking, the number of models represented or their salience may also be affected by the biasing effect of personal beliefs or knowledge about the world (e.g. Gilinsky & Judd, 1994; Oakhill & Johnson-Laird, 1985). When presented with arguments that have to be evaluated, subjects tend to endorse conclusions that they believe to be true (cf. Phillips, Howard and David, in press). These biases are also obvious when subjects are required to make inferences about social attributions.

COMPARISON OF DEPRESSED, PSYCHOTIC, AND NORMAL REASONERS

1. All groups are affected by the emotional content of the task—i.e. biases are more likely to occur when the content is specific to the dominant schematic model whether this is delusional, an attributional style, or simply related to the individual's current positive or negative mood state.

2. The biases are often different. In the Alloy and Abramson (1979) task, students with mild depression were found to be more realistic in their judgements of the amount of influence that they had over the task. In a later replication of this study Kaney and Bentall (1992) found that depressed patients were more realistic, that is, had a more modest view of their control over a task that had in fact been pre-programmed. However, deluded individuals were excessively biased towards reporting high control when they were winning and low control when they were losing, even though in fact they had no control at all. The deluded pattern of responding is in the same direction as normal subjects but appears to be more extreme.

3. The reasoning processes of psychotic individuals are probably also affected by schematic models but these are different from those of depressed people. In some psychoses the schemas may provide a defence against depression, whereas in depression they serve to maintain the dominant schematic model of the self once the negative self has become predominant (Champion & Power, 1995).

4. The 'jumping to conclusions' bias of patients with schizophrenia (Garety et al., 1991) in tasks with little emotional content can be accounted for by reductions in working memory capacity which prevent the representation of complex mental models. Mental models therefore either have to be 'chunked' or only one or two models can be represented at any one time. If there are few models represented, then the provision of only a small amount of information would allow the refutation or the confirming of a particular hypothesis. Depressed patients also show deficits in working memory when required to engage in neutral tasks, although these effects have been investigated mostly in relation to memory performance (e.g. Williams et al., 1988). In a study of dysphoric students Channon and Baker (1994) found that such individuals were less likely to integrate information from the two premises in a syllogistic reasoning task when compared to normal non-dysphoric students; this result is consistent with an impaired working memory capacity in depression. One might speculate that in depression working memory capacity is taken up with self-worth issues,

especially in relation to threatened or failed roles and goals (Champion & Power, 1995); tasks that are ego-involving therefore should be processed more effortfully than tasks that are emotionally neutral or that are of less perceived relevance for the individual.

CONCLUSION

Both depressed and delusional groups appear to be affected by characteristic schematic models about the world in which they live. These models have been built up through experience of the world; for patients who develop psychoses this experience may also include perceptual abnormalities. Such schemas have an automatic effect on the types of models that are likely to be represented in working memory. Reduced capacity also affects the number of models to be represented which may produce inefficient thinking in both groups. However, depressed patients may be able to reason more accurately than non-depressed normal individuals for problems that lead to conclusions which are not consistent with the dominant negative beliefs about the self. Under appropriate circumstances, however, emotional content may either bypass the working memory route and lead to the acceptance of conclusions that are consistent with dominant schematic models, or, alternatively, the emotional content of the material may lead to working memory being filled with task-irrelevant thoughts, memories, or fantasies, thereby reducing the working memory available for the reasoning task.

TAILNOTE

On the importance of reasoning even for professors of psychology and logic, MP recalls as an undergraduate being tortured as a subject in one of Peter Wason and Phil Johnson-Laird's studies of the Wason Selection Task. It was little relief afterwards to discover that even professors of logic had failed to solve the riddle of the cards. However, as a doctoral student of Phil Johnson-Laird's a few years later he witnessed the following piece of reasoning which, in the recounting, goes at least some way to setting the balance straight. Phil's reasoning and consequent actions went as follows:

I parked my car outside the house
My car is no longer outside the house

My car has been stolen.

The inference was good, but the first premise was wrong! The policeman called to the scene of the 'crime' reasoned as follows:

Some people who report their cars stolen are absent-minded
All professors are absent-minded

Therefore, look for the car around the corner.

Needless to say, the policeman's reasoning won on this occasion. We hear, though, that Phil has taken to walking to work in Princeton. One is tempted to suggest that given Phil's earlier work showing that post office workers could easily solve the Wason Selection Task (Johnson-Laird, Legrenzi, & Legrenzi, 1972), perhaps it is time to extend this work to the bastions of logic and rationality in our society, the police (we note that Chan & Chua, 1994, have taken a step in this direction). We are sure that no-one who could begin a sentence with "I was heading in an easterly direction" would have the problems that our psychology undergraduates experienced with spatial syllogisms.

REFERENCES

Abramson, L.Y., Metalsky, G.I., & Alloy, L.B. (1989). Hopelessness depression: A theory-based subtype of depression. *Psychological Review, 96*, 358–372.

Abramson, L.Y., Seligman, M., & Teasdale, J. (1978). Learned helplessness: Critique and reformulation. *Journal of Abnormal Psychology, 87*, 49–74.

Alloy, L.B. & Abramson, L.Y. (1979). Judgement of contingency in depressed students: Sadder but wiser? *Journal of Experimental Psychology: General, 108*, 441–485.

American Psychiatric Association (1987). *Diagnostic and statistical manual of mental disorders* (3rd edn revised). Washington: APA.

American Psychiatric Association (1994). *Diagnostic and statistical manual of mental disorders* (4th edn). Washington: APA.

Arieti, S. (1974). *Interpretation of schizophrenia* (2nd edn). London: Crosby, Lockwood & Staples.

Beck, A.T. (1976). *Cognitive therapy and the emotional disorders.* New York: Meridian.

Beck, A.T. & Emery, G. (1985). *Anxiety disorders and phobias: A cognitive perspective.* New York: Basic Books.

Beck, A.T. & Freeman, A. (1990). *Cognitive therapy of personality disorders.* New York: Guildford Press.

Beck, A.T., Rush, A., Shaw, B., & Emery, G. (1979). *Cognitive therapy of depression: A treatment manual.* New York: Wiley.

Beck, A.T., Ward, C.H., Mendelson, M., Mock, J., & Erbaugh, J. (1961). An inventory for measuring depression. *Archives of General Psychiatry, 4*, 561–571.

Bentall, R.P., Kaney, S., & Dewey, M.E. (1991). Paranoia and social reasoning: An attribution theory analysis. *British Journal of Clinical Psychology, 30*, 13–23.

Bentall, R.P. & Slade, P. (1985). Reality testing and auditory hallucinations: A signal detection analysis. *British Journal of Clinical Psychology, 24*, 159–169.

Berry, D.C. & Broadbent, D.E. (1988). Interactive tasks and the implicit–explicit distinction. *British Journal of Psychology, 79*, 251–272.

Bibring, E. (1953). The mechanism of depression. In P. Greenacre (Ed.), *Affective disorders: Psychoanalytic contribution to their study.* New York: International Universities Press.

Bower, G.H. (1981). Mood and memory. *American Psychologist, 36*, 129–148.

Bradley, B. & Mathews, A. (1983). Negative self-schemata in clinical depression. *British Journal of Clinical Psychology, 22*, 173–182.

Brennan, J.H. & Hemsley, D. (1984). Illusory correlations in paranoid and non-paranoid schizophrenia. *British Journal of Clinical Psychology, 23*, 225–226.

Bruner, J. (1983). *In search of mind: Essays in autobiography.* New York: Harper & Row.

Buchanan, A., Reed, A., Wesseley, S., Garety, P., Taylor, P., Grubin, D., & Dunn, G. (1993). Acting on delusions (2): The phenomenological correlates of acting on delusions. *British Journal of Psychiatry, 163*, 77–81.

Byrne, R. (1989). Suppressing valid inferences with conditionals. *Cognition, 31*, 61–83.

Candido, C. & Romney, D. (1990). Attributional style in paranoid versus depressed patients. *British Journal of Medical Psychology, 63*, 355–363.

Champion, L.A. (1992). Depression. In L.A. Champion & M.J. Power (Eds.), *Adult psychological problems: An introduction.* London: Falmer Press.

Champion, L.A. & Power, M.J. (1995). Social and cognitive approaches to depression: Towards a new synthesis. *British Journal of Clinical Psychology, 34*, 485–503.

Chan, D. & Chua, F. (1994). Suppression of valid inferences: Syntactic views, mental models and relative salience. *Cognition, 53*, 217–238.

Channon, S. & Baker, J. (1994). Reasoning strategies in depression: Effects of depressed mood on a syllogism task. *Personality and Individual Differences, 17*, 707–711.

Chapman, L.J. & Chapman, J.P. (1988). The genesis of delusions. In T.F. Oltmans & B.A. Maher (Eds.), *Delusional beliefs* (pp.67–83). New York: Wiley.

Clark, D.M. (1986). A cognitive model of panic. *Behaviour Research and Therapy, 24*, 461–470.

Fodor, J.D. (1977). *Semantics: Theories of meaning in generative grammar.* Hassocks, UK: Harvester Press.

Fowler, D., Garety, P. & Kuipers, E. (1995). *Cognitive behaviour therapy for psychosis: Theory and practice.* Chichester, UK: Wiley.

Freud, S. (1917). *Mourning and melancholia. The standard edition of the complete works of Sigmund Freud, 14.* London: Hogarth Press.

Frith, C.D. & Corcoran, R. (1996). Exploring "Theory of mind" in people with schizophrenia. *Psychological Medicine, 26*, 521–530.

Garety, P. & Hemsley, D. (1987). Characteristics of delusional experience. *European Archives of Psychiatry and Neurological Science, 237*, 112–114.

Garety, P., Hemsley, D., & Wesseley, S. (1991). Reasoning in delusional schizophrenia and paranoid patients: Biases in performance on a probabilistic reasoning task. *Journal of Nervous and Mental Disease, 179*, 194–201.

Garnham, A. & Oakhill, J. (1994). *Thinking and reasoning.* Oxford: Blackwell.

Gilhooly, K., Logie, R., Wetherick, N., & Wynn, V. (1993). Working memory and strategies in syllogistic reasoning tasks. *Memory and Cognition, 21*, 115–124.

Gilinsky, A.S. & Judd, B.B. (1994). Working memory and bias in reasoning across the lifespan. *Psychology of Ageing, 9*, 356–371.

Gotlib, I.H. & Hammen, C.L. (1992). *Psychological aspects of depression: Toward a cognitive–interpersonal integration.* Chichester, UK: Wiley.

Gray, J., Feldon, R., Rawlins, J., Hemsley, D., & Smith, A. (1991). The neuropsychology of schizophrenia. *Behavioural and Brain Sciences, 14*, 1–84.

Haaga, D.A.F., Dyck, M.J., & Ernst, D. (1991). Empirical status of cognitive therapy of depression. *Psychological Bulletin, 110*, 215–236.

Hemsley, D. (1987). An experimental psychological model for schizophrenia. In H. Hafner, Gattaz, W.F. & Janzarik, W. (Eds.), *Search for the causes of schizophrenia* (pp. 59–76). Stuttgart: Springer.

Huq, F., Garety, P., & Hemsley, D. (1988). Probabilistic judgements in deluded and non-deluded subjects. *Quarterly Journal of Experimental Psychology, 40A*, 801–812.

Jaspers, K. (1913). *General psychopathology.* Manchester: University Press.

Johnson-Laird, P.N. (1983). *Mental models: Towards a cognitive science of language, inference and consciousness.* Cambridge: Cambridge University Press.

Johnson-Laird, P.N. (1994). Mental models and probabilistic reasoning. *Cognition, 50,* 189–209.

Johnson-Laird, P.N., Hermann, D.J., & Chaffin, R. (1984). Only connections: A critique of semantic networks. *Psychological Bulletin, 96,* 292–315.

Johnson-Laird, P.N., Legrenzi, P., & Legrenzi, M.S. (1972). Reasoning and a sense of reality. *British Journal of Psychology, 63,* 395–400.

Johnson, W., Ross, J., & Mastria, M. (1977). Delusional behaviour: An attributional analysis of development and modification. *Journal of Abnormal Psychology, 86,* 421–426.

Kaney, S. & Bentall, R. (1989) Persecutory delusions and attributional style. *British Journal of Medical Psychology, 62,* 191–198.

Kaney, S. & Bentall, R. (1992). Persecutory delusions and the self-serving basis: Evidence from a contingency judgment task. *Journal of Nervous and Mental Disease, 180,* 773–780.

Kotrla, K. & Weinberger, D. (1995). Brain imaging in schizophrenia. *Annual Review of Medicine, 46,* 113–122.

Leventhal, H. & Scherer, K.R. (1987). The relationship of emotion to cognition: A functional approach to semantic controversy. *Cognition and Emotion, 1,* 3–28.

Lewinsohn, P.M. (1974). A behavioral approach to depression. In R.J. Friedman & M.M. Katz (Eds.), *The psychology of depression: Contemporary theory and Research.* New York: Winston.

Lyon, H., Kaney, S., & Bentall, R. (1994). The defensive function of persecutory delusions: Evidence from attribution tasks. *British Journal of Psychiatry, 164,* 637–646.

Maher, B. (1973). Delusional thinking and perceptual disorder. *Journal of Individual Psychology, 30,* 98–113.

Maher, B. & Ross, J. (1984). Delusions. In H.E. Adams & P. Suther (Eds.) *Comprehensive Handbook of Psychopathology* (pp. 383–408). New York: Plenum Press.

Matte-Blanco, I. (1976). Basic logico–mathematical structures in schizophrenia. In D. Richter (Ed.), *Schizophrenia today.* Oxford: Pergamon Press.

Morice, R. & Delahunty, A. (1996). Frontal Executive impairments in schizophrenia. *Schizophrenia Bulletin, 22,* 125–138.

Mullen, P. (1979). Phenomenology of disordered mental functions. In P. Hill, R. Murray, & G. Thorley (Eds.), *Essentials of postgraduate psychiatry* (pp. 25–54). London: Academic.

Murphy, E. (1982). Social origins of depression in old age. *British Journal of Psychiatry, 141,* 135–142.

Oakhill, J. & Johnson-Laird, P.N. (1985). The effects of belief on the spontaneous production of syllogistic conclusions. *Quarterly Journal of Experimental Psychology, 37A,* 553–569.

Phillips, M., Howard, R., & David, A. (in press). A cognitive neuropsychiatric approach to the study of delusions in late onset schizophrenia.

Power, M.J. (1987). Cognitive theories of depression. In H.J. Eysenck & I. Martin (Eds.), *Theoretical foundations of behavior therapy.* New York: Plenum.

Power, M.J. (1991). Cognitive science and behavioural psychotherapy: Where behaviour was, there shall cognition be? *Behavioural Psychotherapy, 19,* 20–41.

Power, M.J. & Champion, L.A. (1986) Cognitive approaches to depression: A theoretical critique. *British Journal of Clinical Psychology, 25,* 201–212.

Power, M.J. & Dalgleish, R. (in press). *Cognition and emotion: From order to disorder.* Hove, UK. Erlbaum (UK) Taylor & Francis Ltd.

Quelhas, A.C. & Power, M.J. (1991). Raciocinio dedutivo na depressao. *Analise Psicologica, 9,* 43–52.

Seligman, M. (1975). *Helplessness: On depression, development and death.* San Francisco: W.H. Freeman.

Spielberger, C.D., Gorsuch, R., & Lushene, R. (1970). *The State Trait Anxiety Inventory (STAI) Manual.* Palo Alto, CA: Consulting Psychologists Press.

Stroop, J.R. (1935). Studies of interference in serial verbal reactions. *Journal of Experimental Psychology, 18,* 643–662.

Teasdale, J.D. (1983). Negative thinking in depression: Cause, effect or reciprocal relationship. *Archives of General Psychiatry, 35,* 773–782.

Teasdale, J. & Barnard, P. (1993). *Affect, cognition and change.* Hove, UK: Lawrence Erlbaum Associates Ltd.

Vazquez, C. (1987). Judgement of contingency: Cognitive biases in depressed and non-depressed subjects. *Journal of Personality and Social Psychology, 52,* 419–431.

Von Domarus, E. (1944). The specific laws of logic in schizophrenia. In J. Kasanin (Ed.), *Language and thought in schizophrenia* (pp. 104–113). Berkeley CA: University of California Press.

Wason, P.C. & Johnson-Laird, P.N. (1972). *Psychology of reasoning: Structure and content.* London: Batsford.

Weishaar, M. (1993). *Aaron T. Beck.* London: Sage.

Williams, E. (1964). Deductive reasoning in schizophrenia. *Journal of Abnormal and Social Psychology, 69,* 447–61.

Williams, J.M.G., Watts, F.N., MacLeod, C., & Mathews, A. (1988). *Cognitive psychology and emotional disorders.* Chichester, UK: Wiley.

Willner, P. (1985). *Depression: A psycho-biological synthesis.* New York: Wiley.

World Health Organization. (1992). *The ICD-10 classification of mental and behavioural disorders. Clinical descriptions and diagnostic guidelines.* Geneva: WHO.

Wykes, T. (1994). Predicting symptomatic and behavioural outcomes of community care. *British Journal of Psychiatry, 165,* 486–492.

12 Applied Mental Models in Human–Computer Interaction

Kate Ehrlich
Lotus Development Corporation, USA

INTRODUCTION

As I contemplated what to write for this chapter, I became intrigued with the idea of exploring the use and meaning of mental models in Human–Computer Interaction (HCI). HCI is a discipline with which I have been associated for over 10 years as a researcher but mostly as a practitioner concerned with building systems that will be easy for people to use. On reflection it seemed that many of these systems rely on the notion that users' interaction is guided by some internal representation of the structure and behaviour of the system. The opportunity to write this chapter seemed an appropriate time to articulate the use and meaning of models in HCI and to explore the important, if somewhat ambitious, goal of relating these notions of models to theories of mental models in cognitive science.

HCI researchers have long been captivated by the idea that users form mental models of computer systems and use those abstractions to guide their interaction with the system (e.g. Halasz & Moran, 1983; Norman, 1983; Young, 1981). Card and Moran (1986, p.595) put it especially cogently when they said:

A user's conceptual model is . . . an abstraction of the system's architecture and software structures—the conceptual entities that the architecture and software implements—that is simple enough for non-technical users to grasp. . . . The user's model provides an integrated package of knowledge that allows the user to predict what the system will do if certain commands are executed, to predict

223

the state of the system after the commands are executed, to plan methods for novel tasks, and to deal with odd error situations (by characterizing the system's state according to the model, then choosing operations necessary to leave that state.)

Despite its intuitive appeal, a model-based approach is neither well understood nor commonly employed as a technique for designing user interfaces. Moreover, there are no agreed terms to describe the user's model. Adding to the confusion is a history of research into cognitive theories of task analysis (e.g. Card, Moran, & Newell, 1983) which has had mixed success in predicting difficulty of learning or using new systems and little applicability to UI (user interface) design.

This chapter tries to revive some of those earlier notions of mental models by first disentangling the various meanings and uses of terms such as mental models, user models, cognitive model, system models, and then reviewing the *research* on models in HCI. Although some of this research has influenced the *practice* of HCI, especially in the area of usability testing, there has been little application of models to the practice of UI design. A preliminary methodology is proposed for incorporating the user's model into the process of UI design. The chapter concludes with some speculation about application of cognitive science theories of mental models to HCI.

MENTAL MODELS IN COGNITIVE SCIENCE

Mental models became a powerful theoretical concept to explain how people construct internal representations of meaning (e.g. Johnson-Laird, 1981). A major contribution of this theory was the linkage between semantics and the world (e.g. Miller & Johnson-Laird, 1976). Where other psychological approaches had emphasised the words themselves—as entries in a mental dictionary, as linked semantic entities, or rules for specifying relations between words—mental models asserted that meaning is derived from the actual state of affairs such as they may exist in the world (Johnson-Laird, 1981, p. 117):

> The psychological theory of meaning that I wish to advance assumes that the mental representation of a sentence can take the form of an internal model of the state of affairs characterised by the sentence.

Evidence supporting the theory comes from studies which demonstrate that the order of sentences can affect the speed, i.e. ease, of comprehension (e.g. Ehrlich & Johnson-Laird, 1982; Garnham, Oakhill, & Johnson-Laird, 1982; Mani & Johnson-Laird, 1982; Oakhill & Garnham, 1985). A similar mechanism can be used to explain how people understand anaphoric references (e.g. Ehrlich, 1980, 1983; Ehrlich & Rayner, 1983; Garnham & Oakhill, 1987).

In constructing a mental model of a discourse, readers and listeners may fill in additional information that is not explicit in the text. Although these experiments demonstrate the ease of constructing a mental model, the power of mental models lies in the operations that can be performed once the model is constructed. Once users have constructed a model, they can infer relations between the items which are represented in the mental model, but not present in the sentences themselves (e.g. Garnham, 1987). The ability to "run" the model is especially powerful in explaining the processes of deduction. Here it is argued that people construct a mental model of the state of affairs described in the problem. They then "run" that model to test it against different inputs or scenarios to draw a conclusion. This model is a better predictor of errors and the relative difficulty of problems than theories that assume people follow conventional syntactic rules of logic and inference (see Johnson-Laird & Byrne, 1991). A large number of experiments now support this theory of mental models (see e.g. Johnson-Laird, 1983, 1989, 1993 for further details) including extensions to various domains of expertise.

The remaining part of this chapter will explore whether some people build and/or use models to guide the way they learn and interact with computers. In this regard all users may be regarded as "novices" in the sense described by Johnson-Laird (1989, p.485):

> An important difference between the way a novice and an expert reason about a physical situation is that the novice's model represents objects in the world and simulates processes that occur in real time, whereas a trained scientist can construct a model that represents highly abstract relations and properties, such as forces and momenta.... The novice reasons qualitatively because appropriate quantitative reasoning calls for the more abstract model.

MENTAL MODELS IN HUMAN COMPUTER INTERACTION

Terminology

Whereas in cognitive science, mental models almost always apply to abstractions in people's heads, in HCI the source of the model is less clear. In the HCI literature, models variously refer to: (a) the actual model of the system, (b) the engineer's model of the system which gets embodied in its implementation, (c) the UI designer's model of the system, or (d) the user's model of the system[1].

---

[1] It should be noted that there is an additional meaning of "model" not covered here which is the system's model of the user, often referred to as user modelling by those in Artificial Intelligence who build adaptive systems and need a way to represent the target user.

Various HCI researchers have posited definitions of mental models. Carroll and Olson (1988) for instance, say that the most common use of the term "mental model" is:

a representation (in the head) of a physical system or software being run on a computer, with some plausible cascade of causal associations connecting the input to the output.

Some researchers have taken pains to point out the specific differences between the user's model and the model of the underlying system employed by the system's implementor e.g. (Gentner & Grudin, 1990, p.277):

A good engineer's model of the system is based on knowledge of the underlying mechanism, and therefore the interface most natural to the engineer is one that provides direct access to the control points in the mechanism. The user, however, is primarily concerned with the task to be accomplished, and a problem arises if the user's model of the task does not map cleanly onto the system mechanism. The user may not need to access control points directly or may wish to access a set of control points in systematically constrained ways. In that case, the engineer's ideal interface will not be a good interface for the user. It may be advantageous to base the user interface on a task model instead.

And Norman (1983, p.244):

it is important for us to distinguish among several different kinds of models and conceptualizations. Our conceptualization of a target system should not be confused with the mental model that a user creates of that system. The designer's conceptualization may also differ from the image that the system itself presents to the user. In the ideal world, the system image will be consistent with the designer's conceptualization, and the user's mental model will thereby be consistent with both.

Norman (1986, p.47) takes this further by explicitly identifying three distinct models: the *Design Model* (the implementor's model of the system), the *User's Model* (the user's model of the system), and the *System Image* which corresponds to the "look and feel", also known as the appearance and behaviour, of the system.

There really are three different concepts to be considered: two mental, one physical. First there is the conceptualization of the system held by the designer; second, there is the conceptual model constructed by the user; and, third, there is the physical image of the system from which the users develop their conceptual models. Both of the conceptual models are what have been called "mental models" but to separate the several different meanings of that term, I refer to these two aspects by different terms. I call the conceptual model held by the designer the Design Model, and the conceptual model formed by the user the User's Model. The third concept is the image resulting from the physical structure that has been built (including the documentation and instruction). I call that the System Image.

This separation of model into three parts is especially useful for bringing the practical elements of UI design into the picture. However, it should be noted that the Design Model (the implementor's model of the system) is in many ways also the system model. There is no representation in Norman's scheme for the UI designer's model of the system, which is distinct from the implementor's view in important ways. This chapter will use a slightly modified version of Norman's terminology as a way of organising the different perspectives and attitudes towards models in HCI. Throughout the rest of the chapter, the terminology will be as follows: *User's Model* (the user's model of the system); *Design Model* (UI designer's model of the system); *System Model* (implementor's model); *System Image* (look and feel).

Early Research

Some of the earliest research on models in HCI displayed a fascination with the mental models that people construct of their computer and other electronic systems. These models, it was posited, would let people understand and predict the behaviour of the system they were using (e.g. Halasz & Moran, 1983; Norman, 1983; Young, 1981, 1983). For instance, Card and Moran (1986) believed that giving users a clear, explicit model would let them understand the system better and perform operations more accurately. Halasz and Moran (1983) conducted an experiment in which half of a group were taught an explicit conceptual model of the calculator's stack and the other half were not given a model but only taught how to perform the necessary tasks. No difference was found between the groups in their accuracy of solving routine or even complex problems. However, when it came to solving problems that required some level of invention—that is, the users had to invent new methods—the group taught the model did get more problems correct. In particular, the model group was better able to perform novel tasks that required more cognitively intense problem-solving. The model, it was argued, helped users construct a better problem space in which to do the problem-solving necessary for creative solutions.

These results provide, at best, weak support for the benefit of mental models. And the research only addresses the role of mental models in learning new systems (see Bibby, 1992 for more recent work on the role of mental models in instruction). Although there continued to be some research on these conceptual models, especially on the mappings between models and tasks (e.g. Moran, 1981; Payne & Green, 1986) the early approach was overtaken by research that focused on users' cognitive models, especially those of the task domain.

Cognitive Models

The approach most closely associated with cognitive models is the seminal work of Card, Moran, and Newell (e.g. Card, Moran, & Newell, 1983; Newell & Card, 1985). Their theory of human information processing as applied to human–computer interaction has roots in cognitive psychology but clearly branches into engineering (Newell & Card, 1985, p.215): "A second principle is the need for an engineering-style theory of how the user interacts with the computer..." They want a model that can represent and characterise the behaviour of the computer user in a way that lets an "engineer" (in practice this could either be a software developer or a user interface designer) build a software system that will be easy to use because it matches the way the user works.

Newell and Card seek to explain and predict human–computer interaction by appealing to a model, called GOMS, which represents the set of tasks performed by a skilled computer user. These tasks are represented as:

● *Goals*.
● *Operators* (actions belonging to a user's repertoire of skills).
● *Methods* (sequences of subgoals and operators often carried out in an automatic fashion to achieve goals).
● *Selectional rules* (for choosing among different possible methods for reaching a particular goal).

The GOMS model was described by Newell and Card, (1985, p. 215):

> The GOMS family of models of the user is an approximate way of characterizing user behavior in terms of goals, basic operations that the user could perform, methods for achieving the goals, and selection rules for choosing among alternative methods.

The GOMS model has been used to predict performance using a text editor, which is described as a "routine cognitive skill" (Card et al., 1983). In the studies, the researchers observe and time skilled users as they carry out a set of designated tasks on the computer. The results demonstrate differences in the speed of operations between different text editors in line with the predictions made by the theory (e.g. Roberts & Moran, 1983).

Another version of this model, the Keystroke-Level model, casts the GOMS model at the level of individual keystrokes to explain and predict expert, error-free performance. The model was used, for instance, to predict the preferred number of buttons on the mouse of a Xerox Star product by first running some tests with novice users and then using the model to extrapolate the data to expert users (Card & Moran, 1986). There has been and continues to be active research in the area of the GOMS model. John and Vera (1992), for instance, have extended it to the world of video games, where they have used the GOMS model to predict the performance and strategy of an expert Super Mario Brothers player. Others have had similar success in domains that focus on primarily sensorimotor activity by skilled operators (e.g. Gray, John, & Atwood, 1993; Gray et al., 1990).

However, the GOMS model has also been subjected to considerable criticism, especially related to its focus on low-level operations, highly skilled users, and error-free performance, as well as its lack of ability to account for individual differences or effects of fatigue (e.g. Carroll & Campbell, 1986; Olson & Olson, 1990). Further criticism and analysis of the underlying experimental methodology can be found in Barnard (1991).

One of the effects of the debate has been to increase awareness, visibility, and the search for better models to account for and predict novice and expert performance with computer systems. Indeed, despite criticism of it, the GOMS formulation has provided the field of HCI with tools for building models of human behaviour. Although the model itself may fall short in focusing too much on low-level tasks by skilled users and in ignoring individual differences and effects of motivation, it does provide a more systematic, principled set of predictions than most other approaches. The predictions that are generated from these and models like them can help to narrow the design space by specifying which kinds of systems are likely to be hard to learn or hard to use. Designers can then focus their attention on the range of system designs that are predicted to be easy to learn and use.

The GOMS approach and its followers have dominated the research on models in HCI. However, to date it has had little influence on the practice of UI design, other than being translated into a technique for evaluating the difficulty of an existing user interface (e.g. Gray et al., 1993).

User Interface Design

Although cognitive models such as GOMS can help to limit the design space, that space may still be very large. As UIs evolved from the glass teletype model of the early 1980s that displayed text only, to the Graphical User Interfaces (GUI) that are now ubiquitous, the practice of designing these interfaces got more complex and has become a profession in its own right. For instance, borrowing an analysis from Moran and others (e.g. Moran, 1981; Payne & Green, 1986 as articulated in Baecker, Grudin, Buxton, & Greenberg, 1995), it can be seen that the UI is composed of many levels:

- *Task level:* the set of tasks the system is intended to accomplish; *e.g. copying text from one location to another.*
- *Semantic level:* the conceptual objects and actions of the system; *e.g. "segments of text", "copy", "delete".*
- *Syntactic level:* the command language with which users communicate with the system; *e.g. a command syntax might be (i) select text; (ii) issue copy command; (iii) move cursor to new location; (iv) issue paste command.*
- *Interaction level:* the physical actions associated with each element of the syntactic level, which corresponds to the "lexical level" in language; *e.g. specifies exactly what happens when each of these actions is taken; e.g. the "paste" operation leaves copied text in a buffer.*
- *Spatial layout level:* the arrangement of input and output devices and the graphics display; *e.g. determined when command names are placed on the display (if at all).*
- *Device level:* all the remaining physical features; *e.g. the pixel pattern used to place a character on a particular display.*

The GOMS approach applies best to the first of these.

If GOMS models and their ilk have not influenced the practice of UI design, does it follow that models have no place in the practical world of designing and developing user interfaces? UI design addresses the *System Image* component of the triad of models outlined earlier. But the System Image is not really a model. As Tognazzini (1992), one of the UI evangelists at Apple Computer Inc described it:

> The system image is an illusion designed to convey the design model.... The system image should make visible every structure, concept, and feature within an application. For example, if users may have difficulty understanding the order in which tasks need to be done, the menu bar titles can bear the name of each task, arrayed in proper order.

The System Image has the most direct, immediate effect on the user. It is through the system's image, its appearance, and behaviour (or "look and feel") that the user interacts with the system.

Developing that System Image, the "look and feel" is now influenced more by UI standards (e.g. Apple Computer Inc, 1992; Kobara, 1991; Microsoft Corp., 1987; Sun Computers Inc, 1990) or guidelines (e.g. Mullet & Sano, 1995) than by a consideration of the user's model or the system's model. Moreover, a process of iterative design has evolved that lets the system's engineers and UI designers evaluate and test the evolving system with users. (See Ehrlich, Stanley, & Shea, 1989; Butler & Ehrlich, 1994; Wiklund, 1994 for some case study descriptions of the design and testing process. See also Nielsen, 1993 for a review of usability testing and Baecker et al., 1995 for a general introduction to and review of all aspects of UI design and testing.) Following this process provides some assurance of building a system that will be easy for users to learn and use. Adhering to these methods and guidelines is often considered sufficient to design good interfaces. Most UI designers and system developers seem to see no need to pay attention to the underlying models when they design and build their systems.

Metaphors in UI Design

Even though most UI designers do not explicitly base their designs on the user's conceptual model, many of them do design a new interface around a metaphor, especially a metaphor that relates to some general knowledge users might be expected to have. But are metaphors a type of model?

When computer systems first began to be used by the general population rather than solely by engineers, it was believed that users learned new systems by drawing on their existing knowledge (e.g. Carroll & Thomas, 1982). The more familiar the system seemed to the user, the easier it would be to transfer existing knowledge of objects and the way they worked to the new computer domain. This belief led to a proliferation of models based on typewriters, filing cabinets, and desks. For instance, describing a computer as like a filing cabinet should help people understand concepts such as saving and organising files.

Metaphors were and still are prevalent as a way of introducing systems to new users, and, as a way for UI designers to organise many of the visual elements of the system (e.g. Lundell & Anderson, 1995; Moll-Carrillo et al., 1995). The most far-reaching use of metaphors has been the "desktop metaphor" first formulated by people working on the Xerox Star system (e.g. Bewley, Roberts, Schroit, & Verplank, 1983; Smith et al., 1983), carried over to the Apple Macintosh and then to Microsoft Windows.

But computer systems are not really desktops and the objects in the system do not really behave quite like their counterparts would in the real world. Messy computer screens are not the same as messy desks. And some of the more sophisticated manipulations that can be done on these computer-based objects have no real counterpart in the world of the physical desk. For this reason, many have preferred to think of these metaphors as user illusions (Kay, 1990) or myths (Rubinstein & Hersh, 1984). Halasz and Moran (1982) note that metaphors are really analogical models not conceptual ones. Users are invited to think that the computer system is like something else. But this approach falls apart when the system introduces elements, such as password protection, that have no real counterpart in the real world. For this reason, metaphors are not sufficient models and need to be supplemented with some level of conceptual analysis of the system.

Use of Mental Models: Information Navigation

The basic assumption of a model-based approach to UI design is that users construct an internal model of the computer system and use that model to guide and predict their interaction with the system. There is a strong intuitive belief that such models are constructed, but little in the way of empirical data. Some evidence that users build such models and use them to guide their interaction comes from a recent study by Campagnoni and Ehrlich (1989) of people's navigational behaviour using an on-line Help system.

The Help system, part of the Sun386i^{TM} workstation, was designed with three levels of hierarchy. The top level (i.e. the level with the most general information) contained a Table of Contents which listed the titles of the eight main "handbooks" (topics) and an entry for the Index. Users could navigate to any one of the handbooks from the top level. From the handbooks, users could go down one more level to the page describing a particular topic. In addition to going to the next or previous page, users could go from a document up one level to a Handbook or up two levels to the main Table of Contents by following the appropriate hypertext link. See Fig. 12.1 for an illustration of the organisation of the contents.

In Campagnoni and Ehrlich's (1989) study people were asked to assume the role of a Help desk administrator. In this role they received Email requests for information from six fictitious users. Their task was to respond to each mail message by finding the name of the handbook, the section, and the page on which the answer could be found. We recorded the time taken to find each answer, the correctness of the answer, and the navigational strategy. We also measured each person's spatial skill using a standardised paper-folding test of spatial visualisation.

If users construct a mental model to guide their navigation, we would expect to find them using that model to jump between levels. Because the different levels were not visible on the screen at the same time, users would have to rely on some kind of internal representation of the overall structure to use this strategy. An alternative strategy would be to navigate by moving through the pages in sequence. In this way, the user would only have to retain memory of the closest page for which there was also some reminder on the screen.

Everyone answered the questions correctly. But there was a significant correlation between spatial visualisation skills and solution time; the people with better visualisation skills took less time to answer the questions. There was also a significant negative correlation between visualisation skill and the frequency of returning to the Top Level Table of Contents; people with better visualisation skills could navigate without having to return to the common starting point. There was no significant correlation between

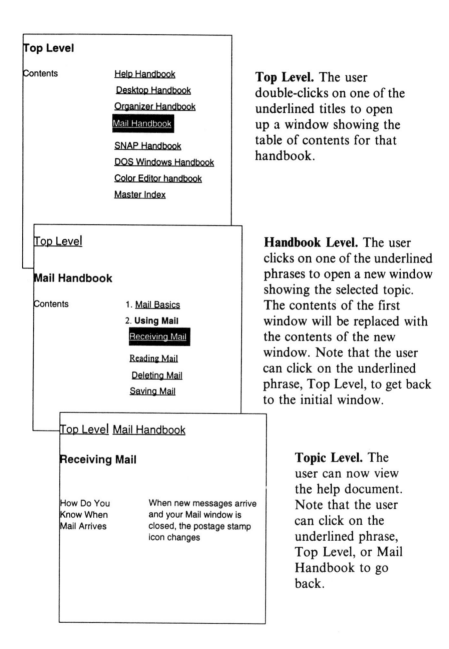

Top Level. The user double-clicks on one of the underlined titles to open up a window showing the table of contents for that handbook.

Handbook Level. The user clicks on one of the underlined phrases to open a new window showing the selected topic. The contents of the first window will be replaced with the contents of the new window. Note that the user can click on the underlined phrase, Top Level, to get back to the initial window.

Topic Level. The user can now view the help document. Note that the user can click on the underlined phrase, Top Level, or Mail Handbook to go back.

FIG. 12.1   Illustration of the information architecture for the Sun 386i on-line Help system.

visualisation skill and computer expertise, implying that experience in using a computer does not necessarily confer better skill in building an internal model of an information system.

These results suggest that people with good visualisation skills can construct a better internal model of an information architecture. The link between visualisation skills and performance also suggests that there is a visual or spatial component to people's internal models, at least for navigating in information spaces. Note that the study argues that people build a mental representation of the information *structure* which they use to guide their search. A similar suggestion was made some time ago by Wright (1983) who argued that during the course of reading, people build up a mental representation of the information given in the document. This representation, she argued, might be built up from the content of the text in much the same way as was proposed in the early research on mental models cited at the beginning of this chapter. But the mental representations might also correspond to the surface structure of the text, perhaps in similar fashion to the information structure in this study. The help system used in the study was quite simple and contained a limited number of documents. Many on-line documentation or information systems are considerably more complex and users frequently feel lost, unable to find their way back or forward to the desired text (see Nielsen, 1995 for a recent review of hypertext systems). It may be argued that one of the failures of these systems is that they are not providing a sufficiently clear model of the organisation of the information.

One can draw an analogy here with physical spaces. For instance, in a fascinating series of studies, Lynch (1960) argues that people's images of the cities in which they live are often partial rather than complete, and made up of elements such as paths, edges, districts, nodes, and landmarks for which there is often an added experiential component. Moreover, poorly laid out spaces can cause tremendous confusion for people. For instance, in Boston there is a public garden called Boston Common. This stretch of land, which is large enough to prevent visual access to more than one boundary at a time, actually has five sides which meet almost at right angles at each corner. People who cross this park frequently exit at unexpected places because they believe the area has four sides not five (Lynch, 1960). Even conscious knowledge of the layout is not sufficient to prevent confusion.

Although concepts from physical spaces may or may not translate into the information space on the computer, the point remains that there is a need for the UI designer to pay attention to the organisation of information, perhaps by constructing a model or some other abstraction to represent the elements of the information space and their relationships. Although that particular task will not be tackled here, a general methodology for developing the *Design Model* (the designer's model of the system) and its relation to the *User Model* (the user's model of the system) will be described.

DESIGN MODELS

The Design Model, as used here, represents the main concepts inherent in a software product and the canonical set of operations that apply to those concepts. For instance, some word processing applications include the concept of a page as an addressable object. As such, users can apply operations to it, such as moving it or deleting it. In applications where a page is not an addressable object, users can delete a page by deleting all the contents of that page, but they cannot delete the page directly.

The Design Model addresses issues of system behaviour. For instance, when an object gets deleted is it removed from the system entirely or simply moved to a holding bin somewhere (e.g. "recycled")? Clearly the user's actions will differ depending on which version is implemented. If the user knows that a "deleted" object is simply moved to a holding bin, he or she may be more likely to delete things and will have different recovery procedures if the deletion was unintended than if deletion resulted in the object being removed from the system entirely.

Design Models also address issues of separation between presentation and specification (similar to the model–view separation in programming languages). For instance graphical and textual objects can have two levels of specification: a level that describes the object itself and another level that describes its particular presentation on the screen. The words also have a presentation level which includes such things as the font, character size, spacing, whether the word is in italics or in bold etc. There are some cases when it is better to separate the underlying specification from the presentation level. For instance, when I copy formatted text from one place to another, only the text remains; the original formatting gets converted to the style in which the copied text is placed. In other cases, the intended meaning is carried by the combination of the underlying specification and presentation, and to separate them is to tamper with the communication. If I send someone a document in which I have underlined certain words, it matters to me if the way they view that document converts italics back to plain text. There is no single answer.

Design Models can address issues of granularity. For instance some word processing systems operate on the level of individual characters. If a user wants to delete a word, he or she would have to select the word by selecting each letter, although not necessarily one by one if the system has a shortcut for making multiple selections. The user would employ a different set of operations if the word processing system represented a word as a unit.

Design Models can address issues of containment and hierarchy. For instance, the system will behave differently and hence create different expectations for the user, if one object is nested inside another than if the objects are equally accessible from some high level, say the desktop itself.

Thinking explicitly about the level of representation can lead to representing objects that were hidden, making them "first class objects". For instance, in most networked systems, there is no explicit representation of the people who are on the system. It may be possible to reach other users by sending Email or typing in a command such as "finger" which returns information about whether a particular user is currently logged in. But there is no notion of "person" as an object. In an innovative design, Tim Shea (Shea, 1989) argued for the concept of "people" as directly represented in the interface. Making the concept of a person a "first class object" enables the design and development of better tools for communicating with people on the system.

Examples of Design Models

In their book, *The human factor*, Rubinstein and Hersh (1984), using a commonplace example such as an ATM (Automated Teller Machine), argue that this system includes such concepts as:

- The overall transaction; how the user identifies themselves to the system.
- Identification codes.
- Balances.
- Deposits.
- Withdrawals.
- Transfers.
- The current state relative to the overall process.

In an early tutorial on designing graphical interfaces, Hemenway, Rosenberg, and Isaacs (1991) compare and contrast the concepts embodied in two popular word processors: Microsoft Word 3.0 and FrameMaker. They argue that there are some concepts in common between the two systems. These common concepts include: character, paragraph, document, margin, page number, footnote, leading, index, graphic, table, table of contents. However, Microsoft Word also offers the concepts of: header, footer, columns, page numbering controls, and footnote format, whereas FrameMaker, with a coarser level of granularity, only offers columns. Hemenway et al. go on to provide examples of how objects have actions associated with them. For instance, if one were to design a tool for creating bibliographies as part of a word processing application, it is likely to include the concept of *Reference*. This concept would have associated with it operations such as: *Display, Add, Delete, Modify, Print, Duplicate*.

Developing the Design Model

The process of developing Design Models as part of the overall design was followed by a number of the UI designers at Sun Microsystems. Matt Belge, for one, developed a Design Model for visualising numeric information in a way that would take advantage of an advanced computing environment (Belge, 1993). The model, by making the concepts and the operations explicit, would reveal (and correct) areas of potential confusion, so that users could better understand the relationships between the different kinds of data elements. For instance, the model included the concept of a Viewer which was used to visually represent data in forms such as bar graphs, scatter plots, tables, and maps. The user could: create, name, save, copy, open, and destroy Viewers. These operations were common across a wide variety of objects that were part of the overall desktop environment.

UI design is a relative not an absolute concept. Designers need to know the purpose and intent of the product and the characteristics of the intended user population before developing the UI. They must take into account the intentions, motivation, background, and experience of potential users. Furthermore, individual differences need to be taken into account in developing the design. A "look and feel" that may appeal to novice users may be considered too simplistic for experienced users; a spreadsheet application that is for people who intend to share their documents may require a different look and feel from an application intended for a single user only.

When the designer constructs the user model of the system, he or she relies on an informed understanding of the goal, user population, and principal features of the product. In addition, the designer may choose to undertake a task analysis (e.g. Rubinstein & Hersh, 1984) to understand how users are carrying out similar tasks now. In doing the task analysis, the designer will be looking to see: what kind of operations the user is performing, what the operations are performed on, what additional materials need to be at hand to complete the task; how often the task is done—for instance, if a task is done frequently the user will probably remember the commands once learned, if done infrequently the user will need to be reminded of the commands—whether the task is done under time pressure, whether the task involves other people and so forth.

Design Models and User Models

In many ways the Design Model is a proxy for the user's model of the system. As such it should guide the user's interaction by predicting or anticipating outcomes, much as the user's own conceptual model might do. But having the Design Model, or rather its instantiation in a particular UI implementation, take an active part in the interaction with the user raises questions of the balance between computer and user in the Human–Computer Interaction. These questions are explored in the next section by seeing what may be learned from notions such as "runnability" which played an important role in theories of mental models.

FROM COGNITIVE SCIENCE TO HCI

Theories of mental models and the development of implementable UI Design Models might, at first blush, appear to have nothing in common. Although this might be true, it is also the case that the process of applying theoretical ideas to a practical, applied domain requires many levels of translation. And there are reasons for believing that HCI is a legitimate arena for application of cognitive science theories (e.g. Card & Polson, 1990, p. 120):

> Human–computer interaction is both an engineering (and design) subdiscipline concerned with how to build human interfaces as well as a set of research topics in supporting sciences. The topic of human–computer interaction plays a different role in design-oriented versus science-oriented disciplines. In the part of computer science concerned with system construction, the human interface is one of the major components of interactive systems—typically more than half of a system's lines of code. In industrial design, the human interface is likewise one of the objects to be designed. But in cognitive science, human–computer interaction is an application domain for the science. Human–computer interaction tasks provide environments to explore numerous important theoretical issues in cognitive science, such as the acquisition and transfer of skills.

On the other hand, cognitive science aims for general theories of human comprehension and processing. There is no "person" here: the correctness of the theory is determined by refutation and counter-example (both argumentative and empirical) rather than by the action or behaviour of any particular person, user or subject. The model is postulated and abstractly characterised but not actually used; models are the subject matter of the theory. In HCI the "model" is one that not only needs to appeal to the person who created it, but must also make sense to the "user" (even a notional one), and the group of UI designers and engineers responsible for the design and implementation of the system.

Many of the distinctions between the use of "model" as a theoretical construct and "model" as part of the practical design of user interfaces refer to the distinction between science and engineering in the guise of psychological theories and design practice. The differences can be clearly seen in the rhetoric used to talk about computers. For instance, in the preface to a book of readings in HCI, Baecker et al. (1995, p.xi) say:

> Computer systems are found throughout our society. Schoolchildren, scholars, secretaries, bank tellers, middle managers, executives, nurses, factory workers, animators, printers, architects, and planners are all discovering that computers are changing roles and expectations, enhancing some careers, trivializing or eliminating others.

Some computer systems run with little or no intervention, but most are interactive—they have human users who are engaged in computer-assisted tasks. The human–computer interface, also called the user interface, is often the single most important factor in the success or failure of an interactive system or application.

There is nothing notional or abstract about computers here; they are a major player visible throughout the discourse on human–computer interaction.

In cognitive science, the computer is more of a ghost-like player who may be heard but not seen (Johnson-Laird & Wason, 1977, p.9):

> An undisputed virtue of the computer is that it provides a metaphorical solution to the traditional dichotomy between the brain and the mind. A computer is an organized physical system, but from a logical standpoint it does not matter whether it is built from relays, valves, transistors or microchips. If its circuitry is appropriate, then it can imitate the behaviour of any other computer. What is crucial is not its physical realisation but the logic of its operations.

However, despite these fundamental differences in assumption, outlook, and outcome, I believe there are some valuable lessons to be learned from applying theoretical concepts from cognitive science to HCI.

Runnability

One of the powerful notions to come from the theory of mental models is the notion of "running" the model to test out possible outcomes in advance of some action such as drawing a deduction from a set of premises. In contrast, say, to schemas, which can be argued to be a static representation, "running" a model is a dynamic process of building, running, and perhaps then changing, the internal mental representation. This also means that the model can be used predictively and in advance of carrying out some action. It is in this sense of generating predictions or hypotheses that it is most applicable to HCI. If it is the case that people construct mental representations in order to guide their interaction with a system, then those representations are really only useful if they direct the user's actions in some fashion. As Card and Moran (1986, p.595) have said:

> The user's model provides an integrated package of knowledge that allows the user to predict what the system will do if certain commands are executed, to predict the state of the system after the commands have been executed, to plan methods for novel tasks, and to deal with odd error situations.

Consider the following observation. A currently popular activity is viewing "pages" on the World Wide Web via a browser. Most pages have hypertext links, which users can follow to get to other related pages. One of these browsers, called Netscape, has a feature commonly referred to as a history list, which is accessible under the "Go" button. As different pages are opened and displayed, the name of that page is added to the list. Many people believe that the way the list is constructed is that the names of pages are added in sequence with each new page being appended to the existing list. Based on this "sequence model" people will often use the list as a quick shortcut to get to a particular page that was opened recently, with the expectation that the page will appear on the list in terms of its recency of being opened; pages opened recently will be near the end of the list. However, the system has implemented a slightly different model which we can call a "linked list model". In this model, the system does indeed keep track of pages in the order in which they are opened. However, if a user returns to a particular page and then follows a hypertext link from that page that is different from the link followed the first time, the system will delete all the originally linked pages. Thus, the system does not simply keep a sequential list of all pages as they are opened, but keeps a much more sophisticated chaining of pages and related pages somewhat akin to dropping breadcrumbs when following a path and then retrieving them as the path is retraced.

In informal observation it is clear that users have a different model from the one implemented. Users will be surprised when they learn that a page that was recently opened is no longer on the list. That is, users have indeed constructed a mental representation of part of the system and used that representation to predict and guide their behaviour. Their model, however, happens not to match the model implemented by the system. But they are constructing and "running" a model. If users simply had a static representation that was not used to generate predictions, they might rely on the history list as it is presented and hence not be surprised by which items are included in that list.

Distribution of Models

A similar idea was recently proposed by O'Malley and Draper (1992). They argued that models don't really guide inferences or help the user make predictions because the model is not in the user's head but distributed amongst several structures, one of which is the user and one of which is the system. Their argument is motivated by experiments which show that people rely on elements of the visual display to guide their interaction rather than their own internal representation. There is a certain appeal to the thought of offloading some of the cognitive demands of using a computer system to the system itself, as well as a resonance with other work. For instance Card, Pavel, and Farrell (1984) argue that:

The display of a computer [can act as] an external memory that is an extension of the user's own internal memory, one with which he can remember and keep track of more information than otherwise.

There is also a prevalent view within social psychology that knowledge, and especially expertise, is distributed among members of a group who work closely together. For instance, Hutchins (1990) reports on a study of how expertise gets distributed among a group of skilled sailors charged with navigating large ships. This work is one example of socially distributed systems which, while not specifically based on mental representations, acknowledge the need and importance of distributing rather than centralising knowledge.

But even if it is the case that mental representations of computer systems are distributed between the user, the system, and other elements such as manuals, there are a number of ways this might occur: (a) The system may have no model, but the user nevertheless infers one. This is quite common, as many systems are designed without an explicit model. (b) The system may have a complete model and the user may have a complete but different model. The example of the history list given earlier would fit this case. I venture that most UI designers who think about mental models at all would probably assume that the user has a complete model, even though it may be fragmentary. (c) A third case is that the system has a complete model and the user only has a partial model. This is the position espoused by O'Malley and Draper. Even within each of these cases, there are questions about whether the user's model of the system is complete or partial, erroneous or fragmentary.

Form of Representations

Discussion of the possible distribution of representations also raises the issue of the form of representation. Based on the study reported earlier in this chapter (Campagnoni & Ehrlich, 1989), it can be argued that users construct spatial models of the information structure. Although such a model can only be a representation and not an exact replica of the structure, the model does have certain visual, concrete properties. By comparison it may also be argued that users construct an abstract model of the rules needed to interact with a computer system. These rules help the user, transfer what they know about one system to learning and using another one. This striving for consistency has been one of the driving forces behind establishing UI standards. For instance, all applications built to run in Microsoft Windows adhere to a certain set of standard methods for common elements such as menus, window controls, item selection, cut and paste etc. Users who become experienced with one system are able to transfer what they have learned to new systems that adhere to the same conventions or standards. It can be argued that users have an internal representation of the system. However, that representation is almost certainly not spatial, in the sense that users represent something like a hierarchical help system. Any notion of mental models in HCI must therefore be able to accommodate a variety of representations.

SUMMARY

This chapter has explored linkages, both historical and intellectual, between mental models as espoused in cognitive science, cognitive models in HCI research, and design models in UI design. The differences between these three disciplines are profound. However, it was argued that important theoretical concepts such as the "runnability" of a model may resonate with UI designers as well as with researchers. If this turns out to be the case, there is an opportunity to build on a theoretical and research foundation in developing a discipline of UI design, and an opportunity for theoreticians and researchers to look to HCI as a fertile area for exploring new ideas.

ACKNOWLEDGEMENTS

This paper benefited enormously from numerous discussions with my colleagues, Arnold Smith and Matt Belge, who took the time to read and comment on several drafts. Many others read and provided valuable comments on the paper. I especially thank Eric Bergman, Don Gentner, and Candy Sidner. Alan Garnham and Jane Oakhill gave me helpful and cogent comments at various junctures despite barriers of time, distance, and technology. I also wish to thank them for the opportunity to write this chapter.

REFERENCES

Apple Computer Inc. (1992). *Human interface guidelines: The Apple desktop interface.* Reading, MA: Addison-Wesley.

Baecker, R.M., Grudin, J., Buxton, W.A.S., & Greenberg, S. (Eds.) (1995). *Readings in human–computer interaction: Toward the year 2000.* (2nd Edn.). San Francisco: Morgan Kaufmann.

Barnard, P. (1991). The contributions of applied cognitive psychology to the study of human–computer interaction. In B. Shackel & S. Richardson (Eds.), *Human factors for informatics usability.* Cambridge: Cambridge University Press.

Belge, M. (1993). *Object visualization user model.* SunSoft internal report.

Bewley, W.L., Roberts, T.L., Schroit, D., & Verplank, W.L. (1983). Human factors testing in the design of Xerox's 8010 "Star" office workstation. In *Proceedings CHI'83 Conference on Human Factors in Computing Systems* (pp.72–77). New York: ACM.

Bibby, P.A. (1992). Mental models, instruction and internalization. In Rogers, Y., Rutherford, A., & Bibby, P.A. (Eds.) (1992). *Models in the mind: Theory, perspective and application.* London: Academic Press.

Butler, M-B., & Ehrlich, K. (1994). Usability engineering for Lotus 1-2-3 Release 4. In M.E. Wiklund (Ed.), *Usability in practice: How companies develop user-friendly products.* Boston, MA: AP Professional.

Campagnoni, F.R., & Ehrlich, K. (1989). Information retrieval using a hypertext-based help system. *ACM Transactions on Information Systems, 7*, 3, 271–291.

Card, S.K., & Moran, T. (1986). User technology: From pointing to pondering. Reprinted in R.M. Baecker, J. Grudin, W.A.S. Buxton & S. Greenberg (Eds.) (1995). *Readings in human–computer interaction: Toward the year 2000* (2nd Edn.). San Francisco: Morgan Kaufmann.

Card, S.K., Moran, T., & Newell, A. (1983). *The psychology of human–computer interaction.* Hillsdale, NJ: Lawrence Erlbaum Associates Inc.

Card, S.K., Pavel, M., & Farrell, J. (1984). Window-based computer dialogues. In B. Shackel (Ed.), *Human–computer interaction—Interact 84 (London, 1984)* (pp.239–243). Amsterdam: Elsevier Science Publishers, BV.

Card, S.K., & Polson, P.G. (1990). Introduction to special issue on foundations of Human–Computer Interaction. *Human–Computer Interaction, 5*, 119–123.

Carroll, J., & Campbell, R. (1986). Softening up hard science: Response to Newell and Card. *Human–Computer Interaction, 2(3)*, 227–249.

Carroll, J., & Olson, J. (1988). Mental models in human–computer interaction. In M. Helander (Ed.), *Handbook of human–computer interaction.* Amsterdam: North-Holland.

Carroll, J., & Thomas, J.C. (1982). Metaphor and the cognitive representation of computing systems. *IEEE Transactions on Systems, Man and Cybernetics, 12(2)*, 107–116.

Ehrlich, K. (1980). Comprehension of pronouns. *Quarterly Journal of Experimental Psychology, 32*, 247–255.

Ehrlich, K. (1983). Eye movements in pronoun assignment: A study of sentence integration. In K. Rayner (Ed.), *Eye movements in reading.* New York: ACM Press.

Ehrlich, K., & Johnson-Laird, P.N. (1982). Spatial descriptions and referential continuity. *Journal of Verbal Learning and Verbal Behavior, 21*, 296–306.

Ehrlich, K., & Rayner, K. (1983). Pronoun assignment and semantic integration during reading: Eye movements and immediacy of processing. *Journal of Verbal Learning and Verbal Behavior, 22*, 75–87.

Ehrlich, K., Stanley, B., & Shea, T. (1989). Incorporating usability studies and interface design into software development. *Proceedings USENIX Technical Conference, summer 1989.* New Jersey: Datapro

Garnham, A. (1987). *Mental models as representations of discourse and text.* Chichester, UK: Ellis Horwood.

Garnham, A., & Oakhill, J.V. (1987). Interpreting elliptical verb phrases. *Quarterly Journal of Experimental Psychology, 39A*, 611–627.

Garnham, A., Oakhill, J.V., & Johnson-Laird, P.N. (1982). Referential continuity and the coherence of discourse. *Cognition, 1*, 29–46.

Gentner, D.R., & Grudin, J. (1990). Why good engineers (sometimes) create bad interfaces. In *Proceedings of CHI'90 Conference on Human Factors in Computing Systems* (pp.277–282). New York: ACM.

Gray, W., John, B., & Atwood, M. (1993). Project Ernestine: A validation of GOMS for prediction and explanation of real-world task performance. *Human-Computer Interaction, 8(3)*, 237–309.

Gray, W., John, B., Stuart, R., Lawrence, D., & Atwood, M. (1990). GOMS meets the phone company: Analytic modeling applied to real-world problems. *Proceedings INTERACT '90* (pp.29–34). Amsterdam: Elsevier (North Holland).

Halasz, F., & Moran, T.P. (1982). Analogy considered harmful. In *Proceedings of the Conference on Human Factors in Computing Systems,* (Gaithersburg, Maryland, 1982) (pp.383–386).

Halasz, F., & Moran, T.P. (1983). Mental models and problem solving in using a calculator. *Proceedings of CHI '83,* (Boston, 1983), (pp.212–216). New York: ACM.

Hemenway, K., Rosenberg, J., & Isaacs, E. (1991). *Designing graphical user interfaces*. Sun Microsystems internal course.

Hutchins, E. (1990). The technology of team navigation. In J. Galegher, R.E. Kraut, & C. Egido (Eds.), *Intellectual teamwork: Social and technological foundations of cooperative work*. Hillsdale, NJ: Lawrence Erlbaum Associates Inc.

John, B., & Vera, A. (1992). A GOMS analysis of a graphic, machine-paced, highly interactive task. *Proceedings of CHI'92, Human Factors in Computing Systems*, (Monterey, California, 1992) (pp.251–258). New York: ACM.

Johnson-Laird, P.N. (1977). Procedural semantics. *Cognition*, 5, 189–214.

Johnson-Laird, P.N. (1981). Mental models of meaning. In A. Joshi, B. Webber, & I. Sag (Eds.), *Elements of discourse understanding*. Cambridge, UK: Cambridge University Press.

Johnson-Laird, P.N. (1983). *Mental models: Towards a cognitive science of language, inference, and consciousness*. Cambridge, UK: Cambridge University Press.

Johnson-Laird, P.N. (1989). Mental models. In M.Posner (Ed.), *Foundations of cognitive science*. Cambridge, MA: MIT Press.

Johnson-Laird, P.N. (1993). *Human and machine thinking*. Hillsdale, NJ: Lawrence Erlbaum Associates Inc.

Johnson-Laird, P.N., & Byrne, R.M.J. (1991). *Deduction*. Hove, UK and London: Lawrence Erlbaum Associates, Ltd.

Johnson-Laird, P.N., & Wason, P.C. (1977). An introduction to the scientific study of thinking. In P.N. Johnson-Laird & P.C. Wason (Eds.). *Thinking: Readings in cognitive science* (pp.1–12). Cambridge, UK: Cambridge University Press.

Kay, A. (1990). User interface: A personal view. In B. Laurel (Ed.), *The art of human–computer interface design*. Reading, MA: Addison-Wesley.

Kobara, S. (1991). *Visual design with OSF/Motif*. New York: Addison-Wesley.

Lundell, J., & Anderson, S. (1995). Designing a "front panel" for Unix: The evolution of a metaphor. In *Proceedings CHI'95 Conference on Human Factors in Computing Systems*, (Denver, Colorado, 1995), (pp.573–579). New York: ACM Press.

Lynch, K. (1960). *The image of the city*. Cambridge, MA: MIT Press.

Mani, K., & Johnson-Laird, P.N. (1982). The mental representation of spatial descriptions. *Memory and Cognition*, 10, 181–187.

Microsoft Corporation (1987). *The Windows interface: An application design guide*. Redmond, WA: Microsoft Press.

Miller, G.A., & Johnson-Laird, P.N. (1976). *Language and perception*. Cambridge, MA: Harvard University Press.

Moll-Carrillo, H.J., Salomon, G., Marsh, M., Suri, J.F., & Spreenberg, P. (1995). Articulating a metaphor through user-centered design. In *Proceedings CHI'95 Conference on Human Factors in Computing Systems*, (Denver, Colorado, 1995), (pp.566–572). New York: ACM Press.

Moran, T. (1981). The command-language grammar: A representation of the user interface of interactive computer systems. *International Journal of Man–Machine Studies*, 15, 3–50.

Mullet, K., & Sano, D. (1995). *Designing visual interfaces*. New Jersey: SunSoft Press.

Newell, A., & Card, S.K. (1985). The prospects for psychological science in human–computer interaction. *Human–Computer Interaction*, 1, 209–242.

Nielsen, J. (1993). *Usability engineering*. Boston, MA: Academic Press.

Nielsen, J. (1995). *Multimedia and Hypertext: The Internet and beyond*. Boston, MA: AP Professional.

Norman, D.A. (1983). Some observations on mental models. In D. Gentner & A. Stevens (Eds.), *Mental models*. Hillsdale, NJ: Lawrence Erlbaum Associates Inc.

Norman, D.A. (1986). Cognitive engineering. In D.A. Norman & S.W. Draper (Eds.), *User centered design*. Hillsdale, NJ: Lawrence Erlbaum Associates Inc.

Oakhill, J. V., & Garnham, A. (1985). Referential continuity, transitivity and the retention of relational descriptions. *Language and Cognitive Processes*, 1, 149–162.

Olson, J., & Olson, G. (1990). The growth of cognitive modeling in human–computer interaction since GOMS. *Human–Computer Interaction, 5,* 221–265.

O'Malley, C., & Draper, S. (1992). Representation and interaction: Are mental models all in the mind? In Y. Rogers, A. Rutherford, & P.A. Bibby (Eds.), *Models in the mind: Theory, perspective & application.* London: Academic Press.

Payne, S., & Green, T. (1986). Task–action grammars: A model of the mental representation of task languages. *Human–Computer Interaction, 2,* 93–133.

Roberts, T., & Moran, T. (1983). The evaluation of computer text editors: Methodology and empirical results. *Communications of the ACM, 26(4),* 265–283.

Rubinstein, R., & Hersh, H. (1984). *The human factor: Designing computer systems for people.* Maynard, MA: Digital Press.

Shea, T. (1989). *User's view of the workgroup environment.* Sun Microsystems internal report.

Smith, D.C., Irby, C., Kimball, R., Verplank, W., & Harslem, E. (1983). Designing the Star User Interface. *Byte, 7(4),* 242–282.

Sun Microsystems Inc. (1990). *OPEN LOOK Graphical user interface application style guidelines.* New York: Addison-Wesley.

Tognazzini, B. (1992). *TOG on interface.* Reading, MA: Addison-Wesley.

Wiklund, M.E. (Ed.) (1994). *Usability in practice: How companies develop user-friendly products.* Boston, MA: AP Professional.

Wright, P. (1983). Manual dexterity: A user-oriented approach to creating computer documentation. In *Proceedings CHI'83 Conference on Human Factors in Computing Systems,* (Boston, 1983), (pp.11–18). New York: ACM Press.

Young, R. (1981). The machine inside the machine: Users' models of pocket calculators. *International Journal of Man–Machine Studies, 15,* 51–85.

Young, R. (1983). Surrogates and mappings: Two kinds of conceptual models for interactive devices. In D. Gentner & A.L. Stevens (Eds.), *Mental models.* Hillsdale, NJ: Lawrence Erlbaum Associates Inc.

13 Interaction and Mental Models of Physics Phenomena: Evidence from Dialogues between Learners

Tony Anderson, Christine Howe and Andrew Tolmie
Centre for Research into Interactive Learning,
University of Strathclyde, UK

INTRODUCTION

In 1983, two influential books were published which both bore the title *Mental models* (Johnson-Laird, 1983; Gentner & Stevens, 1983). As Rogers and Rutherford (1992) note, despite the shared theme, Johnson-Laird's treatment of mental models is relatively general; whilst the various chapters in Gentner and Stevens' collection concern specific examples. These examples focus on causality in such physical domains as heat (Wiser & Carey, 1983), electricity (Gentner & Gentner, 1983) and the motion of objects in free fall (McCloskey, 1983).

Johnson-Laird's notion of mental models derives directly from ideas expressed in Craik's (1943) book, *The nature of explanation*, in which Craik asserted that thought models reality. Although Craik clearly had analogue models in mind (using as an example the workings of the gear wheels of a calculator as a means of modelling the operations of arithmetic), more recent formulations of the idea have argued that human beings model reality by means of manipulating internal symbols. Johnson-Laird's approach is clearly in the latter vein. For example, he argues that reasoning requires the translation of external processes into internal representations in the form of symbols, the derivation of other symbols by an inferential process, and the retranslation of these new symbols into actions or results of some kind (e.g. recognising that a prediction has been confirmed). The mental model

247

functions by virtue of its components having the same "relation-structure" as those of the object or process being modelled.

According to Johnson-Laird, models permit the prediction of events (allowing, for example, the consequences of actions to be anticipated before trying those actions out in reality), and thus confer clear adaptive advantages. Moreover they also permit us to generate explanations of phenomena. In this respect, according to Johnson-Laird, they are to be distinguished from simulations, for simulations serve prediction only (Johnson-Laird, 1983, p.4). Models need neither be wholly accurate nor correspond completely with what they model in order to be useful. For example, a person's model of a television set may vary from "a box that displays moving pictures" to a highly detailed and elaborate representation of its functioning as possessed by a skilled TV repairman. In both cases these are nonetheless useful in that they permit predictions to be made about the course and outcomes of those events the individual has to deal with. Indeed, there are no complete mental models for any empirical phenomena.

Despite the specific nature of the mental models that they describe, the collection of papers published in Gentner and Stevens' book echo many of the points made by Johnson-Laird. For example, Norman (1983) claims that (a) mental models are incomplete, and (b) people's abilities to "run" their models are severely limited, both points that concur with Johnson-Laird's views. There is, however, an important point of contrast between the two accounts. In his 1983 book, Johnson-Laird focuses primarily on the use of mental models in reasoning and language comprehension; his more recent work (e.g. Johnson-Laird & Byrne, 1991) again focuses on deduction. The model theory of reasoning in particular presupposes that mental models can be rather transitory entities: they are constructed as needed and manipulated until a conclusion is reached, and subsequently discarded. In contrast, the chapters in Gentner and Stevens' book allude to models that are held over long periods of time and are relatively stable. Although Johnson-Laird does discuss such models (e.g. in his discussion of different models of how a TV set operates), much of his empirical work concerns the more transitory variety.

The present chapter examines something of the relationship between transitory models created during problem-solving and longer-term conceptions, but in the context of interaction and dialogue: given that dialogue can be viewed as a process of creating or negotiating models of the more transitory kind, what impact might this have on individually held and more enduring conceptions? We examined this question in relation to learners' understanding of phenomena in physics, specifically aspects of kinematics and dynamics, such as motion down an incline and free fall under horizontal motion.

MENTAL MODELS OF DYNAMICS AND KINEMATICS PHENOMENA

Kinematics concerns motion, whilst dynamics concerns not only motion but also the forces that produce motion, and their interplay. The starting point for our work was the growing evidence that individuals build relatively stable and enduring mental models of such phenomena. Indeed, the papers in Gentner and Stevens (1983) are a case in point. That McCloskey (1983), for instance, reviewed a number of studies in which students were asked to make predictions about object motion in various circumstances, and concluded that many adults entertain misconceptions about both the nature of object motion and its causes. For example, imagine a ball sliding along towards the edge of a cliff at a constant speed, rolling over the edge, and free-falling to the ground (see Fig. 13.1). What trajectory will the ball describe, and why?

The physicist's answer is that the ball will describe a parabolic path, as it continues in the forward direction at a constant speed, but accelerates vertically downward due to the effect of gravity. The interaction of these two velocities produces a perfect parabola. In practice many students who are untutored in physics (and even some physics undergraduates) give wrong answers to problems of this type. For example, some claim that the ball will continue with a purely horizontal trajectory after leaving the cliff edge and will subsequently fall through a purely vertical trajectory. Most think that the ball will ultimately describe a purely vertical trajectory immediately

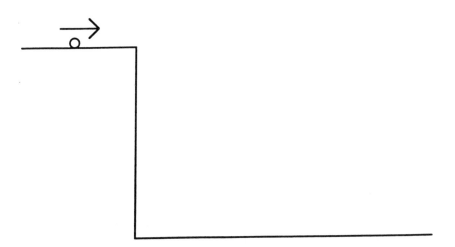

FIG. 13.1   An example of the type of problem presented by McCloskey (1983) to his students. The student's task is to predict the trajectory of the ball after it slides over the edge of the (frictionless) cliff.

prior to hitting the ground. McCloskey claimed that the reason why students make errors on this and other formally similar problems is that they hold a "naive theory" (sometimes referred to as an "alternative conception") of physical events which is remarkably similar to the mediaeval impetus theory, in which objects set in motion somehow "contain" a force that has to dissipate before other forces will exert an effect. Thus, according to this view the ball rolling off the edge of the cliff first has to dissipate its forward impetus, hence it continues in horizontal or quasi-horizontal forward motion. Its forward impetus being exhausted, it then begins to fall.

In an earlier study, we (Anderson et al., 1992) contrasted McCloskey's account with an alternative provided by diSessa (1988; but see also diSessa, 1993). In contrast to McCloskey's claim that naive theories of physics are well-articulated and consistent across individuals, diSessa claims that intuitive physics is a fragmented collection of ideas that are anything but coherent, and which have none of the systematicity normally associated with theories. He argues that, when asked to solve McCloskey-style problems, students rely on phenomenologically primitive notions (such as "force is a mover"). Their answers to superficially different but theoretically related questions will vary as a function of which phenomenological primitives are invoked. They will not appreciate that the problems are solvable by similar principles of physics, and that they have similar correct answers. Good examples are the ball rolling off the cliff quoted earlier, and a ball released from an aeroplane which is flying horizontally at a constant speed. In both cases, the result would be the ball describing a forward parabola. In practice, students will often claim that the ball dropped from the aeroplane will fall straight downwards or even backwards, whereas the ball rolling off the table is more likely to receive a response involving a forward component to its motion. (McCloskey's explanation for the variation in subjects' responses across these two problems is to claim that subjects believe that a body carried by another possesses no impetus; only the carrying vehicle does).

In order to examine these two accounts, we devised 16 force and motion problems, in which objects in either simple linear, disguised linear (i.e. the object is released from a carrying vehicle), circular, or pendular motion commence free-fall. Participants had to predict the trajectory (by drawing the path the object would fall through) and, for four of the problems, explain (using force diagrams and text) why the object would fall through the path depicted. The participants were 12–15-year-old school pupils (there is extensive evidence that from a young age children hold informal conceptions about physical phenomena comparable to those found in adults—see e.g. Driver, Guesne, & Tiberghien, 1985). Across the problems, we systematically varied the mass and velocity of the object. We hypothesised that if diSessa's account was correct then: (a) where mass and speed were both high or both low (e.g. the sail of a windmill breaking away as it revolved at high speed in a storm, and a slowly swinging conker breaking free from its string, respectively), pupils would give predictions that involved a correct or nearly correct response involving both a forward and a downward component to the motion; (b) where mass was high but forward speed was low (e.g. a casket of treasure dropped from a pirate ship), the mass should be salient and vertical-downwards responses should be more common; and (c) where forward speed was high but mass was low (e.g. a bullet fired from a gun), the forward speed should be salient and horizontal-forwards responses should be more common.

This was indeed what was found, and to that extent there was confirmation for diSessa's account rather than McCloskey's. However, the *explanation* responses were much more consistent with each other (consonant with McCloskey's rather than diSessa's account), and we also found that the correlation of prediction quality with explanation quality was close to zero. We concluded that there was evidence in favour of both accounts, and that our pupils, not being physics experts, displayed characteristics that accord well with Johnson-Laird's overall theory: their knowledge took the form of both fragmentary simulation elements (for making predictions) and integrated model elements (for generating explanations), and these two types of elements were largely uncoordinated. These data thus confirm the point made by both Norman (1983) and Johnson-Laird (1983) that an individual's mental model of a domain can be incomplete, inaccurate, and somewhat disorganised.

INTERACTION AND MENTAL MODELS

The work described illustrates that individuals do indeed possess at least some relatively stable mental models of particular domains. Where do these come from? Their initial development, it is suggested (e.g. by McCloskey, 1983), is a function of interacting with the world: in response to events external to us, we build models that permit prediction and explanation, according to what the circumstances require, and these only need to be roughly accurate. Hence the "alternative conceptions" noted in the literature on physics learning; these are inaccurate vis-a-vis a physicist's theory, but they work well enough in the real world most of the time for the individual, and so their inaccuracies endure.

Whatever the truth of this account (and it may be overly simplistic), the question remains as to how such mental models change. A straightforward answer would assert that, when confronted with an inaccurate prediction or explanation, the individual is forced to revise his/her model appropriately. One source of such contradictions is other people: during the course of interactions with others, their predictions or explanations may directly conflict with ours, forcing modification. This might work in a variety of ways, though. For example, suppose two people engage in joint problem-solving. Do they jointly construct a new transitory model (different from each of their prior individual models) that is tested on the spot and used to modify the respective individual enduring models? Or do the events transpiring during their joint problem-solving result not in the construction of a joint, transitory model but instead provoke subsequent individual reflection which results in change to the individual mental models? The key question is whether mental models are changed via a process of social construction of a transitory joint mental model which is subsequently internalised, or whether the individual's enduring model of the domain is adapted in the light of interactions with the others or with the world (without any joint transitory model being essential). This question can only be answered developmentally, i.e. by investigating what changes and why.

Piaget's (1972) theory of development is relevant here, for two reasons. First, Johnson-Laird's "mental models" bear a strong resemblance to Piaget's descriptions of mental transformations "attributed" to and paralleling (primarily physical) causal processes. Piaget also makes the same distinction as Johnson-Laird between these "models", which serve explanation, and an earlier stage of associated regularities "applied" to the world (which can only serve prediction); compare this to the distinction between models and simulations postulated by Johnson-Laird (1983; see earlier). Piaget is thus dealing with a similar notion to that of Johnson-Laird. (It should of course be emphasised that Piaget and Johnson-Laird differ sharply on the mechanisms underpinning performance; nevertheless, there are clear parallels between their views in respect of the distinction between simulations and models). Second, although Piaget (see e.g. Piaget, 1930; Piaget & Inhelder, 1956) certainly acknowledged that social interaction could play a major role in model construction, this process is for Piaget very much an *individual* one. This is because for Piaget (see e.g. Piaget, 1985) conceptual advance occurs as a result of conflict between mental representation and experience. This state of "disequilibrium" forces an adjustment (re-equilibration) of mental structures to take the new experience into account. In this way conceptions become more powerful in the sense of becoming more widely applicable. The point is that social interaction, by exposing the individual to conceptual conflicts that might never be experienced via physical interactions with the world, has considerable potential for forcing the pace of conceptual change. The Piagetian "equilibration" position, then, is that interaction serves to highlight information that is incompatible with aspects of each partici-pant's model, and this incompatibility has an "unsettling" effect, which the individual subsequently resolves. Models are not reconstructed during conversation, but rather are modified *later* as a function of what transpired in the conversation.

There is, however, no shortage of theorists who espouse a more directly social origin for conceptual growth. Perhaps most influential here is Vygotsky (see e.g. Vygotsky, 1978) who holds that individual conceptions derive from the internalisation of socially structured (by more advanced others) activities and experiences. This suggests that in general mental models can be socially constructed, and then internalised. A more refined notion (e.g. Doise & Mugny, 1984) is that models are negotiated, jointly shared products that are created during conversation. Doise and Mugny follow the Genevan school of thought in acknowledging the central importance of "socio-cognitive" conflict between individuals for conceptual advance. However, rather than seeing this as simply a catalyst for individual reconstruction, for Doise and Mugny such conflict is the signal for the parties to pool their ideas and amalgamate them into something better than any of the individual positions. Thus, from this perspective, conceptual conflict is the starting point for a jointly negotiated "compromise" model.

Although it might seem that these two broad views (Piaget's as opposed to Doise and Mugny's) are incompatible, there is another possibility: that they hold true at different stages in development, with Piaget's account being more appropriate for younger learners, and Doise and Mugny's for older learners. This is because younger learners may find it harder to cope with the social process of negotiation, as a result of limitations in the capacity of working memory. Johnson-Laird's (1983) views are again relevant here, for he argues (1983, pp.430–438) that other people's beliefs about something can be represented by embedding a mental model of their beliefs within one's own model of the relevant domain. Clearly, the notion of socially negotiating a transitory model presupposes the representation of the other person's beliefs, as well as comparison of it with one's own beliefs, and the undertaking of various manipulations of those beliefs as new information comes to light during the ongoing dialogue. As the capacity to build and manipulate models (and therefore to embed them one within another) is dependent on the capacity of working memory (Johnson-Laird, 1983), the greater the latter, the greater the capacity to negotiate transitory models.

Three of our studies bear on this hypothesis in that they involve an examination of individual students' conceptions of physics phenomena both before and after an intervention involving peer interaction and dialogue. Our studies therefore allow us to examine both conceptual change and the processes of interaction, and the relation between these two, and as the participants in the three studies varied in age, we can examine whether there was any age trend in the building and use of joint transitory models.

PEER INTERACTION AND MENTAL MODELS OF
PHYSICS PHENOMENA

Three studies were conducted. The first (Howe, Tolmie, & Rodgers, 1992) concerned primary school pupils' understanding of motion down an inclined plane. The second (Tolmie & Howe, 1993) concerned secondary school pupils' understanding of dynamics phenomena, and in particular, the paths followed by objects as they fell to the ground after having been in either linear, circular, or pendular motion immediately previously. The third study (Howe, Tolmie, Anderson, & Mackenzie, 1992) concerned undergraduates' understanding of kinematics phenomena, and in particular of the relative motion of objects from different visual perspectives. All three studies employed a similar three-phase procedure, in which: first, participants were individually pre-tested on a set of problems; second, they were assigned to groups (on the basis of pre-test scores) to work jointly on a set of problems like those used at pre-test, making joint responses and discussing the feedback; and third, they were individually post-tested some time after the group task to ascertain the extent of any conceptual change. The dialogues that took place during the group tasks were also recorded and analysed. This design allowed us to vary group composition in terms of whether the members of a group had initially similar or different ideas. The prediction from Piagetian theory is that different ideas should engender conceptual conflict and thus should act as the springboard for conceptual change, although this need not be achieved via a negotiated compromise; individual reflection is sufficient. The design also allows us to relate any observed conceptual change to the subjects' patterns of dialogue, and hence to their transitory models.

Study 1. Peer Interaction and Mental Models of
Motion Down an Incline

The participants for this study were 113 8- to 12-year old children with roughly equal numbers in each of the four age bands, primary four through seven. Each child was pre-tested to assess their conceptions about the variables relevant to motion down an incline. The pre-test involved using an apparatus to roll toy vehicles down slopes. The toy vehicles varied in weight ("light", "medium" and "heavy"), and the apparatus consisted of a wooden frame supporting four parallel slopes, with the height of the top of the slope (and therefore its steepness of angle of inclination) being adjustable (to give three inclines, "low", "middle" and "steep"). Each slope contained three gates, permitting three vehicle starting positions, "high", "medium" and "low". Lastly, two of the slopes were covered with identical surfaces, one with a higher-friction surface, and the fourth with a lower-friction surface, allowing "high", "middle" and "low" surface friction. The slopes terminated on a mat which was divided into "near", "middle" and "far" sections. The apparatus therefore allowed the manipulation of three variables which are relevant to motion down an incline (angle, starting positions and surface friction) and also one variable which although of negligible significance was known from previous literature to be cited by children as highly important (object weight). Manipulation of the variables formed the basis for interview schedules used in pre-, post- and delayed post-tests, which examined understanding of the variables independently and in combination.

Two types of problem were presented. Three-stage problems involved the presentation of a standard display in which a middle-weight vehicle had rolled down a middle-friction slope set at a medium angle from the middle starting position, and had come to rest in the middle section of the mat. The first stage of the problem involved another situation that varied on one variable only (e.g. a change in the vehicle's starting position). Pupils were required to predict where the vehicle would come to rest in the new situation, and to explain their answer; it was assumed that the explanations given would be revealing of the pupils' alternative conceptions. The second and third stages involved further adjustments, such that there were differences from the standard on two of the variables (e.g. steep angle and low starting position), and then on three (e.g. heavyweight vehicle, steep angle, and low starting position). At each stage, subjects were asked to predict whether the vehicle would travel to the same area of the mat as the standard, and to explain their answer. At no point did children actually observe the outcome of any manipulation. There were six problems of this type.

Interspersed between the three-stage problems were single-stage problems which described real-world situations (e.g. two lorries, both free-wheeling on the same slope but one being empty and the other being loaded with bricks); participants had to predict which (if either) would travel further from the foot of the slope and to explain their answers. Two of these items manipulated object weight, and the other three manipulated two variables of angle, starting position and surface friction. Again, no feedback was provided. Pre-test explanation responses for each of the manipulations (angle, starting position, surface friction, and object weight) on both the three-stage and single-stage items were scored on a scale from 1 to 4 reflecting the degree to which the variable in question was understood and coordinated with other variables. For example, a score of 1 was given when the variable in question was not considered, whereas a score of 4 reflected a full understanding of how the variables coordinated (e.g. distance travelled is directly related to starting position height, and increasing angle will decrease the effects of surface friction when the latter is held constant).

Using these scores children were assigned to one of three levels : Level I children (n = 27) scored only 1 or 2 for at least 50% of their responses; Level II children scored 2 or more for at least 50% of their responses; and level III children scored 3 or more for at least 50% of their responses. The children were then grouped into foursomes to produce the following: (a) Low Different, six groups consisting of two level I children and two level II; (b) High Different, six groups comprising two level II children and two level III; (c) Low Similar, three groups comprising four level I children and three groups comprising four level II children; and (d) High Similar, three groups comprising four level II children (the same three groups as for the Low Similar level II) and three groups comprising four level III children. Members of each group always came from the same school class.

Some six to eight weeks after the pre-test, the children worked on a group version of the task using the same apparatus. This began with children being asked to record private individual predictions about what they thought would happen when each of six different changes had been made from the standard situation on a single variable. Predictions were made by ticking on a card which area of the mat (the same area as in the standard situation, the near area or the far area) would be reached by the vehicle in the new situation. In the subsequent collaborative phase, for each of six problems a book instructed the pupils to set up a display which differed from the standard on one variable, in a manner analogous to the first stage of the three-stage item used in the pre-test. The book then instructed the children to compare their private predictions for that situation (on the cards), and where these were different, to discuss the predictions and come to an agreement. Once they had agreed a prediction, they were invited to test it, and to agree why an outcome had occurred when it was different from what they expected. The same procedure of agreeing a joint prediction, testing it, and explaining any discrepancy between prediction and outcome was repeated for the second and third stages of each problem. In addition to the six three-stage problems, the book also presented groups with five single-stage items for discussion, addressing real-world problems as in the pre-test.

Pre- to Post-test Change and its Relation to Dialogue. Both an immediate post-test (within 24 hours of the group task) and a delayed post-test (around four weeks later) were carried out, the former on a sample of 25% of the children and the latter on the entire sample. Both post-tests employed problems of identical structure to those contained in the pre-test. The delayed post-test, however, concluded with questions designed to elicit information on whether the subjects had tried to find out more about rolling down slopes from other sources following the group task (e.g. from books, other people, or direct observation). Analysis of a composite measure of change on all of the variables from the delayed post-test indicated that the children in the Low Different groups progressed more than the children in the Low Similar groups, regardless of whether they had started at Level I or Level II. In contrast, change in the High Different and High Similar groups was less, and not significantly different, although with hindsight it was realised that the former were less likely to differ over predictions than the Low Different groups, and may therefore have had substantially less occasion to become aware of, and discuss, their differences in understanding.

Further examination of the dialogues was motivated by the question: did groups jointly construct a superior conception which the individuals internalised, and, if not, when and how was change effected? A comparison was made between the pre-test scores of the individuals in each group and their within-group performance scores (computed by identifying from the videotapes the explanation to which each child was subscribing on completion of the relevant dialogue). The values on this measure were largely negative, indicating that the conceptions elaborated in the group context were *inferior* to those held by the same individuals at pre-test. The number of agreements (i.e. the number of other group members by whom a given child's explanations were accepted) of explanations mooted following the testing of predictions were also scored, and were not particularly high, typically averaging 1–2 other members of the group. This suggests that there was considerable failure to resolve conception disagreements; yet learning clearly occurred. Within-group change was regressive, yet pre- to delayed post-test change was generally positive: there must therefore have been many children who advanced from pre- to delayed post-test despite group performances that were worse than their pre-test. This suggests that learning did not involve the internalisation of conceptions that were jointly constructed within the groups. Furthermore, comparison of pre-, immediate post-, and delayed post-test scores indicated that the immediate post-test scores did not differ significantly from the pre-test scores, but were significantly lower than the delayed post-test scores. Further, there was a lack of significant correlation between within-group change and pre- to delayed post-test change. These findings taken together suggest that much of the progress in scores took place after the group tasks were over.

Questioning at the delayed post-test stage suggested that despite the post-group effects, the crucial information was generated within the groups rather than afterwards. Only 19 children reported looking for further information outside and subsequent to the group task, and even then some of the observations made were clearly irrelevant (e.g. attaching varying weights to balloons), some of the answers from parents were wrong (one subject being assured that object weight was critical), and some of the books read (e.g. an account of car manufacture) were unlikely to yield relevant or correct information. In any case, the 19 children who reported seeking further information did not outperform their peers in pre- to delayed post-test change.

Overall, the findings that within-group change was generally regressive, that there was a lack of significant correlation between within-group change and pre- to delayed post-test change, that the gain in learning was between immediate and delayed post-test, together with the lack of convincing evidence of within-group conception resolution, all point to the conclusion that learning was not taking place by groups negotiating a superior conception and this being internalised by individuals during the group sessions. Rather, the findings suggest that the experience created conflicts to be resolved individually and subsequently, rather than solutions to be remembered. In other words, learning was very much a matter of individual equilibration provoked by experience in the group context, and this finding is consistent with the Piagetian view, rather than that of Doise and Mugny. Thus, primary school pupils do not appear to learn by internalising a transitory model that is constructed with their peers at the time of interacting. If groups did construct such models during the course of interaction (and the evidence on agreements indicates that this was not guaranteed), they are clearly not the source of the stable conceptions that pupils hold over time. Our suspicion, outlined earlier, that primary age children would find difficult the process of negotiating a joint conception (a difficulty that is perhaps due to their having insufficient working memory capacity to embed models within one another as suggested by Johnson-Laird) and go on to manipulate and test that conception, would seem to be borne out.

If this difficulty was due to inability to garner sufficient working memory resources to embed others' models within their own in the manner suggested by Johnson-Laird, then it ought to be the case that more in the way of joint negotiation ought to be apparent in older age groups. Two further studies, one involving secondary school pupils and the other involving under-graduates provided the opportunity to check this prediction. It is to the first of these that we now turn.

Study 2. Peer Interaction and Mental Models of Dynamics Phenomena

This study (see Tolmie & Howe, 1993) was concerned with the effects of dialogue on underlying conceptions of the factors that explain the paths followed by falling objects. The participants were 82 secondary school pupils aged between 12 and 15. These 82 pupils were drawn from the larger sample that featured in the Anderson et al. (1992) study outlined earlier. The problems reported by Anderson et al. constituted the pre-test for purposes of this study. As noted already, there were 16 prediction problems: (a) four involved simple linear motion, such as a ball rolling off a cliff; (b) four involved disguised linear motion, i.e. a body released from a carrying vehicle which was in simple linear motion—for example, a food crate dropped from a low-flying aircraft without any parachute; (c) four involved circular motion, such as a spark emanating from a catherine wheel; and (d) four involved pendular motion, such as a trapeze artist letting go of the trapeze and falling into a safety net. Pupils were required to draw the path that they thought the object would follow between the point of beginning to fall until coming to rest (see Fig. 13.2).

We also sought pupils' explanations for four of the paths depicted, one of each initial motion type. These explanations were expressed in terms of force diagrams and text: pupils had to name the forces that they thought would

Emergency Food Supplies. When there is an emergency and people are desperately short of food, aeroplanes bringing relief do not always land. Instead, they fly low without losing speed and drop the food in heavy crates. Suppose the plane pictured below was travelling in the direction shown and dropped a crate from its hatch. Indicate where the crate would be when it hit the ground, and show the path it would follow as it fell through the air. Use X to show where the crate would end up and remember to show the path from the hatch to the ground.

FIG. 13.2 An example of a prediction problem, as used in the pre-test for Study 2, with a typical subject's response.

influence the motion of the object, and to draw arrows that indicated the direction in which each of the identified forces operated (see Fig. 13.3).

The pupils' prediction responses (i.e. the paths that they drew) to each question were scored on a scale from 0 to 5 depending on the degree to which their response approximated the correct answer, i.e. a parabolically shaped path in the same direction as the initial motion. For example, a vertical response (implying no horizontal component to the motion) would

Emergency Food Supplies. The next problem is the one about emergency food supplies, where an aeroplane dropped a crate of food. The following diagram shows what the crate would have looked like when it first left the aeroplane's hatch. Could you draw arrows to indicate the forces that would be operating on the crate?

Could you now number each arrow and explain opposite the appropriate number below what each force was?

Force 1 _____ Wind _____
Force 2 _____ Weight _____
Force 3 _____ _____
Force 4 _____ _____
Force 5 _____ _____
Force 6 _____ _____

FIG. 13.3 An example of an explanation problem, as used in the pre-test for Study 2, with a typical response.

score zero, while an approximately parabolic curve in the correct direction would score 5 (regardless of whether the arc of the parabola was tight or wide: it was the *shape* of the path that mattered). The pupils' explanation responses for each item were scored on a scale from 0 to 6 depending on the number of relevant forces (such as gravity, wind resistance) that had been correctly identified and appropriately used.

Both prediction and explanation scores were used to pair subjects together, as Study 1 had indicated that when subjects do not differ in predictions, they are not moved to compare their explanations. The prediction and explanation scores allowed the computation of "coefficients of dissimilarity", and male, female, and mixed-gender pairs were formed such that there was an even spread of similarity and difference in pre-test responses across the pairs within each gender grouping. Approximately five weeks after the pre-test, the pairs were taken to a quiet room in the school to work jointly on eight of the prediction problems. These were presented on a Macintosh computer, which had been programmed in HyperCard with additional routines in Pascal for simulating motion. For each problem, the program instructed the members of a pair to compare their paper-and-pencil pre-test responses for that problem, and to formulate and enter a joint prediction of the path that would be followed. This prediction was entered into the machine by inserting a fixed number of points using the mouse, each point falling on the predicted path. All points could be modified until the last had been inserted. A record of these joint predictions was held by the computer.

The program then displayed the correct motion of the object, leaving a trace of its path on-screen so that the pupils could compare this correct response with their own joint prediction (see Fig. 13.4). The program asked the pupils to compare the two paths, and agree an interpretation of any apparent discrepancy. The joint activity of all of the pairs was videotaped throughout.

Pre- to Post-test Change and its Relation to Dialogue. Approximately one week after the group task, the subjects were post-tested individually, using a second paper-and-pencil test that was identical to the pre-test in all respects. As our focus was on explanatory understanding, only the responses on the explanation problems were scored, and compared to the pre-test explanation scores to yield a measure of "explanation change" for each individual subject. Overall, there was a small but significant gain in the mean explanation score from pre- to post-test. There was also some evidence that initial dissimilarity of group members' ideas led to a greater degree of explanation change, as the two were significantly correlated. Further analysis revealed that, as anticipated, change was greatest when participants differed on both predictions and explanations (see Howe, Tolmie, &

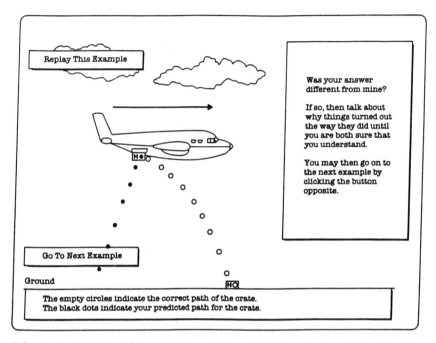

FIG. 13.4   An example of a joint prediction problem, as used in the intervention phase of Study 2, illustrating a typical joint prediction (filled circles) and the computer's feedback showing the correct response to the problem (empty circles).

Mackenzie, 1995). The measures that were recorded from the subjects' dialogues are set out in Table 13.1.

Analysis of the dialogues demonstrated interesting variations across the male, female, and mixed pairs within the broader pattern of results. Taking each type of pair in turn, correlations were computed between scores on all of the interaction indices and the individual subjects' change in explanation scores. Examination of these correlations (see Tolmie & Howe, 1993, for full details) showed that male pairs learned most when perceived differences between initial predictions, and between joint solutions and feedback led them to: (a) attend more to the problem in hand and discuss the factors at work in greater depth; (b) engage in greater discussion of the feedback given to that joint solution; and (c) reappraise factors in the light of feedback, and modify their response to the next problem accordingly. Female pairs, on the other hand, discussed explanations to a much greater extent if they differed in their initial predictions, but did not use this discussion to resolve discrepancies between their input and feedback from the computer. They did, however, tend to discuss explanations *across* problems, and it was this discussion that led to greater individual insight. Male pairs thus coordinated their ideas with the

TABLE 13.1
Measures Taken from the Subjects' Dialogues in Experiment 2

Prediction phase
1. Number of perceived differences between paper-and-pencil predictions.
2. Number of references to explanatory factors.
3. Number of explicit disagreements over explanatory factors.
4. Number of references back to predictions made on previous problems.
5. Number of references back to explanations given on previous problems.

Input phase
6. Number of references to explanatory factors.
7. Proportion of turns taken by input of solution (i.e. relative amount of time spent on this phase).
8. Mean score for joint predictions (on scale used for paper-and-pencil predictions).

Feedback phase
9. Number of perceived differences between joint predictions and computer feedback.
10. Number of references to explanatory factors.
11. Number of explicit disagreements over explanatory factors.

Overall Interaction
12. Total number of communicatory turns.
13. Total number of references to explanatory factors.

Thirteen indices of subjects' on-task interactions were taken, and these are listed, classified in terms of the task phase in which they occurred.

empirical evidence on a problem-by-problem basis; female pairs coordinated explanations across problems but without great reference to the problems themselves. Mixed pairs engaged in rather less dialogue overall (approximately two-thirds the number of turns on average compared to the other gender pairings), and frequently, there was no dialogue at all during the input of solutions. These groups dealt with conflict between predictions by simply ceding control of the input of a joint solution to one member of the pair, and alternating this across problems. Unlike the male pairs, there was no explicit coordination between ideas and empirical evidence, and unlike the female pairs, there was no explicit coordination between the ideas relevant to different problems; the positive explanation change that did occur must have occurred as a function of private reaction to on-screen events (including those controlled by the other) rather than as a function of dialogue.

The male and female pairs therefore both employed *partial* social construction of transitory models, and this was of value in that discussion influenced learning in a reasonably direct fashion. However, the male pairs were still tied to dealing with individual physical events; i.e. there was no explicit *abstraction* of what their transitory models had in common. The female pairs on the other hand did not relate their construction to actual events. The mixed pairs showed *individual* reconstruction of their long-term models in much the same way as did the primary school pupils in Study 1 (though in the latter case this was socially provoked). Thus, the present older group of pupils can, in some circumstances, negotiate transitory models and test them, but the process is incomplete in the same-gender pairs and almost entirely absent in the case of the mixed-gender pairs. In the latter case this was presumably due to the embarrassment that adolescents feel when interacting with a member of the opposite sex, which led to inhibition and a lack of dialogue. Nevertheless, there is evidence that this age group can, under the right circumstances, negotiate and test a transitory model with a greater degree of success than the primary school pupils in Study 1.

Study 3. Peer Interaction and Mental Models of Kinematics Phenomena

The participants here were older again, comprising 108 first-year under-graduate students at Strathclyde University, roughly equal in gender composition and roughly equal in the number from science and arts backgrounds. As in Studies 1 and 2, the participants were individually pre- and post-tested, but in this case both used a Macintosh computer to present computer-based problems, in which the students saw two trains moving across the screen along parallel tracks (see Fig. 13.5). One of the tracks was marked in three places, and the students' task was to decide at which point

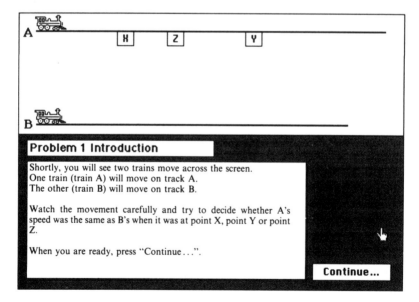

FIG. 13.5   An example of a kinematics problem (Study 3). Problems of this type were used at all stages (pre-test, intervention, and post-test) of the study.

the train on the marked track was travelling at the same speed as the train on the other track. In every problem, the train on the unmarked track moved at a constant speed, while the other's speed increased or decreased uniformly. Simultaneous versus successive start times, and same versus opposite direction of travel were counter-balanced across problems. This gave four "standard" problems in which the students' task was to concern themselves with the problem from their own visual perspective of the situation. In addition there were four other problems, also counter-balanced with respect to start times and direction of travel, in which the students had to decide at which point the speed of the two trains would appear to be the same to an observer located in a third train, depicted as moving from left to right on a track between the other two.

Once the motion of the trains was completed, the students were asked whether they could decide on an answer, or whether they needed more help. If they opted for the former, they simply inserted their solution. If they chose the latter option, they were given the choice of replaying the animation an unlimited number of times, or choosing one of four types of additional information, two of which were redundant (total distances travelled and total times taken) and two useful (graphic displays either of distances travelled in fixed units of time, or of times taken to travel fixed amounts of distance). After a request for information had been made, the students were required to opt for a solution. For the pre- and post-tests, the students undertook these problems individually, with no feedback of any kind being given. They were questioned after each problem by a researcher as to how they had arrived at their solution. All on-screen button presses were saved to a separate disk file. The pre- and post-tests concluded with a series of eight further questions designed to elicit formal kinematics knowledge (e.g. "When you are driving along a road and a car is coming towards you, does it appear to be going at the same speed to you as to someone standing on the pavement?").

Pre- and post-test responses were scored on three dimensions: judgements, strategies and principles. "Judgements" were simply the number of correct decisions about where the trains' speeds would be identical (i.e. a score from 0 to 8 across the eight problems). "Strategies" reflected the conceptual basis offered for a solution, and were scored problem by problem on a scale from 0 to 5, with the points on the scale representing increasing degrees of approximation to a correct and relativistic (for those problems concerning observer motion) conceptual basis. For example, 0 represented a failure to articulate a strategy, while 3 represented a partially correct conceptual basis (e.g. reference to the gaps being the same on the time/distance diagrams). Subjects' scores on this dimension were taken as the total across the eight problems. "Principles" reflected formal kinematics knowledge; students were given the opportunity to articulate up to nine components of formal kinematics knowledge (e.g. speed is the ratio of distance over time; acceleration is independent of specific speed, and so on). Each component was scored between 1 and 4, depending on its complexity, resulting in possible scores which varied between 0 and 18.

Group Tasks. Ninety-six of the pre-test participants were arranged into pairs to take part in the group task; the pairs were composed in such a way that there were three male and three female pairs of each possible combination of similarity or difference in judgements, strategies, and principles (as defined by, respectively, a minimum of five responses the same or five different; Strategy scores equivalent to performing on average at the same scale point or more than one scale point apart; Principle scores equivalent to knowledge at the same level of complexity or more than one scale point apart).

For the group task, the pairs worked through the same set of on-screen problems as used in the pre-test, but were instructed to compare their pre-test answers (provided to them in a printed form) and agree on a joint solution. The existence of written versions of the pre-test responses helped ensure the recognition and discussion of disagreements. Unlike the pre-test, insertion of an answer resulted in feedback (of the form "Well done, that's the correct answer" or "Sorry, that's the wrong answer") being given. In the case of wrong answers, the pairs were instructed to replay the motion and re-examine it jointly. The group session finally concluded with a request for pairs to discuss the information they needed to compare the speeds of objects, and whether this varied if the observer was moving. The group sessions took place approximately eight weeks after the pre-test.

Pre- to Post-test Change and its Relation to Dialogue. The post-test took place about three weeks after the group sessions, the procedure being identical to that used in the pre-test. All but one of the 96 students were post-tested.There were significant pre- to post-test gains in both Strategies and Principles, although the effect was rather stronger for strategy change than for Principles. In fact, Strategy change had virtually no correlation with Principle change ($r = -0.08$).

Subsequent analysis of strategy change showed a significant main effect of Principle group type, such that the students showed greatest gains if they were at the same level of formal physics knowledge. Cutting across this effect was an interaction between Strategy and Judgement group type such that the students gained most if the members of a pair differed in both Strategy and Judgement (i.e. a similar result to that obtained in Study 2); the next most optimal outcome occurred if they were the same in both Strategy and Judgement; and the poorest outcome occurred if the subjects differed on one dimension only. There was no effect of group type on Principle change.

In order to examine the effects of interaction on strategy change, correlations were computed between the frequencies of various categories of interaction (differences between partners' pre-test scores, Group strategy scores and judgements, and individual strategy change: see Howe, Tolmie, Anderson, & Mackenzie, 1992, for full details; see also Table 13.2). Individual change in strategic knowledge was strongly associated with Group Strategy score, which was in turn associated with the incidence of Strategy References Back (i.e. the coordinated use of strategies across items). The discussion of strategies within the groups was influenced by the need to resolve concrete differences, both between members' original judgements and between their negotiated judgements and feedback. Strategy References Back were also correlated with initial differences in judgement, but not with the raw amount of strategy discussion. Consistent with this emerging pattern, further analyses showed that pairs who differed in both judgement and strategy (i.e. who showed greatest pre- to post-test gain in strategy) employed significantly better strategies than any other combination, had better Group Judgement Scores, and made more Strategy References Back.

The implication was that these pairs, given their different initial judgements and ways of arriving at them, realised quickly that there was a need for the explicit generation and testing of ideas, and this testing was coordinated across the problems—i.e. there was a negotiated resolution of their disagreement and repeated application of that resolution. This process

TABLE 13.2
Measures Taken from the Subjects' Dialogues in Experiment 3

Strategy References	Number of distinct references to strategies made by group
Principle References	Number of distinct references to formal principles made by group
Strategy Disagreements	Number of explicit disagreements about strategy occurring within group
Principle Disagreements	Number of explicit disagreements about formal principles occurring within group
Strategy References Back	Number of instances within group of references back to previous mention of strategy
Principle References Back	Number of instances within group of references back to previous mention of formal principle
Moves	Number of button presses
Turns	Number of distinct communications made by either group member

involved both the "empirical testing" element that characterised the behaviour of the male groups in Study 2 and the "generalisation" element that characterised the behaviour of the female groups in Study 2. The latter point underscores the fact that in the present study there was an absence of gender effects on the type of dialogue in which the undergraduate students engaged. It would also seem that this sequence of interaction was assisted if members of a pair shared a common frame of reference for discussing the problems, given the positive effect of *similarity* in Principles score. In the Similar groupings, conceptual change came about as a reaction to getting the answers to the problems wrong, and this was not attributable to the social dynamic: both subjects within the group began with similar ideas, and therefore they had to negotiate and explore *new* ideas. While they ultimately tended to use the same strategies as the Different groups, they arrived at these rather later in the task and performed less well overall.

Overall, there is therefore good evidence from this study that there was social construction and internalisation of a joint model, as Doise and Mugny would predict. It is of note that the undergraduate students in Study 3 did better at negotiating a shared model than did the school pupils in Studies 1 and 2, and that a shared vocabulary clearly facilitated this process. Perhaps both this result and the lack of an effect of gender can be explained by the undergraduates being at a developmentally more sophisticated level, which allows them not only to negotiate and test a strategy and evaluate its success against feedback, but also to hold different strategies in mind simultaneously and compare them in terms of the outcomes from different trials; younger subjects may well lack the metacognitive skills required to achieve this.

CONCLUSIONS AND IMPLICATIONS

Our data seem to imply that although the Piagetian "equilibration" position gives a good account of mental model change in younger learners, in older, more sophisticated learners there is a real possibility of social negotiation and testing of a joint transitory model, provided certain conditions are met .

Thus, Study 1 found that primary school children could improve in their knowledge about the factors that influence motion down an incline, but there was little evidence from the dialogues that the groups jointly constructed a conception of the situation that was superior to those of its members, which was then internalised. Rather, the evidence suggested that group discussion was a catalyst for change that took place individually subsequent to participation in the group. This finding has been replicated with children of the same age. For example, Howe, Rodgers, and Tolmie (1990) found the same absence of relation between group task performance and post-test gain in a study of primary school children's understanding of the factors that influence whether an object floats or sinks. Tolmie, Howe, Mackenzie, and Greer (1993) found gains between a four-week and eleven-week post-test, again in relation to floating and sinking. Piaget's individualistic account of mental model change therefore appears to hold good for children of primary school age, in these domains of learning at least, whereas Doise and Mugny's more social-constructionist account receives little support. These young children do not appear to be capable of negotiating and manipulating a transitory, jointly held mental model as a prelude to integrating the results of those manipulations into their more enduring model of the domain. Instead, the interaction with peers provides a spur to provoke individual reflection and consequent modification of the child's long-term mental model of the domain, and this modification clearly occurs subsequent to the interaction.

Study 2 found that secondary-aged pupils gained significantly in knowledge about the influential factors involved in free fall under various conditions of prior motion as a result of peer interaction, especially where groups comprised individuals who differed in both predictions and explanations. Examination of the dialogues, however, revealed that only partial social construction of models had taken place, in that male groups dealt empirically with individual problems but failed to engage in abstraction, whereas female groups coordinated across problems at the expense of generating explanations for the problem at hand. Secondary-age pupils therefore show some ability to construct transitory models jointly and internalise the results of testing them, but the process is incomplete, with pupils failing to integrate some of the usable information into their long-term models, as revealed by the differences across the gender groupings.

Study 3 obtained evidence that undergraduates could socially construct a joint transitory model, and internalise the results of testing that model, thus capitalising on their experience in the group context. However, the effect was in fact stronger for improving their strategies for tackling the problems than for improving their knowledge of the abstract principles at stake (although the latter were not an explicit focus of discussion).

The varying results across the three studies could be taken to support a view that with development there is an increasing ability to negotiate, hold in mind, and test a jointly held, transitory model, and to extract lessons from the experience of working in a group that can be incorporated in the individual's own more stable mental model of the domain. There are in fact two aspects to this process of change in long-term models. The first concerns the individual's capacity to build and manipulate a transitory model at all. The fact that primary-age children can perform reasonably well on syllogistic reasoning tasks (at least the simpler varieties: see Johnson-Laird, Oakhill, & Bull, 1986) suggests that this is possible, even in young children. The second concerns the capacity to negotiate a *joint* transitory model. Our studies particularly concerned the latter. Nevertheless it is important to note that there is evidence for developmental variation in both the individual's capacity to build and manipulate their own individual transitory models, and in their capacity to negotiate a joint transitory model.

Evidence for a developmental trend in the individual's capacity to build and manipulate transitory models comes from studies of childrens' reasoning (e.g. Johnson-Laird et al., 1986). As noted earlier, the degree of success with which mental model construction and use can be achieved depends on such variables as the capacity of working memory and the meta-ability to reflect on one's own performance. Johnson-Laird and Byrne (1991) argue that the acquisition of deductive competence is the acquisition of a capacity to build models of the world, which in turn is therefore dependent on working memory and metacognition. Accordingly, children will show a developmental variation in their deductive abilities as the capacity of their working memory increases and their metacognitive skills become increasingly sophisticated. For example, Johnson-Laird, Oakhill, and Bull (1986) found that children's (both 9–10 year olds and 11–12 year olds) ability to solve some syllogistic reasoning problems but not others was readily explicable in terms of the number of mental models that had to be constructed in order to solve a given problem. Performance was best with problems that can be solved by building a single mental model (and manipulating its contents in order to test a putative conclusion), whereas performance on syllogisms requiring the building and manipulation of two models was poorer (but better than chance level), and only 2% of syllogisms requiring the building and manipulation of three models were solved correctly by the children. Adults show a similar pattern of performance (best on one-model problems, poorest on three-model problems) but the number of problems of each type that they solve correctly is typically greater than that for the children. Given a restricted amount of time in which to solve syllogisms, adults show a decrement in performance such that they perform like the 11-year-olds. The explanation of these effects in terms of changes in the capacity of working memory ties in with the views of Case (1984, 1985) who argues that, while the overall capacity of short-term memory does not increase as a function of development, the effect of practice at tasks results in more efficient use of short-term *operating* space, leaving greater capacity in short-term *storage* space. This explanation for the acquisition of deductive competence clearly bears on our results summarised earlier. As learners get older, they become more adept at building, maintaining in memory, and testing a transitory mental model. Increases in the capacity to store information would clearly have a beneficial effect on learners' capacity to achieve this.

Evidence for a developmental trend in the capacity to negotiate a joint transitory model comes from studies of reference in dialogue. Anderson and

Garrod (1987) and Garrod and Anderson (1987) found in undergraduates that the requirement to specify locations precisely within a jointly visible (on physically separate VDU screens) spatial network resulted in their setting up joint models to underpin their reference generation and interpretation. These models involved setting up, for example, arbitrary coordinate systems, or establishing tacit agreements on the referential meaning of nouns like "line" or "row", or phrases (like "one node along") which would otherwise have been rather ambiguous. Subsequently, Clark and Garrod (1991) tested 9- to 13-year-old school children with the same task, and found that, although adults progressively develop more abstract and efficient description schemes, younger children tended to converge on single description schemes which they stuck with, failing to continue to revise and refine their schemes to increasingly high levels of abstraction in the way that adults do. Thus younger participants do not adopt novel schemes once they have converged, nor do they readily employ more abstract descriptions, suggesting that there is a limit to the level of complexity of what they can socially construct.

In their overview of a collection of readings on mental models (Rogers, Rutherford, & Bibby, 1992), Rogers and Rutherford (1992) note that in recent years some researchers have shifted emphasis away from a focus on the cognitive processes of the individual (as exemplified by Johnson-Laird, 1983 and many of the contributions in Gentner and Stevens, 1983) to one that takes account of the social and cultural context, and acknowledges that individuals frequently interact with external representations and/or with other individuals when immersed in a cognitive activity. They assert that further development in mental models research would benefit from examining the role played by social, cultural and external factors in mediating the development and use of mental models. They propose (1992, p.305) that "...the construct of a mental model as exemplified in Johnson-Laird's work or Gentner and Stevens' collection could be elaborated to provide an account of the extent to which individuals share and construct similar mental models when interacting together...". Much of the work that they review in the context of shared mental models concerns "situated cognition" in occupational settings (e.g. Cicourel, 1990; Hutchins, 1990) and invokes such theoretical issues as distributed cognition and intersubjectivity.

Our work described here suggests that the general issue of how interaction between individuals impacts on their respective mental models of the topic under discussion is relevant to many of the domains studied in the classic works on mental models (e.g. McCloskey, 1983). It also implies a developmental progression in the extent to which individuals are capable of negotiating, holding in mind, and testing a jointly held transitory model, and comparing the outcomes of using it with the predictions derived from their individual more enduring model of the domain, as a prelude to modifying the latter.

ACKNOWLEDGEMENTS

The research described in this chapter was supported by the Economic and Social Research Council of Great Britain, under grant C000232426 to Christine Howe and grant R000231287 to Anthony Anderson, Christine Howe, and Terry Mayes. We would like to extend our grateful thanks to the staff and pupils of the various schools involved in our studies, and also the undergraduate students who willingly gave their time to participate.

REFERENCES

Anderson, A., & Garrod, S.C. (1987). The dynamics of referential meaning in spontaneous conversation: Some preliminary studies. In R. Reilly (Ed.), *Communication failures in dialogue and discourse* (pp.161–183). Amsterdam: Elsevier.

Anderson, A., Tolmie, A., Howe, C., Mayes, T., & Mackenzie, M. (1992). Mental models of motion. In Y. Rogers, A. Rutherford, & P. Bibby (Eds.), *Models in the mind: Theory, perspective and applications* (pp.57–71). London: Academic Press.

Case, R. (1984). The process of stage transition: A neo-Piagetian view. In R.J. Sternberg (Ed.), *Mechanisms of cognitive development*. New York: Freeman.

Case, R. (1985). *Intellectual development: Birth to adulthood*. New York: Academic Press.

Cicourel, A.V. (1990). The integration of distributed knowledge in collaborative medical diagnosis. In J. Galecher, R.E. Kraut, & C. Edigo (Eds.), *Intellectual teamwork: Social and technological foundations of cooperative work* (pp.221–242). Hillsdale, NJ: Lawrence Erlbaum Associates Inc.

Clark, A., & Garrod, S. (1991). Conceptual and semantic coordination in children's dialogue. In J. Verschueren (Ed.), *Pragmatics at issue* (pp.67–80). Amsterdam: John Benjamins Publishing Company.

Craik, K. (1943). *The nature of explanation*. Cambridge: Cambridge University Press.

diSessa, A. (1988). Knowledge in pieces. In G. Forman & P.B. Pufall (Eds.), *Constructivism in the computer age*. Hillsdale, NJ: Lawrence Erlbaum Associates Inc.

diSessa, A. (1993). Towards an epistemology of physics. *Cognition and Instruction, 10*, 105–225.

Doise, W., & Mugny, G. (1984). *The social development of the intellect*. Oxford: Pergamon.

Driver, R., Guesne, E., & Tiberghien, A. (1985). *Children's ideas in science*. Milton Keynes, UK: Open University Press.

Garrod, S.C., & Anderson A. (1987). Saying what you mean in conversational dialogue: A study in conceptual and semantic co-ordination. *Cognition, 27*, 181–218.

Gentner, D., & Gentner, D.R. (1983). Flowing waters or teeming crowds: Mental models of electricity. In D. Gentner, & A.L. Stevens (Eds.), *Mental models* (pp.99–129). Hillsdale, NJ: Lawrence Erlbaum Associates Inc.

Gentner D., & Stevens, A.L. (1983). *Mental models*. Hillsdale, NJ: Lawrence Erlbaum Associates Inc.

Howe, C., Rodgers, C., & Tolmie, A. (1990). Physics in the primary school: Peer interaction and the understanding of floating and sinking. *European Journal of Psychology of Education, 5*, 459–475.

Howe, C.J., Tolmie, A., Anderson, A., & Mackenzie, M. (1992). Conceptual knowledge in physics: The role of group interaction in computer-supported teaching. *Learning and Instruction, 2*, 161–183.

Howe, C.J., Tolmie, A., & Mackenzie, M. (1995). Computer support for the collaborative learning of physics concepts. In C.E. O'Malley (Ed.), *Computer supported collaborative learning* (pp.41–68). Berlin: Springer-Verlag.

Howe, C.J., Tolmie, A., & Rodgers, C. (1992). The acquisition of conceptual knowledge in science by primary school children: Group interaction and the understanding of motion down an incline. *British Journal of Developmental Psychology, 10*, 113–130.

Hutchins, E. (1990). The technology of team navigation. In J. Galecher, R.E. Kraut, & C. Edigo (Eds.), *Intellectual teamwork: Social and technological foundations of cooperative work* (pp.191-220). Hillsdale, NJ: Lawrence Erlbaum Associates Inc.

Johnson-Laird, P.N. (1983) *Mental models*. Cambridge: Cambridge University Press.

Johnson-Laird, P.N. & Byrne, R.M.J. (1991). *Deduction*. Hillsdale, NJ: Lawrence Erlbaum Associates Inc.

Johnson-Laird, P.N., Oakhill, J., & Bull, D. (1986). Children's syllogistic reasoning. *The Quarterly Journal of Experimental Psychology, 38A*, 35–58.

McCloskey, M. (1983). Naive theories of motion. In D. Gentner & A.L. Stevens (Eds.), *Mental models* (pp.299–324). Hillsdale, NJ: Lawrence Erlbaum Associates Inc.

Norman, D. (1983). Some observations on mental models. In D. Gentner & A.L. Stevens (Eds.), *Mental models* (pp.7–14). Hillsdale, NJ: Lawrence Erlbaum Associates Inc.

Piaget, J. (1930). *The child's conception of physical causality*. London: Routledge & Kegan Paul.

Piaget, J. (1972). *The principles of genetic epistemology*. London: Routledge & Kegan Paul.

Piaget, J. (1985). *The equilibration of cognitive structures*. Chicago: University of Chicago Press.

Piaget, J. & Inhelder, B. (1956). *The child's conception of space*. London: Routledge & Kegan Paul.

Rogers, Y., & Rutherford, A. (1992). Future directions in mental models research. In Y. Rogers, A. Rutherford, & P. Bibby (Eds.), *Models in the mind: Theory, perspective and applications* (pp.57–71). London: Academic Press.

Rogers, Y., Rutherford, A., & Bibby, P. (Eds.). (1992). *Models in the mind: Theory, perspective and applications*. London: Academic Press.

Tolmie, A., & Howe, C.J. (1993). Gender and dialogue in secondary school physics. *Gender and Education, 5*, 191–209.

Tolmie, A., Howe, C.J., Mackenzie, M., & Greer, K. (1993). Task design as an influence on dialogue and learning: Primary school group work with object flotation. *Social Development, 2*, 183–201.

Vygotsky, L.S. (1978). Mind in society. Cambridge, MA: Harvard University Press.

Wiser, M., & Carey, S. (1983). When heat and temperature were one. In D. Gentner, & A.L. Stevens (Eds.), *Mental models* (pp.267–297). Hillsdale, NJ: Lawrence Erlbaum Associates Inc.

14 Causality by Contact

Giuliano C. Geminiani
Center for Cognitive Science, University of Turin, Italy

Antonella Carassa
Center for Cognitive Science, University of Turin, Italy
Department of General Psychology, University of Padua, Italy

Bruno G. Bara
Center for Cognitive Science, University of Turin, Italy

1. INTRODUCTION

The major objective of this chapter is to investigate within the mental model framework a central domain of everyday reasoning: physical causality. We shall provide both an account of folk psychological knowledge of causation in the physical world, and a computer simulation of causal reasoning in naive subjects. We consider our work as a development of the seminal analysis of causation initially offered by Johnson-Laird (1983). Thus, our goal is to explore people's competence in understanding causal relations between events and objects.

The chapter is structured around a series of points, which we sketch here for clarity:

1. What are the evolutionary precursors of causality that one can find in animals? We adopt the notion of weak causal knowledge, realised through associative learning.

2. In human psychology causality has been investigated through two different strategies: a domain-general approach (general principles dictate behaviour), and a domain-specific one (there are different mental mechanisms that explain causality in different domains). We adhere to the second tradition, in keeping with the emphasis in contemporary developmental psychology. As already stated, the domain investigated in this paper is causality as experienced in the physical world.

3. Within physical causality one may distinguish elementary and complex phenomena. As far as elementary phenomena are involved, e.g.

in infants' perception of causality, a hard-wired, automatic interpretation of appropriate stimulation has been postulated. But with complex phenomena, higher cognitive processes become important. In essence, complex physical causality is conceived as the result of contact between objects (see Fig. 14.1).

4. In order to detail the cognitive aspects of physical causality, we postulate three levels of knowledge (see Fig. 14.2):

● abstract level: knowledge about facts in the domain and causal relations between events;

● analogical level: knowledge about the causal roles (Agent, Medium and Target) of objects;

● subcognitive level: knowledge about elementary physical interactions between objects.

5. According to our hypothesis a cognitive analysis in the domain of physical causality has two different levels (see Fig. 14.3), an abstract level in which a causal link between events is assumed, and an analogical level in which the causal role of objects and dynamics of causal processes are considered.

6. Two types of reasoning may be used in the causal domain.

● *forward* reasoning, where a cause-event is given and an effect-event has to be inferred (prediction);

● *backward* reasoning, where an effect-event is given and a cause-event has to be inferred (retrodiction).

7. As a prototypical case of physical causality, we have chosen poisoning. On the one hand it is common enough to be easy to explore even in children, and on the other hand it is complex enough for explanations to range from simple intuition to refined expert models; in this paper, however, we shall consider only the commonsense naive treatment of poisoning. The analysis is conducted with the help of a computer program (SNAKE) which reproduces each of the steps discussed.

8. We classify the basic commonsense models of poisoning, first according to the medium—which is our core notion for the analogical level of knowledge—and then according to the agent and target. In the case we consider, the causal objects are the blood (medium), the poison (agent), and the heart (target). An object possesses physical properties, each of which is characterised by quantitative variables (see Fig. 14.4).

9. Reasoning processes are based on a recursive comparison between two models, a base model and a progressively more refined modified model (Fig. 14.6). In accordance with the spirit of mental model theory, we divide inferential processes into three phases:

● A *construction* phase, which takes as input the premises expressing causal events, and generates mental models of the involved physical phenomena.

● A *comparison* phase, which receives dynamic models as input, carries out a series of comparisons between them, and produces as output a first putative conclusion.

● A *falsification* phase, which attaches various degrees of confidence to the generated conclusions.

A series of examples is described in detail, to illustrate how people reason about poisoning, and what are the dynamics of the interactions among the different levels of knowledge (see Fig. 14.2).

The chapter is organised as follows. Section 2 provides the necessary background to our analysis. In section 3 we describe the structure of causal models and in section 4 the reasoning process. In section 5 we briefly describe the technical features of a computational model based on our hypothesis.

2. BACKGROUND TO OUR ANALYSIS OF CAUSAL REASONING

From an evolutionary perspective, causality is an interpretation of reality that has a profound influence on the capacity of higher species to interact adaptively with the world. The ability to apprehend regularities in sequences of events is crucial for influencing the environment by prediction and action. Animals are able to relate two contiguous events after many repetitions through the process of associative learning.

In animals, arbitrary *sensu* (Premack & Premack, 1995) or weak causal knowledge (Kummer, 1995) allows connection of any two events in temporal order so long as both are perceived in the same motivational state. This means that motivation causes an animal to admit only stimuli and rewards that are relevant to its present needs. Contiguity is the cue: no previous or "hard-wired" knowledge establishes which events are likely to be construed as causally related.

However, to survive, animals must have the ability to detect connections between non-contiguous events. In a clearly circumscribed repertoire of cases, higher animals demonstrate that they "know" that a certain causal connection between two events widely separated in space and time is highly probable. Such pairs of events are those that occur frequently and are crucial for survival. For example, rats are able to relate illness to ingestion of a particular food (Garcia, Hankins, & Rusiniak, 1974); furthermore house mice (Perrigo, Cully Bryant, & Vom Saal, 1990) and dunnocks (Davies, Hatchwell, Robson, & Burke, 1992) are able to "know" their paternity by connecting mating with the appearance of offspring. This natural *sensu*, or strong causal knowledge, is based on adaptive genetic programs highly specific for each species. Evidence shows that animals use a sort of knowledge of interdependent events to exert a variable amount of control over their environment. However, only humans are known to have a conceptual interpretation of reality in terms of causation, and to perform explicit causal reasoning (Premack, 1993, 1994).

Strong causal knowledge in animals performs the same role that causal reasoning does in humans, but the former does not require the ability to entertain causal beliefs, i.e. to represent the consequences of an event or an action. Thus, if a rat detects the odour of a certain food on a dead rat, it will avoid that food, but its behaviour is not dictated by a mental state of the type: "If I eat that food I will die".

Causal reasoning, as observed in humans, is the explicit use of causal analysis. Humans engage in causal reasoning when, in a problem-solving context, they appreciate the final state of a process and try to infer or reconstruct the intermediate events. For example, consider a damaged car after an accident. Spectators observing this situation will ask themselves: "Why? What happened?". Inferences are made on the basis of observations of the immediate circumstances and on prior knowledge of the world. Thus, a spectator might conclude that the accident occurred because the speed was too high for the slippery road conditions. Causal reasoning is relevant to the success of future behaviour. In the case of the car accident, future behaviour would be not to drive so fast on that tract of road when it is raining. Causal reasoning is the first step toward the construction of conceptual knowledge in a certain domain. Pursuing the example, a generalisation would be to slow down on slippery roads.

It is distinctive of human beings that they can consciously analyse what happens in the world and in themselves; they can advance hypotheses and try to test their validity; and can reflect on their own knowledge. The ultimate result of this kind of mental activity is the elaboration of a sort of "theory" about the domain of phenomena being considered, and this theory has to be coherent, relatively stable, and able to explain things (e.g. the generalisation that fast-moving objects constrained to follow a curve tend to fly off at a tangent). Figure 14.1 illustrates the constituents of causal relations from a psychological point of view.

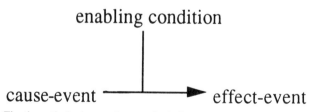

FIG. 14.1.   The theoretical schema of a causal relation.

When subjectively interpreting a situation in terms of causality, people assign specific roles to facts. The core of a causal relation is a cause–effect link (represented by the horizontal arrow in Fig. 14.1) between the cause-event and the effect-event. This link can only be realised when a series of enabling conditions obtain (vertical arrow in Fig. 14.1) and the corollary is that if one or more of these conditions do not hold, the link is not activated. The crucial aspect of causal reasoning in establishing and enabling conditions for the link to be realised, and this is the case of both backward and forward inferences.

In backward inferences an effect-event is given and a cause-event has to be inferred. When the cause-event has been established, reasoning concentrates on identifying the enabling conditions that increase the plausibility of the link. When both the cause-event and the effect-event are given, the focus is exclusively on the enabling condition(s). For example:

James was driving very fast (cause-event)
James skidded off the road (effect-event)

The road was wet (enabling-condition)

In forward inferences, a cause-event is given and an effect-event has to be inferred. If only an elementary prediction is required, enabling conditions can be omitted or assumed by default (an exhaustive treatment of this topic can be found in Shoam, 1988). For example:

James was driving fast (cause-event)
The road was wet (enabling-condition)

James skidded off the road (effect-event)

Our aim in this article is to analyse how people draw causal inferences by assuming a set of enabling conditions, given that the cause–effect link is already known. It is not our purpose to investigate how people proceed in postulating the cause–effect link (the attribution process).

2.1 Developmental Constraints

In psychology the study of causal reasoning falls into two distinct traditions. The logical tradition focuses on the general principles governing causal inferences. Its main idea is that people establish causal connections between events by appealing to statistical relations between variables, as if events were related probabilistically. The "attribution theory" in social psychology falls within the logical tradition. This theory is concerned with how and why people explain events with reference to the interpersonal and social domain

(Einhorn & Hogart, 1986; Heider, 1958; Jones & Davis, 1965; Kelley & Michela, 1980).

The explanation-mechanism tradition (Carey, 1995), on the other hand, sees the task of causal analysis as that of elucidating the mechanisms that explain how one event (the cause) gives rise to another (the effect). This approach is mostly embraced by developmental psychologists.

The differences between the two paradigms are marked. The logical tradition treats causal cognition as domain-general: the algorithms that causally connect events are the same, whatever the type of event; whereas the other paradigm stresses that causal explanation-mechanisms are different for each domain. Developmental psychologists such as Spelke (1988, 1990, 1994), Baillargeon (1986, 1993, 1995), and Carey (1985, 1995) search for forms of causal analysis that are specific to different cognitive domains, such as commonsense physics, psychology, and biology.

Anyway, the distinction between domain-dependence or independence should not be drawn too strongly. We have defined our approach as domain-dependent, but things are slightly more complicated. As a matter of fact, mental models have always been supposed to be a general representation structure: so general as to subsume any possible kind of reasoning process (Garnham & Oakhill, 1994). For example, the three phases of model construction, revision, and falsification are present in all the theories proposed for the different domains (Johnson-Laird & Byrne, 1991), and in all the computer programs designed to simulate human behaviour (Bara, Bucciarelli, Johnson-Laird, & Lombardo, 1994). However, the different applications of model theory depend on the specifics of particular domains: e.g. spatial reasoning requires different inference processes from syllogistic reasoning (Bara, Bucciarelli, & Johnson-Laird, 1994). In the case of physical causality, such domain-specific aspects are the principle of contact, and the mechanisms that implement the (domain-independent) phases of model construction, revision (here called comparison), and falsification.

We have domain-specificity as soon as we apply a model to a situation in which different types of agent, target and medium may be found; at this level the dynamics of the different models may follow quite different paths. For example, think of electric propagation versus the flowing of a fluid in a conduit.

In conclusion, there is both domain-generality and domain-specificity, in that particular models will differ from one another, and that models from the same domain are likely to have more in common than models from different domains. The link with the general principles of the mental models approach is that, because mental models are models of specific situations, they will inevitably have components that are specific to the domain being modelled. But there are also general principles for constructing mental models, and these provide the domain-general component.

Once the view that causal cognition is domain-dependent is accepted, a major task of this work will be to develop a description of what constitutes a domain as far as physical causality is concerned. We will now try to trace the boundaries between different types of causal models. Before beginning, however, we shall briefly review some of the basic presuppositions of the explanation-mechanism approach insofar as they are important for understanding our approach.

The initial postulate is that there are at least two domains of causal reasoning which are treated and represented in the mind differently: the domain of physical objects and the domain of intentional objects.

Premack (1990; Premack and Premack, 1995) argues that in infants simple analysis of the motion of two or more interacting objects is crucial for the interpretation of those objects as either physical (non-self propelled) or intentional (self propelled). Infants interpret as physical objects that change their state of motion only as a consequence of the action of another object. For example, a toy car changes trajectory when touched by another toy car. Motion *per se* is not the critical parameter, it is change that is critical: from rest to motion and vice-versa, from one speed to another or one direction to another.

Infants are also predisposed to perceive that there is a second type of object, one that has internal control of its own motion; such objects are able, for example, to pass autonomously from rest to motion. Premack emphasises how a precocious analysis of motion allows, independent of characteristics like form or colour, the identification of the two different domains of objects; each domain having unique properties. For example, when two objects are perceived as self-propelled, there is also the perception that one object intends to affect the other and vice-versa; thus predicates such as positive valence or negative valence can be applied to their behaviour.

In a prototypical experiment, the following scene is presented to an infant on a computer screen. A simple circle keeps jumping up, going higher and higher in front of a vertical line, without ever reaching the top of the line. The object is perceived as intending to escape confinement by the line and to pass over the barrier it represents. Another circle approaches, touches the first and the two pass over the barrier together. The action of the second object is interpreted as positive, as helping behaviour. Clearly, this kind of interpretation does not occur if objects are perceived as merely physical.

As in the case of Premack's investigation, evidence for a restricted number of core domains and for domain-specific systems of knowledge is sought through studies on so-called initial knowledge. Initial knowledge is the innate knowledge that "appears to capture fundamental constraints on ecologically important classes of entities in the child's environment and appears to remain central to the common-sense knowledge systems of adults" (Spelke, 1994). Initial knowledge is investigated by means of experimental methods that involve variations of the habituation–dishabituation paradigm or preferential looking or listening; they were expressly developed for studying very young children.

Initial knowledge in the domain of physical objects has been thoroughly investigated. There is good evidence that, at a very early age, children interact with the world by appealing to a rich set of expectations concerning the behaviour of objects. Thus, according to Spelke (1994), and in sharp contrast to Piaget, the development of a child's knowledge of the physical world does not begin as a confrontation with chaotic perceptual input, nor is it acquired entirely as a result of a period of sensory and motor experience; on the contrary, the development of knowledge is strongly influenced by innate predispositions.

Thus, Spelke and her collaborators have demonstrated that infants perceive certain properties of objects and certain basic principles governing their behaviour; they are able to detect subtle violations of these principles as early as 3–4 months of age. Spelke compares children's acquisition of knowledge of the physical world with the acquisition of knowledge of language according to Chomsky (1980). Spelke's principles of object behaviour (1994), which she maintains also hold for object perception and reasoning in older children, are as follows: objects move as connected wholes on connected paths, they cannot pass through each other and they cannot act on each other unless they are in contact.

The principle of contact ("action on contact"; "no action at a distance") was first enunciated by Michotte in his famous book, *The perception of causality* (1946) and elaborated from a developmental perspective by Ball (1973), Leslie (1984) and Leslie and Keeble (1978), with later corroboration by Oakes (1993). The experimental methods these authors employed were varied, but all point to the conclusion that the principle of contact is pervasive in infancy.

Accepting therefore that causality is at the elementary level a hard-wired, automatic interpretation of appropriate stimulation, we shall now concentrate on the cognitive level of causal reasoning. Our basic idea is that at this level also, contact is assumed as the necessary condition for the realisation of a causal link. A main point to be noted is that different interactions in the physical world happen without apparent contact among objects. However, people explain these interactions in terms of waves or fields which are an invisible medium connecting agent and target.

The implication for our theory of causal models (developed later) is that for reasoning with mental models in the domain of physical causality, both objects and their motions have to be represented in order for contact to be possible. The initial knowledge possessed by infants establishes the ontology of the physical domain, constraining the construction of mental representations.

The point of departure of our analysis of physical causality is the consideration that three levels of knowledge are implicated in causal reasoning (see Fig. 14.2). On the one hand there is abstract knowledge about the causal links between events in the physical world. It is, for example, our abstract knowledge that allows us to causally connect the throwing of a stone and the breaking of a window. On the other hand, in order to understand the dynamics of the process it is essential to be able to call upon non-explicit knowledge that we have about elementary physical phenomena such as the trajectories of thrown objects—knowledge that derives directly from our sensory-motor interactions with the physical world.

The final element necessary for a full understanding of the causal process is analogical knowledge concerning how a certain event happened, given certain circumstances. Analogical knowledge is that which allows us to understand what made the physical process possible and what could have prevented it from occurring. This level of knowledge derives from causal inferences, and allows us, for example, to discern that only by getting into a certain position could we have intercepted the stone thrown in the previous example and prevented its collision with the window. This type of knowledge is necessary if the individual is to act and react effectively in his or her environment. It is genuinely informative about causality and is the level of knowledge we will be chiefly concerned with in what follows. We shall describe first the structure of the mental representation of analogical knowledge and then discuss the processes involved in causal reasoning.

3. CAUSAL MODELS: STRUCTURE

We shall now describe the characteristics of causal models, which are a subset of mental models of the physical world; later we shall examine these

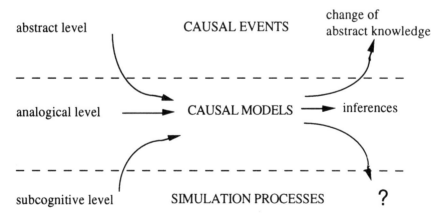

FIG. 14.2.   Levels of knowledge in naive causal reasoning.

characteristics in the context of a prototypical example of causality by contact, viz: poisoning.

According to Johnson-Laird (1983) there are six major types of mental model of the physical world, one of which is the kinematic model. A kinematic model has a time dimension; it is psychologically continuous and represents changes in and motions of depicted entities. Dynamic models are a subset of kinematic models, and represent causal relations between certain events in temporal sequence. Because our goal is to explain causality by contact, we shall be concerned only with a subset of dynamic models—i.e. causal models—in which causal events are represented as physical objects and physical processes. In the causal domain, two features of Johnson-Laird's models become important:

i. *Analogicity.* This refers to the fact that the entities and the relations present in the representational structure correspond directly to the entities and their relations in which is being represented. In causal models, physical objects and their physical properties are represented. These physical properties are based on knowledge about the world acquired through sensory and motor interactions, and conditioned by innate predispositions, as discussed in the previous section.

ii. *Constructability.* Models are not general structures but are constructed for the particular goal the cognitive system is pursuing. As a model represents a specific situation, it is an instance of a class of models. Reasoning by example consists in building a series of models and in comparing them with each other.

The structure of any mental model of the physical world is constrained by how the cognitive system perceives the world, and by its in-built possibilities for interacting with the world. Mental models serve as an interface between the external world (according to the subject's perception and action), and how the subject behaves within that world.

Our hypothesis about causality in the physical world is that it is conceived mentally as the result of contact between objects (Carassa, Geminiani & Bara, 1993). We attribute causality from object contact because this interpretation is "hard-wired" into our brains, as we saw in section 2. From a subjective point of view, contact, as the *sine qua non* of causality, is appreciated and learned as a result of two types of experience. First, experience of changes in the world generated by our own actions, i.e. by physical interaction between our bodies and external objects. Second, because in every physical happening that we are able to perceive directly and in its entirety, the involved objects interact with one another only if they are spatially contiguous. Examples are: a liquid wets a surface only if it spreads over it; or a fist breaks a glass only if it hits it. In these examples the phenomena occurring may be defined as elementary, and are to be compared with complex causal processes which we shall discuss later.

Knowledge of elementary phenomena is handled by subcognitive processes derived from sensory-motor experience. For example, when a glass of water is spilled over the table, people usually act quickly to avoid further inconvenience and this action requires naive knowledge. The same happens when a person throws a ball against a wall; he knows where it will rebound and is able to catch it (McLeod and Dienes, 1993). This kind of action does not depend on conscious thought; on the contrary it is controlled by "reflexive" reasoning (Shastri & Ajjanagadde, 1993), which in its turn is based on direct experience of perception and action.

We turn now to complex processes. Consider these two situations:

(a) Observing a match scraped over a rough surface followed immediately by its ignition.

(b) Inferring that a fire lit in a clearing started a blaze in the forest.

The second is an example of a complex causal inference: the dynamics cannot be directly observed, but have to be inferred from a series of clues.

Our basic idea is that when human beings are reasoning about two events that they judge as causally linked, they try to represent a physical interaction between objects. Such objects would correspond to tokens in the mental models of Johnson-Laird.

The starting point of causal reasoning is that of assigning causal roles to two specific objects and simulating how they can come into contact. Considering how contact can be realised and how it can be facilitated or hindered are essential for planning how to modify or direct the course of events, i.e. planning to act in the world.

The fundamental assumption is that people do not reason in terms of causal links between events but in terms of dynamic physical processes, in which different objects are involved. Contact is seen as the necessary condition for the realisation of the causal link between events at a more abstract level. This analysis of the mental processes involved in causal reasoning is presented in Fig. 14.3.

The figure shows the conceptual and analogical levels of cognitive analysis in the domain of physical causality. The first level depicts a cause–effect link between two events. Event 1 and Event 2 (causal attribution). At the second level the linked events are analysed in terms of objects which play the role of agent and target; the effect of the contact is a new state of the target. The causal roles can be derived from perception, given by information, or hypothesised on the basis of general or domain knowledge. Event 1 (cause) and Event 2 (effect) are in temporal sequence; furthermore, Event 1 is characterised by the fact that the agent and the

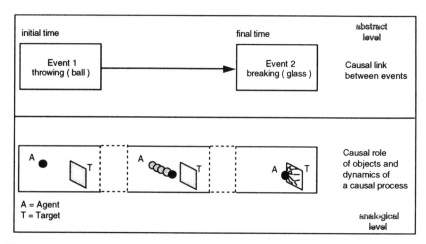

FIG. 14.3. The abstract and analogical level of naive cognitive analysis in the domain of physical causality.

target are not yet in contact, as they will necessarily be in Event 2. At this level the dynamics of the causal process are analysed.

In order to reason about the dynamics of the causal process it is necessary to postulate the presence of a medium, which is an object or a set of objects that allow the agent to act on the target in spite of spatial non-contiguity. Like the agent and the target, the medium has physical features that are relevant to the dynamic evolution of the process. The causal process is what allows contact between the agent and the target, and therefore it precedes the contact in time. An example is a solid object (agent) transported by a fluid (medium) so as to reach another solid object (target).

In our analysis, the medium is the central notion. In fact, the physical properties attributed to the medium determine directly the type of causal model, while the physical properties of agents and targets have a smaller influence on the model. For this reason, our classification of causal models is based primarily on the medium, and only secondarily on agent and target. The roles of agent, target, and medium are not absolute: no object is naturally an agent, target, or medium. It is human minds that attribute one of these roles to a specific object.

We now introduce the concept of a kinematic function, which is responsible for the movement of agents and targets. A kinematic function may apply to any combination of agent, target, and medium as we illustrate here:

i. Agent moves toward target: e.g. a ball hits a glass, as in Fig. 14.3 (agent has kinematic function).

ii. Target moves toward agent, e.g. a ship collides with a mine (target has kinematic function).

iii. Agent and target meet: e.g. two cars collide (agent and target have kinematic function).

iv. The agent, the target, or both may be carried by the medium (poison reaches the heart carried there by the blood).

Poisoning: A Case of Causality by Contact

We now analyse poisoning, a case of contact causality. Figure 14.4 illustrates several possible naive models about how poisoning may occur. It emerges that there are a series of ways of conceptualising poisoning, each corresponding to a different type of causal model. In a common model of poisoning the cardiovascular system is the key concept. However, if we hypothesise a medium that is not the circulatory system, but for instance nervous tissue, we would expect a completely different model. Such a model could lead to the hypothesis of cardiac arrest, as the nervous system regulating heart-rate could either be inhibited to the point of fatally slowing contractions, or excited, leading to heart fibrillation so that no blood is pumped.

Let us consider the commonest of the models illustrated in Fig. 14.4, type A. Here the medium corresponds to blood flowing in the circulatory system. The vascular conduits (blood vessels) may be considered either elastic [A1] or rigid [A2]. For both types of medium, the agent (poison) may either be a solid [s] or a fluid [f]. In the latter case, a liquid enters another liquid's flow. For example a naive person might conceptualise poison as a sort of paint melting into the blood: when the heart becomes painted by the poisonous

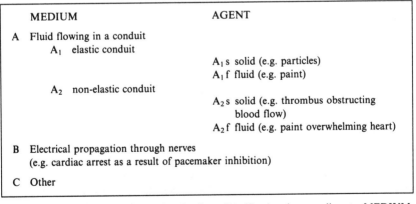

FIG. 14.4. Some naive models of poisoning. Classification is according to MEDIUM, followed by AGENT and TARGET.

colour (becoming green instead of red), then death occurs. In the case of a rigid conduit, a solid agent [A2s] could be envisaged as a substance able to solidify blood, generating an obstruction or "thrombus" in the circulatory system. The only case investigated experimentally was that of a solid agent in an elastic conduit [A1s].

It should be noted that the status of the agent and the target are not important for determining the type of causal model. It is the medium that defines the type of model. Thus, type A is defined on the basis of a fluid flowing in a conduit. In subtype A1 the conduit is elastic and in subtype A2 the conduit is not elastic. The type of agent, solid or fluid, has a minor effect on the reasoning procedures. In the other possible causal models (A1f; A2f; A2s; B; and C; see Fig. 14.4), the type of model modifier can also change. Thus in [B] an antidote (modifier) could be an anti-depolariser, in [A2s] a solvent and in [A1f] and [A2f] a blood-purifying filter.

Let us now delve more fully into our model of contact causality. To keep the analysis simple we shall refer only to [A1s] (Fig. 14.4)—a naive example of a poisoning process. By means of a snake bite, poison is injected into a human body. The poison does not enter the circulatory system directly but remains in the wound area, which functions as a filter gradually releasing poison particles into the bloodstream. The particles are carried through the blood vessels, which are considered as elastic conduits, whose cross-section may change. Once the particles reach the heart, they progressively impair its function.

In causal model [A1s], the position is the agent and the heart is the target. Contact between the poison and the heart occurs via the flow of blood through the vessels (medium). To understand the central role of the medium in causality by contact, one must appreciate how contact can be impeded or facilitated by the medium. Thus, contact would be facilitated by increasing the blood flow (e.g. by making the subject run); and contact could be impeded by removing part of the poison (e.g. by ablation of the puncture site), or by slowing the flow (e.g. by use of a tourniquet; see Fig. 14.5). Figure 14.5 shows two possible causal models each representing a series of facts:

Model 1:
Cleopatra was bitten by an asp. Cleopatra died.

Model 2:
Cleopatra was bitten in the hand by an asp; a tourniquet was applied to the arm. Cleopatra was saved.

This illustrates that causal models can contain objects able to modify the evolution of the poisoning process. These objects are called modifiers and represent points where a complete model may diverge from an initial standard model.

Model 1   Model 2

FIG. 14.5. Mental models of Cleopatra's poisoning. In Model 1 Cleopatra dies, while in Model 2 she is saved by a tourniquet.

A crucial feature of our approach to causal reasoning is that quantities are always treated as multiples or fractions of those used in the initial standard model, or base model. Modifiers utilise the standard values of each parameter (those used in the base model) as their unit of measurement, and new values generated in modified models are expressed relative to these. This evens out the difference between the qualitative and quantitative treatment of the parameters of a model and is, furthermore, in accord with findings from developmental studies of causality. Thus Baillargeon (1991) has shown that when reasoning about the height and location of a hidden object, infants between 4.5 and 6.5 months old start with relational (qualitative) models and only later use more precise quantitative models.

Modifiable components are the quantitative aspects of objects and of physical relations: both have to be defined in order to bring about a specific temporal evolution of the model. The quantitative properties of models we considered were:

(i) Physical properties. For example: quantity of poison (a property of agent), strength of the heart (property of target), and blood flow (property of medium);

(ii) Spatial and temporal relations between objects. For example the distance between the point of entry of the poison and the heart, or the time between the snake biting and application of a tourniquet.

Therefore, an object is defined by:

● physical properties (e.g. solid particles, elastic conduits, etc.);
● quantities pertaining to physical properties (e.g. number and hardness of particles, length and resilience of the duct, etc.);
● its causal role as *agent*, *medium*, or *target*.

An object has one or more physical properties (Property), each of which is characterised by one or more quantitative variables (Quantity) and by one or more causal roles (Role). Physical properties and causal roles define the relationships between the objects of the model, or in other words specify the relations between the tokens of the mental model. Thus, an object is formally specified as follows:

Object (Property (Quantity(Q)), Role).

For example:

Poison (solid-particles (number(low)), agent)

This formula expresses the fact that "few particles of a solid substance are the causal agent (i.e. cause poisoning)" within the model.

In summary, a causal model consists of:

(i) A structural component which is invariant; it comprises different objects, their physical properties, and physical relations between them. In our example, the objects are the poison (agent), the heart (target), blood flowing through the blood vessels (medium), plus all possible modifiers (antidote, cutting out the poison, tourniquet, etc).

(ii) A modifiable component, represented by the quantitative properties of the objects, responsible for the various instances of the model. In our case, the modifiable component comprises the quantity of poison, the location of the snake bite with respect to the heart, blood flow, etc.

We shall now go on to examine how model components are manipulated in reasoning processes.

4. CAUSAL MODELS: REASONING PROCESSES

The main consequence of our qualitative approach to modelling physical processes is that reasoning is considered essentially as a comparison between two or more models. We assume that the starting point is to build a base model, which serves as the standard model for the manipulation processes. The conclusions derived from the base model are compared with the results obtained from more complex models. For forward inferences, two models are constructed, the base model and a modified model based on the content of the premises. In backward inferences, reasoning is constrained by a fixed final state; in this case, complex models are constructed by means of two strategies. In the first, new objects—modifiers—are introduced; these are added one at a time to the initial model, generating progressively more complex models. The second strategy is to change quantitative aspects of the objects already represented. In neither case is there an explicit rule that prescribes how the model should be modified so as to approach the fixed final state.

Revision proceeds by trial and error. Trials are evaluated by comparing pairs of successively generated models. Comparison proceeds by selection of changes that bring the final state of a modified model closer to the desired conclusion; the other model of the pair is rejected. This procedure is justified by the fact that, as it is based on analogical representations of physical processes, causal reasoning is bounded by the unidirectionality of time. In other words, systems in a universe of increasing entropy experience phenomena whose dynamics necessarily follow the time arrow (Bara,

1995). It follows that the only way to draw a backward inference is to generate different forward simulations, until the desired final state is reached: given an initial and a final state of a causal process, there are different ways of connecting them. In real life our sensory-motor competence is learned by trial and error. For example, to hit a can with a stone, you do not try to reconstruct the trajectory from the can back to your hand, but try several launches from your hand towards the target.

Causal models share three general principles of reasoning with other types of mental models, roughly corresponding to three different phases of reasoning: constructing models, drawing conclusions, and falsifying putative conclusions. In the construction phase, the model is built up from descriptions of states-of-affairs. For drawing a conclusion, relations between objects which were not defined in the construction phase are made explicit. In causal reasoning this phase is based on the comparison of quantities between different mental models; for this reason we have called it the *comparison* phase in causal reasoning.

The *falsification* phase involves testing the validity of the model by searching for counter-examples. In causal reasoning, falsification does not check the validity of a putative conclusion, but evaluates the extent to which the conclusion can be considered acceptable. In forward inferences, the system tries to find alternative conclusions. In backward inferences, where the conclusion is fixed, the falsification system introduces modifications to the causal path and evaluates the final state of the new model compared to that of the initial model. Because everyday reasoning is located in the realm of the possible, and not the realm of the necessary, falsification procedures aim to guarantee the soundness of the initially reached conclusion. In fact, in forward inferences the system modifies the models in order to assess the well-foundedness of the first conclusion. In an analogous way, in backward inferences the key point is to vary modifiers and their quantities, in order either to increase the confidence in the first conclusion, if it is the only one to fulfil the requirements, or to decrease its confidence value, if other modifiers are able to reach the same final point.

We are therefore able to divide causal inference processes into three main phases. The interactions among them are illustrated in Fig. 14.6.

In the following sections we specify the procedures corresponding to these three phases in causal models.

4.1 The Construction Phase

In this phase, the inferential system takes, as input, premises expressing causal events and generates mental models of the physical phenomena involved in those events. Closely connected to this phase, but conceptually distinct from it, are subcognitive processes (simulation processes, Fig. 14.5)

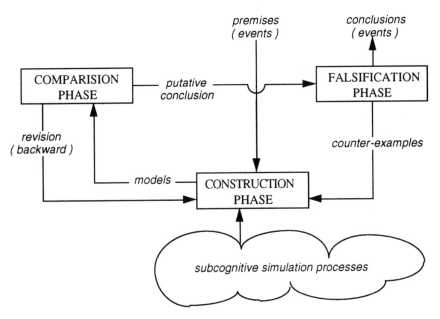

FIG. 14.6.   The inferential system.

which drive the dynamic evolution of the physical mental models that generate the causal mental models.

Two main processes occur within the construction module: premodelling and quantification; the first involves qualitative features of the model, the second is concerned with assigning relational values. Starting from events described by the premises and knowledge of a specific causal connection, the objects constituting the tokens of the model are defined.

4.1.1 Premodelling Processes

Premodelling processes identify objects (tokens of the model) and their causal roles. Causal roles define causal relations between tokens.

A procedure identifies the basic objects involved in the physical causal process, specifying the relations between them, i.e. their roles within the process (which can be agent, medium, or target) and their physical properties. It is important to bear in mind that there are two roles for the medium in the causal process: that of container (structural function) and that of carrier (kinematic function). The various possible physical properties of the medium result in several classes of causal models.

Thus the premodelling processes generate a PRE-MODEL which is defined purely in qualitative terms. Agent, target, and medium may consist of elementary objects or complex objects (i.e. several elementary objects). A single object may have several roles. Consider a bullet hitting a target: the bullet functions as agent and partly as medium. In the poisoning example, the three objects are the poison, the heart, and the circulatory system. For example "particles of poison transported by the blood in the blood vessels to the heart" is represented in the pre-model as follows:

A (particles, agent)
T (recipient, target)
Mcont (elastic conduit, medium-container)
Mcarr (running fluid, medium-carrier)

Modifiers are objects that change the quantitative parameters of the objects of the previously constructed pre-model. The causal function of a modifier is derived from general knowledge of the physical world and is defined in terms of modifying functions between objects. Modifying functions are connections between modifier objects and the objects—agent, target, medium—making up the pre-model:

modifying the function
    (modifier object, object to be modified, modify function)

For example, a tourniquet would be represented as:

tourniquet (cord, modifier)

and would be integrated into the pre-model by defining its causal function as follows:

modifying function
    (cord, elastic, conduit, constrict)

This modifying function states that a cord has a constrictor function on (is able to constrict) an elastic conduit. Thus the tourniquet is integrated into the pre-model as modifier of the object elastic conduit or:

Modifier (cord, constrict [medium-container])

4.1.2 Quantification Processes

Quantification processes fix the values of the parameters of models. They consist of two sub-routines, value fixing and time assignment.

i. Value Fixing.   The value fixing procedure assigns a point on a scale to each quantity expressed in the premises. The scale is: high, medium-high, medium, medium-low, low. The procedure assigns the value medium by default. In this way a quantified or physical model is generated.

As an example consider the following description: "a few particles of poison were introduced into the blood and carried by the circulatory system; a very small number of particles accumulated in the heart; the heart is rather vulnerable (perhaps because the individual is weak); the particles were introduced a short distance from the heart (perhaps the arm)." This state of affairs is represented in the physical models as follows:

A (solid-particles (number [med–low]), agent)
T (recipient (capacity [med–low], fill [low]), target)
Mcont (elastic-conduit(diameter[med], distance[low]), medium-container)
Mcarr (running fluid (velocity[med]), medium-carrier)

ii. Time Assignment. Time assignment procedures define the duration of a dynamic model relative to the duration of the base model.

The duration of the *base model* functions as the unit of time measurement and this is compared with the duration of the successive causal models; in this way a value for each causal model is assigned. Duration is expressed by assigning one of the values on this scale: much shorter, slightly shorter, about equal, slightly longer, much longer.

4.2 Subcognitive Simulation

The physical model generated in the construction phase activates sub-cognitive *simulation processes* which, using knowledge implicit in the dynamics of the elementary physical phenomena, and under control of the physical model, cause the model to change in time. In other words: the physical phenomena underlying the causal process are simulated. The result is a dynamic model. We distinguish the following steps in the simulation process:

(i) Activation of implicit knowledge of the dynamics of the elementary physical phenomenon by objects having carrier and container functions.
(ii) Generation of instantaneous changes in quantities during the simulated physical process (temporal evolution of the physical model).
(iii) Simulation of the temporal evolution of a base model.

4.3 The Comparison Phase

In this phase, the inferential system receives dynamic models as input; after carrying out a series of comparisons between them, it produces as output a putative conclusion which will be evaluated in the falsification phase. In forward inferences the values of the target parameters are considered. In backward inferences any quantitative property not included in the premises is rendered explicit. In this phase, the inferential system also makes explicit those causal relations between tokens (functional dependencies) which were not defined in the construction phase; for example, it specifies the inverse relation between how much the tourniquet constricts and the speed with which the target is reached by the agent:

> functional dependency
> (cord (constriction), target (fill), INVERSE).

These processes compare the quantitative parameters of the simulation of the causal model to be investigated with the parameters of the simulation of the base model, thus identifying quantity changes in dynamic models. Specifically the processes compare the initial and final values of target, agent, medium, and modifier parameters. Subsequently, the procedures work differently in forward and backward inferences: in forward inferences they select the final state of the target parameters within the model passed on from the comparison phase. In backward inferences they work in either of two ways:

(a) if modifiers not mentioned in the premises were introduced, then the last modifier introduced—with the values of its parameters—is selected as a conclusion. For example,

> Premises
> Cleopatra was bitten by an asp. Cleopatra was saved.
> Conclusion
> A tourniquet was applied to her arm.

(b) if no such modifiers were introduced, the output non-default values of one or more parameters are chosen as a conclusion. For example,

> Premises
> Cleopatra was bitten on the hand by an asp; A tourniquet was applied to the arm. Cleopatra died.
> Conclusion
> The tourniquet was too loose.

In this phase, there is a set of procedures called *revision procedures*, which apply only to backward inferences. Because the inference system proceeds only towards the future, this procedure is required to modify and select dynamic models whose final states are compatible with the initial premises. Their goal is to assess the compatibility of the causal model generated in the forward procedure with the states of affairs described by the premises. These procedures are applied recursively only to backward inferences until the final state of the causal model generated is compatible with a final state defined by the premises. They consist of two sub-routines:

i. Final-states matching. This procedure compares the final state of the dynamic model generated in the construction phase with what is specified in the premises. Specifically, it compares quantitative properties of the target in the final state of the causal model generated with the properties expressed in the premises, and calculates the difference (in relative terms). If there are other quantitative properties of the final state determined by the premises, it compares them in the same way. If the differences are zero, the dynamic model is accepted and the reversion procedures terminate. As more than one cycle of these procedures may be repeated, a local working memory is checked for other previously memorised differences; the model with the greatest difference is then rejected. The system then passes to the next set of procedures.

ii. Updating. This procedure modifies structural parameters of the dynamic model, possibly adding modifiers, thus generating a revised causal model in accordance with the change; this procedure continues to generate revised causal models until the final state and premises are consistent.

4.4 Falsification Phase

Unlike in formal logical reasoning, this phase is not necessary for producing conclusions, because in causal reasoning there are no necessarily valid conclusions that require validation. We can only attach various degrees of confidence to the conclusions of causal reasoning. Assigning a confidence level is not essential for drawing a conclusion and may be carried out in a non-systematic way.

In the falsification phase, the inferential system performs two tasks:

(i) It searches for counter-examples to the generated causal model which are compatible with the state of affairs described by the premises.

(ii) It assesses the plausibility and probability of the conclusions derived from any dynamic model.

These steps are achieved by the two different processes described in the following.

4.4.1 Counter-example Processes

Counter-example processes depend on the type of inference:

(i) In forward inferences a final state is selected that is opposite to that selected by the previous procedure.

(ii) In backward inferences, either new modifiers not mentioned in the premises are introduced, or the values of the parameters of the model are changed.

In either case, the change selected is passed to the construction phase so that it can then construct a model compatible with that result, while keeping the other parameters unchanged.

4.4.2 Evaluation Processes

These processes compare the causal model from which the conclusion was obtained with the counter-examples. Specifically they assign a high or low degree of confidence to the selected conclusion by comparing the final state of the dynamic model with that of the counter exemplifying model. For forward inferences, obtaining the same final state in the dynamic model and counter-examples increases confidence in the conclusion, as it implies that that final state may be obtained under several different initial conditions. On the other hand, for backward inferences, if the change in the parameter considered important by the comparison phase leads to a different final state, this implies that that parameter plays an important role and hence confidence in the conclusion is increased.

5. A COMPUTATIONAL MODEL

The theory presented in this chapter has been developed at the competence level; in other words, we claim that it is a viable possibility for a human system for reasoning about physical causality. The computer model that simulates the hypothesised structures and processes guarantees the formal soundness of the theory itself.

A computational model of causal reasoning based on our theory has been developed by Carassa, Valpiani, Geminiani, and Bandini (1995). Two general considerations guided the construction of this model, one of a theoretical, the other of a heuristic nature:

(a) The model had to be organised into modules reflecting three essential features: general principles of reasoning by mental models, reasoning by examples, and qualitative treatment of quantities.

(b) Within each module we had to be able to identify specific procedures for manipulating models. The construction of a computational model required the specification of procedures which we hypothesise to be similar to those that realise human inference processes.

The computational model is based on Qualitative Process Theory or QPT (Forbus, 1984) for representing quantitative aspects of models and simulating their dynamic evolution. QPT identifies the fundamental components of a physical phenomenon to be the objects involved, the quantities describing the interesting parameters of the objects, and the processes operating on or between the objects. The QPT interpreter allows the simulation of different physical phenomena, provided that they are represented in QPT language. The inferential system is based on an extended version of QPT (EQPT). EQPT is remarkable for the following reasons:

• it allows an accurate representation of the quantities of the objects and of the relationships between these quantities;
• when conflicting influences impinge on a single quantity, it is able to determine the resulting direction of change for the quantity;
• it allows the introduction of actions and new objects during the simulation of a process.

The inferential system was developed in the language Prolog at the Expert Systems Lab of the Department of Computer Science, University of Milan; the system is being currently tested at the Cognitive Science Center, University of Turin.

6. CONCLUDING REMARKS

A fundamental feature of commonsense reasoning, which includes causal reasoning, is that it is characterised by extensive and complex interactions between different types of knowledge. Any theory that seeks to explain or model commonsense reasoning must therefore take these interactions into account. The starting point of our approach to causal reasoning was to identify three levels of knowledge: abstract knowledge, analogical knowledge, and subcognitive knowledge. These levels of knowledge are not equally involved in the different types of causal reasoning about the physical world, and depending on the type of causal reasoning, inference processes take place preferentially within one or other level.

Thus, processes involving the "perception" of causal relations between events take place mainly at the subcognitive level. These processes start from subcognitive sensory-motor knowledge ("background" knowledge) regarding causal interaction by contact between objects, and then pass to the analogical level in which that knowledge is made explicit by reference to examples, to then become explicit at the abstract level.

In processes involving "attribution" of a causal link between events, the formation of the hypothesis of such a link is guided by knowledge at the abstract level.

During the exploration of an already known causal link—a process that we call causal reasoning in the strict sense, and which we have explored in this article—the main level in which knowledge is elaborated is the analogical level, i.e. the level of representation of mental models.

An interesting aspect of our theory is the dynamics of the interactions among the different levels of knowledge. As we show later, the functioning of the inferential system during the phase of construction of mental models, particularly during the premodelling phase, is dependent on the subcognitive background, especially for the generation of temporal change. Conversely, the results of inference processes occurring at the analogical level modify knowledge at the abstract level and probably also knowledge at the subcognitive level, although we have not explored this later aspect here. Figure 14.2 illustrates this information flow between the three knowledge levels in causal reasoning.

We shall now examine briefly how information flow takes place through the various levels of knowledge. The starting point for dynamic models that represent physical causality are objects. Objects are characterised by three fundamental aspects: causal roles, physical properties, and quantitative features; each of these properties is mainly associated with a level of knowledge.

Thus, abstract knowledge allows the definition of causal roles on the basis of the hypothesis of contact—a general hypothesis valid for all the domains of physical causality. In particular, definition of the causal roles of agent and target is essential for identifying objects that play the central role of medium in dynamic models.

The subcognitive level contains background knowledge essential for the temporal evolution of the dynamic model. What mainly distinguishes the different types of model are the physical properties of the medium in each. Given that the medium has two functions—structural and kinematic—and that a limited number of physical properties characterise different objects, it follows that the number of types of causal model is limited. The obviously relevant physical properties of the medium are its physical state (solid, liquid, or gas) and kinematic state (at rest, in uniform motion, or undergoing acceleration).

Finally there is the analogical level of knowledge, the most important level as far as causal reasoning is concerned. Relations between the different quantitative features of the model are explored at this level, and this is essential for understanding how the various objects that interact in the causal process are causally interrelated. Abstract knowledge and analogical knowledge interact in a complex fashion. On the one hand conceptual knowledge about the functions of modifiers is essential for dealing with quantities (for example, conceptual knowledge tells us that in the case of a snake bite a tourniquet reduces the diameter of the blood vessels, see Fig. 14.5). On the other hand, at the level of analogical knowledge, the construction of different dynamic models (for example placing the tourniquet between the bite point and the heart, or alternatively placing it peripheral to the bite point) allows discovery of the fact that to effectively reduce the flow of poison to the heart the tourniquet must be applied between the bite and the heart, and that the nearer the heart it is, the later it can be applied.

In general then, exploration of the analogical level is important for reasoning about complex situations in which many modifiers can intervene: it is unlikely that there is sufficient abstract knowledge to foresee all possible interactions between modifiers. The analogical level is also important for processing anomalous situations, i.e. those in which circumstances evolve contrary to the expectations of abstract knowledge. Suppose, for example, that Cleopatra is poisoned but notwithstanding the timely administration of an antidote, she dies. Exploration of the analogical level can suggest the possibility that the target's sensitivity threshold may be important. The analogical model may even lead to the hypothesis that too much antidote was given, or when administered early can be harmful because it is not bound to the poison. All this is possible by modifying the quantities characterising the model and exploring their consequences. Our model therefore emerges as having an important general property: the types of processes that allow the model to deal with quantities are constant for different types of causal model.

To conclude we restate three general characteristics peculiar to our theoretical approach to causal reasoning:

i. that at the level of abstract knowledge, the postulate is that contact mediates causal roles;
ii. that the physical characteristics of the medium are such as to define a fixed number of types of model at the level of subcognitive knowledge;
iii. that there is a basic machinery which allows manipulation of quantities at the level of analogical knowledge.

Mental models are a vital part of causal reasoning because they perform the task of exploring the complex and unpredictable aspects of known causal links; such exploration also leads to enrichment of knowledge at the abstract level, not only relative to the domain explored, but also in similar domains. However an aspect of interest from the point of view of the evolution of the subcogitive remains to be investigated: the mechanisms by which subcognitive knowledge is modified by causal reasoning.

ACKNOWLEDGEMENTS

We thank Alan Garnham and Jane Oakhill for many helpful criticisms on earlier drafts of this paper.

The research has been supported by the Italian *Ministero della Pubblica Istruzione* (MPI 40%) for the years 1995–1996, project "*Nuovi modelli della comunicazione e nuove tecnologie*", Unit of Torino.

REFERENCES

Ball, W.A. (1973). The perception of causality in the infant. Paper presented, *Society for Research in Child Development*. Philadelphia.

Ballargeon, R. (1991). Reasoning about the height and location of a hidden object in 4.5 and 6.5-month-old infants. *Cognition*, 38, 13–42.

Baillargeon, R. (1993). The object concept revisited: New directions in the investigations of infants' physical knowledge. In C.E. Granrud (Ed.), *Visual perception and cognition in infancy, Carnegie Mellon Symposia on Cognition*. Hillsdale, NJ: Lawrence Erlbaum Associates Inc.

Baillargeon, R., Kotovsky, L., & Needham, A. (1995). The acquisition of physical knowledge in infancy. In D. Sperber, D. Premack, & A.J. Premack (Eds.), *Causal cognition*. Oxford: Clarendon Press.

Baillargeon, R., Spelke, E.S., & Wassermann, S. (1986). Object permanence in five months old infants. *Cognition*, 20, 191–208.

Bara, B.G. (1995). *Cognitive science: A developmental approach to the simulation of the mind.* Hove, UK: Lawrence Erlbaum Associates Ltd.

Bara, B.G., Bucciarelli, M., & Johnson-Laird, P.N. (1994). Development of syllogistic reasoning. *The American Journal of Psychology*, 108 (2), 157–193.

Bara, B.G., Bucciarelli, M., Johnson-Laird, P.N., & Lombardo, V. (1994). Mental models in propositional reasoning. *Proceedings of the 16th Annual Conference of the Cognitive Science Society*.

Carassa, A., Geminiani, G.C., & Bara, B.G. (1993). Causalità per contatto: Un modello computazionale di ragionamento quotidiano. *Sistemi Intelligenti*, 3, 371–400.

Carassa, A., Valpiani, A., Geminiani, G.C., & Bandini, S. (1995). A cognitive model of causal reasoning about the physical world. *Lecture Notes in Artificial Intelligence* (pp. 217–230). Berlin: Springer Verlag.

Carey, S. (1985). *Conceptual change in childhood*. Cambridge, MA: Bradford/MIT Press.

Carey, S. (1995). On the origin of causal understanding. In D. Sperber, D. Premack, & A.J. Premack (Eds.), *Causal cognition*. Oxford: Clarendon Press.

Chomsky, N. (1980). *Rules and representations*. New York: Columbia University Press.

Davies, N.B., Hatchwell, B.J., Robson, T., & Burke, T. (1992). Paternity and parental effort in dunnocks *Prunella modularis:* How good are male chick-feeding rules? *Animal behaviour*, 43, 729–745.

Einhorn, H.J., & Hogart, R.M. (1986). Judging probable cause. *Psychological Bulletin*, 99, 3–19.

Forbus, K.D. (1984). Qualitative Process Theory. *Artificial Intelligence*, 24, 85–168.

Garcia, J., Hankins, W.G., & Rusiniak, K.W. (1974). Behavioural regulation of the milieu interne in man and rat. *Science*, 185, 824–831.

Garnham, A., & Oakhill, J. (1994). *Thinking and reasoning*. London: Blackwell.

Heider, F. (1958). *The psychology of interpersonal relations*. New York: John Wiley & Sons Ltd.

Johnson-Laird, P.N. (1983). *Mental models*. Cambridge: Cambridge University Press.

Johnson-Laird, P.N., & Byrne R. (1991). *Deduction*. Hillsdale NJ: Lawrence Erlbaum Associates.

Jones, E.E., & Davis, K.E. (1965). From acts to dispositions: The attribution process in person perception. In L. Berkowitz (Ed.), *Advances in experimental social psychology*. New York: Academic Press.

Kelley, H.H., & Michela, J.L. (1980). Attribution theory and research. *Annual Review of Psychology*, 31, 457–501.

Kummer, H. (1995). Causal knowledge in animals. In D. Sperber, D. Premack, & A.J. Premack (Eds.), *Causal cognition*. Oxford: Clarendon Press.

Leslie, A.M. (1984). Spatiotemporal continuity and perception of causality in infants. *Perception, 13,* 287–305.

Leslie, A.M., & Keeble, S. (1978). Do six-month-old infants perceive causality? *Cognition, 25,* 265–288.

McLeod, P., & Dienes, Z. (1993). Running to catch the ball. *Nature, 362,* 23.

Michotte, A. (1946). *La perception de la causalité.* Louvain: Publications de l'Institut Superieur de Philosophie (Etudes de Psychologie), VIII, *The perception of causality.* London: Methuen [reprinted 1963].

Oakes, L.M. (1993). The perception of causality by 7 and 10 months old infants. Paper presented, *Society for Research in Child Development.* New Orleans.

Perrigo, G., Cully Bryant, W., & Vom Saal, F.S. (1990). A unique neural timing system prevents male mice from harming their own offspring. *Animal Behaviour, 39,* 535–539.

Premack, D. (1990). The infant's theory of self-propelled objects. *Cognition, 36,* 1–16.

Premack, D. (1993). Prolegomenon to evolution of cognition. In T.A. Poggio & D.A. Glaser (Eds.), *Exploring brain functions: models in neuroscience.* Chichester, UK: John Wiley & Sons Ltd.

Premack, D. (1994). Levels of causal understanding in chimpanzees and children. *Cognition, 50,* 347–362.

Premack, D., & Premack, A.J. (1995). Intention as psychological cause. In D. Sperber, D. Premack, & A.J. Premack (Eds.), *Causal cognition.* Oxford: Clarendon Press.

Shastri, L., & Ajjanagadde, V. (1993). From simple associations to systematic reasoning: A connectionist representation of rules, variables and dynamic bindings using temporal synchrony. *Behavioral and Brain Sciences, 16,* 417–494.

Shoam, J. (1988). *Reasoning about change.* Cambridge, Mass: The MIT Press.

Spelke, E.S. (1988). The origins of physical knowledge. In L. Weiskrantz (Ed.), *Thought without language.* Oxford: Clarendon Press.

Spelke, E.S. (1990). Principles of object perception. *Cognition Science, 14,* 29–56.

Spelke, E.S. (1994). Initial knowledge: Six suggestions. *Cognition, 50,* 431–445.

15 The Blues and the Abstract Truth: Music and Mental Models

Mark Steedman
University of Pennsylvania, USA

INTRODUCTION

The idea that there is a grammar of music is probably as old as the idea of grammar itself, and the idea that there should be *formal* grammars of music followed equally hard on the Chomskean application to natural languages of the formal techniques used to analyse logical and mathematical languages—see Winograd, 1968; Lindblom and Sundberg, 1972; Steedman, 1973, 1977; Longuet-Higgins, 1978; Johnson-Laird, 1991; and many others reviewed by Sundberg and Lindblom, 1991.

Nevertheless, it is probably fair to say that such musical formal grammars have lagged behind the linguistic ones in terms of descriptive adequacy, constraint on formal generative power, psychological plausibility, and computational practicality, especially as far as harmonic analysis goes.

For example, Steedman 1984 offers a generative grammar for chord progressions in jazz twelve-bar blues. The grammar is used to account for the fact that the chord sequences shown in Fig. 15.1—the last of which

a)	I(M7)	IV(7')	I(M7)	I7	IV(7')	IV(7')	I(M7)	I(M7)	V7	V7	I(M7)	I(M7)
b)	I(M7)	IV(7')	I(M7)	Vm7, I7	IV(7')	♯IV ○ 7	I(M7)	VI7	IIm7	V7	I(M7)	I(M7)
c)	I(M7)	IV(7')	I(M7)	Vm7, I7	IV(M7)	IVm7	IIIm7	VI7	IIm7	V7	I(M7)	I(M7)
d)	I(M7)	IIm(7'), ♯II ○ 7	IIIm(7')	Vm7, I7	IV(M7)	IVm7, ♭VII7	IIIm7	♭IIIm7	IIm7	V7	I(M7)	I(M7)
e)	I(M7)	VII♭7, III7	VIm7, II7	Vm7, I7	IV(M7)	IVm7, ♭VII7	♭III(M7)	♭IIIm7, ♭VI(7')	IIm7	V7	I(M7)	I(M7)
f)	I(M7)	IV(7')	I(M7)	♭IIm7, ♭V7	IV(7')	♯IV ○ 7	IIIm7	VI7	IIm7, V7	♭VIm7, ♭II7	I(M7)	I(M7)
g)	♭II7, ♭V7	VII7, III7	VII7, II7	V7, I7	IV(7')	♯IV ○ 7	IIIm7	♭III7	VIm7	♭II7	I(M7)	I(M7)

FIG. 15.1. Some jazz 12-bars (adapted from Coker, 1964).

shares no bars in common with the first, other than the fifth and final bars— are perceived by jazz musicians as being in some sense "paraphrases". That is, they are all instances of the twelve-bar form, one of the basic forms of the music. (The notation, which is for the most part standard, is explained in an appendix to the present chapter.)

The 1984 paper attempts to capture this fact in a small number of rules modelled on the linguist's device of a "rewriting rule". The principal rules are shown in Fig. 15.2, in which X is a variable over relative chord roots I, II, etc., and IV_X is to be read as "the chord that is X's IV (so that if X is II, IV_X is V).[1] I will briefly summarise the motivation for these rules, but the reader is directed to the earlier paper for a fuller account.

Rule 0 simply defines the skeleton of the twelve bar as two-bar units of tonic I harmony, followed by two two-bar units constituting a "plagal cadence"—a progression from IV to I—followed by two two-bar units constituting a "perfect cadence", from V to I.

Rule 1 recursively expands this framework as a binary tree. There is a convention not indicated in the rules whereby the total number of bars or fractions thereof on the right equals that on the left—hence each of the Xs on the right of rule two lasts half as long as the one on the left. The brackets round the minor annotations m mean that the relevant chords can optionally be minor, and there is another convention that says that if the thing on the left is minor, the things on the right must be. Bracketed 7 means that those chords are optionally dominant sevenths and a similar inheritance convention applies. Note that the dominant seventh when present passes down the *right branch*. This is important because a dominant seventh strongly constraints the chord that follows.

Rule 2 is another binary tree expansion rule, with the same conventions, which says that a chord X *other than* a dominant seventh can be expanded as that chord and its subdominant IV_X. Rules 0 to 2 are all

0.			*12bar* →	*I I7*	*IV I*	*V7 I*
1.			$X(m)(7)$ →	$X(m)$	$X(m)(7)$	
2.			$X(m)$ →	$X(m)$	IV_X	
3a.		*W*	$X7$ →	$V_X(m)7$	$X7$	
3b.		*W*	$Xm7$ →	V_X7	$Xm7$	
4.		V_X7	$X(m)(7)$ →	$bII_X(m)(7)$	$X(m)(7)$	
5.	X	X	X →	X	II_Xm	III_Xm
6a.	$X(m)$ $X(m)$	V_X →	$X(m)$	$\sharp X \circ 7$	V_X	
6b.	$X(m)$ $X(m)$	II_Xm7 →	$X(m)$	$\sharp X \circ 7$	II_Xm7	
6c.	$X(m)$ $X(m)$	VII_Xm7 →	$X(m)$	$\sharp X \circ 7$	VII_Xm7	

FIG. 15.2. Chord substitution rules for jazz 12-bars (adapted from Steedman, 1984).

that is required to generate the chord roots for the mind-numbingly dull twelve-bar (a) in Fig. 15.1.

The remainder of the rules are rules that substitute more interesting chords in this somewhat boring framework, to achieve the variety illustrated in the remainder of Fig. 15.1. Rule 3, which comes in two instances, does most of the interesting work in this respect. 3a says that any chord W preceding a major dominant seventh chord $X7$ can be replaced by the dominant seventh of X, V_X7 or the minor dominant seventh of X, V_Xm7. 3b says the same applies to the chord preceding a *minor* dominant seventh on X, except that the new chord has to be major. The chord W in these rules is further limited to chords that have not been affected by any previous substitution by a root-changing rule like 3 itself (see Steedman 1984, p.63).

Rules 4, 5, and 6 introduce various passing chords whose detailed motivation need not detain us here.

Together with the trivial rules shown in Fig. 15.3 for optionally adding further notes to the basic chord types X, $X7$, Xm, $Xm7$ the earlier paper shows that the grammar covers a small corpus of Jazz twelve-bars including the above representative examples. (Again the conventional interpretations of these chord symbols are given in the appendix.)

There are a number of things that are unsatisfactory about this grammar. One is its minute coverage. However, the work of Johnson-Laird (1991) shows that rather similar kinds of rules can be generalised to a more diverse set of harmonic "skeletons" common in jazz, including the very frequent "I've Got Rhythm" family.

Another objection that has been raised is that the rules give the appearance of Context-sensitive PS rules, a very powerful class of grammars indeed. I shall show later that this appearance is actually illusory. We can replace these rules (and the corresponding rules in Johnson-Laird, 1991— see p.311) by strongly equivalent context-free rules.

The third objection is that, while rules 2–7 capture the musician's intuition that elaborated chord sequences are derived from simpler ones by a process of chord substitution, the way the rules are phrased, and in particular the presence of the variable W, even with the rather nasty condition that W should not have been altered by any previous substitution, means that the search space for the parser is large. This difficulty can to

$$7a.\quad X \quad \rightarrow \quad \{X(M7), X(7'), X9, X13\}$$
$$7b.\quad X7 \quad \rightarrow \quad \{Xb9, Xb10, X7+5\}$$
$$7c.\quad Xm \quad \rightarrow \quad \{Xm(7'), Xm6\}$$
$$7d.\quad Xm7 \quad \rightarrow \quad \{Xm9, X\phi7\}$$

FIG. 15.3. Surface "spellings" of chords (adapted from Steedman, 1984).

some extent be overcome by suitable search strategies. However, these have proved hard to identify without compromising the integrity of the grammar itself (see Mouton & Pachet, 1995). Moreover, the most promising search strategies merely point to a further implausibility in the grammar, as follows.

Rule 3 has the effect of propagating perfect cadences backwards. That is, successive substitutions in the basic skeleton (a) of Fig. 15.1 generate examples like those in Fig. 15.4, in which the elaborated cadence is underlined: this means that the value of, for example, the *IIIm7* chord in *a‴* in Fig. 15.4 is dependent on a chain of substitutions working back from a quite distant *V7* to its right. This suggests that a good parsing strategy to minimise search is to parse from right to left. (The same strategy was also a forced move for the parser proposed by Winograd 1968.)

Musically it is quite correct to claim that the *IIIm7* is dependent on the *V7* to its right, and as this grammar is in Chomsky's terms a "competence grammar", distinct from the performance mechanism that delivers the analysis, there is nothing in principle wrong with this assumption about the parser. Nevertheless, it is in psychological terms quite surprising to find that the optimum processor for our grammar is right to left. Our own experience of such music does not suggest that we need to wait to the end of a chord sequence like *a‴* to interpret the role of that *IIIm7* chord. As in the case of natural language processing, our intuition is that we interpret sequences more or less note by note and chord by chord, from left to right. In the case of natural language processing, at least, there is abundant experimental evidence to back up this intuition (see Marslen-Wilson, 1975; Tyler & Marslen-Wilson, 1977; and much subsequent work.)

LONGUET-HIGGINS' THEORY OF TONAL HARMONY

To devise a better grammar, we need to get away from the whole idea of substituting one chord for another, and to seek something founded more straightforwardly in musical semantics.

The first completely formal identification of the nature of the harmonic relation is in Longuet-Higgins (1962a, b), although there are some earlier incomplete proposals, including work by Weber, Schoenberg, Hindemith,

a.	I(M7)	IV(7′)	I(M7)	I7	IV(7′)	IV(7′)	I(M7)	I(M7)	V7	V7	I(M7)	I(M7)
a′.	I(M7)	IV(7′)	I(M7)	I7	IV(7′)	IV(7′)	I(M7)	I(M7)	IIm7	V7	I(M7)	I(M7)
a″.	I(M7)	IV(7′)	I(M7)	I7	IV(7′)	IV(7′)	I(M7)	VI7	IIm7	V7	I(M7)	I(M7)
a‴.	I(M7)	IV(7′)	I(M7)	I7	IV(7′)	IV(7′)	IIIm7	VI7	IIm7	V7	I(M7)	I(M7)

....etc..

FIG. 15.4. Effect of recursive application of rule 3.

and the important work of Ellis (1874, 1875). Longuet-Higgins showed that the set of musical intervals relative to some fundamental frequency was the set of ratios definable as the product of powers of the prime factors 2, 3, and 5, and no others—that is as a ratio of the form $2^x.3^y.5^z$, where x, y, and z are positive or negative integers. (The fact that ratios involving factors of seven and higher primes do not contribute to this definition of harmony does not exclude them from the theory of consonance. In real resonators, overtones involving such factors do arise, and contribute to consonance. Helmholtz realised that the absence of such ratios from the chord system of tonal harmony represented a problem for his theory of chord function, and attempted an explanation in terms of consonance—see Ellis [translation] 1885, p.213.)[2]

Longuet-Higgins' observation means that the intervals form a three-dimensional discrete space, with those factors as its generators, in which musical intervals can be viewed as vectors. Since the ratio 2 corresponds to the musical octave, and since for most harmonic purposes, notes an octave apart are functionally equivalent, and have the same note-names, it is convenient to project the three dimensional space along this axis into the 3 × 5 plane, assigning each position its traditional note-name. It is convenient to plot the plane relative to a central C, when it appears as in Fig. 15.5, adapted from Longuet-Higgins (1962a).

The traditional note-names are ambiguous with respect to the intervals, and the pattern of names repeats itself in a south-easterly direction, although each position necessarily represents a unique frequency ratio when played in just intonation. (That is to say that the note-names "wrap" the

E	B	F#	C#	G#	D#	A#	E#	B#
C	G	D	A	E	B	F#	C#	G#
Ab	Eb	Bb	F	C	G	D	A	E
Fb	Cb	Gb	Db	Ab	Eb	Bb	F	C
Dbb	Abb	Ebb	Bbb	Fb	Cb	Gb	Db	Ab

FIG. 15.5. (Part of) The space of note-names (adapted from Longuet-Higgins, 1962a).

plane of musically significant frequency ratios onto a cylinder, which is here projected back onto the plane). Nevertheless, every vector in the infinite plane from some origin necessarily corresponds to a distinct frequency ratio, and potentially to a distinct musical function. There is a traditional nomenclature which distinguishes among the different functions corresponding for example to the two Ds relative to the central C in Fig. 15.5, as between the "major tone" and the "minor tone". However, this nomenclature is confusing and not entirely systematic. Instead we will display the intervals relative to an origin or tonic I using the same roman numeral notation as is used for the chord roots in Fig. 15.1, as in Fig. 15.6. In this figure the intervals are disambiguated. The prefixes # and b roughly correspond respectively to the traditional notions of "augmented" intervals, and to "minor" and/or "diminished" intervals, while the superscripts plus and minus roughly corresponds to the "imperfect" intervals. (However the intervals here identified as II^-, $bVII^-$, and bV^- would usually be referred to as the minor tone, dominant seventh, and minor fifth, rather than as imperfect intervals, and the interval shown as $\#IV$ should be referred to as the tritone, rather than the augmented fourth.) The positions with no prefixes and suffixes are "major" and/or "perfect" intervals.

Crucially for our purpose, if we choose a particular position X in the plane of note-names of Fig. 15.5 as origin, and then superimpose the plane of intervals in roman numeral notation of Fig.15.6, with the I over the X, then we can calculate note-names corresponding to intervals like II_X, VII.[3]

Longuet-Higgins' harmonic representation therefore bears a strong resemblance to a "mental model" in the sense of Johnson-Laird, 1983.

III^-	VII^-	$\#IV^-$	$\#I$	$\#V$	$\#II$	$\#VI$	$\#III^+$	$\#VII^+$
I^-	V^-	II^-	VI	III	VII	$\#IV$	$\#I^+$	$\#V^+$
bVI^-	$bIII^-$	$bVII^-$	IV	I	V	II	VI^+	III^+
bIV^-	bI^-	bV^-	bII	bVI	$bIII$	$bVII$	IV^+	I^+
$bbII^-$	$bbVI^-$	$bbIII^-$	$bbVII$	bIV	bI	bV	bII^+	bVI^+

FIG. 15.6. (Part of) The space of disambiguated harmonic intervals.

That is to say, it builds directly into the representation some of the properties of the system that it represents. It will be obvious to musicians that the intervals they refer to as harmonically remote, such as the imperfect and augmented intervals, are spatially distant from the origin in the representation. Similarly, the definition of musically coherent chord sequences such as the twelve-bar blues has something to do with orderly progression to a destination by small steps in this space.

For example, the basic sequence in Fig. 15.1a, repeated as Fig. 15.4a, is a closed journey around a central *I* visiting the immediately neighbouring *IV* and *V*. Figure 15.4a′ makes a jump to the right to *II*, then returns via *V*. Figure 15.4a‴ is perhaps the most interesting, because it takes a step up to *III*, then proceeds via leftward steps to end up on *I⁻*. (This is a progression used to great effect by Louis Armstrong (1928) in *Basin Street Blues*, although its original discovery is at least as early as Beethoven's G major Piano Concerto, as Longuet-Higgins has pointed out.)

I⁻7 is musically distinct from the original *I*, and if perfectly intoned (as opposed to being played on an equally tempered keyboard), would differ from the original in a ratio of 80:81. Nevertheless, we are able to treat it as the tonic.

This theory also explains why the dominant seventh chord creates such a strong expectation of a following chord to its left, whereas the same chord without does not. The major chord on a root *V*, shown in Fig. 15.7 as made up of a circled *V*, *VII*, and *II*, is extremely unambiguous as to its interpretation, like all such triads. Thus, even if the major triad is played on

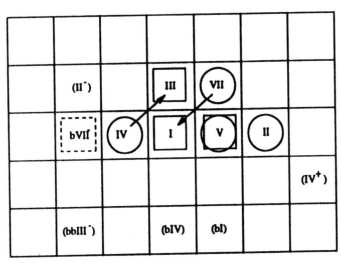

FIG. 15.7. The interpretation of the dominant seventh chord (circles) and its resolution (squares).

an equally tempered instrument, obscuring the distinction between the frequency ratios of the pure intervals, having picked *that* *V*, the representation makes it obvious why the harmonically closest interpretations of the *VII* and the *II* are not any of the imperfect or diminished alternatives shown in brackets. However, it is the addition of the dominant seventh of *V*, the circled *IV*, that makes the *V* chord have a hole in its middle, into which a triad on *I* (squared *I*, *III*, *V*) fits neatly, sharing one note with the first chord, and with the two remaining notes standing in semitone "leading note" relations with two other notes in the first chord.[4] A chord of *I* is indeed the expectation produced by a dominant seventh chord *V*7. Moreover the addition of a dominant seventh b*VII*⁻ to the *I* major triad (dotted square) makes the *I* in turn lead onto the *IV* to its left. The effect of adding dominant seventh chords to *minor* triads is suggested as an exercise at this point. (Why is an alternation of major and minor dominant seventh chords so effective?)

This "semantics" for the dominant seventh chord, showing why it generates a leftward shift in the space and a "need" or expectation for the corresponding tonic, is crucial to explaining why the grammar developed in the next section takes the form that it does. This representation or mental model is what underlay the earlier grammar, as I pointed out in passing at the time (Steedman, 1984, p.56, n.4). However, to make explicit the way in which this works points the way to a different "type-driven" kind of grammar, which makes explicit in the category of a dominant seventh chord its need for the tonic. Such a grammar will point the way to removing the distressingly right-branching analyses of the earlier version.

CATEGORIAL GRAMMAR

Categorial Grammars for natural languages have been mainly advanced as competence grammars, for linguistic reasons (see Wood, 1993 for a review). However, one branch of the family, the flexible or "combinatory" categorial grammars, which include associative operations like function composition, have also been defended on the grounds that they allow left-branching analyses of what are traditionally viewed as right-branching constructions, and are therefore more directly compatible with processors that make available incrementally assembled semantic analyses at an early stage in processing (see Steedman, 1989, for the argument).

Like other lexicalist approaches, categorial grammars put into the lexicon most of the information that is standardly captured in context-free phrase-structure rules. For example, instead of using rules like 1 to capture the basic syntactic facts concerning English transitive sentences, such grammars associate with English transitive verbs a category that we will usually write as in 2:[5]

(1) $S \rightarrow NP\ VP$
$VP \rightarrow TV\ NP$
$TV \rightarrow$ {eats, drinks, ...}

(2) eats := $(S\backslash NP)/NP$

The category says that *eats* is a *function*, combining with an NP to its right to yield a predicate, which is itself a function bearing the caregory $S\backslash NP$, which in turn combines with an NP to its left to yield an S.[6] Combination takes place via the following rules of functional application, which in a pure categorial grammar are the only rules of combination:

(3) *Functional Application:*
  a. $X/Y \quad Y \quad \Rightarrow \quad X$
  b. $Y \quad X\backslash Y \quad \Rightarrow \quad X$

These rules have the form of very general binary PS rule schemata. In fact Categorial Grammar is just binary-branching context-free grammar written in the accepting, rather than the producing, direction. There is a consequent transfer of the major burden of specifying particular grammars from the PS rules to the lexicon. Although it is now convenient to write derivations as in a, below, they are equivalent to conventional trees, as in b.

(4) a. Keats   eats   apples   b.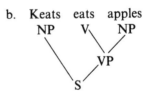
  $\overline{NP}$ $\overline{(S\backslash NP)/NP}$ $\overline{NP}$
       $\overline{} \rightarrow$
       $S\backslash NP$
  $\overline{} \rightarrow$
       S

(The annotations > and < on combinations in a, above, are mnemonic for the rightward and left function application rules 3a,b.)
   Flexible categorial grammars typically handle relative clauses by allowing rules of functional composition, such as the following:

(5) *Forward Composition* (> B):
  $X/Y \quad Y/Z \quad \Rightarrow_{B} \quad X/Z$

Together with "type-raised" categories that can be substituted in the lexicon or introduced by rule for argument categories like subject NPs, rule 5 allows extractions as follows:

(6) $\underline{\text{(a man)}}$ $\underline{\text{who(m)}}$ $\underline{\text{I}}$ $\underline{\text{like}}$

$(N \backslash N)/(S/NP)$ $S/(S \backslash NP)$ $(S \backslash NP)/NP$
$$\dfrac{\qquad\qquad\qquad}{S/NP} \rightarrow {}_B$$
$$\dfrac{\qquad\qquad\qquad\qquad\qquad\qquad}{N \backslash N} \rightarrow$$

Such extractions are immediately predicted to be unbounded:

(7) $\underline{\text{(a man)}}$ $\underline{\text{who(m)}}$ $\underline{\text{I}}$ $\underline{\text{think}}$ $\underline{\text{that}}$ $\underline{\text{I}}$ $\underline{\text{like}}$

$(N \backslash N)/(S/NP)$ $S/(S \backslash NP)$ $(S \backslash NP)/S'$ S'/S $S/(S \backslash NP)$ $(S \backslash NP)/NP$
$$\dfrac{\qquad\qquad\qquad}{S/S'} \rightarrow {}_B$$
$$\dfrac{\qquad\qquad\qquad\qquad\qquad}{S/S} \rightarrow {}_B$$
$$\dfrac{\qquad\qquad\qquad\qquad\qquad}{S/NP} \rightarrow {}_B$$
$$\dfrac{\qquad\qquad\qquad\qquad\qquad\qquad}{S/NP} \rightarrow {}_B$$
$$\dfrac{\qquad\qquad\qquad\qquad\qquad\qquad\qquad\qquad}{N \backslash N} \rightarrow$$

The interesting thing about such grammars for present purposes is that they allow left-branching analysis of structures like the English clause, which we usually think of as predominantly right-branching. Although we will not go into the details here, it is also crucial that the combinatory rules allow the immediate assembly of a correct semantic interpretation for non-standard constituents like *I think that I like*. The implications of this fact for the theory of natural language grammar are quite far-reaching, and are explored in Steedman, 1996 (in press).

Such grammars afford an equally natural expression for the harmonic semantics of the last section. Figure 15.8 gives a categorial lexicon that

$$
\begin{aligned}
(1.) \quad & X(m) \quad := \quad X(m)(7)/X(m)(7) \\
& \qquad\qquad\qquad\quad X(m) \\
(2.) \quad & X(m) \quad := \quad X(m)/IV_X \\
(3a.) \quad & Xm7 \quad := \quad Xm7/IV_X(7) \\
(3b.) \quad & X7 \quad := \quad X7/IV_X(m)(7) \\
(4.) \quad & X(m)7 \quad := \quad \|IV_X(m)7/VII_X(m)(7) \\
(5.) \quad & X \quad := \quad (X/III_X m)/II_X m \\
(6.) \quad & X \circ 7 \quad := \quad bV_X/bV_X \\
& \qquad\qquad\qquad\quad bII_X/bII_X \\
& \qquad\qquad\qquad\quad bVII_X m7/bVII_X m7
\end{aligned}
$$

FIG. 15.8. A categorial grammar equivalent to Fig. 15.2.

corresponds point for point with the earlier grammar in Fig. 15.2. The categories are numbered accordingly to facilitate the comparison [conventions for inheriting optional properties like (*m*) are as before]. Together with the same "spelling" rules as before (Fig. 15.3), and function composition and type-raising as well as function application, this grammar gives rise to (incomplete) derivations like the following for the chord sequence *c* in Fig. 15.1:

(8)

I(M7)	*IV(7)*	*I(M7)*	*V7, I7*	*IV(7')*	*IV(7')*	*IIIm7*	*VI7*	*IIm7*	*V7*	*I(M7)*	*I(M7)*
I	*IV*	*I*	*V7, I7*	*IV*	*IV*	*IIIm7*	*VI7*	*IIm7*	*V7*	*I*	*I*
I/IV	*IV*	*I*	*V7/I(m)7, I7/IV(m)(7)*	*IV/IV*	*IV*	*IIIm7/VI(7)*	*VI7/II(m)(7)*	*IIm7/V(7)*	*V7/I(m)(7)*	*I/I*	*I*

$\xrightarrow{\quad}$ *I* $\quad$ *V7/IV(m)(7)* $\xrightarrow{}B$ *IV* $\xrightarrow{}$ *IIIm7/II(m)(7)* $\xrightarrow{}B$ *I* $\xrightarrow{}B$

$\xrightarrow{\quad\quad}$ *V7* $\quad\quad$ *IIIm7/V(7)* $\xrightarrow{}B$

$\xrightarrow{\quad\quad}$ *IIIm7/I(m)(7)* $\xrightarrow{}B$

$\xrightarrow{\quad\quad}$ *IIIm7*

There are a number of things to notice about this fragment. First, unlike its predecessor, it does not work by substitution on a previously prepared skeleton. Second, it is still incomplete, in that it does not yet specify the higher levels of analysis that stitch the sequences of cadences together into canonical forms like twelve-bars, and variations on *I Got Rhythm*. (Notice that it as yet includes no lexical categories corresponding to Rule 0 in the old grammar of Fig.15.2). However, the lineaments of Johnson-Laird's more elaborated 1991 cadence grammar are visible to the willing eye in the categories of Fig. 15.8.

We can show this by including some further unary type-changing rules, analogous to the type-raising of categories like subjects in natural language CG mentioned in connection with example 6. (These rules actually smuggle the equivalent of Rule 0 or Johnson-Laird's PS rules back into the grammar.)

First, instead of just applying an extended cadence to its target, we will give the target a higher-order type that labels the result explicitly as *C*, the category of a non-initial cadence:

(9) $\quad X \quad \Rightarrow \quad C(X) \backslash (Y7/X)$

Second, we add a trivial rule that makes *X* into *X/X*—that is, which allows strings of *X*s to combine into one *X* (this rule renders redundant the categories 1 in Fig. 15.8).

(10) $\quad X \quad \Rightarrow \quad X/X$

With these rules we can continue the earlier derivation as follows:

(11)

The analysis is not yet complete, but we are at least in a position to distinguish twelve-bar sequences made up from cadences onto I, IV, and V from other less coherent sequences. (We assume as before that the combination of two categories X and Y each respectively occupying x and y bars creates an object occupying $x + y$ bars.)

Although more work remains to be done before this fragment will support analysis or generation, this is a much nicer *kind* of grammar than the one I offered in 1984. The fact that the only rules are "order-preserving" presumably means that it is weakly context-free (although more needs to be said about the type-changing rules). And although I have not provided anything like a formal semantics or model theory, the fact that this is a one-level grammar, rather than one based on substitutions, suggests that such a semantics would be rather easily specifiable in terms of the Longuet-Higgins theory, as the resemblance to Montague Grammar (Montague, 1974) should suggest. It also looks as if this grammar will be fairly simply parsable, and incrementally interpretable from left-to-right. To that extent, it may constitute an advance on its predecessor, and perhaps lead to similar simplifications in the more ambitious but similarly right-branching grammars of Winograd and Johnson-Laird.

NOTES

[1] This notation is different from, but equivalent to, that in the original paper.

[2] The history of these developments and some related developments in work of Balzano (1982), Shepard (1982), and Lerdahl (1988), is reviewed in greater detail by Steedman (1994).

[3] A simple analogue calculator for this purpose can readily be built by photocopying the roman numeral interval plane of Fig. 15.6 onto transparent film, and then sliding it over the note-name plane. Fig. 15.5.

[4] The addition of the new note also makes the V chord rather ambiguous. The added IV could be the south-easterly IV^+, making this a minor seventh $V(7')$ chord rather than a dominant seventh $V7$.

[5] This is the "result leftmost" notation for categories. There is another "result on top" notation in use, in which this category would be written $(NP\backslash S)/NP$.

[6] Of course, example 2 is not the *only* category that the verb *eats* bears. Like many other transitives, it can also be used intransitively, as $S\backslash NP$, like *walks*. For parsing purposes, we might combine such categories into a single disjunctive lexical entry, including optional arguments. However, such considerations are irrelevant to competence grammar, and we shall here treat such alternatives as independent lexical categories.

ACKNOWLEDGMENTS

The research described here has its origins in many hours of work with Phil Johnson-Laird, Keith Oatley, and Mark Georgeson in the Epistemic Spasm Band at the University of Sussex in the mid-70s, while the author was a postdoctoral fellow in Phil's lab under SSRC grant HR 2351/1. (They don't write numbers like that any more.) The author hereby records his lasting gratitude for this appointment, which allowed him to switch fields into Natural Language Processing, and from which he learned much of what he knows about the subject.

More recent phases of the research have been supported in part by NSF grant nos. IRI91-17110, IRI95-04372, ARPA grant no. N66001-94-C6043, and ARO grant no. DAAH04-94-G0426. Thanks to Brian Butterworth and Oliver Nelson for suggesting the first part of the title, and to Alan Garnham for a close reading of the draft.

REFERENCES

Armstrong, L. (1928). *Basin Street Blues*. Columbia.

Balzano, G. (1982). The pitch set as a level of description for studying musical perception. In M. Clynes (Ed.), *Music, mind and brain*. New York: Plenum Press.

Coker, J. (1964). *Improvising jazz*. New Jersey: Prentice Hall.

Ellis, A. (1874). On musical duodenes. *Proceedings of the Royal Society, 23.*

Ellis, A. (1875). Appendix XX to the 1st edn. of this translation of Helmholtz, 1862 (q.v.), as *On the sensations of tone*. London: Longmans.

Ellis, A. (1885). 2nd edn. of his translation of Helmholtz, 1862, as *On the sensations of tone*. Longmans. [Republished by Dover, New York, 1954.]

Helmholtz, H. (1862). *Die Lehre von dem Tonempfindungen*. Braunschweig: Vieweg.

Howell, P., West, R., & Cross, I. (Eds.) (1991). *Representing musical structure*. London: Academic Press.

Johnson-Laird, P.N. (1983). *Mental models*. Cambridge, MA: Harvard University Press.

Johnson-Laird, P.N. (1991). Jazz improvisation: A theory at the computational level. In Howell et al., 1991, pp.291–326.

Lerdahl, F. (1988). Tonal pitch space. *Music Perception, 5,* 315–350.

Lindblom, B. & Sundberg J. (1972). Towards a generative theory of melody. *Swedish Journal of Musicology, 52,* 71–88.

Longuet-Higgins, H.C. (1962a). Letter to a musical friend. *The Music Review, 23,* 244–248.

Longuet-Higgins, H.C. (1962b). Second letter to a musical friend. *The Music Review, 23,* 271–280.

Longuet-Higgins, H.C. (1978). The grammar of music. *Interdisciplinary Science Reviews, 3,* 148–156.

Marslen-Wilson, W. (1975). Sentence perception as an interactive parallel process. *Science, 189,* 226–228.

Montague, R. (1974). *Formal philosophy,* (Ed. R. Thomason). New Haven: Yale University Press.

Mouton, R., & Pachet, F. (1995). The symbolic vs. numeric controversy in automatic analysis of music. *Proceedings of the Workshop on Artificial Intelligence and Music*, International Joint Conference on Artificial Intelligence, Montreal, August 1995, pp.32–39.

Shepard, R. (1982). Structural representations of musical pitch. In D. Deutsch (Ed.), *The psychology of music*. New York: Academic Press.

Steedman, M. (1973). *The formal description of musical perception*. Unpublished PhD dissertation, University of Edinburgh.

Steedman, M. (1977). The perception of musical rhythm and metre. *Perception, 6,* 555–569.

Steedman, M. (1984). A generative grammar for jazz chord sequences. *Music Perception, 2,* 52–77.

Steedman, M. (1989). Grammar, interpretation and processing from the lexicon. In W. Marslen-Wilson (Ed.), *Lexical representation and process* (pp.463–504). Cambridge, MA: MIT Press/Bradford Books.

Steedman, M. (1994). The well-tempered computer. *Philosophical Transactions of the Royal Society, A, 349,* 115–131.

Steedman, M. (1996) (in press). *Surface structure and interpretation.* Cambridge, MA: MIT Press.

Sundberg, J., & Lindblom, B. (1991). Generative theories for describing musical structure. In Howell et al. 1991, pp.245–272.

Tyler, L. & Marslen-Wilson, W. (1977). The on-line effects of semantic context on syntactic processing. *Journal of Verbal Learning and Verbal Behavior, 16,* 683–692.

Winograd, T. (1968). Linguistics and the computer analysis of tonal harmony. *Journal of Music Theory, 12,* 2–49.

Wood, M.McG. (1993). *Categorial grammars.* London: Routledge.

APPENDIX: CONVENTIONS USED IN FIG. 15.1

The sequences (a) to (g) represent the twelve-bar chord sequences. Vertical columns represent the twelve successive bars, further grouped into four-bar sections. Where only one chord symbol occurs in a bar it is to be understood to last for all four beats of the bar. Where there are two symbols, they each occupy two beats. The root of each chord is identified by a Roman numeral. This indicates a degree in the major scale of the keynote of the piece, *I* being the tonic and *VII* the seventh. The prefixes b and # identify the root of the chord in question as being one diatonic semitone above or below the degree in question. For example, b*III* indicates a chord whose root is the minor third of *I*. All chords are understood to be based on the major chord unless explicit indication is given that they are based on the minor by a small *m* immediately following the Roman numeral, as in b*IIIm*. Further numerical suffixes indicate that additional "passing" notes are to be included with the notes of the basic minor or major chord. The ones in brackets are less harmonically significant, in the sense spelled out earlier in the discussion of the original rules in Fig. 15.3. Their identity is indicated in a rather obscure (but standard) way. The suffix 7 means that the "dominant" seventh note, a tone below the tonic, is to be included, as in b*III7* and *IIIm7*. The nonstandard suffix (7') also denotes a keyboard tone below the tonic. However, in these chords the additional note functions as the *minor* seventh, rather than the dominant seventh—cf footnote 4. The suffix (M7), in contrast, indicates the inclusion of the leading note or major seventh, a semitone below the root, as in *IV(M7)*. The suffix + 5 indicates the addition of the note an augmented fifth above the tonic (G# for the chord of C). It often occurs in combination with the dominant seventh, as in *V7 + 5*.

The suffix 6 indicates that the major sixth is added. The suffix φ7 indicates that the minor third, the diminished fifth (Gb for the chord of Cφ7), and the dominant seventh are included. The suffix o7 indicates that the minor third, the diminished fifth, and the diminished seventh (Bbb for the chord of C o7) are all included—this is the so-called diminished seventh chord.

16 Afterword. The Model Theory of Reasoning: Current Standing and Future Prospects

Jonathan St.B.T. Evans
University of Plymouth, UK

Everyone who is old enough is supposed to remember where they were when they heard that President Kennedy had been shot. Actually, I can't—but I do have my share of "flash-bulb memories". The questions to ask reasoning researchers is "Where were you when you first encountered the Wason selection task?". I know where I was: in a small lecture theatre in Gordon Square—the building that once housed the Psychology Department of University College London (UCL). The year was 1968, the lecturer was Phil Johnson-Laird who had recently completed his doctorate under the supervision of Peter Wason. Phil presented the now famous four card problem to the class and invited us to solve it before telling us the answer[1]. This was part of a brilliant series of undergraduate lectures on thinking and psycholinguistics that did much to stimulate my early interest in higher cognitive processes.

Because Phil's standing as a reasoning researcher is now so closely tied to the theory of mental models developed in the 1980s, it is easy to forget that he was in at the very beginning, in that crucial period at UCL when Peter Wason was laying the foundations for the field we now know as the psychology of reasoning (see Evans & Newstead, 1995). Wason and Johnson-Laird's 1972 book *Psychology of reasoning: Structure and content* was the first of a number of influential and important books that Phil has been involved in writing. The book was in final preparation during the period in which my own doctoral research on reasoning was conducted at UCL, also with Peter Wason supervising, between 1969 and 1971. The same

319

period saw the birth of the Italian connection: a young Italian researcher called Paolo Legrenzi visited UCL at Phil's invitation, speaking barely a word of English when he arrived. Phil and Paolo became lifelong friends and occasional collaborators.

After helping Wason to found the modern psychological study of reasoning, Phil left UCL and moved to the University of Sussex where he concentrated mostly on research on the psychology of language during the 1970s. I remember that during a visit of Phil's to Plymouth in 1979—to examine Paul Pollard's PhD thesis—I recklessly remarked that I intended to run no further experiments on the Wason selection task, believing at the time that it had been worked out. Phil shook my hand and said "Likewise". His self-insight was evidently a deal better than mine: history records that he stuck to his resolve, whereas I lapsed time and again in years to come.[2]

In the early 1970s, the discipline of cognitive psychology had barely found its identity and the meta-discipline of cognitive science was in its infancy. Yet Phil Johnson-Laird, even then, was a cognitive scientist. He was already unconvinced that experimental psychology could solve the problems unaided and was deeply interested in the theory of computation, in linguistics, and in philosophy. He presented early computational models of the selection task (Johnson-Laird & Wason, 1970) and the three-term series problems of transitive inference (Johnson-Laird, 1972). During the 1970s he actively campaigned for the development of cognitive science, berating approaches that he regarded as "brute empiricism" (Johnson-Laird & Wason, 1977, Introduction). To a young experimentalist like myself, such arguments were surprising and difficult to accept at the time. But, of course, we are all cognitive scientists now.

It may appear to an outside observer that—unlike other authors writing in this book—I am not a collaborator of Phil Johnson-Laird's. This is true only in the sense that there are no joint papers to be found in the literature featuring the names Johnson-Laird and Evans—at least none so far. The truth, however, is that Phil and I have argued, debated, and interacted over the years about almost every facet of reasoning theory and our respective research programmes. Not only do we frequently read and criticise drafts of each other's papers and books, but we continually argue about ideas and set each other theoretical challenges and suggestions for future research work. The Emails flow thick and fast between Princeton and Plymouth on a regular basis.

MENTAL MODELS AND MENTAL LOGIC

Phil Johnson-Laird is, of course, a prolific author of books and papers. The most significant, in my view, is *Mental models* (1983)—a truly innovative, imaginative, and seminal work. This was one of the most widely read and discussed works in cognitive science of its time. Almost every cognitive psychologist that I met in the year or two after it was published greeted me with the question "Have you read *Mental models*? What do you think of it?'. Many admired it and a few hated it, but the point was that everyone had read the book and wanted to discuss it. Few researchers ever write a single work with such impact.

In line with the emphasis of Phil's work in the previous decade, *Mental models* applied the theory to language as well as reasoning. Nevertheless it was the new theory of reasoning that it contained which came to dominate Phil's subsequent work, so marking a shift into a new period of predominantly reasoning research. The theoretical and experimental research programme on human deduction that followed was astonishing in its scope, energy, and ambition. Originally, the theory was applied to the explanation of syllogistic reasoning and quantifiers (Johnson-Laird & Bara, 1984). In the mere eight years that passed before the publication of *Deduction* (Johnson-Laird & Byrne, 1991) the programme had expanded to encompass propositional reasoning, relational reasoning, and meta-deduction. What impressed me particularly was not only that the theory had been worked out in detail for all of these areas, but that together with Ruth Byrne and other collaborators Phil had managed to produce a whole host of new experimental studies and findings. A cognitive scientist ahead of his time he may have been, but Phil has not forgotten his roots in experimental psychology, nor the importance of data.

To be so strongly associated with one theory, as Phil is with mental models, is in a sense a hard burden to carry. The theory was born—and remains—highly controversial, and has attracted admirers and critics in roughly equal numbers. Some of the criticisms are highly vigorous if not downright hostile, as examination of some of the commentaries in the peer review treatment of *Deduction* illustrates (*Behavioral & Brain Sciences*, 1993, vol.16, pp.323–380). To see why the theory is so controversial we need a little historical perspective on the traditional approach that it seeks to refute: an approach aptly labelled by Phil himself as the "doctrine of mental logic" (Johnson-Laird, 1983).

There is a strong logicist tradition in philosophy which holds that formal logic is a descriptive and not simply a normative theory of human reasoning. In psychological writings, logicism is most clearly seen in the writings of Jean Piaget (e.g. Inhelder & Piaget, 1958) and his followers. Smedslund (e.g. 1990), for example, has argued that reasoning experiments can only be sensibly interpreted on the assumption that subjects are invariably logical in their reasoning, whilst Henle (1978) has apparently "never found errors which could ambiguously be attributed to faulty reasoning". Although such strong logicist positions are almost impossible to sustain in light of the now very large experimental psychological literature on deductive reasoning, a more subtle form of mental logic has emerged as a powerful contemporary theory.

Mental logicians argue that people possess innate logical systems of a type known in philosophy as *natural* logics or natural deduction systems—a term embodying the philosopher's own assumption that people must reason using a logic of this kind. Natural logics are comprised of a set of inference schemas which are abstract and general purpose in nature. Contemporary mental logic theories propose that some inferences are easier than others because they are direct rather than indirect (Braine, Reiser, & Rumain, 1984; Braine & O'Brien, 1991) or made forward rather than backwards (Rips, 1983, 1994). However, such theories also concede that many findings in the experimental literature cannot be accounted for within this system and need therefore to propose the operation of pragmatic reasoning schemas as well as the influence of response biases (e.g. Rips, 1994; O'Brien, 1993, 1995). All this makes the contemporary mental logic theory a lot more flexible (or slippery, depending on your point of view) than the logicist tradition from which it grew. As O'Brien (1995, pp.210–211) puts it:

> Mental logic ... provides an accurate and natural representation that is not equivalent to a standard formal logical system of the sort found in logic textbooks. On the one hand, mental logic makes only some of the inferences that are sanctioned in standard-logic systems; on the other hand, mental-logic inferences cohabit easily in a line of reasoning with pragmatic inferences that go beyond those of a standard-logic system.

Now, I should say that there definitely *is* evidence of abstract deductive competence that needs to be explained (see Evans & Over, 1996, Ch.6). However, given the high incidence of error and bias, and given the huge influence of pragmatic factors that dominate the experimental literature on reasoning, one may feel—as I do—that the mental logic proposal is simply implausible. Why should we have an innate and complex formal reasoning system—comprising large sets of rules and procedures—that actually accounts for such a small amount of the variance in observed reasoning? In fact, evidence for deductive competence is based entirely on the results of laboratory experiments with abstract and artificial problem materials. As the problems are semantically enriched—and therefore more real-world-like—the dominance of pragmatic over formal reasoning is manifestly obvious, and not even denied by the mental logic theorists.

If there were no alternative to the formal rules account of the mental logicians, we would be stuck with this account—however implausible we may find it. That there is an available alternative account of competence is due almost entirely to the work of Phil Johnson-Laird and his collaborators. The technical account of the model theory of deduction includes the notion that models are structural isomorphs of the situations they represent, that they consist in tokens, and that there are three stages of reasoning: model construction, provisional formation of a conclusion, and a validation stage in which counter-examples to the conclusion are sought. However, I prefer to think of the model theory in terms of the simple semantic principle that Phil has put forward (Johnson-Laird & Byrne, 1993, p.194): "an inference is valid provided that there is no model of the premises in which its conclusion is false." To put it another way, if an inference holds in all the states of affairs that you can imagine, then that inference must be valid.

The first attraction of this theory is its simplicity. Deductive competence resides in the grasp of this simple semantic principle, rather than in the complexity of innate rule systems. Of course, competence requires more than just understanding of this principle. People must also be capable of formulating mental models that represent actual, possible, or counter-factual states of the world. However, this is not some arbitrary, technical assumption analogous to the need of mental logicians to postulate, say, a disjunction elimination rule. No contemporary cognitive scientists—including mental logicians—could deny that people must have such an ability to formulate mental models of this kind. It is not simply deduction that (may) require this but also language comprehension and any form of hypothetical thinking or decision making that involves consideration of how the world is, might be, or might have been.

The second attraction of Phil's theory is its genuinely psychological nature. True, the theory has been formalised and implemented in computer programs both in the domain of quantified reasoning (Johnson-Laird & Bara, 1984) and propositional inference (Johnson-Laird, Byrne, & Schaeken, 1992). It can take on the mental logic theory within the cognitive science agenda. That is not what makes it attractive to me, however, or other similarly empirically oriented psychologists. What I see as the great strength of the theory is first that it can—at least potentially—provide within one framework an account of deductive competence, biases, and pragmatic effects. We have already seen that the mental logic account can only explain biases and pragmatic influences by adducing factors *external* to the theory of deduction.

Let me give an important example of how the model theory captures the psychological process of reasoning better than the rule theory. The predominant finding in all the various literatures on deductive reasoning is this: people make more inferences than can be warranted by the information given. In syllogistic reasoning, for example, people frequently endorse invalid inferences: conclusions that are possible, but not necessary, given their premises (see Evans, Newstead, & Byrne, 1993, Ch.7). Similarly, in conditional reasoning, subjects frequently endorse fallacies such as Affirmation of the Consequent: *if p then q, q*, therefore *p*. The mental logic theory has no specific account to offer of fallacious inferences because there are no rules for fallacies in its system. Instead mental logicians rely on vague references to pragmatic factors and "invited inferences" (e.g. Braine & O'Brien, 1991). The model theory, however, is a theory of possible inference with a validation stage tacked on (searching for counter-examples to the possible conclusion). In other words, the primary act of inference is to form a model consistent with the premises and a provisional conclusion consistent with them. Fallacies will occur when the validation stage fails to generate counter-examples.

There is increasing evidence that this validation stage is rather weak. As Johnson-Laird and Byrne (1993, p.194) put it:

> Individuals who have no training in logic appear to have a tacit grasp of this meta-principle [quoted earlier], but they have no grasp of specific logical principles, and no systematic or comprehensive procedures for drawing conclusions according to the meta-principle. They have no principles for valid thinking, i.e. for searching for models that refute conclusions.

In other words, although inferences will be rejected when counter-examples are thought of, subjects may not be very good at seeking them out. There are psychological considerations that make this a plausible proposition and which can explain the frequent endorsement of logically fallacious inferences. First, as Phil has long argued (e.g. Johnson-Laird & Bara, 1984), working memory capacity is limited and so validation is limited by the difficulty of considering more than one model at a time. Second, inductive reasoning may be our habitual mode of thinking: we may tend to focus on single mental models when thinking hypothetically and rely on provisional conclusions until or unless conflicting evidence is encountered. If this is correct, then validation will only occur when experimental instructions for deductive inference are provided by the experimenter. Even when they are provided, subjects may lose track of these instructions and revert to habitual methods of reasoning. In support of this, a recent study by Evans, Allen, Newstead, and Pollard (1994) found that increased instructional emphasis on drawing only necessary conclusions inhibited fallacious inferences and belief bias effects (i.e. accepting invalid but believable conclusions).

THE FUTURE OF THE MODEL THEORY

The model theory in its specific current formulation is neither correct nor complete. This is hardly a controversial statement, as Phil himself will agree immediately with it. Come to that, there is no cognitive psychological theory to my knowledge that is either correct or complete. So what persuades psychological researchers to follow one theoretical approach rather than another when designing their research programmes? The fitting of theories to data is something you do in the course of the research work, but data–theory fits are not the prime motivator for the work itself. I suspect that it is much more fundamentally to do with the inherent attractiveness and plausibility of a theory and the degree to which it gels with the investigators' intuitions about the problems they study.

Although the theory is wrong in its details, the mental models *approach* is one for which I see a great future. I have already indicated why I think it is both more plausible and more psychological than the mental logic theory. However, there is another factor favouring the continuation of this approach which I have yet to mention. A number of psychologists are currently interested in forging direct links between research on reasoning, probabilistic thinking, and decision making. Among these are David Over and myself, and we have recently completed the manuscript of a new book in which we lay out our theory of rationality and inference across the domains of deduction, judgement, and decision making (Evans & Over, 1996). In the course of this work we consider the issue of deductive competence and the rival accounts based on models and rules. We favour the model theory, but *not* on the basis of the specific arguments in the literature about which theory provides the better account of specific experimental findings (e.g. O'Brien, Braine, & Yang, 1994; Johnson-Laird, Byrne, & Schaeken, 1994). We are not even sure that such arguments are decidable, as there are too many free parameters on both sides for the theories to be strictly testable.

In addition to the reasons already given here, we like the model theory because it can span the gap between research on reasoning and decision making. Phil himself is well aware of this and has already published some provisional thoughts about the application of the theory to probabilistic thinking (Johnson-Laird, 1994). Let us consider a super-ordinate category of thought, which we may call *hypothetical thinking*. Psychologists interested in studying hypothesis testing have suggested that subjects tend to focus on a single hypothesis (Mynatt, Doherty, & Dragan, 1993). A hypothesis is a belief about a possible state of the world, so we could rephrase this suggestion as one of focusing on a single mental model. Now, as already suggested here, the primary mode of reasoning may be inductive—i.e. focused on the single most plausible (or psychologically available) model— and effort at deduction is only induced, somewhat uncertainly, by experimental instructions. Phil himself, of course, has been working on extension of the theory to inductive inference (Johnson-Laird, 1993).

Another form of hypothetical thinking is decision making. In order to make a decision, the subject must choose between one of several actions. All rational analyses of decision making assume that this requires imagination of the future possible worlds that might result when different actions are taken. The probability and utility of these possible worlds must be taken into account in order to achieve a rational decision. Now, the evidence for rational choice is as sparse in the decision literature as is the evidence for deductive competence. However, both rational choice and rational deduction require exactly the same thing: hypothetical thinking about possible states of the world—i.e. mental models. The cognitive constraints that operate in either case may be similar: for example in decision making as well as in reasoning, people tend to focus on specific models and fail to consider a sufficient number of alternatives (e.g. Legrenzi, Girotto, & Johnson-Laird, 1993). In contrast to the insights that the model approach may yield, the mental logic theory would seem to offer nothing at all to the study of decision making. For all the emphasis on normative theory in the decision-making literature, no-one suggests that rules of logical inference have any part to play.

The exciting theoretical opportunity that now faces us is the development of an integrated theory of hypothetical thinking that will encompass both reasoning and decision making, and allow us to bridge the gap between these unhappily dissociated literatures. It is clear that the progress that is now starting to be made with this enterprise owes a large debt to the fundamental insights provided by Phil Johnson-Laird.

NOTES

[1] In case anyone is interested, I got the answer wrong. I chose the P and Q cards—the error pattern that I was later to characterise as demonstrating a "matching bias".

[2] A near lapse occurred when Phil ran some experiments on the reduced array selection task (RAST)—Oakhill and Johnson-Laird (1985). Recently, he has become more interested in providing theoretical accounts of the task in terms of mental model theory—see Johnson-Laird (1995).

REFERENCES

Braine, M.D.S., & O'Brien, D.P. (1991). A theory of If: A lexical entry, reasoning program, and pragmatic principles. *Psychological Review*, 98, 182–203.

Braine, M.D.S., Reiser, B.J., & Rumain, B. (1984). Some empirical justification for a theory of natural propositional logic. In G.H. Bower (Ed.), *The psychology of learning and motivation*, Vol 18. New York: Academic Press.

Evans, J.St.B.T., Allen, J.L., Newstead, S.E., & Pollard, P. (1994). Debiasing by instruction: The case of belief bias. *European Journal of Cognitive Psychology*, 6, 263–285.

Evans, J.St.B.T., & Newstead, S.E. (1995). Creating a psychology of reasoning: The contribution of Peter Wason. In S.E. Newstead & J.St.B.T. Evans (Eds.), *Perspectives on thinking and reasoning*. Hove, UK: Lawrence Erlbaum Associates Ltd.

Evans, J.St.B.T., Newstead, S.E., & Byrne, R.M.J. (1993). *Human reasoning: The psychology of deduction*. Hove, UK: Lawrence Erlbaum Associates Ltd.

Evans, J.St.B.T., & Over, D.E. (1996). *Reasoning and rationality*. Hove, UK: Psychology Press.

Henle, M. (1978). Foreword. In R. Revlin & R.E. Mayer (Eds.), *Human reasoning*. Washington, DC: Winston.

Inhelder, B., & Piaget, J. (1958). *The growth of logical thinking*. New York: Basic Books.

Johnson-Laird, P.N. (1972). The three-term series problem. *Cognition, 1*, 57–82.

Johnson-Laird, P.N. (1983). *Mental models*. Cambridge: Cambridge University Press.

Johnson-Laird, P.N. (1993). *Human and machine thinking*. Hillsdale, NJ: Lawrence Erlbaum Associates Inc.

Johnson-Laird, P.N. (1994). Mental models and probabilistic thinking. *Cognition, 50*, 189–209.

Johnson-Laird, P.N. (1995). Inference and mental models. In S.E. Newstead & J.St.B.T. Evans (Eds.), *Perspectives on thinking and reasoning*. Hove, UK: Lawrence Erlbaum Associates Ltd.

Johnson-Laird, P.N., & Bara, B.G. (1984). Syllogistic inference. *Cognition, 16*, 1–62.

Johnson-Laird, P.N., & Byrne, R. (1991). *Deduction*. Hove & London: Lawrence Erlbaum Associates Ltd.

Johnson-Laird, P.N., & Byrne, R.M.J. (1993). Models and deductive rationality. In K.I. Manktelow & D.E. Over (Eds.), *Rationality*. London: Routledge.

Johnson-Laird, P.N., Byrne, R.M.J., & Schaeken, W. (1992). Propositional reasoning by model. *Psychological Review, 99*, 418–439.

Johnson-Laird, P.N., Byrne, R.M.J., & Schaeken, W. (1994). Why models rather than rules give a better account of propositional reasoning: A reply to Bonatti and to O'Brien, Braine, & Yang. *Psychological Review, 101*, 734–739.

Johnson-Laird, P.N., & Wason, P.C. (1970). A theoretical analysis of insight into a reasoning task. *Cognitive Psychology, 1*, 134–148.

Johnson-Laird, P.N., & Wason, P.C. (1977). *Thinking: Readings in cognitive science*. Cambridge: Cambridge University Press.

Legrenzi, P., Girotto, V., & Johnson-Laird, P.N. (1993). Focusing in reasoning and decision making. *Cognition, 49*, 37–66.

Mynatt, C.R., Doherty, M.E., & Dragan, W. (1993). Information relevance, working memory and the consideration of alternatives. *Quarterly Journal of Experimental Psychology, 46A*, 759–778.

Oakhill, J., & Johnson-Laird, P.N. (1985). Rationality, memory and the search for counter-examples. *Cognition, 20*, 79–94.

O'Brien, D., Braine, M.D.S., & Yang, Y. (1994). Propositional reasoning by mental models? Simple to refute in principle and practice. *Psychological Review, 101*, 711–724.

O'Brien, D.P. (1993). Mental logic and irrationality: We can put a man on the moon, so why can't we solve those logical reasoning problems. In K.I. Manktelow & D.E. Over (Eds.), *Rationality*. London: Routledge.

O'Brien, D.P. (1995). Finding logic in human reasoning requires looking in the right places. In S.E. Newstead & J.St.B.T. Evans (Eds.), *Perspectives on thinking and reasoning*. Hove, UK: Erlbaum.

Rips, L.J. (1983). Cognitive processes in propositional reasoning. *Psychological Review, 90*, 38–71.

Rips, L.J. (1994). *The psychology of proof*. Cambridge, MA: MIT Press.

Smedslund, J. (1990). A critique of Tversky and Kahneman's distinction between fallacy and misunderstanding. *Scandinavian Journal of Psychology, 31*, 110–120.

Wason, P.C., & Johnson-Laird, P.N. (1972). *Psychology of reasoning: Structure and content*. London: Batsford.

Author Index

AUTHOR INDEX 333

Shastri, L. 285, 303
Shaw, B. 201, 219
Shea, T. 230, 243, 245
Shehata, M. 144, 152
Sheldon, A. 59, 75
Shepard, R. 316n, 317
Sherman, S.J. 149, 153, 166, 167, 173
Shoam, Y. 279, 303
Shoben, E.J. 54, 75
Silveri, M.C. 30, 33
Sim, D. 107, 118
Simon, H.A. 179, 196
Simonson, I. 123, 137
Simpson, G.B. 28, 29, 33
Skov, R.B. 149, 153
Slade, P. 213, 219
Slovic, P. 140, 143, 144, 151, 152, 153
Small, S. 15, 17
Smedslund, J. 321, 327
Smith, A. 214, 220
Smith, D.C. 231, 245
Smith, E.E. 54, 75, 140, 153
Smith, G.F. 123, 136
Smyth, R. 59, 75
Snyder, M. 148, 149, 153
Solomon, G. 183, 196
Solomon, S. 56, 75
Spears, R. 167, 172
Spelke, E.S. 280, 281–282, 302, 303
Sperber, D. 98n, 115n, 118
Spielberger, C.D. 208, 222
Spreenberg.P 231, 244
Stalnaker, R.C. 162, 166, 174
Stanley, B. 230, 243
Stanners, R.F. 12, 17
Steedman, M.J. 67, 75, 305, 307, 312, 314, 316, 316n, 317
Stein, N.L. 86, 94, 181, 196
Steiner, R. 81, 94
Stenning, K. 39, 52, 59, 60, 75
Stevens, A.R. 247, 248, 249, 271, 272
Stevens, K.V. 36, 51
Stevenson, R.J. 59, 60, 62, 65–71, 73n, 75, 76
Stothard, S. 79, 94
Strathman, A.J. 167, 173
Stroop, J.R. 207, 222
Stuart.R. 229, 243
Sun Microsystems Inc. 230, 245
Sundberg, J. 305, 317, 318

Suri, J.F. 231, 244
Swann, W.B. 149, 153
Swinney, D.A. 13, 18, 26, 27, 28, 29, 33
Tabossi, P. 20, 24, 25, 27, 28, 29, 34, 160, 173
Tanenhaus, M.K. 29, 34, 64, 71
Tasso, A. 98, 117, 156, 163, 165, 170–171, 172
Taylor, B.R. 167, 174
Taylor, P. 210, 220
Teasdale, J. 200, 202, 205, 219, 222
Tengi, R. 13, 17
Thaler, R.H. 144, 153
Thomas, J.C. 231, 243
Thomas, R.G. 12, 13, 17
Thorndyke, E.L. 13, 18
Tiberghien, A. 250, 272
Tognazzini, B. 230, 245
Tolmie, A 250, 254, 258, 261, 262, 267, 268, 269, 272, 273
Tooby, J. 120, 136
Toulmin, S. 119, 121, 122, 126, 137
Trabasso, T. 181, 196
Trollip, S.R. 36, 51
Tu, S. 162, 174
Tunmer, W. 92, 94
Turtle, J.W. 167, 174
Tversky, A. 96, 107–108, 115, 118, 123, 126, 137, 140, 143, 144, 145, 150, 151, 151, 152, 153, 166, 167, 169, 173, 174
Tweney, R.D. 102, 117
Tyler, L. 308, 318
Tyler, S.W. 122, 137

Urbanowicz, A. 70–72, 76

Valpiani, A 298, 302
van der Pligt, J. 167, 172
van Dijk, T.A. 39, 52, 54, 75
Varey, C.A. 166, 173
Vazquez, C. 204, 222
Vera, A. 229, 244
Verplank, W.L. 231, 242, 245
vom Saal, F.S. 277, 303
von Domarus, E. 198, 222
Voss, J.F. 122, 137
Vygotsky, L.S. 120, 137, 184, 196, 253, 273

Walker, M. 63, 76
Ward, C.H. 208, 219
Ward, D.W. 187, 195
Warrington, E.K. 30, 34
Wason, P.C. xiii–xvi, xvi, 50, 51, 109–11, 109n, 117, 118, 125, 136, 137, 149, 152, 207, 218, 222, 239, 244, 319, 320, 327
Wassermann, S. 280, 302
Watson, J xv
Watts, F.N. 207, 217, 222
Weber, C.M. 308
Weeks, D.J. 142, 153
Weick, K.E. 122, 137
Weinberger, D. 216, 221
Weinstein, S. 62, 63, 64, 74
Weishaar, M. 203, 222
Wells, G.L. 155, 166, 167, 172, 174
Wesseley, S. 210, 214, 216, 217, 220
Wetherick N. 215, 220
Whitney, P. 25, 34
Whiten, A. 120, 136
Wickens, C.D. 142, 153
Wiener, M. 79, 81, 94, 94
Wiklund, M.E. 230, 245
Wilke, A. 140, 153
Wilkes-Gibbs, D. 37, 51
Williams, E. 211, 222
Williams, J.M.G. 207, 217, 222
Willner, P. 200, 222
Winograd, T. 305, 308, 316, 318
Wiser, M. 247, 273
Wittgenstein, L. xv, 35, 51
Wood, M, M. 312, 318
World Health Organization 199, 222
Worth, L.T. 187, 188, 190, 195
Wright, P. 234, 245
Wyer, R.S. 187, 195
Wykes, T. 35, 215, 222
Wynn, V. 215, 220

Yang, Y. 325, 327
Yates, J.V. 65, 69, 74
Yengo, L.A. 122, 137
Young, R. 223, 227, 245
Yuill, N.M. 79, 81, 82, 83, 84, 86, 90, 91, 92, 94

Zardon, F. 28, 34
Zipf, G.K. 12, 18

Subject Index